"For nearly four decades Paul Wachtel has been one of tl
ers in the field of psychotherapy. In *Cyclical Psychodyn*
Self he has really outdone himself! Wachtel applies his cyclical psychodynamic
perspective breathtakingly to a wide range of clinically central issues, including
the importance of the larger social and cultural context. A must read!"

—**Robert D. Stolorow**, PhD, author of *World, Affectivity, Trauma: Heidegger
and Post-Cartesian Psychoanalysis* (Routledge, 2011)

"Wachtel has once again produced a mighty work of astonishing brilliance and
enduring value. *Cyclical Psychodynamics and the Contextual Self* is a rich and
ambitious contemplation on the contemporary debates in psychotherapy and psychoanalysis by a pioneering clinician, a teacher and thinker with sparkling eru-
dition, and a gifted writer. He examines our clinical beliefs and practices with
a keen eye, an attuned ear, and a humane heart. His perceptive critiques on the
world of society and culture are dispatches from the trenches. I love this book for
its vividness, vitality, and vision."

—**Spyros D. Orfanos**, PhD, ABPP, Clinic Director, New York University Postdoctoral Program in Psychotherapy and Psychoanalysis

"Paul Wachtel's cyclical psychodynamic theory may be the most important integrative theory of psychotherapy, bringing together a dizzying array of diverse
literatures. Wachtel's range is astonishing, but he doesn't stop with mere compre-
hension. Even more interesting and significant than Wachtel's grasp is his capacity to bring all these theories into meaningful relation with one another."

—**Donnel B. Stern**, PhD, William Alanson White Institute; NYU Postdoctoral
Program in Psychoanalysis and Psychotherapy

"Paul Wachtel is in the vanguard of a group of seminal thinkers who are shaping what might be seen as the entrance of psychoanalysis into its 'relational era.'
This book makes it even clearer why Wachtel's integrative theory of cyclical psychodynamics is acknowledged within and beyond the field of psychoanalysis as
such a unique and powerful force in the ongoing evolution of personality theory
and psychotherapy. Wachtel has written both a theoretical tour de force and an
immensely practical guide to clinical practice."

—**Philip Bromberg**, author of *The Shadow of the Tsunami: and the Growth of the
Relational Mind* (Routledge, 2011)

"How an integrationist approach relates to clinical work is masterfully demonstrated by Paul Wachtel in his brilliant new book. Wachtel writes in an engaging and accessible style and offers numerous clinical examples of the relational
processes that influence the perpetuation of suboptimal patterns in our daily lives,
as well as the vicious circles that characterize social phenomena, such as race
relations. It is an outstanding contribution to the psychoanalytic field and one that
I unreservedly recommend to novice and experienced clinicians alike."

—**Paul Renn**, author of *The Silent Past and the Invisible Present: Memory,
Trauma, and Representation in Psychotherapy* (Routledge, 2012)

Cyclical Psychodynamics and the Contextual Self

Cyclical Psychodynamics and the Contextual Self articulates in new ways the essential features and most recent extensions of Paul L. Wachtel's powerfully integrative theory of cyclical psychodynamics. Wachtel is widely regarded as the leading advocate for integrative thinking in personality theory and the theory and practice of psychotherapy. He contributes to cutting-edge thought in the realm of relational psychoanalysis and to highlighting the ways in which the relational point of view provides especially fertile ground for integrating psychoanalytic insights with the ideas and methods of other theoretical and therapeutic orientations.

In this book, Wachtel extends his integration of psychoanalytic, cognitive-behavioral, systemic, and experiential viewpoints to examine closely the nature of the inner world of subjectivity, its relation to the transactional world of daily life experiences, and the impact on both of the larger social and cultural forces that both shape and are shaped by individual experience. Here, he discusses in a uniquely comprehensive fashion the subtleties of the clinical interaction, the findings of systematic research, and the role of social, economic, and historical forces in our lives. The chapters in this book help to transcend the tunnel vision that can lead therapists of different orientations to ignore the important discoveries and innovations issuing from competing approaches.

Explicating the pervasive role of vicious circles and self-fulfilling prophecies in our lives, *Cyclical Psychodynamics and the Contextual Self* shows how deeply intertwined the subjective, the intersubjective, and the cultural realms are, and points to new pathways to therapeutic and social change. Both a theoretical tour de force and an immensely practical guide to clinical practice, this book will be essential reading for psychoanalysts, psychotherapists, and students of human behavior of all backgrounds and theoretical orientations.

Paul L. Wachtel is CUNY Distinguished Professor at City College and the City University of New York Graduate Center. He is Past President of the Society for the Exploration of Psychotherapy Integration and is the winner of the 2010 Hans H. Strupp Memorial Award for Psychoanalytic Writing, Teaching, and Research, the 2012 Distinguished Psychologist Award by Division 29 of the APA (Psychotherapy), and the 2013 Scholarship and Research Award by Division 39 of the APA (Psychoanalysis).

RELATIONAL PERSPECTIVES BOOK SERIES
LEWIS ARON & ADRIENNE HARRIS
Series Co-Editors

STEVEN KUCHUCK & EYAL ROZMARIN
Associate Editors

The Relational Perspectives Book Series (RPBS) publishes books that grow out of or contribute to the relational tradition in contemporary psychoanalysis. The term *relational psychoanalysis* was first used by Greenberg and Mitchell (1983) to bridge the traditions of interpersonal relations, as developed within interpersonal psychoanalysis and object relations, as developed within contemporary British theory. But, under the seminal work of the late Stephen Mitchell, the term *relational psychoanalysis* grew and began to accrue to itself many other influences and developments. Various tributaries – interpersonal psychoanalysis, object relations theory, self psychology, empirical infancy research, and elements of contemporary Freudian and Kleinian thought – into this tradition, which understands relational configurations between self and others, both real and fantasied, as the primary subject of psychoanalytic investigation.

We refer to the relational tradition, rather than to a relational school, to highlight that we are identifying a trend, a tendency within contemporary psychoanalysis, not a more formally organized or coherent school or system of beliefs. Our use of the term *relational* signifies a dimension of theory and practice that has become salient across the wide spectrum of contemporary psychoanalysis. Now under the editorial supervision of Lewis Aron and Adrienne Harris with the assistance of Associate Editors Steven Kuchuck and Eyal Rozmarin, the Relational Perspectives Book Series originated in 1990 under the editorial eye of the late Stephen A. Mitchell. Mitchell was the most prolific and influential of the originators of the relational tradition. He was committed to dialogue among psychoanalysts, and he abhorred the authoritarianism that dictated adherence to a rigid set of beliefs or technical restrictions. He championed open discussion as well as comparative and integrative approaches, and he promoted new voices across the generations.

Included in the Relational Perspectives Book Series are authors and works that come from within the relational tradition and that extend and develop the tradition, as well as works that critique relational approaches or compare and contrast it with alternative points of view. The series includes our most distinguished senior psychoanalysts along with younger contributors who bring fresh vision.

Vol. 1
Conversing with Uncertainty:
Practicing Psychotherapy
In a Hospital Setting
Rita Wiley McCleary

Vol. 2
Affect in Psychoanalysis:
A Clinical Synthesis
Charles Spezzano

Vol. 3
The Analyst in the Inner City:
Race, Class, and Culture
through a Psychoanalytic Lens
Neil Altman

Vol. 4
A Meeting of Minds:
Mutuality in Psychoanalysis
Lewis Aron

Vol. 5
Holding and Psychoanalysis:
A Relational Perspective
Joyce A. Slochower

Vol. 6
The Therapist as a Person:
Life Crises, Life Choices, Life Experiences,
and Their Effects on Treatment
Barbara Gerson (ed.)

Vol. 7
Soul on the Couch:
Spirituality, Religion, and Morality
in Contemporary Psychoanalysis
Charles Spezzano &
Gerald J. Gargiulo (eds.)

Vol. 8
Unformulated Experience:
From Dissociation to Imagination
in Psychoanalysis
Donnel B. Stern

Vol. 9
Influence and Autonomy
in Psychoanalysis
Stephen A. Mitchell

Vol. 10
Fairbairn, Then and Now
Neil J. Skolnick & David E. Scharff (eds.)

Vol. 11
Building Bridges:
Negotiation of Paradox in Psychoanalysis
Stuart A. Pizer

Vol. 12
Relational Perspectives on the Body
Lewis Aron & Frances Sommer
Anderson (eds.)

Vol. 13
Seduction, Surrender, and Transformation:
Emotional Engagement in
the Analytic Process
Karen Maroda

Vol. 14
Relational Psychoanalysis:
The Emergence of a Tradition
Stephen A. Mitchell &
Lewis Aron (eds.)

Vol. 15
The Collapse of the Self and
Its Therapeutic Restoration
Rochelle G.K. Kainer

Vol. 16
Psychoanalytic Participation:
Action, Interaction, and Integration
Kenneth A. Frank

Vol. 17
The Reproduction of Evil:
A Clinical and Cultural Perspective
Sue Grand

Vol. 18
Objects of Hope:
Exploring Possibility and Limit
in Psychoanalysis
Steven H. Cooper

Vol. 19
Who Is the Dreamer,
Who Dreams the Dream?
A Study of Psychic Presences
James S. Grotstein

Vol. 20
Relationality:
From Attachment to Intersubjectivity
Stephen A. Mitchell

Vol. 21
Looking for Ground:
Countertransference
and the Problem of Value
in Psychoanalysis
Peter G.M. Carnochan

Vol. 22
Sexuality, Intimacy, Power
Muriel Dimen

Vol. 23
September 11: Trauma and
Human Bonds
Susan W. Coates, Jane L. Rosenthal,
& Daniel S. Schechter (eds.)

Vol. 24
Minding Spirituality
Randall Lehman Sorenson

Vol. 25
Gender as Soft Assembly
Adrienne Harris

Vol. 26
Impossible Training:
A Relational View of
Psychoanalytic Education
Emanuel Berman

Vol. 27
The Designed Self:
Psychoanalysis and
Contemporary Identities
Carlo Strenger

Vol. 28
Relational Psychoanalysis, Vol. II:
Innovation and Expansion
Lewis Aron & Adrienne
Harris (eds.)

Vol. 29
Child Therapy in the
Great Outdoors:
A Relational View
Sebastiano Santostefano

Vol. 30
The Healer's Bent:
Solitude and Dialogue in
the Clinical Encounter
James T. McLaughlin

Vol. 31
Unconscious Fantasies and
the Relational World
Danielle Knafo & Kenneth Feiner

Vol. 32
Getting From Here to There:
Analytic Love, Analytic Process
Sheldon Bach

Vol. 33
Creating Bodies:
Eating Disorders as
Self-Destructive Survival
Katie Gentile

Vol. 34
Relational Psychoanalysis,
Vol. III: New Voices
Melanie Suchet, Adrienne Harris, &
Lewis Aron (eds.)

Vol. 35
Comparative-Integrative Psychoanalysis:
A Relational Perspective for the
Discipline's Second Century
Brent Willock

Vol. 36
Bodies in Treatment:
The Unspoken Dimension
Frances Sommer Anderson (ed.)

Vol. 37
Adolescent Identities:
A Collection of Readings
Deborah Browning (ed.)

Vol. 38
Repair of the Soul: Metaphors of
Transformation in Jewish Mysticism
and Psychoanalysis
Karen E. Starr

Vol. 39
Dare to be Human:
A Contemporary Psychoanalytic Journey
Michael Shoshani Rosenbaum

Vol. 40
The Analyst in the Inner City,
Second Edition:
Race, Class, and Culture through
a Psychoanalytic Lens
Neil Altman

Vol. 41
The Hero in the Mirror:
From Fear to Fortitude
Sue Grand

Vol. 42
Sabert Basescu:
Selected Papers on Human Nature
and Psychoanalysis
George Goldstein &
Helen Golden (eds.)

Vol. 43
Invasive Objects: Minds under Siege
Paul Williams

Vol. 44
Good Enough Endings:
Breaks, Interruptions, and
Terminations from Contemporary
Relational Perspectives
Jill Salberg (ed.)

Vol. 45
First Do No Harm: The Paradoxical
Encounters of Psychoanalysis,
Warmaking, and Resistance
Adrienne Harris &
Steven Botticelli (eds.)

Vol. 46
A Disturbance in the Field:
Essays in Transference-
Countertransference Engagement
Steven H. Cooper

Vol. 47
Uprooted Minds:
Surviving the Politics of Terror
in the Americas
Nancy Caro Hollander

Vol. 48
Toward Mutual Recognition: Relational
Psychoanalysis and the Christian
Narrative
Marie T. Hoffman

Vol. 49
Understanding and Treating
Dissociative Identity Disorder:
A Relational Approach
Elizabeth F. Howell

Vol. 50
With Culture in Mind:
Psychoanalytic Stories
Muriel Dimen (ed.)

Vol. 51
Relational Psychoanalysis, Vol. IV:
Expansion of Theory
Lewis Aron & Adrienne Harris (eds.)

Vol. 52
Relational Psychoanalysis, Vol. V:
Evolution of Process
Lewis Aron & Adrienne Harris (eds.)

Vol. 53
Individualizing Gender and Sexuality:
Theory and Practice
Nancy Chodorow

Vol. 54
The Silent Past and the Invisible
Present:
Memory, Trauma, and Representation
in Psychotherapy
Paul Renn

Vol. 55
A Psychotherapy for the People:
Toward a Progressive Psychoanalysis
Lewis Aron & Karen Starr

Vol. 56
Holding and Psychoanalysis:
A Relational Perspective
Joyce Slochower

Vol. 57
The Play Within the Play: The Enacted
Dimension of Psychoanalytic Process
Gil Katz

Vol. 58
Traumatic Narcissism: Relational
Systems of Subjugation
Daniel Shaw

Vol. 59
Clinical Implications of the
Psychoanalyst's
Life Experience: When the Personal
Becomes Professional
Steven Kuchuck (ed.)

Vol. 60
The Origins of Attachment: Infant
Research and Adult Treatment
Beatrice Beebe & Frank M. Lachmann

Vol. 61
The Embodied Analyst: From Freud
and Reich to Relationality
Jon Sletvold

Vol. 62
A Relational Psychoanalytic Approach
to Couples Psychotherapy
Philip A. Ringstrom

Vol. 63
Cyclical Psychodynamics and the
Contextual Self: The Inner World, the
Intimate World, and the World
of Culture and Society
Paul L. Wachtel

Vol. 64
Traumatic Ruptures: Abandonment and
Betrayal in the Analytic Relationship
Robin A. Deutsch (ed.)

Cyclical Psychodynamics and the Contextual Self

The Inner World, the Intimate World, and the World of Culture and Society

Paul L. Wachtel

Routledge
Taylor & Francis Group

LONDON AND NEW YORK

First published 2014
by Routledge
27 Church Road, Hove, East Sussex BN3 2FA

and by Routledge
711 Third Avenue, New York, NY 10017

Routledge is an imprint of the Taylor & Francis Group, an informa business

British Library Cataloguing-in-Publication Data
A catalogue record for this book is available from the British Library

Library of Congress Cataloging-in-Publication Data

Wachtel, Paul L., 1940–
  Cyclical psychodynamics and the contextual self : the inner world, the intimate world, and the world of culture and society / Paul L Wachtel.
    pages cm. — (Relational perspectives book series)
  1. Personality. 2. Psychotherapy. I. Title.
  BF698.W23 2014
  155.2—dc23   2013040535

ISBN: 978-0-415-71394-8 (hbk)
ISBN: 978-0-415-71395-5 (pbk)
ISBN: 978-1-315-79403-7 (ebk)

Typeset in Times
by Apex CoVantage, LLC

For my friends — pillars of support, co-conspirators in life-affirming fun, endless sources of inspiration and stimulation. I have been blessed by my friendships and am grateful for the opportunity to dedicate this book to all of you, both individually and collectively.

Contents

About the Author   xv
Acknowledgments   xvii

PART I
Psychotherapy, Personality Dynamics, and the
World of Intersubjectivity   I

1   Cyclical Psychodynamics: An Integrative, Relational Point
of View   3

2   The Good News: To Mess Up Your Life, You Need
Accomplices. The Bad News: They Are Very Easy
to Recruit   31

3   The Inner and Outer Worlds and Their Link through Action   39

4   Attachment in Psychoanalysis and Psychotherapy:
A Two-Person, Cyclical Psychodynamic Approach   50

5   The Surface and the Depths: Reexamining the Metaphor
of Depth in Psychoanalytic Discourse   67

6   Repression, Dissociation, and Self-Acceptance: Reexamining
the Idea of Making the Unconscious Conscious   83

7   Active Intervention, Psychic Structure, and the Analysis
of Transference   97

8   Incorporating the Panther: Toward a More Clinically
Seamless Integration in Therapeutic Practice   109

9   Thinking about Resistance: Affect, Cognition, and Corrective
Emotional Experiences   117

10 Should Psychoanalytic Training Be Training to Be
    a Psychoanalyst?   131

11 Epistemological Foundations of Psychoanalysis:
    Science, Hermeneutics, and the Vicious Circles of
    Adversarial Discourse   139

PART II
Race, Class, Greed, and the Social Construction
of Desire   153

12 Psychoanalysis and the World of Cultural Constructions:
    The Contextual Self and the Realm of Everyday Unhappiness   155

13 Full Pockets, Empty Lives: Probing the Contemporary
    Culture of Greed   168

14 Greed as an Individual and Social Phenomenon   184

15 Psychoanalysis, Psychotherapy, and the Challenges
    of Race and Class   195

16 The Vicious Circles of Racism: A Cyclical Psychodynamic
    Perspective on Race and Race Relations   207

    References   221
    Index   237

About the Author

Paul L. Wachtel, PhD, is CUNY Distinguished Professor in the doctoral program in clinical psychology at City College and the Graduate Center of the City University of New York. He received his doctorate in clinical psychology from Yale and is a graduate of the postdoctoral program in psychoanalysis and psychotherapy at New York University, where he is also a faculty member. Dr. Wachtel has lectured and given workshops throughout the world on psychotherapy, personality theory, and the applications of psychological theory and research to the major social issues of our time. He has been a leading voice for integrative thinking in the social and behavioral sciences and was a cofounder of the Society for the Exploration of Psychotherapy Integration. He has received the Hans H. Strupp Memorial Award for Psychoanalytic Writing, Teaching, and Research, the Distinguished Psychologist Award from Division 29 of the American Psychological Association (Psychotherapy), and the Scholarship and Research Award from Division 39 (Psychoanalysis).

Acknowledgments

A key theme of this book is that human beings always live, behave, and experience in the context of a web of relationships. It now seems to me that an acknowledgments section of the sort I once thought was sufficient – acknowledging those who read the manuscript or directly discussed the ideas – seems to fly in the face of the very point the book is making. We are by no means *merely* the sum of our relationships; this is a serious distortion and misunderstanding of the relational point of view that I have critically discussed in some detail in a previous book, *Relational Theory and the Practice of Psychotherapy*. But, as the present book further elaborates, it is equally a distortion to think we can understand an individual *apart from* the web of relationships that are so intricately entwined with our very nature.

In my own life, I am acutely aware of the way that my friends, family, colleagues, and students have sustained me through all the ups and downs that life presents. My life, it seems to me, does not belong exclusively to me but is a *joint* product of my own inclinations and the ways those inclinations have been met, shaped, amplified, and modified by the people with whom I have shared my days. Those who have contributed to this book are thus not just the people with whom I have directly discussed the ideas introduced here, but the people who, in being part of my life, have, for better or worse, made me *me*. I cannot saddle my friends with the responsibility for what is written in this book, but I can certainly acknowledge their contribution even if they have not read a single word. In making the somewhat unusual decision of dedicating this book to my friends collectively, I am in part avoiding the daunting – and ultimately thankless – challenge of naming some individuals and, thereby, leaving others out. But I am also acknowledging with gratitude a lesson learned during a successful battle with illness during the period in which this book was being created – that I have been truly blessed by the remarkable network of friends who share and give meaning to my life. Their love, support, and simple reminder of how much sheer *fun* life can be was perhaps the most powerful medicine of all. In dedicating this book to my friends, I am making but a small down payment on a debt that – happily – continues to grow.

One very specific context that has sustained me over the years, especially in the kinds of efforts presented in this book, has been the clinical psychology doctoral program at the City College of New York. The program has had an unwavering commitment to understanding people in depth and to the pursuit of clinical psychology as a discipline that is rooted both in rigorous intellectual effort and research and in humane, empathic immersion in the experiences of others. There are many pressures in our society today to trim the sails of such ambitions and pursue instead a narrow vision guided by purported economic necessity or by a cramped, ideologically blindered, and, in fact, scientifically unsophisticated program of supposedly "empirically supported" treatment methods. (See Wachtel, 2010 for a critique of these misuses of science that is rooted not in a rejection of science but in respect for its complexity.) The program at City has steadfastly resisted these pressures while pursuing serious intellectual inquiry and intensive clinical training with openness, energy, and rigor. I am both lucky and proud to be a part of that community.

As always, providing the most day-to-day sustenance and stimulation, offering both the love that keeps me going and the intellectual firepower that makes me stop and think, my wife Ellen has been by my side through all the challenges and the triumphs, sharing my life in such a profound way that it is impossible to say who I would be without her.

I also wish to acknowledge the specific contributions to this book of the editors and publishers who gave me permission to include here work that had previously appeared in somewhat different form or context in various journals or edited books. It has all been at least partly reworked to eliminate redundancy and to give a coherence and direction to the book's argument. But the generous permission of the publications listed below has greatly aided my efforts to create a book that states as effectively as I can the implications of cyclical psychodynamic theory both for clinical work and for understanding the ways in which cultures and societies shape us and are simultaneously shaped by the daily experiences of the people who live within them.

Earlier versions of many of the chapters appeared in various books and journals. I gratefully acknowledge the following journals for permission to include material I had previously published: *Journal of Abnormal Psychology* (Chapter 1), *Psychoanalytic Psychology* (Chapters 3 and 15), *The International Journal of Psycho-Analysis* (Chapter 4), *Contemporary Psychoanalysis* (Chapter 5), the *Journal of Psychotherapy Integration* (Chapters 6, 8, and 9), *Psychoanalytic Dialogues* (Chapter 7), *Journal of European Psychoanalysis* (Chapter 11), *American Journal of Psychoanalysis* (Chapter 13), and *Psychoanalytic Review* (Chapter 16). An earlier version of Chapter 2 appeared in R. Curtis & G. Stricker (Eds.), *How people change: Inside and outside therapy* published by Plenum. Parts of Chapter 12 appeared in C. Strozier & M. Flynn (Eds.), *Trauma and self* published by Rowman & Littlefield. An earlier version of Chapter 10 appeared in M. Meisels & E. Shapiro (Eds.), *Tradition and innovation in psychoanalytic education* originally published by Erlbaum. An earlier version of Chapter 14 appeared in J. Auerbach, K. Levy, & C. Schaffer (Eds.), *Relatedness, self-definition and mental representation: Essays in honor of Sidney J. Blatt* published by Brunner-Routledge. I am grateful to all these publishers for permission to include this material here.

Part I

Psychotherapy, Personality Dynamics, and the World of Intersubjectivity

Chapter 1

Cyclical Psychodynamics

An Integrative, Relational Point of View

This book extends and further explores a point of view that has characterized my work over the course of many years. The theoretical perspective I have come to call cyclical psychodynamics originated in my efforts to come to terms with challenges to psychoanalytic thought deriving from the arguments and research efforts of behavior therapists and social learning theorists; but as the cyclical psychodynamic perspective has continued to evolve, it has addressed additional challenges and sought additional opportunities in relation to an expanding array of observations and viewpoints, both from outside of psychoanalysis and from within. Among the important nonpsychoanalytic influences in shaping the trajectory of cyclical psychodynamic theory have been the ideas and practices of family therapists and family systems theorists, emotion-focused and humanistic-experiential therapists, and acceptance and mindfulness-oriented cognitive-behavioral therapists. Alongside the influence of these diverse clinical traditions, cyclical psychodynamic thought and practice have been nourished by attachment theory and research and by developments in social and affective neuroscience. Additionally, its particular characteristics were shaped in important ways by efforts to pay more serious attention than is common in clinical theorizing to the powerful influence of cultural values and of race, class, and ethnicity upon the phenomena addressed by clinicians and by the reciprocal effort to explore the ways in which our understanding of the complexities of psychological dynamics could, in turn, shed light on a number of pressing social challenges, especially in the realm of race relations (Wachtel, 1999) and in the interlocking phenomena of materialism, obsession with economic growth, and despoilation of the environment (e.g., Wachtel, 1983, 2003).

An especially important element in the evolution of cyclical psychodynamic theory was its encounter with the concurrently evolving relational movement in psychoanalysis. At first, the relational point of view and cyclical psychodynamics proceeded on parallel tracks, developing very similar ideas in many important respects but remaining separate strands in the overall landscape of the field. But over time, the consonances became more and more apparent (Wachtel, 1997, 2008, 2011a). The beginnings of the relational movement are generally viewed as being marked by the publication of Greenberg and Mitchell's (1983) book on *Object Relations in Psychoanalytic Theory* and Mitchell's (1988) publication of *Relational Concepts in Psychoanalysis*, though certainly there were numerous precursors, which these two works built upon and integrated. Thus, the first formulations of cyclical psychodynamic theory (Wachtel, 1973, 1977a, 1977b) predated the appearance of relational theory by a number of years, and hence were built on an independent conceptual foundation. Moreover, whereas relational theory was designed to integrate diverse strands of thought within the spectrum of psychoanalysis, cyclical psychodynamic theory aimed at a still broader integration, including not only psychoanalytic theories and observations but those that derived from outside the world of psychoanalysis as well. These differences in origin led to differences in terminology and emphasis that for a time made the substantial overlap between cyclical psychodynamic theory and other versions of relational thought not as readily apparent as they might be today.

One-Person, Two-Person, and Contextual Points of View

Among the various features that cyclical psychodynamic theory shares with the majority of relational theories, one of the most fundamental is the shared emphasis on what has come to be called the two-person point of view. As I have discussed in detail elsewhere (Wachtel, 2008), there are actually several dimensions to the two-person point of view that are not always sufficiently distinguished. Most common in all relational theories is a two-person *epistemology*. Here, the emphasis is on a critique of the objectivist assumptions that led early analysts to regard themselves as neutral observers, simply commenting on the dynamics of the other person. This objectivist element in psychoanalytic thought was, in fact, never as total as the neat distinction between one-person and two-person theory suggests, but there are certainly important differences between the epistemological foundations of classical psychoanalytic thought and those of relational thought, as has been well articulated by writers such as Aron (1996), I. Z. Hoffman (1998), and Mitchell (1988, 1993, 1997). Cyclical psychodynamics is, in this sense, clearly a two-person theory, and there are very few differences in this regard between the cyclical psychodynamic point of view and those of other relational theorists.

But when consideration moves from matters of epistemology to the understanding of personality dynamics or the essentials of clinical practice, new complexities enter. Not all writers who manifest a two-person point of view with regard to epistemology are as thoroughly two-person in their thinking when it comes to personality dynamics or to the practice of psychoanalysis or psychotherapy. In these realms, what I have called the *default position*, the largely unexamined set of assumptions carried over from older psychoanalytic conceptualizations, finds its way into relational thinking to a surprising extent (Wachtel, 2008). As discussed later, and throughout this book, the cyclical psychodynamic understanding of personality dynamics and development highlights the *pervasive* relevance of the relational context in contributing to the individual's behavior and experience, not just in the analytic session, but in every facet of the person's life throughout the day. The relational matrix is not just the shaping context for development in the earliest years of life or the epistemological foundation for observations in the analytic session. It is an inextricable element in personality dynamics throughout life. When this critical point is lost, and what Mitchell (1988) called the metaphor of the baby and the developmental tilt take center stage, then relational theories unwittingly take on crucial properties of the one-person theories they were created to replace.

Although the one-person versus two-person distinction served very valuably in highlighting the differences between older classical models in psychoanalysis and the newer relational models, it is a misleading term when applied to the dynamics of personality. The crucial contexts in which personality continues to evolve include not just two-person contexts. They include as well the triangular configurations highlighted both by family therapists and by psychoanalysts in relation to the Oedipus complex; the groups of varying sizes encountered in school, at work, and at play; and the larger context of culture and society. For this reason, although cyclical psychodynamics falls squarely on the two-person side of the *epistemological* divide between one-person and two-person theories, its understanding of personality dynamics is more accurately described as contextual than as two-person (Wachtel, 2008).

The observations that psychotherapists make in the therapeutic session are two-person observations because there are two people in the room, and each is contributing to what transpires and what is observed. But in formulating a more complete understanding of the person sitting across from her,[1] what is essential for the therapist to achieve is a *contextual* understanding, an understanding of the person in the context of *his life*, of the ways in which his experiences are shaped by the myriad forms of relational matrices that he encounters and participates in throughout the day and week. As discussed in various ways throughout this book, the two-person form of that context can at times be overvalued in clinical theory because the observations most immediately available to the therapist or analyst are two-person observations. But for that very reason, it is essential that our understanding of the patient not be shaped too exclusively by the emotional experience of the two parties in the room alone. That experience, to be sure, is of enormous importance in developing a deep and personally substantive understanding of the patient's experience. It is a crucial element in the approach to therapeutic practice and therapeutic understanding depicted in this book. But it is also a potential trap, a seductive and partial substitute for the even broader and deeper understanding that can only be achieved when attention to the co-created emotional experience in the room, no matter how compelling, is complemented and illuminated by equal attention to what we learn from the patient's accounts of his life outside the room.

It is certainly true that those accounts lack the immediacy of what is happening right at the moment, and they require, in certain ways, more filling in, because we are not there with the patient at the time and must rely on his recollections and his selective attention and memory. Our knowledge of these events is always partial and in certain ways conjectural, but there are ways to inquire about the patient's experiences outside the room that give us a better chance to achieve at least a therapeutically useful approximation (see, for example, Wachtel, 2011a, 2011b; E. F. Wachtel & Wachtel, 1986). And, of course, our understanding of what is transpiring in the room right at the moment, notwithstanding our immediate presence and participation, is *also* limited and subject to selectivity and personalized constructions. Indeed, *both* facets of the more complete and accurate picture to which we aspire – the observations from within the room and the reports of what transpire outside – are more adequately understood and more adequately evaluated in relation to each other. It is not that either realm can *validate* the other; if we have made up a story for ourselves about the patient, we are capable of imposing that story on both kinds of observations. But the complementarity of observations and formulations helps to shed light on each in ways that underline both their consonances and their contradictions, and thus, for the best of clinicians, can serve to continually *raise questions* about formulations that have become too comfortably or confidently settled.

Constructivism and Other Shared Themes

Another element of convergence between cyclical psychodynamic theory and most other relational perspectives is their shared emphasis on constructivism. The constructivist epistemology that underlies cyclical psychodynamic and most other relational theories dovetails with the two-person point of view in important ways (see, for example, Aron, 1996; I. Z. Hoffman, 1998). It dovetails as well with the findings of contemporary research on perception and memory (e.g., Schacter, 1996; Schacter, Norman, & Koutstaal, 1998). The older understanding that informed Freud's theorizing, a vision of camera-like registration of perceptual input and of fixed memory traces that are stored in an original form and then distorted in the service of defense (see Schimek, 1975), has been replaced in subsequent years by a vision of perception and memory in which it is understood that memory and perception are active processes whereby we select, construct, and reconstruct anew each time we remember or, indeed, perceive.

Further characterizing the shared assumptive world of cyclical psychodynamics and most other relational approaches is an emphasis on mutuality, reciprocity, co-construction, intersubjectivity, and the powerful interconnectedness of people and their experiences and perceptions. Each of these terms refers to something slightly different, but they converge and overlap both with each other and with the previously noted concepts of the two-person point of view and of constructivism. In this, they imply as well an approach to the therapeutic relationship that is more collaborative and egalitarian than had been typical of psychoanalysis previously or than is typical of some contemporary cognitive and cognitive-behavioral approaches. I shall have more to say about these latter points as I proceed.

The Integrative Aims of Relational Theory and Cyclical Psychodynamics

Another key theme that unites cyclical psychodynamic theory and most other relational theories is the emphasis on integrating different points of view into a larger, more comprehensive theoretical vision. Central to the origins of the relational turn in psychoanalysis was the effort to highlight convergences between object relations theory, interpersonal theory, and self-psychology. Greenberg and Mitchell (1983) first articulated these convergences in their distinction between the drive/structure model and the relational/structure model, and a wide range of relational writers has noted them subsequently. This original integrative thrust in relational theorizing has been complemented by efforts to integrate as well a variety of other perspectives, especially attachment theory (e.g., Beebe & Lachmann, 2003; Mitchell, 1999; Wallin, 2007) and critical elements of feminist thought (e.g., Aron, 1996; Benjamin, 1988; Dimen & Goldner, 2002; Goldner, 1991; Harris, 2005). This latter feature of the relational synthesis overlaps in important ways with the already mentioned emphasis on mutuality, collaboration, and awareness of the *constructed* nature of what is often taken as just the way things are, in matters of gender as well as in other realms of living.

Cyclical psychodynamic theory too originated in an effort at integration, but, as has already been noted, the integration sought included not just diverse psychoanalytic perspectives but also points of view that were outside the psychoanalytic spectrum altogether and that, in some cases, were conceived of as *in opposition* to psychoanalysis. Thus, to reconcile these competing points of view required a still more probing examination of the assumptions underlying each. The key to addressing this challenge was to look to each facet of the emerging integration not in terms of its received formulations (the official or standard versions of psychoanalytic thought, cognitive-behavioral thought, and so forth – which often *were* formulated in ways that looked incompatible), but to focus instead on what clinicians or researchers from each tradition actually did and actually observed. As I further elaborate as I proceed, this strategy was predicated on the assumption that the differences in viewpoint by proponents of different theories and approaches at least in part reflected primary focus on and attention to certain phenomena and relationships and a marginalizing or even outright failure to notice certain others. The construction of a more comprehensive and integrative theory required close attention to how each theoretical perspective foregrounded different phenomena and, where strong incompatibilities appeared, placed at the margins some of the very observations that were central to the other point of view. The challenge, thus, was to develop more comprehensive formulations that included, in a single coherent framework, the observations central to each perspective without excluding those central to the others.

As a consequence of its broader integrative aim, cyclical psychodynamic theory, although strongly rooted in the psychoanalytic point of view and in the relational reconceptualization of that point of view, also has important differences from other psychoanalytic viewpoints, including other relational viewpoints (Wachtel, 2008). Both the broader integrative ambitions of cyclical psychodynamic theory and the fact that for a number of years its evolution proceeded apart from that of the relational movement gave it a different cast and attuned it to different phenomena. It thus makes sense to think of cyclical psychodynamic theory as a theory whose foundations lie *both* in the relational point of view *and* in the larger psychotherapy integration movement (Wachtel, Kruk, & McKinney, 2005).[2]

Alternative Conceptions of the Dynamics of Psychological Development

Cyclical psychodynamics shares with virtually all psychoanalytic perspectives, relational and nonrelational, an emphasis on unconscious motivations, conflicts, and defenses, but it conceptualizes the dynamics of those unconscious phenomena – and especially the dynamics of their persistence over time – in a different fashion. In place of the emphasis in much psychoanalytic theorizing on processes such as fixation and developmental arrest – that is, on how portions of the psyche are split off and prevented from growing and changing, remaining instead infantile, archaic, primitive, and out of touch with the reality of the person's everyday life – the cyclical psychodynamic conceptualization understands the influence of early experiences rather differently. Cyclical psychodynamic theory too treats early experiences as of critical importance, but their importance lies in how they skew the *later* experiences the person has. That is, people with different early experiences are likely to have different *later* experiences as well, because the early experience leads them to interact with others differently, to interpret and give meaning to events differently, and so on.

Now, of course, all theories that stress the importance of early experiences posit that later experiences are changed as a consequence. Otherwise, there would be little meaning to claiming that the early experience is consequential. But from a cyclical psychodynamic perspective, these differences in the person's later experiences are not just a result of the earlier representations having been deeply etched into the psyche or rendered persistent and relatively unchangeable because they have been internalized. Rather than depicting psychological inclinations, once internalized, as playing themselves out more or less independently of what is transpiring in the present, the cyclical psychodynamic understanding is that there is a *continuing and mutually consequential* transaction between the person's existing predispositions and the people and events he or she encounters. The maintenance over time of the pattern of behaving and experiencing established early in life requires repeated confirmation of the assumptions that early experience has engendered, ongoing repetition of the same kinds of experiences again and again.

This is not to say that the proclivities that were established early are easy to change. The cyclical psychodynamic emphasis on the need for patterns to receive repeated confirmation, to elicit repeated experiences consistent with the early-engendered structural inclinations, in order to be maintained, does not mean that just one or two disconfirmations will result in radical change. Far from it. Change *is* difficult. Expectations – especially unconscious expectations – *are* hard to change. But the existing pattern, while having a good deal of drag, is by no means inexorable or invulnerable to new input. If the patient were to repeatedly encounter experiences that differed from those he learned to expect in childhood, the patterns of expectation/perception/behavior learned in childhood would also, over time, begin to change. But the tragedy of the patterns that patients bring to our offices is that they are patterns that *prevent* such new input from developing. The behavior and affective tone that derive from the patient's prior experiences are likely to elicit still more such experiences, evoking feelings and reactions in others that once again make the original inclinations and original patterns of behavior and affect likely to be manifested. This dynamic holds whether the pattern is problematic or salutary. Thus, as I have described elsewhere:

> The two-year-old who has developed an engaging and playful manner is far more likely to evoke friendly interest and attention on the part of adults than is the child who is rather quiet and withdrawn. The latter will typically encounter a less rich interpersonal environment, which will further decrease the likelihood that he will drastically change. Similarly, the former is likely to continually learn that other people are fun and are eager to interact with him; and his pattern, too, is likely to become more firmly fixed as he grows. Further, not only will the two children tend to evoke different behavior from others, they will also interpret differently the same reaction from another person. Thus, the playful child may experience a silent or grumpy response from another as a kind of game and may continue to interact until perhaps he does elicit an appreciative response. The quieter child, not used to much interaction, will readily accept the initial response as a signal to back off.
>
> If we look at the two children as adults, we may perhaps find the difference between them still evident: one outgoing, cheerful, and expecting the best of people; the other rather shy, and unsure that anyone is interested. A childhood pattern has persisted into adulthood. Yet we really don't understand the developmental process unless we see how, successively, teachers, playmates, girlfriends, and colleagues have been drawn in as "accomplices" in maintaining the persistent pattern. And, I would suggest, we don't understand the possibilities for change unless we realize that even now there are such "accomplices," and that if they stopped playing their role in the process, it would be likely eventually to alter. (Wachtel, 1997, p. 52)[3]

The pattern changes over time, of course. In many of its details, it obviously does not look the same in a 40-year-old as in a 3-year-old – another reason why internalization or fixation are not sufficient explanations. But without some significant shift in the tone and nature of what is elicited from others in the course of daily experience, the emotional essence of the pattern is likely to remain fairly constant, constituting what Sullivan (1953, p. 103) called an "envelope of insignificant differences." It is the tendency for entrenched psychological patterns to elicit from others the very responses that will keep the pattern going that constitutes the ironic heart of psychopathology, and it is the repeated cycle of internal states of motivation, affect, and expectation eliciting external responses that once again maintain that internal state (and thereby make likely a similar external response still again) that gives the *cyclical* psychodynamic model its name and its conceptual structure.

Thus, from a cyclical psychodynamic vantage point, what maintains the unconscious persistence of the fantasies, desires, or images of self and other that analysts often refer to as infantile, primitive, or archaic, is the way those seemingly infantile psychological structures repeatedly elicit experiences that confirm them.[4] I say "seemingly" infantile because I question the assumption that these ubiquitous psychological structures and inclinations are just holdovers from the earliest years of life, anomalies out of touch with the realities of adult living. Rather, I suggest, what is crucial to understand about the unconscious fantasies and longings that psychoanalytic inquiry reveals is that if one looks closely enough, one sees that, either directly or symbolically, they are in fact *exquisitely in touch* with the realities of the person's daily life. They may seem odd and anomalous if they are viewed against the background of what we take to be ordinary adult living. But if we look at the *particular version* of ordinary that the patient actually lives, at the subtleties and particularities of affect, tone, and meaning that lie at the heart of his interactions and experiences with others, those "infantile" wishes, feelings, and fantasies make more sense. When it comes to the experiences that actually fuel and maintain the patient's unconscious desires and fantasies, each of us lives in a rather idiosyncratic world; with apologies to Heinz Hartmann, none of us lives in an "average expectable environment."

Viewed differently, the common distinction in psychoanalytic discourse between the inner world and the more superficial world of everyday experience dissolves from the vantage point of a cyclical psychodynamic analysis. Inner and outer are mutually and reciprocally co-determinative, and depth lies not in the direction to which one turns one's attention (inward or to the past), but rather in the thoroughness of one's understanding of how inner state and outer reality re-create each other over and over (as well as in the adequacy of one's understanding of how attention to each can be employed in the effort to *change* the other).

The Origins of Cyclical Psychodynamic Theory in the Confrontation of Psychoanalysis and Behavior Therapy

By now, this emphasis on the pervasive role of vicious and virtuous circles in maintaining patterns of personality and on the critical importance of understanding how our behavior and experience vary in different social or relational contexts seems to me so obvious it feels remarkable that it entailed such a struggle to articulate this point of view. As I listen to my patients now, the ways in which their actions in the world so frequently feed back to maintain the inner state that generated them – a phenomenon illustrated throughout this book – are repeatedly and strikingly apparent.[5] Similarly, it now seems to me equally obvious that no adequate theory of personality can ignore the often quite enormous differences in the way people behave – and *feel* – in different contexts or in interacting with different people. When we compare how we feel and how we behave at a party or a bar or at a dissertation orals; with our closest friends or with people we have met at a formal occasion; with our children, our supervisors at work, or our sexual partners, it is remarkable that we can maintain at all the sense of sameness that enables a feeling of a coherent identity or self. For these differences are not only in manifest behavior but also often in the very way we experience ourselves. Not only our behavior but also our basic sense of competence or incompetence, of shyness or boldness, of self-worth or worthlessness can vary from context to context to a noteworthy degree. There are people with whom we feel funny, interesting, and uninhibited, and people with whom our entire sense of well-being, adequacy, or vitality seems to disappear. Any understanding of personality that does not take into account these enormous variations in behavior and even self-experience, or that dismisses them as mere surface waves atop an internal world whose nature was long ago set by the experiences of childhood, seems to me one that is just not paying attention to the actual data of lived experience.

These differences of behavior and experience are of central importance to a range of contemporary relational theorists who organize much of their understanding around conceptualizations of multiple self-states (e.g., Benjamin, 2010; Bromberg, 1998; Davies, 1996; Mitchell, 1993; Slavin, 1996). They were similarly a key element of Erikson's (1950, 1959) classic writings on identity, which pointed to and were grounded in not a simple sameness across situations, but a *constructed* sense of coherence across the enormous *diversity* of our behavior and experience, a sense that we are one *despite* being many. We "contain multitudes," as Walt Whitman famously said.

Indeed, it is one measure of mental health that this differentiation among the multiple ways we can act and feel in different contexts be well and solidly established. At the extremes, of course, if someone, say, behaves with one's children as one does with one's sexual partner, we are clearly in the realm of very serious pathology. But even short of this, if one is no more relaxed and intimate with a close friend than with a casual acquaintance, or, conversely, if one is no more cautious and attentive to image with one's boss than one is with a friend or family member, then one is likely to be seriously hampered in full and satisfying living. Moreover, it must again be noted that I am not referring here merely to manifest behavior. The differences I am referring to in these different contexts and relationships are likely to also be evident in the way we feel about ourselves and feel about our lives. Although the proportions of the experiences will differ from person to person, for virtually all of us there are times when we feel strong and competent and times when we feel inadequate, fraudulent, or overwhelmed, and those differences have a good deal to do with the setting or relationship in which we find ourselves. There are times when the shyest person feels social, relaxed, even gregarious, and times when even the most extraverted person feels uncomfortable or insecure, and here again, the setting and the relationship play a significant role. Any adequate theory of personality must not only take these variations into account but also must be grounded in their very centrality; in the ways that our consistencies across time and situations and our simultaneous acute responsiveness to the constantly varying circumstances and challenges we encounter are the twin poles of personality dynamics, with neither more real nor more fundamental than the other.

Yet as I look back at the psychoanalytic landscape during the period of my early training, I can also readily understand why what now seems so obvious took so long to see clearly. The psychoanalysis of that day was dominated by a vision of psychological development and organization in which the very variations in behavior and experience I have just been discussing were relegated to the realm of the superficial (see Chapter 5). As a consequence, observations that could have highlighted those variations were filtered through a conceptual prism that rendered them either invisible or marginal. The interlocking set of ideas and clinical and investigative methods that constituted the heart of what could be called the received version of psychoanalysis (for example, neutrality, interpretation, free association) brought forth again and again the particular subset of observations that were consistent with those ideas and thereby further buttressed the same set of ideas (and the methods that both derived from and supported them). At the same time, this closed circle of methods and the observations that derived from them unwittingly suppressed or excluded other observations that could have challenged or expanded the entire framework (see Chapter 11).[6]

Similarly restrictive was the effect of psychoanalysis as a *social* group or network – that is, not just a set of ideas, but a set of concrete and affectively important personal ties with people whose good opinions I valued, whose ideas and perceptions I honored and listened to, and so forth. Here again, the closed circle that is thereby created, channeling thoughts and perceptions and screening out or invalidating alternative ways of seeing things is by no means unique to psychoanalysis. It is common to *all* systems of thought, whether intellectual, social, religious, or ideological. The particular community in which I was rather thoroughly immersed at the time was the psychoanalytic community, but the phenomenon I am addressing here is no less true for those whose almost exclusive reference group is cognitive-behavioral or any other of the tribes (I use the word advisedly) that constitute our field. This process of reverberating reinforcements of shared ideas, filtering out alternative and potentially more complex and multidimensional understandings, can be seen to play a critical role in ethnic or class conflict and in war and political strife (Wachtel, 1999), but it operates as well in scientific circles, as Kuhn (1962) and others have long pointed out.

Indeed, another important implication of what is called, as a shorthand, the two-person point of view is that individual perception per se must often be understood in a larger context. What we think we are just seeing with our own eyes is in fact seen through the eyes of the community to which we belong, which powerfully, though usually invisibly, leads us to notice certain phenomena and not others, to draw certain connections and not others, and to reach certain conclusions and interpretations and not others. These various processes influencing and filtering our thoughts and perceptions can lead as well to not noticing as clearly as one might ways in which one has *already* begun to differ from the received view of one's reference group. When this happens, the differences can remain unformulated almost in the sense discussed in a clinical context by D. B. Stern (1997). Or, in this slightly different context, they can be articulated in a way that keeps them dissociated from the (now more shaky) core beliefs that anchor one's continuing membership in the community. In my own case, for example, I had been increasingly struck by the variations in people's experience from context to context and, relatedly, by our *responsiveness* to our present context; but I had not articulated for myself (or had kept dissociated or marginalized) the ways in which such observations challenged the standard psychoanalytic thought of the time.

Interestingly, not having articulated sufficiently the *challenge* to a core element of my intellectual identity, I was not yet in a position to see the ways in which these new perceptions could – with some conceptual diligence – be *reconciled* with at least a transformed version of the core observations of psychoanalytic work. That reconciliation, between observations of our responsiveness to the events and experiences of our ongoing lives and the older core of psychoanalytic thought, ultimately became a key focus of cyclical psychodynamic theory. But the social and psychological constraints I have just noted rendered that task difficult to achieve and, indeed, made it difficult at first even to envision its necessity.

It thus took the challenge of essentially being *forced* to confront a point of view outside the confines and worldview of my community to enable me to be clear about and to articulate the ways in which I had begun – much more than I had let myself realize – to question some of the fundamental assumptions of the intellectual community of which I was a part. In my case, the challenge came in the form of Walter Mischel's 1968 book *Personality and Assessment*. Mischel, a social learning theorist and advocate of behavior therapy, was highly critical both of psychoanalysis and of the academic research traditions that emphasized the search for personality traits that were stable over time and across situations. Although the book was highly tendentious and excessive in its advocacy of a preponderantly situationist understanding of the sources of behavior and experience (Bowers, 1973; Wachtel, 1973), it made a very strong impact in the world of academic clinical and social psychology and, for all its flaws, also raised serious and substantial questions about the empirical and conceptual foundations of psychoanalytic thought.

My own serious attention to the book derived from being invited, as essentially in the role of defender of psychoanalysis, to participate in a panel on the book to be held at the annual meeting of the American Psychological Association (APA). As it happened, for reasons I can no longer remember, the panel was canceled close to the time of the APA meetings, but by then the die had been cast. I had spent much time preparing for it, and my immersion in Mischel's arguments led to the rethinking that eventuated in the cyclical psychodynamic point of view.

Two elements of my encounter with Mischel's book were especially important. The first was being confronted with a powerful (if again also flawed) argument for the importance of behavioral and experiential variability and responsiveness to circumstances. Mischel's argument was excessive and one-sided, but in its mustering of an enormous body of evidence, it did get me to think. And, very importantly, although the initial experience was that it was a *challenge* to psychoanalysis that I needed to fend off or rebut, as I thought further, I realized clearly for the first time that the version of psychoanalysis toward which I had been implicitly moving for some time actually included many of the observations that Mischel was highlighting. Put differently, I came to see that the evidence and viewpoint that Mischel was presenting was not as incompatible with psychoanalytic thought as I had originally thought (and as Mischel continued to think). Although I had not articulated it to myself as fully and clearly as I did after my encounter with Mischel's arguments, I had become increasingly restless with some of the unexamined, blandly accepted features of psychoanalytic thought and, beneath the surface of my own consciousness one might say, was beginning to fashion an alternative or critical version that sat better with what I was observing both in my clinical work and in my daily life. Thus, I came to see, I didn't so much need to *defend* psychoanalysis against Mischel's assault (and it *was* an assault; Mischel's understanding of psycho-analysis was rudimentary, and his arguments had a blunderbuss quality); rather I needed to *refine* my own understanding of what was continuingly of value in psychoanalysis, to sort out the premises that underlay my own thinking, to be clear both about what I had learned from my psychoanalytic training *and* where it left me unsatisfied – unsatisfied not just theoretically but, in important ways, clinically as well.

This clinical side of the rethinking initiated by Mischel's arguments leads me to the second important impetus for the development of the cyclical psychodynamic point of view – my immersion, for the first time in any serious way, in the rapidly accumulating evidence for the effectiveness of behavioral methods[7] and, perhaps even more important, in the world of actual behavioral practice. Here again, my initial instinct was to rebut, but serious attention led to a more complex response. After first feeling that the impressive evidence for behavior therapy *threatened* my psychoanalytic identity, further thought made me realize that it *amplified* and refined that identity, that it helped me to articulate intuitions, observations, and impressions that my identity as an analyst had prevented me from fully articulating for myself and enabled me to intervene more effectively in the very dynamics that my psychoanalytic perspective had enabled me to identify. As I further immersed myself in the actual practice of behavior therapy, I came to see that, in the hands of its best practitioners, it was not nearly as mechanical or superficial as I had been led to believe, and that in interesting and important ways it intersected fascinatingly with aspects of psychoanalytic practice.

At the same time, the overlaps and compatibilities I began to see did not entail a redundancy. There were still very considerable differences between what behavior therapists paid attention to and what psychoanalysts paid attention to and between what each did as clinicians. The challenge was thus to bring together the differing observations and differing methods into an overarching theoretical and clinical framework that did justice to both. The more opportunities I had to observe the work of leading behavioral clinicians, both on videotape and through their generosity in letting a member of a different tribe observe their work through a one-way mirror, the more impressed I was with their clinical sophistication,[8] and the more possibilities I saw for integrative combining of the strengths of each approach. I saw clearly ways in which their methods – especially their greater readiness to intervene actively in their patients' dilemmas rather than merely interpret them – could enhance my own clinical work. At the same time, it was also clear that behavioral work could benefit greatly from incorporating key elements in the psychoanalytic approach to understanding and to the clinical encounter. They had paid rather little attention to some of the most important contributions of the psychoanalytic tradition, such as attention to unconscious motivation, to conflict, to the ways that people defensively misrepresented their experience to protect their images of self and significant others. They were much more prone than analysts to accept social clichés about what people really want and to limit their attention to the person's conscious report of his or her experience. Each brought different strengths to the table, and each brought limitations. The key to taking clinical work and clinical theory to the next level, it seemed to me, was to develop a framework for practice and theory that could put all of this together in coherent fashion.

My initial efforts to incorporate behavioral methods into the work aimed to implement those methods as much as possible in the way that behavior therapists themselves used them. That was, after all, the mode of practice for which there was the most direct evidence for their effectiveness. In addition, I was not yet experienced enough in the use of these methods to innovate or improvise. I thus tried to do what the master behavioral clinicians I had observed had done and then, in the more psychoanalytic part of the work, to explore the impact and meaning of these interventions for the patient.

Over time, however, I began to be aware that there were differences in the way I was employing these procedures from how they were employed by exclusively behavioral therapists. As I have described it in various contexts examining this evolution, I found that having initially learned to practice psychotherapy from a psychoanalytic point of view, and having practiced from that perspective for my entire career up to that point, had given a psychoanalytic "accent" to my behavioral work. Rather than strictly following the protocol, I was communicating to a much greater degree than the behavioral clinicians I had observed that I was interested in the patient's ongoing subjective experience while participating in the procedure, in the feelings about me that were generated by our using these methods, and so forth. This was conveyed not so much by an explicit and conscious inquiry but, one might say, by the very core of my being with patients; it was just how I *am* with patients, and it got across even when I had no conscious intent to engage in such exploration but was still thinking that I was being "just behavioral" at certain points. As a consequence, my use of behavioral methods was evoking much more "material" than was evoked by the more straightforward employment of these methods by strictly behavioral clinicians. Behavioral procedures such as systematic desensitization or other exposure techniques thus became, in my idiosyncratic use of them, not just a complement or alternative to psychodynamic exploration but a *means* for such exploration as well.

Eventually, I became aware that I had moved from using discrete behavioral methods but with a psychoanalytic accent to having begun to develop a new dialect altogether, one in which the boundaries between what was psychodynamic and what was behavioral in the work began to blur. These days, it is difficult to identify when I am being psychodynamic in the session and when I am being behavioral. Both perspectives are often evident and woven together in any given intervention or mode of inquiry or exploration. As I describe in Chapter 8 of this book, my work has become more seamless.

To be sure, there are times, even today, in which I introduce a specific, readily identifiable behavioral intervention or, as the integration has subsequently further expanded (see discussion later in this chapter), when a specific method from some other orientation is introduced as something new or different at a given point. More often, however, the very way in which I engage in the therapeutic dialogue and therapeutic relationship with the patient has elements of several perspectives so thoroughly woven together that is it difficult to say where one begins and the other ends. The overall form of the work most closely resembles a modified psychoanalytic approach; that remains, after all, my home orientation. But beneath the surface, a sophisticated observer can readily observe a set of other dimensions that complement the psychodynamic without necessarily calling attention to themselves.[9]

The result of all these explorations and efforts at differentiation, reconciliation, and innovation was an integrative clinical and theoretical approach that I have spelled out in some detail elsewhere (see especially Wachtel, 1977a, 1997, 2008, 2011a). It included, for example, a perspective on what analysts called interpretation that highlighted similarities with what behavior therapists thought of as exposure, and illuminated how this yielded a more experiential approach to the former and a deeper and more comprehensive version of the latter. It highlighted the value of attending to the contingencies of the person's daily life, both as a way of achieving a more differentiated understanding of psychodynamic patterns and as a way of attending to and potentially disrupting the vicious circle patterns I came increasingly to realize were the central engine by which early vulnerabilities and maladaptations were carried forward into adult life. It offered a variety of routes into addressing the impact of the person's inhibitions and conflicts on the capacity to experience and express emotions and to hone the capacity to interact with others in satisfying and enhancing ways.

As I further pondered these challenges and surprising convergences, taking into account what observers and thinkers of *both* traditions had contributed and pursuing the reconciliation of the contradictions that were also beginning to feel like maybe they weren't really contradictions after all, my sense of the pervasive influence of vicious and virtuous circles began to increase still further. I realized that such circular patterns were essential to understand not just in the clinical situation but also as well in evaluating the implications of controlled psychological experiments, which writers like Mischel relied on almost exclusively to validate their formulations. The structure of most psychological experiments, with its division of the world into independent and dependent variables, is a kind of pure culture of situation, with much less possibility of the person *influencing* the situation he is in (Wachtel, 1973). As a consequence, theorists who rely too exclusively on experiments can erroneously downplay the role of individual psychological characteristics because they are artificially minimized in the very way the experiment is structured. When people are observed in their ecologically typical contexts, it is in fact in this very impact on the situation that personality so often is expressed. Personality often plays its role not in overriding the constraints of the situation, not *in spite of* the situation, but by *changing* the situation.

This is not to say that Mischel's emphasis on situation or context was unimportant or did not lead to an important corrective in my own way of thinking. Coming to terms with Mischel's arguments did highlight for me how important the situation or context was and called attention to the differences between those versions of psychoanalysis that strongly took context into account and those that did not. Situations may not operate as the kind of omnipotent independent variable that Mischel depicted them as, but they *do* play a major role in shaping behavior and experience. It is a role, however, in which personality is *also* critical, because personality itself determines to a significant degree the situations the person encounters. As I worked to formulate my understanding of what was faulty in the overreliance of Mischel and many other academic theorists on the results of controlled experiments, without sufficient tempering by attention to other sources of data about human behavior and experience, what emerged, in essence, was the first articulation of the cyclical psychodynamic point of view. I insert here a substantial part of my critique of Mischel's critique of psychoanalysis (Wachtel, 1973) because it represents the earliest emerging formulation of the cyclical psychodynamic point of view and illustrates some of the initial considerations on which the more mature theory eventually was built:

> The data generated and examined by most behaviorally oriented students of normal and abnormal behavior involve changes in clearly denotable behaviors in response to clear, unambiguous changes in environmental events. The subject, or the model in some studies, is given money or has it taken away, he is shocked or he escapes from shock, he is allowed privileges or they are denied him, etc. Under such circumstances, a kind of lawfulness tends to emerge in which the complicated formulations of psychodynamic theorists

seem very much beside the point. Behavior varies closely with changes in environmental events. The individual's "learning history with similar stimuli" is, of course, relevant, but one hardly needs to conceptualize complex personality structures with considerable cross-situational application. Change the situation and you change the behavior.

To the analyst, however, such studies are likely to seem irrelevant to the phenomena of interest to him. The data he observes consist largely of statements such as: "I feel angry at my girlfriend because she smiled in a condescending way. She said it was a warm smile, but it didn't feel that way to me." Or, "My boss criticized me for being so insistent with him, but I could tell from his tone of voice he was really proud of my assertiveness, and I had a good feeling that he supports me." Or, "It seemed to me you were more silent this hour. I felt you were angry with me because I complained about the fee, and I was afraid you'd say we should stop therapy. I know you'll think *I'm* the angry one, and want to stop, but I think you're wrong, and I resent your distortion of my feelings."

Such reports do describe behavior in response to environmental events. In principle, a girlfriend's smile, a boss' tone of voice, or an analyst's silence are events that can be observed just as the administration of a food pellet to a rat or a token to a back-ward patient. But whereas the latter two events are specifically chosen to be clear and unequivocal, the interpersonal events scrutinized by the analyst are often exceedingly ambiguous. The experimenter, no less than the subject, must judge on largely idiosyncratic grounds whether a smile is warm or condescending, and observer reliability regarding a tone of voice is unlikely to be impressive. Views may and do differ as to whether it is a wise *strategy* to study such ambiguous events at this point in the development of our discipline, but it must be acknowledged that we all spend a good portion of each day responding more or less adequately to just such ambiguous "stimuli." (p. 328). . . .

Still another way in which differing strategies of investigation may lead dynamic and behavioral investigators to differing conclusions is illuminated by an interpersonal perspective on human behavior. If each person's behavior is largely a function of the interpersonal situation in which he is engaged, then when two or more people interact, they are each not only influenced by the behavior of the other (in the familiar sense of a response to a stimulus); each also *influences* the behavior of the other, by virtue of the stimulus properties of his own behavior. Person A responds to the stimulus properties of Person B, but Person B in turn is responsive to the behavior of Person A which he has in part determined. Further, these are both continuous adaptations, not simply sequential. From such a systems orientation, the understanding of any one person's behavior in an interpersonal situation solely in terms of the stimuli *presented to* him gives only a partial and misleading picture. For to a very large extent, these stimuli are *created by* him. They are responses to his own behaviors, events he has played a role in bringing about, rather than occurrences independent of who he is and over which he has no control. . . .

From the above considerations we may see that the postulation of consistency of personality need not be incompatible with the view that people may be acutely sensitive to changes in the stimulus situation. For consistency need not be the result of a static structure that moves from situation to situation and pays no heed to stimuli. Much of the rigidity and persistence of human behavior can be accounted for without conceiving of an id, cut off from the perceiving, adapting aspect of the personality; and the striking tendency, observed by Freud and many others, for human beings to persist in beating their heads against countless proverbial walls does not require the postulation of a repetition compulsion (Freud, orig. publ. 1920). Rather, one can, in many cases, view consistency as a result of being in particular situations frequently, but situations largely of one's own making and themselves describable as a characteristic of one's personality.

These considerations suggest that the finding in many experiments of rather minimal consistency in behavior from situation to situation (Mischel, 1968) may be in part an artifact of the conceptual model and research strategy that has typically guided American personality research. Mischel noted the discrepancy between these research findings and the persistent impression that people are characterizable by their typical way of acting. He attributed the discrepancy largely to a documented tendency for observers to *falsely* construe consistency when diversity is the fact. But genuine consistency may also occur in most life situations and yet not be evident in the laboratory. For the typical experiment, with its emphasis on standardized independent variables as antecedents of the behavior to be studied, may short-circuit the mutual influence process described above, which is importantly involved in the generation of consistency.

In most experiments, some stimulus event is designated as the independent variable, and every effort is made to assure that this independent variable is presented to each subject in the same fashion. Research assistants are trained to behave similarly with each subject, and if they do vary their behavior in response to some feature of the subject's interpersonal style, this is generally viewed as a failure of the experimental method; the "independent variable" is supposed to be "standardized." Such a model of research, with the experimenter preprogrammed to occur independently of the myriad interpersonal cues of the subject may be designated as the model of the "implacable experimenter."

Such a model is well suited for testing the isolated effect of a particular independent variable, for it assures, if proper controls are included, that that variable is what accounts for the differing behaviors in the various experimental groups. Mischel's survey suggests that in experiments conducted in this fashion, the behavior of individuals will vary considerably when the "independent variable" is varied (subject, of course, to the limiting parameters discussed above, e.g., degree of psychopathology and ambiguity of the situation encountered).

But let us note what such a research procedure does *not* examine. Although the highly practiced and routinized behavior of the experimenter does not rule out all opportunity for observing individual differences in the subjects of the study – differences in perception or interpretation of events, or in response to the same situation, may be noted – it does effectively prevent the subject from recreating familiar stimulus situations by evoking typical complementary behavior by the experimenter in response to the subject's behavior. In most life situations, whether someone is nice to us or nasty, attentive or bored, seductive or straightlaced is in good part a function of our own behavior. But in the typical experiment the subject has little control over the interpersonal situation he encounters. It has been determined even before he enters the room. Borrowing the language of the existentialists, such experiments reveal a person in his "thrownness," but do not make clear his responsibility for his situation.

Mischel (1968) suggested that the impression of identity or constancy in personality may be reinforced by regularities in the environmental contexts in which a person is observed. Mischel's focus is on the occasions when the regularity is a function of the conditions of observation rather than of the person's life, as when we only see someone in a particular context, though he in fact operates in a wide variety of situations. But what if the person is *usually* in a particular situation? In such a case, it may be true that his behavior is describable as a function of his situation, and perhaps also that he could act differently if the situation were different. But then we must ask why for some people the situation is so rarely different. How do we understand the man who is constantly in the presence of overbearing women, or constantly immersed in his work, or constantly with weaker men who are cowed by him but offer little honest feedback? Further, how do we understand the man who seems to bring out the bitchy side of *whatever* woman he encounters, or ends up turning almost all social encounters into work sessions, or intimidates even men who usually are honest and direct?

Certainly we need a good deal more data before we are sure just how general such phenomena are, how characterizable people are by the situations they "just happen" to run into. What should be clear, however, is that, piecemeal observation of "stimuli" and "responses" or "independent" and "dependent" variables, divorced from the temporal context of mutually influencing events, can shed little light on these questions. If experiments in the implacable experimenter model are the central source of data for one's view of man, it is understandable that conceptions of man as constructing his life or his world, or of personality as a self-maintaining system, would have little appeal. (p. 331)

Ultimately, Mischel's critique led me to look more closely at a number of habits of thought that were very prominent in psychoanalytic discourse – both to see them more clearly *as* habits of thought in psychoanalysis and to see more clearly as well their limitations. But it also led me to realize that although my thinking had remained grounded in the psychoanalytic tradition, I had been using psychoanalysis selectively, placing more weight on and taking more seriously certain aspects of psychoanalysis than others. That is, it led me to look more closely at how my own psychoanalytic thinking had evolved, at the ways in which I had been implicitly differentiating among psychoanalytic positions, not swallowing psychoanalysis whole but rooting my thinking in some features of psychoanalytic thought and in fact being skeptical about some others. As I examined more closely what my own psychoanalytic assumptions were, and which psychoanalytic thinkers had most profoundly influenced my own thinking about clinical and theoretical matters, I realized that, notwithstanding Mischel's hatchet job on psychoanalysis, in fact the versions of psychoanalytic thought to which I was increasingly drawn were not at all threatened by the findings reported by Mischel, and were in fact *enhanced* by them. At the time of my initial encounter with Mischel's work, it was particularly the ideas of Erikson, Sullivan, and Horney[10] that had been increasingly informing my thinking. As both the field and the cyclical psychodynamic point of view continued to evolve, that mix was enriched by the incorporation of the range of psychoanalytic thinkers that are now described as relational. In all these versions of psychoanalytic thought, the specificity of behavior and experience and their responsiveness to the relational context, far from representing a challenge, are an intrinsic part of the understanding. But in contrast to the dismissive inattention to both personality structure and the complexities of personality dynamics manifested by Mischel, these psychoanalytic formulations *embrace* those complexities even as they attend to the variability emphasized by Mischel. Mischel's critique was framed in relation to a global psychodynamic point of view, but in fact different psychodynamic theorists differed substantially in relation to the very issues that Mischel was addressing.

The Individual and the System: Assimilating Family Systems Thinking into the Evolving Cyclical Psychodynamic Point of View

Once the basic framework of cyclical psychodynamic theory was shaped in the effort to integrate observations and methods deriving from the psychodynamic and behavioral traditions, the next challenge entailed the assimilation of ideas and methods from family therapy and family systems theories. At the time I was working on *Psychoanalysis and Behavior Therapy: Toward an Integration* (Wachtel, 1977a), my wife, Ellen, having recently completed her PhD in clinical psychology, was engaged in postdoctoral study in family therapy at the Ackerman Institute. As she was being introduced to the ideas and methods of family therapy and simultaneously hearing about my own explorations of the interface between psychoanalysis and behavior therapy and the emerging theory of cyclical psychodynamics, she was struck by similarities between what she was learning at Ackerman and what was emerging from my own work. Both, she pointed out, emphasized circular and reciprocal rather than linear accounts of causality and highlighted how the older linear formulations could be subsumed in a framework that looked through a broader lens to incorporate a fuller picture of human experience and interaction. Our discussions led eventually to a joint book on the interface between the theories and methods deriving from psychoanalytic explorations and those deriving from the world of family therapy (E. F. Wachtel & Wachtel, 1986). Most of the writing for the book was done by Ellen, who was the senior author, but participating in this joint project strongly introduced a family systems perspective into my thinking, and this has remained an important dimension of my thinking and my work ever since.

The emphasis on understanding people in the context of the systems in which they daily participate (the family, of course, as a crucially important one, but by no means the only system that plays a critical role in people's lives) was both consistent with the emerging contextual nature of the cyclical psychodynamic point of view and an extension of that view. Family therapists and family systems theorists and researchers had developed a range of concepts and clinical methods that were both distinct from those of psychoanalysis and, importantly, very largely compatible at least with the version of psychoanalytic thought from which I was increasingly operating (for another valuable take on the interface between psychoanalytic thought and family systems thinking, see Gerson, 2010).

One especially important point of intersection between family systems approaches and that of cyclical psychodynamics is the emphasis on the consequentiality of the actual transactions that constitute the person's life. We live not just in our heads but also in our interactions, and the reciprocal webs of interaction that anchor and give context to our lives are central both to cyclical psychodynamic theory and to family systems theories. This point of view will be evident throughout this book, but is especially prominent in Chapters 2, 3, and 4.

Cyclical Psychodynamics and the Humanistic-Experiential and Emotion-Focused Therapies

More recently, as a result especially of attending meetings of the Society for the Exploration of Psychotherapy Integration (SEPI), an international organization devoted to integrative thinking in psychotherapy and personality theory, I have been drawn to the contribution of the humanistic-experiential tradition (see, for example, Greenberg, 2008; Greenberg & Goldman, 2008; Greenberg & Pascual-Leone, 2006; Greenberg & Watson, 2006; Pos & Greenberg, 2007; Pos, Greenberg, & Elliott, 2008) and have been working to further expand and rework the cyclical psychodynamic model in order to incorporate its insights and practices. Concern with making psychotherapy more experiential has in fact been a central impetus for my integrative efforts from the very beginning. A key element in what originally drew me to incorporate behavioral methods into my psychoanalytically guided work was that the behavior therapy of that time, contrary to stereotype, seemed to me one of the most experiential of the approaches then in clinical use. Far from being behavioristic, as both its proponents and detractors tended to portray it, behavior therapy had seemed to me a highly *experiential* way of working, in which people were directly confronted with the sources of their fears or their social difficulties rather than just *talking about* them. Indeed, as I noted earlier, when behavior therapy began to turn from this more experiential way of working toward a more predominantly *cognitive* model, it had seemed to me to be a step backward clinically. Although there were important ways in which the introduction of a cognitive perspective into behavior therapy represented a *theoretical* advance – the earlier behavior therapy had been largely grounded in an anticognitive stimulus–response psychology that to a growing number of experimental psychologists, not to mention psychoanalytic and other insight-oriented clinicians, was increasingly seen as anachronistic and untenable – the *clinical* fallout of the cognitive shift was far less salutary. The cognitive therapy and cognitively dominated cognitive-behavior therapy (CBT) that began to dominate the field moved back from the directly experiential quality that had drawn me to behavior therapy and toward a more intellectualized, in-the-head way of approaching people. Even more troubling, this highly rationalistic way of working verged on trying to *talk people out of their feelings.*[11] (For a more detailed discussion of these issues, as well as a discussion of newer forms of CBT that are more experiential and affect focused, see Wachtel, 2011a, 2011b).

The experiential and emotion-focused perspectives in our field represent a sharp contrast with this overly cognitive approach. Their emphasis is on promoting awareness of emotion and addressing those factors that impede access to painful or conflicted emotions, clearly an agenda that dovetails well with that of more psychoanalytic approaches. But these approaches complement the psychoanalytic modes of accessing and working through emotions with a range of additional methods designed to further promote deep emotional experiencing and to integrate that experiencing with reflection and integration with ongoing life goals (Greenberg, 2002, 2004; Greenberg & Paivio, 1997). Incorporation of these clinical methods into a therapy that is rooted in the insights and complexities of the psychoanalytic point of view is an important part of the current agenda of the cyclical psychodynamic perspective.

The Larger Social Context

One final important element in the evolution of cyclical psychodynamic theory has been the attempt to address the larger social and cultural context. Consistent with the general thrust of the cyclical psychodynamic viewpoint, this effort has been approached in a bidirectional way that does not privilege either direction of causality. Thus, on the one hand, the cyclical psychodynamic point of view directs attention to the ways that individual patients' experiences and dilemmas reflect larger cultural, economic, and historical trends along with the more personal and familial concerns that are more typically addressed by psychotherapists;

on the other, it applies the insights of psychoanalysis and other psychological theories to understanding aspects of the culture that are obscured by the very way that cultures tend to render themselves invisible by conveying that "this is just the way things are" rather than that this is one of many ways to make sense of the challenges that living presents.

It is surprising how often therapists fail to take into account the powerful and important impact of the patient's culture and the impact of his or her socioeconomic circumstances. From a cyclical psychodynamic perspective, these influences on the patient's psychological state are not something extra or different from the realm of psychodynamics but are part and parcel of it. The patient's dynamics *always* play themselves out in a cultural and social context, and their meaning is inseparable from that context. At the same time, the significance of that context is different for each individual and reflects the individualized way that each person registers and *gives particularized meaning to* that context. Purely psychological analyses that omit the social context and purely social analyses that ignore or minimize the individual ways that each person makes sense of his or her cultural surround are both limited. Repeated individual experiences, writ large, shape or maintain the social order and, simultaneously, the evolved patterns of larger social, cultural, and economic relations significantly shape the lives of individuals and families. Individuality and participation in a shared culture are but two sides of the same coin. Part II of this book is especially focused on these issues, exploring both the ways that members of marginalized groups in society face a special set of challenges and dilemmas over and above those faced by those more privileged or more in the mainstream and the ways that a cyclical psychodynamic understanding can help shed light on a range of social patterns and problems. Building on previous cyclical psychodynamic analyses of race relations (Wachtel, 1999) and of materialism and the psychological consequences of organizing our society around unceasing economic growth (Wachtel, 1983), the chapters in Part II reflect the way that a cyclical psychodynamic analysis addresses the reciprocal interaction between individual psychodynamics and larger social and cultural dynamics.

The Inner World, the Intimate World, and the World of Culture and Society

The subtitle of this book points to a continuity that is a central theme of this book. For many years, psychoanalytic writing was most characteristically focused on what came to be called the inner world. What exactly was meant by "inner" could vary from theorist to theorist, but for many years there was a robust tendency to posit dynamics that played themselves out with little reference to the "outer" world of everyday events, which was regarded as but a superficial overlay. In some versions of inner world theorizing, or discussions of internalization or internalized objects, once a representation has been internalized it becomes more or less autonomous, playing itself out according to a script that requires no prompts from any current players. To the degree that inner world theorizing reflects such ways of thinking, this book departs from it rather substantially.

I include the term *inner world* in the very subtitle of the book, however, because there is another version of inner world thinking that comports very well with the cyclical psychodynamic project and mode of thought. This second version essentially points to the realms of subjectivity and of individuality, both of which are essential features of the cyclical psychodynamic point of view. In contrast to some versions of CBT, in which the person's conscious report of his experience, usually in response to a fairly structured set of questions, is as far as the probing of subjectivity goes,[12] the perspective explored in this book is concerned with the depths and subtleties of subjectivity in much the way as in most other psycho-analytic approaches. When attention to the inner world means attention to those subtleties and complexities of subjectivity, to a probing of experience *in depth*, then attention to the inner world is very much a characteristic of cyclical psycho-dynamic work.

Relatedly, attention to the inner world can be understood as attention to the pro-cesses whereby the person's individuality is expressed and reflected in her every thought, feeling, and perception. Here, the notion of the inner world points to the ways in which, whatever the situation we encounter, we each make sense of it in terms of our unique history and unique (and continually evolving) set of psycho-logical structures and inclinations. The concept of schema, especially as framed by Piaget as a continuing dialectical tension between processes of assimilation and accommodation, is much to the point here, for the schema concept does not pit individual interpretation against the influence of the situation or context but rather illuminates how we do not adequately understand the role of either without taking into account the other (see, for example, Wachtel 1981, 2008). Likewise, the inner world referred to in the subtitle of this book is not a world apart, sealed off from the world of everyday life, but rather a concept that points to the ways that the very experience of one's everyday life is infused with individuality and subjectivity *even as* it is also – and always – a *response to* that life as it is lived from moment to moment.

The second component of the book's subtitle similarly refers not to an entirely separate realm but rather to a convenient way to refer to a set of phenomena and processes that have to do with experiences in relation to one or several other people. Such transactions with others, which constitute a huge proportion of our waking lives, were often relegated to the realm of the superficial in earlier psy-choanalytic theorizing. This "superficiality" was the flip side of the form of inner world thinking that I was just distinguishing from my own use of the term. It reflected the view that what was "deep" was "inside" (and usually buried) and what was on "the surface" was "superficial" (see Chapter 5 in particular for further critical discussion of how psychoanalytic writers long conceptualized what was superficial and what was deep). In recent years, however, there has been increas-ing attention paid in the psychoanalytic literature to the actual exchanges between people that constitute what I am calling here the intimate world. This attention largely began with Sullivan's (1953) interpersonal theory, but it remained very much a minority point of view in psychoanalysis until the emergence of the relational movement in the 1980s and its continuing growth into a major component of psychoanalytic thought.

Of course, our interactions with others are not all intimate in nature. Even our interactions with lovers, family members, or close friends consist very largely of transactions such as requests to "pass the butter," discussions of what movie to see, exchanges about the day's news, and so forth. And many of our immediate interactions with other people are with people we hardly know, from store clerks, to fellow passengers on an elevator, to rather casual acquaintances. In referring to the intimate world, I am, with less than pinpoint accuracy, essentially referring to an intermediate zone of interaction, a realm between the world of primarily private and subjective experience – dreaming, daydreaming, private fantasies, the subjective experience of pain or delight – and the world of the social and cultural to be discussed next. The intimate world is thus in part a term designed to direct our attention to the dyadic or triadic (or sometimes slightly larger) interactions that frame so much of our daily experience and that are the zone of the multiple feedback processes that constitute so much of the texture of daily living and, simultaneously, as cyclical psychodynamic theory especially highlights, the way that patterns of personality are maintained or gradually evolve.

But I did not use the term *intimate world* just to be perversely imprecise. Rather my choice of terminology here reflects that – notwithstanding both the statistical frequency of *non*intimate transactions, or even the fact that such transactions too play a significant role in maintaining the personality patterns we often attribute just to the person herself (or to the inner world) – it is nonetheless the subset of those interactions that truly are in the realm of the intimate[13] that constitute the center of interest for psychoanalysts and most other therapists and that probably also play an outsize role in shaping the patterns that are of particular interest in the therapeutic work. It is the world of consequential transactions with others, transactions with meaning and import and affective resonance for each party, which is usually the center of our attention. Especially is this the case in recent years, as attention to countertransference experience, to enactment, and to other perspectives on what is actually transpiring in the room – as a phenomenon engaging *two people*, not just as the expression of what is inside one – have increasingly become a center of psychoanalytic attention, not only among relationalists but in a still broader segment of the psychoanalytic community (Gottlieb, 2010).[14]

Thus, in referring to the intimate world in the subtitle of this book, I am in part calling attention to the important role of direct interactions with others in maintaining or modifying what had once been thought of as personality traits that lay within a single individual. We are shaped – and we shape ourselves – by countless direct transactions with others and by the ongoing and reciprocal feedback processes that characterize those transactions. But I am indeed also calling attention to the particular importance of those interactions that lie on the more intimate end of the spectrum of such transactions. And in placing the intimate world in a kind of intermediate position between the inner world and the world of society and culture, I am highlighting both the ways in which each facet of experience shapes and is reciprocally *shaped by* the others and the ways in which they are, indeed, part and parcel of each other.

The third element in the subtitle, the world of society and culture, may seem to require the least explication. In some ways, the terms seem to point to a realm that is clearly distinguishable both from the inner world and the intimate world. Yet central to the entire message of this book is that these are *not* completely separate realms. Including attention to society and culture in our clinical training is not just an add-on, not just icing on an already baked cake. Nor, as some more sociologically oriented writers suggest, is the realm of culture and society the "real" substructure to our daily lives, the material reality that underlies the "superficial" subjective realm. Here, vulgar Marxism parallels vulgar Freudianism, placing its preferred explanatory level at the core and the elements it disparages or marginalizes at the "surface" (again, see Chapter 5).

Rather, from a cyclical psychodynamic point of view, the inner world, the intimate world, and the world of society and culture are reciprocally consequential for each other, continually maintaining and changing each other. Put differently, they are realms that not only border on each other but also interpenetrate and are fundamentally constitutive of each other. None of them exists without the other or has meaning apart from each other.

Similar cyclical processes can be found in all three realms – the inner world, the intimate world, and the world of society and culture. Within each realm and between each realm, vicious and virtuous circles and self-fulfilling prophecies are the key dynamic that maintains and generates subjective experience and social interaction. This central vision of human psychological experience and social behavior is the core of the cyclical psychodynamic point of view, and it unites the clinical discussions and theorizing in Part I and the social analyses in Part II, as well as the cyclical psychodynamic understanding of why these three realms – artificially divided here in order to get a conceptual handle on what is ultimately a unity rather than a trinity – are inseparable and mutually constitutive.

Elsewhere (e.g., Wachtel, 1997, 2008, 2011a, 2011b) I have spelled out in more detail some of the concrete implications for daily clinical work of the cyclical psychodynamic point of view presented here. These include a particular attention to the patient's strengths, and a focus on those strengths that does not brush aside the more problematic aspects of the person's makeup or way of life or what is more typically discussed in terms of psychopathology (see especially Wachtel, 2011a, for detailed accounts of how this can be accomplished and why it promotes moving the clinical process in a deeper rather than a more superficial direction). Relatedly, I have highlighted, again from the vantage point of the cyclical psychodynamic perspective spelled out in this book, the differences between a psychoanalytic or psychotherapeutic practice whose deep explorations are rooted in an "attitude of suspicion" (e.g., Messer, 2000; Ricouer, 1970; Schafer, 1997;

Wolff, 2001) or in a (realistic and hard-headed) attitude of support and nurturance (see Wachtel, 2008).

As part of this shift from what I have referred to as the "default position" in psychoanalytic practice (Wachtel, 2008), I have highlighted as well the inadvertently pejorative ways in which patients' dilemmas are often conceptualized and, unfortunately, are also communicated to the patient, generating a degree of resistance that is likely to be viewed as coming from inside the patient but that is at least equally iatrogenic (see especially Wachtel, 2011a). When, in contrast, clinical practice is enabled to transcend the default position, therapeutic change can be facilitated and enhanced by new ways of constructing one's narratives and communications (Wachtel, 2011a, 2011b), by a readiness to employ a range of active interventions that derive from the full spectrum of theoretical perspectives in our field (Wachtel, 1997), and by the probing examination of theoretical presuppositions so that this expanded range of methods, conceptualizations, and communications reflects not a fly-by-the-seat-of-the-pants eclecticism but rather a thorough and coherent integration and reconciliation of diverse observations and perspectives. The current book is concerned with all of these levels and aims of clinical theory and practice, from the concrete and practical to the more conceptual realm of theory construction and clarification of unexamined premises, but it is especially focused on the latter. Ultimately – whether in discussions of the relation between interpretation and exposure, of the role of new relational experience both in the session and in daily life, of the role of procedural learning as a complement to the traditional psychoanalytic focus on interpretation and promoting recovery of memories in the declarative realm, or in its emphasis on making therapeutic work both more deeply experiential and more attentive to the actual behaviors and emotions that constitute the stuff of daily living – the cyclical psychodynamic perspective explicated in this book is concerned most of all with how life as subjectively experienced can only be adequately understood by simultaneously attending to life *as it is lived*.

Notes

1. For purposes of clarity, throughout this book terms like *therapist* or *analyst*, when intended generically rather than pointing to a specific therapist, are referred to by the feminine pronouns *she*, *her*, and *hers*, and *patient* is referred to by the masculine pronouns *he*, *him*, and *his*.
2. Relational theory itself, it is useful to remind ourselves, is really an umbrella term, referring to a *set* of theories with both overlaps and significant differences (Wachtel, 2008).
3. I discuss the role and dynamics of accomplices further in Chapter 2.
4. The discussion here and elsewhere in this book of the ways we create and re-create the same situation over and over again may seem similar to Freud's concept of the repetition compulsion; we act in ways that bring about again and again the very experiences that were so problematic for us in the past. But in Freud's formulation, that repetition is *intended* (of course, usually *unconsciously* intended). It is – apart from the more speculative and arcane aspects associated with the concept of the death instinct – an

attempt (usually a vain attempt) to master an experience that previously overwhelmed us by bringing it on again. In the cyclical psychodynamic account, in contrast, the repetition is seen as often *un*intended, the ironic consequence of the very effort to *prevent* its coming about. The implications of this difference are apparent throughout this book (see also Wachtel, 2008 for further clarification of the differences between these two concepts).

5. It is also now clear that a wide range of research studies similarly support this view of the pervasive role of vicious and virtuous circles in the dynamics of personality and human social interaction (see, for example, Wachtel, 1994; Wachtel, Kruk, & McKinney, 2005).

6. As also discussed in Chapter 11, this kind of closed circle is by no means unique to psychoanalysis. It is a significant challenge for *any* system of thought and *any* methodological tradition.

7. It is important to point out here that there is an unfortunately broad segment of clinical psychologists who believe that behavior therapy (or these days, cognitive-behavior therapy) is the *only* approach that has strong empirical support. That is a seriously erroneous and misguided view (see, for example, Shedler, 2010; Wachtel, 2010). At the same time, it must be noted that my serious attention – really for the first time – to the evidence that, if by no means exclusive to behavior therapy nonetheless pointed strongly to the clinical *value* of behavior therapy, led to a significant reworking of my understanding of the sources of clinical gain – indeed, even my understanding of the clinical impact of more psychodynamic approaches (see, for example, Wachtel, 1997, 2008, 2011a).

8. Some years later, I was troubled to find that, as a narrowly rationalistic version of cognitive behavior therapy began to emerge, some of these very same clinicians began to turn their backs on what amounted to a deeply experiential attention to the realities of their patients' lives and to try, essentially, to *talk them out of their feelings*, to show them that their feelings were irrational. I have described this disillusion in Wachtel (2011a, 2011b), where I have also described some important new trends in cognitive-behavior therapy that represent a return to affect and to clinical sensitivity.

9. As I discuss shortly, there are now additional dimensions beyond the behavioral that similarly complement (and modify) my core psychodynamic point of view – in particular, those deriving from the systemic and experiential points of view.

10. Erikson is not a thinker usually grouped with Horney and Sullivan. In the politics and sociology of psychoanalysis, Erikson was grouped with the ego psychologists and Sullivan and Horney with the interpersonalists. But it seemed to me that in Erikson's highly contextual thinking and in his emphasis on the powerful role of reciprocal transactions between people and the continuing evolution of personality, rather than its remaining embalmed in a particular developmental stage, he resembled the interpersonalists more than he did those on "his" side of the political divide.

11. It is important to note in this context that in recent years, prominent representatives of the cognitive-behavioral tradition have themselves pointed out this turn away from affect and have highlighted the importance of reintegrating affect into cognitive-behavioral practice (e.g., Burum & Goldfried, 2007; Samoilov & Goldfried, 2000).

12. It is important to note that this limitation is by no means characteristic of all cognitive-behavioral approaches. Some of the newer third-wave versions of cognitive-behavior therapy, as well as the more constructivist cognitive approaches engage in much more thorough exploration of subjective experience. But I have seen in recent years a disturbing tendency for cognitive-behavioral therapists to "stick to the protocol" in ways that do not really leave room for the subtleties or complexities of the patient's subjective experience. On several occasions, I have been the discussant at conferences in which videotapes were shown of some of the most prominent figures in the

cognitive-behavioral world, and, notwithstanding my own strongly integrative inclinations, I have had to acknowledge real dismay at seeing levels of clinical responsiveness
and skillfulness that would disappoint me if I saw them in one of my first-year graduate
students.

13. It should be understood that actions or subjective experiences and interpretations that
impede or *ward off* intimacy belong in this realm as well. Such actions and defensive
operations are part of the core dynamics of intimacy in a way that asking a grocer "how
much are the cucumbers today?" clearly is not.

14. As I discuss especially in Chapter 3, but in fact throughout this book, it is important
not to limit our attention to the patient's interactive dynamics and their consequences
solely to the therapeutic interaction. The process of evoking in others behavior and
affective reactions that feed back to shape our own internal experience occurs in every
aspect of our lives, and it has been problematically limiting when therapists assume too
blithely that every important facet of the patient's interactional style will be manifested
in the transference and countertransference.

Chapter 2

The Good News
To Mess Up Your Life, You Need Accomplices

The Bad News
They Are Very Easy to Recruit

A neurosis is a wondrous thing. In the face of plentiful guidelines from reality and from the rough edges of daily experience, our patients somehow persist in the same self-defeating patterns day after day and year after year. The sheer staying power of neurotic patterns is little short of miraculous. But we are prone to give the neurosis – and the neurotic – too much credit for this prodigious, if unfortunate, tenacity. Maintaining a neurosis is hard, dirty work that cannot be successfully achieved alone. To keep a neurosis going, one needs help. Every neurosis requires accomplices.

I am aware, of course, that the term *neurosis* has gone out of favor. Partly as a result of its seeming lack of precision, and very largely as a result of the politics that produced that camel of a document called *The Diagnostic and Statistical Manual of Mental Disorders* (DSM), the term has rapidly taken on a measure of quaintness. I use it here, however, not only because astute investors know that charming antiques have a tendency to appreciate in value, but for the very generality that so annoyed those psychiatrists who hoped to be writing a manual about particular medicines for particular diseases. My focus here (and throughout this book) is on the psychological dynamics that maintain maladaptive behavior, particularly those dynamics that are evident across a wide range of problematic ways of living and that are largely independent of the imitations of medical diagnosis that may be written on the patient's chart or insurance form.

Thus, in the same spirit, I wish to suggest that the processes described in this chapter (and, by and large, throughout this book) are relevant as well for those difficulties that clinicians these days often call borderline, narcissistic, or some other term that aims to distinguish a different "level of personality organization" from that of neurosis. Relatedly, I aim here to discuss psychological difficulties and complaints that cannot so readily be distinguished by the contrivance of recording separate Axis I and Axis II diagnoses. The problematic psychological phenomena I am focusing on here and throughout this book entail forms of suffering and of less-than-full living in which "symptoms" and personality patterns are so intertwined that it is the very connectedness between them that is of most significance. In many respects, then, I use the term neurosis here in the sense that Horney (e.g., 1937, 1939, 1945) and Shapiro (1965) did, to refer to the self-perpetuating traps in which people get caught and the multiple, intricate, and ironic ways that certain problematic patterns of living and the pain they cause (their "symptoms") become mutually reinforcing.

When I suggest, as I did at the start of this chapter, that maintaining a neurosis is hard work, and that in fact it cannot be successfully achieved alone, I am only in part being whimsical. I am certainly aware, both from the literature and from my own experience as a therapist, of how *difficult* it is to bring about change in these patterns. Psychotherapists of every stripe have found that once one moves away from the treatment of isolated symptoms and takes on the task of dealing with broader and more pervasive complaints – the personal and interpersonal troubles that characterize the real agenda of most therapy patients (e.g. Kazdin, 2008; Westen, Novotny, & Thompson-Brenner, 2004) – the clinical enterprise becomes a daunting challenge. Improved methodologies in psychotherapy research in recent years have simultaneously made clear both that the more symptom-focused forms of psychotherapy do help people and that their impact all in all is less than earthshaking (e.g., Kazdin, 2006; Shedler, 2010; Westen & Morrison, 2001; Westen et al., 2004).

But what I wish to convey in my focus on how it "takes help" to maintain a neurosis is that in attempting to gain some leverage for the therapist's difficult endeavor, it is useful to notice that, hard as it is to change neurotic patterns, it also takes work to keep them going. By understanding just how they are maintained, we can see better where there are possibilities for change. Of course, in suggesting, even if partly tongue in cheek, that maintaining a neurosis is so difficult we can only do it with help, it is necessary to ask why its maintenance *appears* to be so effortless and why efforts to bring about change in fact prove so arduous? The answer, I believe, lies in our ability to recruit – indeed in our considerable *in*ability *not* to recruit – the very help that is needed to keep the neurotic patterns going. As I illustrate shortly, we are often unfortunately and unwittingly experts in turning other people into accomplices in our neuroses.

Being effective in helping people to achieve deep and lasting change requires understanding the ways in which neurosis is a joint activity, a cooperative enterprise of a most peculiar sort. Without the participation of the cast of characters in the patient's life – or, to put it differently (because nothing in human behavior occurs in a vacuum) with *different* participation by the significant others in the patient's life – the neurosis would not continue. Indeed, one might even argue that the process whereby others are continually recruited into a persisting maladaptive pattern *is* the neurosis.

An Illustration

Let me illustrate with an example. Consider the individual who is extremely cautious and distant in interpersonal relationships, who is perhaps excessively self-sufficient and self-contained, who (consciously or unconsciously) makes a very high priority of preventing himself from being hurt and as a consequence also prevents himself from being touched or reached. Such a person may seem rather sad, but he may equally well look to the world like a successful, independent, highly competent person. Even in the latter case, however, if one looks closely, one sees a tinge of bitterness and a feeling of loneliness, emptiness, maybe even desperation.

Many readers will have a favorite diagnostic term for such people. I prefer instead a simple description of the pattern. First of all, these people have enough troubles already. They are vulnerable enough without therapists calling them names. But even more important, the diagnostic labels usually imply – problematically – a one-person system; what is being described is something "in" the patient since childhood. That is precisely the perspective I want to question here.

This is not to say that the pattern may not well have started early in life, most likely in relation to the parents. I assume that the kind of person I am discussing had good reason for being cautious, for expecting the worst of opening himself up to needing another person. The question, though, is why that fear, mistrust, and consequent deprivation *persists*. Why, now that he is an adult and no longer subject to the inordinate neediness of early childhood or the unreliable parenting that first produced his caution, does he continue to live as if the circumstances, needs, and limited capacities of his early years were still the reigning reality?

To many in our field, the answer lies in an internal structure or internal world that is largely impervious to the potential lessons of new realities. Such explanations, however, seem to me to border on the tautological: old patterns persist because they persist; internal worlds don't change because that is their nature.

It is not that the careful delineation of the person's subjective experience, of his fantasies and wishes and of the images to which they are tied, is irrelevant. Far from it. Rather, the problem lies in an excessively dichotomous view of human beings and their relation to the world, in a split vision that distinguishes far too sharply and artificially between, on the one hand, an inner world, a subjective world, internal dynamics, what have you, and on the other hand, the so-called outer world, the social world, the world of overt interactions. These are not two separate realms. They are part and parcel of each other. Efforts to understand the one without the other are basically nonsensical and incoherent. The phenomena to which "internal world" theorists point are ignored at our peril. But the peril is equally great if they are discussed without an appreciation of their continued rooting in a social and interpersonal context.

To illustrate this further, let us look more closely at the daily experience of an individual of the sort just described. Let us see how the pattern of his life – indeed how his inner world – is maintained by the ways he induces others, even if unwittingly and unwillingly, to become accomplices in his unfortunate life patterns.

Consider what happens when this individual, who we will call Jim, goes out on a date with a woman, Marcia, he has recently begun to see. He has initially been lively and engaged – there is not yet a threat of his becoming vulnerable to her charms – and she in response has been interested in him and eager both to hear him and to talk to him. A relationship has begun to form, and it is at a crucial stage.

Today he begins to be aware that he feels something for her, and, sensing her interest and her good sense, he is tempted to ask her for help in sorting out some difficult things that have been happening at work. He starts to, but as he does he begins to feel uneasy. Some dim recollection emerges of the last time he opened up to a woman. He felt then that he stuck his neck out and the woman was unresponsive – either she complained that he was not open enough or she essentially ignored his needs by making light of what to him was serious or by going on to another subject. This woman was the last accomplice in a long chain, and Marcia is about to become the next.

Neither Jim nor Marcia quite knows what is going on. The elaborate and all-too-familiar dance they are about to begin goes on largely outside of awareness, though they are both aware of many of the steps – for example, of the painful feelings of awkwardness and vulnerability, of being let down, unappreciated, perhaps even betrayed.

Jim thinks he is reaching out to Marcia, that he is baring his soul, and he feels hurt and disappointed at her response. She seems not to be very sensitive, not to quite get what he is saying, sometimes even to be annoyed at him for reasons he can't quite comprehend. Rather than the warm glow with which the evening began, the experience is increasingly one of frustration, anxiety, and futility.

What Jim does not appreciate is how hedged is his reaching out, how tentative and cautious. He does not see how excessively self-sufficient he appears to be because he does not realize how threatened he feels by the feelings of neediness that Marcia's previous responsiveness to him drew forth. Because the feelings of neediness are largely unacknowledged, he cannot let himself see that he is reacting defensively to that neediness by an exaggerated demonstration (more for his own benefit than for Marcia's) of how little he really needs any help, of how on top of things he really is.

Jim thinks he is asking for help and not getting it, indeed not even getting the respect, caring, and attention that is the necessary precondition for getting help. In fact, what he is doing is telling Marcia about an "interesting" problem that – so far as most people could make out without reading between the lines in an unusually perceptive way – he neither wants nor needs much help with. If one hears primarily what he is actually saying, it seems he is basically on top of things, he is not really very upset about what happened, and indeed, he thinks little of people who do get upset about such things or who can't handle things on their own.

What Marcia experiences is being with someone who doesn't seem to need her very much, who doesn't seem to really *want* much response from her, except perhaps for a casual, relatively uninvolved response. Taking her cue from him, she acts as if – and perhaps feels as if – he doesn't need very much; and the result is that *he*, notwithstanding the message of self-assured independence that his behavior seemed to convey, goes home feeling not attended to or understood, with a not quite articulated – or in D. B. Stern's (1997) felicitous term, an unformulated – sad and hurt feeling that translates, in its consequences for his life, into a strengthening of his conviction that you can't expect very much of women. And of course you *can't* – if you are going so out of your way to keep strong needs under wraps and to ensure that she does not mean too much to you.

So the next time he sees Marcia (or sees some other woman; neither of them may have much desire to get together again), he begins the encounter still more convinced that women won't come through for him – and thus still more resolved (whether conscious of the resolve or not) not to be hurt by opening himself up. And given his skewed history, there is a certain inevitable logic to his actions and point of view. The upshot is thus likely to be that in his next encounter he will once again, acting on the basis of past experience, be hesitant, play it close to the vest, and get one more confirmation of the view with which he started – a view that to most of us seems a distortion, but which squares quite well with what he actually has experienced over and over.

But what if Marcia were not to go along with Jim's signals so readily? What if her own history and her own inclinations led her instead to try hard to connect with him? Could she avoid becoming an accomplice in his neurosis? Perhaps. As I discuss in more detail shortly, the therapeutic impact of people other than therapists is seriously underestimated in most of our discussions of the therapeutic process. But the odds are against it. Consider what is likely to happen:

Marcia tries hard to connect. She responds to Jim's cues, subtle and hedged as they are. And what he does is back off, convinced – on the basis of experience after experience – that no good can come of this.

And indeed, no good does. After a while Marcia becomes frustrated with what she experiences as his tease, his lack of follow-through, his withholding; and she starts to complain. She tells him perhaps – as each week thousands of women tell thousands of men (who tell thousands of therapists) – that he is cut off from his feelings. And so he leaves the encounter still more thoroughly persuaded that it is like entering a meat grinder to begin to bare your feelings. Marcia has become an accomplice – an unwilling and unwitting one, perhaps, but an accomplice nonetheless.

Now, to be sure, the outcomes I have described thus far are not the only ones possible. If Marcia were able to just keep listening and being there, neither backing off nor complaining about *his* backing off, and if she could she do this over and over, and – another big if – if Jim were able to stay in the relationship through instance after instance of this, the pattern would very possibly begin to shift. In that case, Marcia would become not an accomplice in Jim's neurosis but an accomplice in change.

But this is a lot to ask. It's hard enough, after all, to do this even in the protected role of psychotherapist. We all get regularly drawn into enactments with our patients, and truth be told, we do not always spin straw into gold by stepping back and calling the patient's attention to how we have both been drawn in in familiar ways. We do not always find ways to inhabit the metaperspective of the therapeutic third (Aron, 2006; Benjamin, 2004), or to repair the ruptures that have occurred in the therapeutic alliance and thereby build new more healthy psychic structure (Kohut, 1977; Safran, Muran, & Eubanks-Carter, 2011). For "civilians" like Marcia, with no commitment to such efforts as the primary reason for being in the relationship with the patient, and without the unusual structure of the therapeutic setting to make such benign transformation more likely (Wachtel, 2011a), it is even more difficult to avoid becoming an accomplice in the patient's all-too-familiar patterns.

Nonetheless, in understanding how change occurs in entrenched patterns of living, it is important to recognize that sometimes accomplices – or potential accomplices – *do* manage not to play the old familiar game. And when that happens, when significant figures in the person's daily life become instead accomplices in change, they are the most potent therapeutic force a person can encounter. Daily life is the power source to which our neuroses are plugged in, but it is also potentially the most powerful source of cure.

This is by no means to say that it is easy for this to happen. Most neuroses are perpetual motion machines, generating their own justification over and over again and making a kind of depressing, self-defeating sense that is exceedingly hard to overcome (cf. Horney, 1939, 1945; Shapiro, 1989; Wachtel, 1987, 1997, 2008). Outside of Hollywood, happy endings do not come easily.

Psychotherapists do earn their keep. The people who come to see us tend to be the people for whom the unplanned therapeutic events of daily life have been insufficient or simply not forthcoming. But the accomplice perspective highlights two aspects of our influence that tend to be insufficiently appreciated. First, a great deal of our effect as therapists derives from our own role as potential accomplices – *potential* accomplices who, because of our training and because of the protective structure of the therapeutic situation, manage fairly successfully not to get chronically drawn into the role but rather to respond to the patient in ways that differ from his accustomed interactions and that promote new perceptions and new ways of being with people (and with himself). Note, however, that even in my depiction of how we function when we are working well, I refer to our not *chronically* getting drawn in. It is almost impossible to avoid getting drawn in altogether, and managing to do so might indeed not even be optimal. I discuss the complexities of this process at various points in this book as I discuss such concepts as enactments, new relational experience, and the repair of ruptures in the therapeutic alliance.

The second way in which attention to the accomplice dimension aids our therapeutic work is that although an important portion of the change resulting from successful psychotherapy derives from the patient's direct experience of the therapeutic relationship and what transpires in the room – particularly from our being benign, understanding good objects who modify the patient's inner world through his new experience with us (see, for example, Fairbairn, 1952; K. A. Frank, 1999; Loewald, 1960; Weiss & Sampson, 1986) – another very crucial source of change is whether the therapeutic process promotes change in the patient's life *outside* the therapy room. In a successful therapy, the events of the session have their impact very largely through serving as a *catalyst*. They bring about change in the patient's interactions with *others* in his life, and it is the sum of those countless interactions day after day that determines whether whatever changes occur in the sessions become permanent or are undermined.

If the therapist is attentive to the patterns of interaction of daily life and to the role played in those patterns by accomplices, she can direct her efforts not only to the emotional climate in the room but also toward promoting change in the ironic dynamics (Wachtel, 1979) that have maintained the patient's difficulties over the years. This attention to the dynamics of daily life not only can be a potential parallel source in the service of *promoting* change; it is crucial to ensure that whatever gains are achieved in the session do not dissipate when the patient walks out. When the patient leaves the session, he is reentering the world of (mostly unwitting) accomplices who have for so long been co-authors of his difficulties. Without proper attention to and preparation for the impact of the by-now chronic expectations of others and the ways in which he continues to evoke and maintain those expectations, the prospects for change are seriously compromised.

Sometimes the interactions with the accomplices in the patient's problematic patterns undermine change in ways that at least enable the therapist to *notice* that something is not going smoothly. There is little incremental momentum; some sessions seem to yield real insights or changes, but over time, or even in the next session, what has seemed to be achieved begins to dissolve. That is, the undermining effects of the experiences the patient has had between sessions may render fragile and unstable the change that had seemed to be evident just a session or two before. We are certainly all familiar with the pattern of patients evidencing change, reverting to older patterns, moving toward change again, and so on. To some degree, the recognition that this is an expectable feature of much therapeutic work, and the readiness to persist in working through, in patiently providing a holding presence, and so forth is a critical therapeutic asset. But if the focus is too much on the patient's inner life or on the experience the patient and therapist are having together in the session, and insufficient attention is paid to the two-person dynamics of *all* of the patient's life and the consequent power of the feedback loops in which the patient and his accomplices are caught, then the therapist is likely to have too much faith in her benign persistence – the patient's problems are "deep"; perhaps they derive from traumas that are "early"; and if not much stable change is achieved in 5 years, then it may take 10, or more. In contrast, attention to the feedback loops of daily life that is as probing and systematic as attention to the intersubjective experiences in the consulting room – or to the intricacies of mother–infant interactions (see, for example, Chapter 3) – can reveal other sources of the slow and fragile course of change and point to ways to address it that may help to more effectively consolidate and amplify the changes that become evident.

The importance of attention to the dynamics of accomplices in everyday life may further be understood by appreciating a different kind of scenario. In the circumstances described in the preceding paragraph, the therapist is at least aware that change seems slow and fitful. But on other occasions, the experience of the therapist is that things are going rather well. The critical importance of the patient's interactions outside the session with the various people who have played the role of accomplices in maintaining his difficulties – and the ways that this can undermine change – may be obscured because the therapist is better at not falling into the problematic patterns in which the patient had been enmeshed than others in his life are. As a consequence, the patient may learn, in effect, that it is safer to be fully himself in relation to the therapist than it is to be himself outside.[1]

Thus, the therapist may see with her own eyes what appear to be deep and meaningful changes in the patient and not fully appreciate how limited is the degree to which that change is carried over to the patient's daily life. In the therapist's benign presence, the patient may be considerably more related, more real, and more emotionally alive than he was when he began the work. But the improvement that is palpably evident in the sessions may not be paralleled by similar improvement in his daily life. The patient's conclusion that it is only safe to be more fully himself in the special circumstances of the session, after all, is not likely to be a conscious one; it is implicit and automatic, and cannot be reported. So in order for the therapist to understand and gauge the ways in which daily life interactions are undermining the process of change and maintaining old patterns despite a genuinely warming and facilitative relationship in the therapy room, it is essential for the therapist to be alert to the ways that others in his life are drawn in as accomplices in maintaining the painful or constricting patterns he has come to therapy to resolve.

In effective psychotherapy, change in the sessions and change in daily life work hand in hand, mutually enhancing and promoting each other. When insufficient attention is paid by the therapist to how the insights achieved in the sessions are carried forth into the patient's daily interactions, and to how they can lead to changes in the transactions that keep other people accomplices in the neurosis, then the result is likely to be that good work in the sessions is undermined by the interactions that occur outside. In the chapters that follow, I offer further considerations that point to ways that the therapist can take into account the powerful impact of daily life without abandoning the attention to the depths that has been the signal contribution of the psychoanalytic point of view.

Note

1. This occurs, of course, not because therapists are more evolved human beings than others, but for reasons having to do with the therapist's training and with the structure and aims of the therapeutic situation. In their own lives outside the consulting room, there is little indication that therapists interact with their friends, children, or intimate partners any more effectively or benignly than anyone else.

Chapter 3

The Inner and Outer Worlds and Their Link through Action

Traditionally, it has been the patient's inner life that the analyst has tried to illuminate – thoughts, feelings, affectively charged images of self and other, unacknowledged wishes, fears, and fantasies. The patient's *behavior*, the actual actions he or she takes in the world and the impact of those actions on others in the patient's relational world, has tended to be a secondary concern. Manifest behavior has been viewed as a surface phenomenon, something more suited to the focus of social psychology than to the deeper concerns of psychoanalysis about what *underlies* that behavior (see Chapter 5). Thus, self-knowledge is typically pursued from the inside out (Boston Change Process Study Group, 2007).

In this chapter, I want to look at the role of understanding oneself *from the outside in* – looking further at how one's actions in the world lead to consequences that in turn maintain or reshape the very nature of the inner world. Such a perspective regards the inner world not merely as a residue of early relational experiences that, once they are internalized, reside in the psyche as more or less fixed or enduring features of the personality, sealed off from the influence of later "external" events. Rather, it views the inner world as genuinely dynamic, fluctuating and continually reconstituting itself in response to the ongoing experiences of daily life, even as it simultaneously *shapes* those daily experiences in a repeated pattern of bidirectional reciprocal causality.

As I hope will be clear as I proceed, what I mean by understanding from the outside in is not a *replacement* for understanding from the inside out. Rather, each perspective expands, illuminates, and deepens the understanding of the other. Just as the shaping and maintenance of the inner world by daily experience is complemented by the simultaneous shaping of daily experience by the expectancies and schemas of the inner world, so too are the dynamics of the psyche and the dynamics of overt behavior bidirectional, reciprocal, and mutually contextually embedded. The two perspectives are inseparable in the lived experience of self and in coming to know oneself more deeply and thoroughly. We cannot adequately know ourselves from the inside out without knowing ourselves from the outside in, and we cannot adequately know ourselves from the outside in without knowing ourselves from the inside out. Stating the matter somewhat differently, and anticipating a point I develop further as I proceed, understanding one's impact *on others* is utterly central to understanding *oneself*; and this not just because how we are experienced by others affects what our lives are like, but because the very nature of the inner world is constructed from the ongoing dialectic between our already existing proclivities, desires, fears, and representations (our preexisting psychological structures) and the life experiences that these structures and inclinations both bring about and are continually either maintained or changed by. Here again, the influences are simultaneous and bidirectional, not a matter of one perspective replacing the other. We do not know ourselves in any deep or meaningful way unless we know and understand our impact on others, nor do we understand very well our impact on others without understanding the affective and motivational wellsprings of the behavior that overtly expresses itself in our daily living. Especially is this the case because the impact of our behavior on others resides not simply in the acts per se but in the subtle qualities of affect and meaning that inevitably accompany them.

Much of the time, especially in cases of relatively severe pathology, it may *look like* the inner world is more or less autonomous, that it is sealed off from the influence of daily life, that it persists in infantile modes of thought and fantasy that are quite divorced from the mental activity that is more familiar to us from daily experience. Viewed through the lenses that have been traditional in psychoanalytic thought, the causal priority of the inner world is so obvious and compelling that the reciprocal feedback loops, the ways in which the inner world is *shaped by* the experiences of daily life as much as it is the *source of* those experiences, are hardly visible or, at best, recede into the background. That these equal and opposite force fields jointly maintain the consistency of personality patterns and self-experience, that the inner world is as much a product of current daily living as it is of the early experiences that originally gave rise to the images and affective predispositions that constitute it, has clearly not been the mainstream view in the psychoanalytic tradition. I argue here that it should be. Without understanding how responsive to the continuing events of our lives are the fantasies, images, representations, desires, and affects that constitute the inner world, we problematically restrict our understanding of the inner world's dynamics. Daily life and enduring psyche are not two separate realms. They are part and parcel of each other and of the experience of living.

A Clinical Example: The Case of Karl

Let me offer some examples of what I have in mind when I state that the inner world must be understood from the outside in as much as from the inside out. Karl was a handsome, charming man from a family of high-achieving financiers and philanthropists. He was married to a woman, Eleanor, who was attractive, intelligent, and very nice. If that trio of adjectives sounds both positive and bland, it is intended to. The relationship between Karl and Eleanor had been marked more by stability than vitality. By all external appearances, Karl's family life and marriage were successful and unproblematic. They lived on Park Avenue and had two sons who were both excellent students and budding tennis stars. Indeed, the marriage was not at all the focus of the concerns that brought Karl into therapy, which centered more on certain inhibitions and conflicts in his work life. But over time, the focus of the therapy shifted, as Karl began to be more and more unhappy about the lack of passion in the marriage. This lack of vitality and passion was evident not only in their infrequent and lackluster sexual experiences together, but also in the general tenor of the relationship. Karl felt hurt by Eleanor's lack of passion for him, but he also felt guilty about his own lack of passion for her.

These nagging concerns had been in and out of Karl's awareness for a long time, but they only became an experienced problem in the safe confines of the therapy. Previously, he had been too hampered by his guilt and self-disparagement to permit himself to dwell much on his dissatisfactions in the marriage; indeed, even to believe he *had a right* to be dissatisfied. But when the therapy began to make room for the more vital, confident, and expansive side of Karl, which he had previously – for reasons I elaborate on shortly – viewed as excessive and narcissistic, he began to want more from the marriage and – very important – to feel less *guilty about* wanting more.

In understanding how the inside-out and outside-in directions simultaneously shaped Karl's life and subjective experience, it is important to note – and equally important not to overemphasize – that, in the fashion we have come to expect, Eleanor evoked in Karl many affective responses and self- and object-representations originally associated with and evolving out of Karl's relationship to his mother. Karl's mother was a very moralistic and critical figure in his life, an overseer of standards virtually impossible to meet, because to please her Karl had to be both the high achiever/master of the universe that his father was *and*, at the same time, to be irreproachably modest, not too big for his breeches, free of any taint of unseemly self-regard. Karl was always both *too much* and *not enough* in her eyes, and he experienced himself as that in Eleanor's eyes as well. On both a conscious and an unconscious level, this experience of Eleanor as the inheritor or carrier of his mother's affect-laden representations evoked a painful set of feelings and self-reproaches for Karl, as well as images of the potentially disastrous consequences of his being fully himself, whether as a high achiever on the one hand or as someone hurting and longing to gratify unmet needs on the other.

In the work Karl and I did together, many hours were spent exploring, in a fashion intimately familiar to a psychoanalytic readership, the unconscious desires, fantasies, and self- and object-representations that were associated with Karl's conflicted relationship with Eleanor. But to understand Karl in the most clinically useful way, something else was needed as well. For every feature of this "internal" configuration was intimately related to the ways that Karl *behaved* in his daily life and to the ways it led Eleanor and others to behave toward him. The mix of expectations inherited from his relationship with his mother – but also constituting Karl's longstanding and *still ongoing* schemas of intimate relationships – led him to be deeply conflicted. He felt humiliated by the perception that he was insufficiently successful in the world (measured, that is, against the almost mythic figure of his father in his mother's eyes) and by what felt almost like a motivated refusal by his wife to be turned on by him sexually. At the same time, he felt guilty about (and humiliated in a *different* way by) the anger this circumstance evoked in him and even by his very desire to *be* admired and responded to. The result was that he often became sullen and withdrawn at home.

Karl could not find a way to actually talk to his wife about his wishes for more vitality in their relationship or to approach her in a way that might actually lead to that happening. Indeed, until he had worked through some other issues in the therapy, he could not even permit himself to appreciate very clearly that he *was* dissatisfied in the marriage. Instead, he simply felt vaguely unhappy, grumpy, and withdrawn – a way of experiencing himself (and of presenting himself) that fed on itself, further increasing his unhappiness and sense of unworthiness, and making it even harder to feel he had the right to ask more of Eleanor. Hence, it led him still again into impotent, silent withdrawal and the next repetition of the cycle. He experienced Eleanor as dissatisfied with him, and much of his behavior at home was designed to ward off her criticisms. But because his most frequent way of shielding himself from those criticisms was to withdraw from her, he ended up perpetuating and exacerbating the very circumstance he was trying to evade, because Eleanor's greatest dissatisfaction was with the withdrawal itself.

Those of you familiar with the literature of family therapy will recognize here a version of the pattern that family therapists refer to as pursuer and distancer (e.g., Betchen, 2005; Napier, 1978), with Eleanor in the role of pursuer and Karl in the role of distancer. The situation was further complicated, however, by Eleanor's *also* having a strong element of withdrawal and distancing as her own way of warding off the painful experience of rejection. Even more ironic, both of them also engaged in such withdrawal as a means of warding off another painful feeling – emptiness. Of course, that withdrawal only added to that feeling.

In his subjective experience of this pattern of behavior on his own part and this pattern between them, Karl experienced himself as, on the one hand, deadened and dull, and on the other, as unjustifiably expecting what it was unreasonable and childish to expect. He literally ran past mirrors, fearful he would catch himself being narcissistic if he looked at himself and thought himself handsome – a sort of forbidden truth about himself that he both feared acknowledging and *yearned* to acknowledge. This latter conflict was further exacerbated by one additional – and not surprising – response by Karl to this complex of feelings and attitudes. When he was at parties and other social gatherings, and especially when he had had a couple of drinks, he was far more seductive than he dared let himself realize, and women responded to his behavior very obviously and enthusiastically. He thus further had to cope with guilt over experiences that he both sensed and *could not bear* to sense he had contributed to bringing about, as well as with the further pain of the contrast between the responsiveness of women who were not really part of his life and the *lack* of response shown by his wife.

Further adding to the ways in which the patterns of both behavior and subjective experience between Karl and Eleanor dovetailed with – and perpetuated – the internal representations that his relationship with Eleanor had inherited from his relationship with his mother, Eleanor, like his mother, derided him for the very expressions of vitality and expansiveness that Karl was struggling to accept and liberate in himself. Indeed, she, like his mother, was palpably and conspicuously *hurt* by Karl's popularity and ease with people, which contrasted sharply with her own *unease* with people. Part of her hurt and unease derived from the very obvious interest that other women showed in Karl, but it went well beyond that. It might arise just as readily after a gathering of family or friends, and be about the response of other men, who enjoyed Karl's wit and social ease, or of her own parents, who she felt liked and enjoyed Karl more than they did her. When Eleanor referred to how much everyone loved Karl, how funny and charming they found him, as she did frequently, the tone of her observations was more reproachful than complimentary. Just as was the case with Karl's mother, Eleanor's depressive experience of herself became an implicit criticism of Karl for the very qualities that he was struggling to own, qualities that he had painfully submerged in order to preserve whatever tie he did have to mother, and then to Eleanor. These were, of course, also the qualities that it was one of the therapy's aims to liberate in Karl.

However the pattern began – and much of what transpired between Karl and Eleanor had to do with the ways that the preexisting inner worlds of each of them intersected – once it got going, as it did rather early in their relationship, it became largely self-perpetuating. The response of each kept the response of the other the same, and hence kept his and her own response (and his or her own *subjective experience*) the same, over and over. The internal configuration of affectively charged images and perceptual inclinations that shaped Karl's experience of Eleanor and of what was happening between them left him feeling unable to reach out to Eleanor *or* to complain to her, at least in an explicit and manifest way. And both his experience of his own behavior with her (which made him feel ashamed both of his passivity and of his silent hostility) and his experience of *her response* to his behavior (which left him experiencing her as the repetition of the implacably unresponsive and critical mother of his inner world) kept the images and representations that dominated his inner world firmly fixed in place – and ready to generate anew the very pattern of mutual relational behavior that *kept them* firmly fixed.

Karl's actions – in response to a longstanding configuration of subjective images, affects, and expectations – led to consequences that further maintained those very images, affects, and expectations. And in turn, those images, affects, and expectations prompted once again the same set of *actions*, perpetuating still again that same inner state. Put differently, the resemblances and continuities between Karl's inner state as an adult and his inner state as a child did not just persist because his internal world was sealed off, buried, like an archaeological shard, beneath covering layers (of defenses and countercathexes). His inner state was, rather, a living (though largely unconscious) response to the dynamically generated but largely unchanging conditions *of Karl's life*. His inner world was both cause and effect of that life, as his life was both effect and cause of his inner world.[1]

A Second Illustration: The Case of Arlene

A similar dynamic interplay between the patient's longstanding inclinations and representations and the actions and reactions of everyday life could be seen in the very different case of Arlene (as, I think it is important to note, it may be seen in just about *every* case at which one looks sufficiently closely). Arlene had grown up in a family that was rather stressed and preoccupied, with little time or psychic energy for the ins and outs of their children's experience. The family was an intact one, and even a loving one (accounting for Arlene's many strengths), but it was not an attentive one. Arlene's parents were, one might say, overly "efficient." As soon as they "got" what Arlene wanted or was saying, they took action. Often the actions were reasonably close to the mark, but they missed the subtleties of her experience and gave her little sense that she had the space to *elaborate* on her experience or to think out loud in the presence of a supportive and attentive parental figure. As she described her current experiences with her boyfriend, her parents, or with friends or acquaintances, it seemed clear that, like Karl but with a different set of specifics, Arlene was caught in a vicious circle in which inner and outer events continuously prompted and maintained each other.

In Arlene's case, it became apparent that from rather early in her life, Arlene's response to the often perfunctory parental attention to what she was saying was to repeat herself in a fashion that could feel rather obsessional to others. Elaborating here imaginatively on the bare bones of an incident she once described in the therapy, one might imagine her, at age 12, trying to decide whether to sleep over at a friend's house the night before an exam for which they were studying together. Discussing the pros and cons with her parents, she might indicate that, on the one hand, she didn't want to hurt her friend's feelings by saying no, and also that there was a possibility they might actually get more studying done if she spent the night there, but on the other hand, she felt that she would do better on the exam if she had a good night's sleep in her own bed. After discussing it for a while, with her clear (if conflicted) preference being to come home after studying, her parents would, with a touch of impatience (because the discussion had gone on so long) indicate that it seemed that Arlene preferred to come home and they thought that was a good idea. Then, after agreeing that this was the best course, but not having really had the sense that she had been carefully listened to, Arlene might say, repeating in essence what she had just said a moment ago, "So I think I'll call Sally and tell her that I don't want to stay over at her house after we study together, that I'd prefer to come home and be rested at home before the test."

Having just gone over this with Arlene, and having already affirmed this thought of Arlene's more than once, her parents, this time around, would perhaps just give a perfunctory nod or "uh huh," while hardly looking up from their newspaper. This in turn would leave Arlene *still* feeling unsure she had been heard and had had an attentive sounding board to check out the logic of her decision. And so, she would *again* say some variant of the same thing. "Because I think I will do better on the exam if I sleep in my own bed and can go to sleep early in familiar surroundings." Here again, her parents – who were basically good-natured and did not wish to be rejecting, but were also preoccupied and impatient (and, as the pattern had evolved and repeated itself frequently, were in essence confident there was *no new content* in what Arlene was saying) would give some perfunctory response to what was, for them, a rather tiresome feature of their otherwise loved daughter. But the perfunctoriness of their response would elicit still another repetitive variation of the same response from Arlene in a sequence that could go on for a surprisingly long number of repetitions.

In her adult life, this pattern had been extended to her boyfriend and close female friends, and even to teachers and colleagues, who similarly seemed to genuinely care about Arlene and, even, to listen with real interest to her *initial* presentations of her thoughts (Arlene was very smart and often had an interesting take on things). But they also, it seemed, began to feel a little crazy and frustrated at the repetitive and obsessional nature of Arlene's reassurance-seeking and going over things again and again. And thus with them too, over time Arlene's response to their response to Arlene's response fueled the perpetuation of the pattern.

Arlene's expectancies and representations of the attitudes of others were, from one vantage point, distortions; most people in her life were *not* almost automatically predisposed to listen perfunctorily and with minimal attention, as her parents were. Had Arlene approached them in the fashion that *most* people approach thinking something through with a friend or loved one, they would probably have been attentive and responsive. And had that happened, Arlene's own tendency to repeat herself in seemingly interminable fashion would likely have gradually diminished, creating a *positive* dynamic or *virtuous* circle, in which each move toward greater cogency or succinctness made it easier for others to pay attention, which made it easier for her to be more concise, which made it easier for others to listen, and so on and so forth. But because the relational schemas that guide us from within do not change on a dime, Arlene would continue to relate to others *as if* they were going to need a dozen repetitions to be wrestled into paying attention. And before her schemas could begin to accommodate to the differences between the way people were actually responding to her and the way she expected them to, they would begin to respond to her repetitiveness and – without having had an initial inclination or tendency to be inattentive – they would begin to unintendedly "confirm" her expectations.[2]

Much of this would go on without awareness, either on Arlene's part or on the part of the other people in her life who served as accomplices (see Chapter 2) in maintaining the pattern. Arlene was largely unaware of the inner expectations that drove her, *or* of the behavior itself; that is, she was not really aware of how repetitive she actually was. She had, to be sure, been told this at times, and could be aware of it *momentarily*. But in the midst of being driven to try to get the full attention of the other, she was aware only of what she was saying, of what she was thinking out loud about, not of the glazed look in the other's eyes or the relentless repetition in her own chewing over of the issue. In the fashion that is familiar to psychoanalytic clinicians, although she in some way *registered* both the other's response and the way it affected her own contribution to the conversation, she defensively warded off *focal* awareness of this, *effective* awareness that can lead to new behavior (Allen, Fonagy, & Bateman, 2008; Fonagy, 1991; Wallin, 2007). In similar fashion, the accomplices too were registering what was going on; that was why their attention was beginning to flag. But they too were largely doing this on automatic pilot rather than with focal awareness.

Not surprisingly, the pattern was evident in the therapy sessions too, and indeed, it was in part my own response to Arlene's obsessional repetitiveness – at first in the more automatic fashion that characterizes an enactment, and later with reflective awareness – that enabled me to discern the pattern more clearly and to understand its pervasiveness in her life. Such attention to the two-person processes occurring in the patient–therapist relationship is, of course, the stock-in-trade of contemporary psychoanalytic clinicians. My main focus in this chapter, however, is on the ways that such patterns are repeated again in the patient's daily life.

Daily Life and the Inner World

Far from distracting from or abandoning concern with the inner world, attention to the details of the person's daily life – including not just how the patient sees things or feels about things (as important as those are) but also what he *does* – is the only way to adequately *understand* the inner world, both theoretically and clinically. The inner world is not set in stone in the preoedipal years, but is an alive, continually responsive attribute of a *person* who is *living-in-the-world*. There are ways, to be sure, in which the inner world can seem to be rigidly adherent to old images and old programs, can *seem* to be unresponsive to what is presently going on. It is these ways that lead numerous clinicians and theorists to depict the patient's desires or expectations as infantile, primitive, or archaic, and to refer to those expectations as *fantasies*. But the image of a fixed inner world, unresponsive to the play of actual events and constituting instead a world of fantasy (or "phantasy") is a reflection of the traditional *lack of attention* to daily life experiences that has been a part of the psychoanalytic point of view for a long time.

In a number of conversations I have had recently with respected people in our field, they have conveyed that one of the most helpful features of my book on the clinical implications of a thoroughgoing relational perspective (Wachtel, 2008) is that it enabled them to feel less guilty about spending a significant amount of session time discussing the patient's daily life. They were aware that they were probably not at all exceptional in paying such attention to the events of the patient's life – in truth, almost everyone does – but they had a nagging sense that they were not being "psychoanalytic" while doing so and that this material was more "superficial" (cf. Chapter 5).

In the history of psychoanalysis, this attitude derived at first from the prominence of free association and the interpretation of transference as central to the clinical method of psychoanalysis and from the archaeological model of depth as a key theoretical metaphor (Spence, 1982; Stolorow & Atwood, 1997; Stolorow,

Orange, & Atwood, 2001; Wachtel, 2003, 2008). More recently, it has derived particularly from the advances in our understanding of enactments (e.g., Aron, 2003; Bass, 2003; Bromberg, 1998; Hirsch, 1998; Jacobs, 1986; Maroda, 1998; McLaughlin, 1991; D. B. Stern, 2003, 2004) and the move from viewing countertransference as a therapeutic error or sign of personal flaws in the analyst to the appreciation that countertransference is not only pervasive and inevitable but an invaluable source of therapeutic understanding. These have been enormous advances, and they have enabled our clinical interventions to be more powerful, sophisticated, and grounded in the clinical process. But it is also essential to recognize that in certain ways we have made one of our great advances simultaneously into one of our most significant constraints and blinders. There has evolved a tendency to be what we might call session-centric; that is, to focus on the therapeutic relationship and the experiences of the two parties in the room almost to the exclusion of everything else.

As I have just noted, this has probably not kept analysts from hearing a good deal about the patient's daily life; most patients, after all, would not tolerate this being ignored. But the tendency to view clinical work directed to the patient's daily life as superficial or not really psychoanalytic has hampered the development of a well-thought-through psychoanalytic *theory* of everyday life or, put differently, a well-thought-through theory of the relation between the inner world and the world of daily transactions. As a result, guidelines for exploring the everyday life of the patient, sophisticated methods of inquiry that can reveal or uncover as powerfully in this realm as free association does in the realm of the patient's conflicted desires and associative networks, have been slow to evolve.[3]

In turn, the failure to inquire in sufficient detail in this realm has meant that analysts were not confronted with the very kind of data that would make it clear that such inquiry was essential. Consequently, they could comfortably continue with the familiar clinical procedures that would ensure still further disinterest in daily life. Relatedly, the absence of compelling observations regarding the role of everyday life in maintaining the inner world – observations that are not readily forthcoming without the very methods of inquiry that are marginalized in standard psychoanalytic technique – has fed back to seemingly give further credence to the theories that placed everyday life in a secondary position to begin with. We thus encounter an epistemological vicious circle that, in a sense, parallels the clinical vicious circles that I have been emphasizing thus far: the absence of attention to (or of effective methods for investigating) the fine-grained reciprocal feedback processes of daily life outside the consulting room – in contrast, say, to the close attention to such feedback processes among contemporary mother–infant researchers – has led to the bolstering of theories that privilege the past and the internal and manifest a relative lack of interest in everyday life – and hence to still further impediments to developing the methods of inquiry that would *make* everyday life more interesting to analysts.

From another vantage point, the theoretical gap to which I am referring reflects a failure to notice that in large measure the evolution of the two-person point of view has been largely restricted to two domains, the transactions between patient and analyst in the session and the transactions between mother and infant early in life. In these two realms, a thoroughgoing two-person model, emphasizing the mutual co-construction of experience by the two parties, is strongly evident. In the realm of infancy, for example, this emphasis on the way that the early evolution of personality is co-constructed, mutual, and reciprocal is evident from Winnicott's early observation that "there is no such thing as a baby" but only a "nursing couple" (Winnicott, 1975), through a wide range of contemporary relational formulations, to the groundbreaking studies of psychoanalytically oriented infant researchers such as D. N. Stern (1985), Beebe (2000), Beebe & Lachmann (1998, 2002), and Tronick (Cohn & Tronick, 1988). Similarly, in the understanding of the patient's experience in the session and the way that the phenomena observed in the session emerge, it is now widely apparent that they do not simply bubble up from the unconscious but reflect an intricate back-and-forth in which *both* parties are both observers *and* observed (see, for example, Aron, 1991; I. Z. Hoffman, 1983; Mitchell, 1997), bringing forth responses from the other even as they simultaneously *respond to* the other. But the rest of the patient's life, the huge swath of living between the nursery and the consulting room, has been very largely addressed, even by relational writers, in essentially one-person terms (see Wachtel, 2008). The painstaking analysis of mutual, bidirectional co-construction of experience that is evident in the two "anchor areas" (the nursery and the consulting room) is not nearly as evident in the discussions of why the patient is having difficulty *in his daily life*. There the patient's difficulties are more often described as but a reflection of a deeper world of internalized objects, exerting their influence from the past and from within.

Even in contemporary relational accounts, one sees little indication in discussions of the patient's daily life of the reciprocal, two-person dynamics that are so prominent in discussions of infancy or the therapeutic relationship. The understanding that the internal world is a product as well as a cause of what is transpiring is far more evident in those realms than in the understanding of daily life experiences. Indeed, part of why so much more attention is paid to the two anchor points is that they are thought to be where the action is. That is, they are understood as dynamically shifting, continuously in dialectical tension, and subject to a reciprocal play of forces and of intersubjective transactions, whereas daily life is but a stage on which a play already written (and stored in the internal world) is performed.[4]

The very acuity of attention to intersubjective or two-person processes at the two anchor points, it might be said, has served to obscure the relative *absence* of a thoroughgoing two-person perspective in addressing the rest of the patient's life (Wachtel, 2008). The aim of the clinical examples presented in this chapter is to highlight what a two-person conception of daily life would look like and to highlight as well the *consequentiality* of daily life. When it is understood how central the experiences of daily living are for maintaining (or modifying) the patient's deepest personality dynamics, it is no longer necessary, as some have suggested (see, for example, Ghent, 1989; Modell, 1984), to supplement the two-person perspective with a dash of one-person thinking in order to address the deeply unconscious roots of our behavior and experience or to understand the stubborn persistence of patterns that originated years or decades earlier. That persistence, it becomes clear, is not additional to or separate from our responsiveness to the events and experiences of daily life (see Wachtel, 1973, 1977b, 1981), but is *part and parcel of* that responsiveness (and of the responsiveness of the other, in similar fashion, to our own behavior, affective tone, and enduring characteristics).

The case material I offer in this chapter is intended to illustrate not only how the two-person and reciprocal nature of psychological causality extends well beyond the consulting room but also how the reciprocal *actions* of the patient and those he or she interacts with are a crucial part of the glue that holds together and maintains each party's persisting personality and individuality. It should be clear, however, that in emphasizing overt actions and their consequences more than is common among psychoanalytic writers, I am not downgrading the importance of affect, motivation, or representations of self and other. Rather, I am suggesting that it is only when we also take into account the effects of the mutual actions that occur in patterned ways millions of times in every person's life that we in fact understand adequately those more traditional foci of psychoanalytic thought and inquiry. In the chapters that follow, I further illustrate and elaborate on this point from a variety of vantage points. It is a central feature of the cyclical psychodynamic point of view.

Notes

1. It should be clear that I am not contending that Karl's subjective experience was a simple product of what was "objectively" transpiring. The idiosyncratic construction of experience out of the materials of one's lived life, the ways in which prior experiences shape our expectations and perceptions, the role of both wishful and defensive thinking on what we make of experiences, even the simple sheer *impossibility* of seeing social reality free of our situated perspective, is at the heart of contemporary psychoanalytic thought, and at the heart of my own thinking as well (see, e.g., Wachtel, 2008). But it is essential not to confuse these insights with the idea that we simply "distort," or to fail to acknowledge, how powerfully what is actually going on does shape the subjective world, how much it is responsive, not sealed off (cf. Aron, 1996; Gill, 1982, 1983, 1984; I. Z. Hoffman, 1998; Mitchell, 1988).
2. Recall here the discussion in Chapter 2 of the race between confirmation and disconfirmation.
3. One exception to this general trend is psychoanalytic work that has been inspired by the ideas of Harry Stack Sullivan. Outside the psychoanalytic realm, important contributions can be found in the systemic inquiries of family therapists, which are aimed at revealing sequences and patterns which may not be readily apparent without such inquiry (see Wachtel & Wachtel, 1986).
4. It might be objected that concepts such as projective identification fill this theoretical gap. See Wachtel (2008) for an extended discussion of how the conceptualization offered here differs from projective identification and some of the limitations of the latter concept.

Chapter 4

Attachment in Psychoanalysis and Psychotherapy

A Two-Person, Cyclical Psychodynamic Approach

In recent years, there has been an increasing interest in attachment among therapists of many orientations, and especially among psychoanalytic therapists. As part of this development, there has also been an increasing integration of attachment theory and the findings of attachment research into the ways that therapists conceive of the therapeutic process (e.g., Eagle, 2003; Eagle & Wolitzky, 2009; Fonagy, 2001; Fonagy, Gergely, & Target, 2008; Renn, 2012; Slade, 1999, 2004, 2008; Wallin, 2007). These developments represent a marked change in attitude. For many years, the development of attachment theory and research proceeded largely independently of the mainstream of psychoanalytic thought, even though John Bowlby, the originator of attachment theory, was an analyst. At the time Bowlby was writing, his emphasis on what actually transpired between mother and infant departed from the primary emphasis in psychoanalytic writing on the infant's *phantasies* regarding the mother or representations of a mothering figure. In recent years, however, there has been increasing psychoanalytic interest in attachment processes and in research exploring the impact of the actual transactions between mother and infant in shaping the development of personality (e.g., Beebe & Lachmann, 2002; Fonagy, 2001; Mitchell, 1999; D.N. Stern, 1985; Wallin, 2007). In this chapter, I want to further explore the implications of this theoretical turn, especially in light of developments in the relational branch of psychoanalytic thought.

A central feature of relational theorizing is advocacy of a two-person point of view and a critique of the one-person viewpoint that relational theorists argue was characteristic of psychoanalytic formulations for many years (Aron, 1990; Ghent, 1989; Lyons-Ruth, 1999). In this chapter, I examine more closely the distinction between one-person and two-person theorizing and further elaborate on how the cyclical psychodynamic perspective provides an alternative to that distinction in the form of a more thoroughgoing *contextual* version of psychoanalytic thought. I pursue these lines of thought via consideration of attachment phenomena and their theoretical and therapeutic implications, and in doing so also attempt to contribute to further sharpening our understanding both of attachment and of relational theory.

I begin with a clinical account that bears on two of the key points I want to make in this chapter. On the one hand, this clinical vignette illustrates how attention to the implications of attachment theory and research can enhance the clinical inter-action, alerting the therapist to dimensions of the patient's experience and dynam-ics that might otherwise be overlooked or not seen as sharply. On the other hand, I also want to use this illustration as a jumping-off point for introducing some *caveats* about the way attachment is often thought about and discussed. In addi-tion, I aim to extend this examination of the conceptual foundations and clinical implications of attachment theory to the broader framework of relational theory in general and cyclical psychodynamic theory in particular and to do so through a distinction between what might be called one-person attachment theory and two-person attachment theory.

The Case of Andrew

The patient, who I will call Andrew, was a grants officer in a large foundation. His work meant a lot to him, and his mood often depended to a significant degree on the quality of the proposals that he was being asked to evaluate. When the propos-als were innovative and high quality, he felt he was engaged in a meaningful and important activity that contributed to the welfare of others and of society at large. When they were mediocre, he felt he was wasting his time, that he had chosen a career that depended on the creativity of others rather than deriving from crea-tive contributions of his own. At these latter times, other insecurities had more room to emerge and invade his consciousness. This particular feature of Andrew's self-evaluations and their relation to the input from others is part of the story that I relate.

The central concern that brought Andrew into therapy was a distressingly conflictual experience of his marriage. He felt at times that he was only in the marriage for the sake of his daughter, Emily, who was just entering her teenage years and who, he felt, would be very distressed to have to deal with her parents' divorce. Apart from feeling that leaving would be detrimental to Emily, he also was aware that he himself would experience it as a great loss to have less contact with her. In contrast, his relationship with his wife, Jane, felt to him much more functional. They handled household and childcare issues well, but he did not feel they really *connected*, and felt that in reality they never really had.

It had become apparent fairly early in the work that a central factor in Andrew's conflictual experience of the marriage was an enormous sensitivity to feel-ing coerced and crowded. He experienced his wife as controlling him, though a broader look at the pattern between them made it clear that her control – as is often the case – was in good measure a function of his own acquiescence. Put dif-ferently, part of what happened was that Andrew – both because of his concerns about his daughter and because of his own *guilt* over his wish to pull back from his wife – often went out of his way to be compliant with Jane's wishes, and then felt intruded on and controlled. In a number of important sessions, I had inquired of Andrew what made it seem like Jane was controlling him rather than that she *wanted something different* from what he wanted – that is, something he could say no to if he wished or could discuss and negotiate with her so that *both* of their interests and desires were represented.

In the course of discussing and exploring this question, it became more apparent to Andrew just how frighteningly intrusive *his mother* had been in the course of his growing up and the ways that he had attempted to deal with this by submitting to her on certain large and symbolic choices, while secretly channelling the real affect and personal meaning in his life into the time that he was alone reading, thinking, or walking in the woods. That is, Andrew was officially a good boy – pursuing a career choice his parents would approve of, being a faithful attendee at family functions, and so forth – while privately, in his guilty heart of hearts, he was extremely isolated, inaccessible, and disconnected from them. In the kind of vicious circle that I argue in this book is central to almost every problematic pattern that brings people to analysis or therapy, Andrew's private sense of isolation and disconnection fed his need to publicly submit and comply, and his compliance and submission to his mother's demands in turn fed his need to be physically and psychologically alone. It will not surprise most readers that a similar dynamic was evident in his relationship with Jane.

In the particular in-session event that I wish to discuss here, my interest in the clinical implications of the attachment perspective called my attention to aspects of what had transpired for Andrew that I might otherwise have overlooked, or at least might not have seen from the particular angle that I did – an angle which resonated especially strongly for Andrew. Andrew had been talking about Jane having said he seemed to be feeling depressed and asking if it was because the proposals he had received recently didn't seem so promising. This was in fact Andrew's own understanding of his mood, and he explicitly commented to me, in relating this experience, that he could see where many men might feel pleased that their wife noticed their mood and understood what it was about. But instead, Andrew felt *intruded* upon by Jane's comment, and it felt uncomfortable and unpleasant. It made him think, once again, that he would be happier alone, that he had to get away. And in turn, in the fashion that had become familiar to both of us, this then cast him into painful conflict and led to a self-deprecating judgment that there was something wrong with him for feeling this, a self-criticism that, it should be noted, did not diminish his anger at Jane or feeling of wanting to leave her.

This time, having been stimulated by a recent immersion in the attachment literature and the related literature on mother–infant interaction, I articulated my understanding of Andrew's experience just a little differently than I had previously (and than I otherwise might have thought to). Instead of saying that Jane's comment had felt intrusive (though it did, and though that would certainly have *also* been an empathically responsive comment), I said that it felt like Jane had been "overtracking" his experience. His eyes lit up, and he said, excitedly, "Yes, that's *exactly* it. I love that word, *overtracking* – that's it!"

I used that particular word because this time Andrew's description of his experience brought to mind what I had been reading about the way that infants seem to do best with a moderate degree of tracking of their experience; that is, of the mother's interacting in a way that was responsive to the baby's cues. Too little responsiveness, of course, is hardly a good experience for the infant. He or she will feel, in some preverbal fashion, misunderstood, misread, unhelped. But, it turns out, *too much* tracking, too high a correlation between the cues coming from the infant and the behavior coming from the mother seems not to feel so good either (Beebe & Lachmann, 2002; Wallin, 2007). Though such close correspondence between the baby's behavior and the mother's could be seen, in the abstract, as a very high degree of empathy, it turns out that sometimes what is required to be genuinely and *effectively* empathic is *not to be* quite so empathic, to leave the baby free not to be understood and not to be followed quite so closely (cf. Winnicott, 1960). Put differently, and pointing to the *dynamic* nature of attachment patterns – the way in which, like all other aspects of human psychology, attachment patterns represent an attempt to address *conflicting* feelings and desires – the mother's not tracking quite so thoroughly and precisely allows the infant some room for the other side of the attachment dynamic, the needs for autonomy and exploration as well as contact.[1]

The babies of mothers who undertrack tend to be insecure in the fashion that is called ambivalent or resistant in the attachment literature. They keep flailing about trying to get their mothers to be more responsive. But the babies of mothers who *over*track, who are *too* in sync, seem to have difficulties too; they tend to be insecure in the fashion that is described as avoidant. They withdraw from contact in order to have any room for autonomy at all (Beebe & Lachmann, 2002; Malatesta, Culver, Tesman, & Shepard, 1989; Tronick, 1989). In contrast, mothers who track in a moderate fashion, who, as in the attachment version of the Goldilocks story, are not too far and not too close, but "just right," seem more likely to engender secure attachment in their infants.

As Andrew and I continued to talk about the experience I had labeled as overtracking, Andrew conveyed both his great pleasure at the way I had labeled the experience and his experience of almost horror at what it felt like to *be* overtracked. In the midst of this, he suddenly did something I found very striking, but which I might well not have noticed (or might not have noticed with as much clarity or interest) had we not been talking about this particular experience in this particular way (that is, had I not had the concept and the experience of overtracking reverberating in my consciousness). What happened was that Andrew continued to talk to me about the experience, but while he was doing so he turned his head so that he was not only facing away from me but was basically looking at right angles to me while he spoke. This continued for a few seconds, and then he turned back to look at me. He did not seem to notice at all that he had done this, and he continued to speak continuously and coherently through both the turning away and the turning back to face me. Someone listening to an audiotape of the session would have no idea that anything unusual had happened.

Several things struck me about this discussion and this experience. First of all, it reminded me of the images from attachment and other mother–infant research of the mother who *looms in* at the child and does not seem to recognize that the infant is turning away from contact – and, indeed, who often further zeroes in on the infant as the infant turns away, seemingly trying to *force* the very contact that the infant is clearly trying to avoid. What Andrew did, in a fashion that seemed completely outside his awareness, seemed to me to be both a confirmation and a poignant playing out of the very concern about overtracking we had just been discussing. Andrew had clearly felt keenly understood by me in my labeling of his overtracking experience. In many respects, this was a gratifying and positive experience for him. But the very fact that I had understood him so well, I believe, also raised the anxiety that I too would understand him *too* well, that I too would overtrack, not leave him room for his needed zone of privacy. From that vantage point, turning away from me was a way of seeing whether he could still control our interaction, whether he could be understood and in contact when *he* felt like it rather than as an inexorable consequence of my "looming empathy."

In this sense, what happened between us in this interaction could be seen as a version of what Weiss, Sampson, and their colleagues (e.g., Silberschatz, 2005; Weiss, 1998; Weiss & Sampson, 1986) depict as the patient unconsciously posing a test for the therapist. In this instance, I think that the unconscious test that Andrew was posing was whether he could control the degree of contact between us and whether we could remain in contact under *his* terms – that is, with his regulation of the intensity and nature of the contact. (In discussing Andrew's relationship with Jane, I had, in several of the sessions preceding this experience, mentioned that Andrew did not feel sure he would be *welcome* upon trying to reconnect with Jane if he acknowledged that he had enjoyed a number of temporary respites when either he or she was out of town. Things felt all-or-nothing to Andrew; either he submitted to what felt to him like *relentless* relating by Jane or he had to be completely alone and *without any* real contact with her. What Andrew was thus testing out with me was whether it could be different with me, whether he could enjoy, in a small way, diminishing our contact and yet still be welcome and still be able to have the contact when he wanted it.)

Given this understanding on my part of what was transpiring between us, I did not comment on his having turned away, which I felt would feel to Andrew like one more instance of being overly observed, of having no breathing room to simply "be." Instead, I permitted the experience with me to register unconsciously, as an instance of implicit or procedural learning rather than change pursued through explicit or declarative channels, as is stressed in interpretations. For many years, explicit interpretation was the most highly valued intervention in psychoanalytic circles, sometimes being viewed as virtually a sine qua non of working psychoanalytically (e.g., Bibring, 1954; Friedman, 2002; Laplanche & Pontalis, 1973). In recent years, however, a growing number of influential psychoanalytic writers have emphasized that interpretive efforts must be complemented with ways of working that are more on the procedural level and that seek to generate change via new relational experiences, "moments of meeting," and implicit relational knowledge (e.g., Eagle, 2003; Fonagy, 1999; Fosshage, 2003; K. A. Frank, 1999;

Lyons-Ruth, 1999; D.N. Stern et al., 1998; Wachtel, 2008). Summarizing this trend, and explicitly relating it to the study of attachment processes, Eagle (2003) has stated,

> The basic idea that noninterpretive factors play a central role in all psycho-therapy and psychoanalysis has gained a new currency and vitality from the recognition, gained from attachment research and theory, as well as devel-opmental and cognitive psychology, that early, overlearned, and nonverbal representations – procedural knowledge and "rules" – are not easily and fully translatable into reflective (symbolized) knowledge, and *are not always sus-ceptible to change via interpretation and insight, but require noninterpretive, interactional, and strong emotional experiences in order for them to change.* (p. 50, italics added)

At no point in the session did I interpret or call attention to Andrew's essen-tially unconsciously turning away from me. But I did *register* what had transpired and worked with it as the session proceeded. For example, later in the session I commented that what he wished was possible between him and Jane was to be able to talk to her and not have to be gazing into her eyes at every moment, to be able to know that she is there and listening, but that he can glance over at the mail or do something else while talking to her. I offered this essentially in a metaphori-cal sense, as an image that captured *the kind* of experience with her that he desired rather than as a literal description of a specific mode of interaction. I also offered it without reference to what had transpired between us earlier in the session, but clearly with that experience in mind. Andrew was enthusiastically receptive to this comment, saying that yes, it captured very well what he longed for, and it seemed to create at least a small opening for him to imagine a way of *approach-ing* Jane rather than having to retreat from her in order to prevent himself from feeling invaded.

Securely Attached People or Patterns of Secure Attachment?

The clinical account I just offered hopefully illustrates the potential value of the attachment perspective in generating additional ways of making sense of the clini-cal material and pointing to ways of responding that enable the patient to feel better understood. But there are also ways in which the images generated by attach-ment theory and research, if not examined very carefully, can potentially *impede* our clinical and theoretical understanding. The impediments are not intrinsic to attachment theory; indeed, they represent a failure to read its literature carefully and to take seriously the overall theoretical perspective that guided Bowlby's work. Nonetheless, the problematic way of discussing attachment phenomena that I wish to discuss here – categorizing individuals as "securely" or "insecurely" attached – reflects deeply ingrained habits of discourse, evidenced frequently even by sophisticated theorists and researchers who in more careful and reflective moments know better. Without examining more closely how attachment is conceived and discussed, the incorporation of concepts from attachment theory and research into psychoanalytic theory and practice can end up bolstering the very features of psychoanalytic thought most in need of rethinking and renovation.

The issues I wish to raise here are especially relevant to those psychoanalytic thinkers who identify with and seek to advance the relational version of psychoanalytic thought, because the potentially problematic applications of attachment theory parallel rather similar vulnerabilities in the broader realm of relational theory. In particular, both the literature on attachment and the literature of relational psychoanalysis represent, at the heart of their intended illuminations, quintessentially two-person modes of conceptualization.[2] And yet prominent versions of both often retain insufficiently appreciated traces of the one-person and essentialist modes of thought that it was the very aim of the two-person point of view to replace. (See Wachtel, 2008, for a fuller discussion of this with regard to relational theory in general.)

Bowlby's vision was very clearly what is today called a two-person vision, although at the time Bowlby was introducing his new ideas, the distinction between one-person and two-person theorizing was not yet the common feature of the psychoanalytic literature that it is today.[3] Appropriately understood, attachment status is not a quality residing inside a single individual. Attachment is always attachment *to* someone.[4] It is about a relation *between* two people, and is thus a quintessentially two-person concept. And yet, in so much of the literature, and in the way many clinicians, and even researchers, regularly discuss attachment in informal conversation (always a revealing window into the "working models" that actually guide our thinking), attachment is depicted as if it were a property of the individual alone. We describe people as securely or insecurely attached, as avoidantly or ambivalently attached, and so forth, as if they were that way with everyone and at all times – as if, that is, this were just "the way they are." This linguistic form, seeming to suggest that attachment status is a property the individual simply carries around with him in his head, reflects what Mitchell (1995) called "a view of mind as monadic, a separable, individual entity," in contrast to "a view of mind as dyadic, emerging from and inevitably embedded within a relational field" (p. 65; see also Stolorow & Atwood, 1994). I used such monadic language myself earlier in this chapter, referring to how particular patterns of tracking by the mother led to "securely," or "ambivalently," or "avoidantly" attached individuals. And if, on being pressed, I, or any other writer on attachment, might say that that is just a convenient shorthand, that *of course* we are referring to attachment *to* an attachment figure, at the very least it must be acknowledged that the shorthand version tends to get a lot more ink than the explicitly two-person version.

In part, this is simply a problem of the limitations of ordinary discourse – of the linear, sequential nature of our sentences – to convey certain ideas in a fashion that is both true to the phenomena being discussed and able to be listened to without an unbearable sense of tediousness. Imagine if each time we might ordinarily use a term like *securely attached* or *insecurely attached*, we said something like "This person experiences certain relationships with certain people in ways that leave him feeling that the other will not be usefully available when he is anxious, but in some other relationships he may have quite different experiences and antic-ipations, and even with the person with whom he is usually secure, certain mutual cueings can occur that lead to a different experience that time." Locutions such as this are closer to the truth, to the complexities of attachment in daily life, than the simple adjectives *secure* or *insecure*; but they are also extraordinarily well designed to ensure that whomever we are speaking to will suddenly remember that he has to make a phone call or will feel an urgent need to take a nap.

And yet, it is necessary that we *understand* terms like securely attached or insecurely attached in precisely that way, even if we don't generally articulate that understanding in such a long-winded fashion. Otherwise, we fall into an essen-tialist mode of thought that has encountered increasing challenges in recent years (e.g., Benjamin, 1988; I. Z. Hoffman, 1998; Mitchell, 1993; D. B. Stern, 1997). We begin to think that this is the way the person "is," when it is more accurate to say that this is the way he is *with me* (and, moreover, how he is with me *when I am acting in a particular way*, and he may *not* be that way even with me when I am being different). Thus, a fully contextual or two-person conceptualization of attachment not only attends to how the person varies in the attachment experi-ences that are evoked with one person or another; it also requires us to ask *what is happening* that leads the person to relate and to perceive and experience in a secure fashion, in an ambivalent or avoidant fashion, and so forth. It attends to what each party to the exchange or to the relationship is *doing* and *feeling* at any particular moment, and it asks what each person's participation in the attachment relationship at any given moment is *in response to* and what it *evokes* in the other.

It is certainly true that each of us enters any interaction with certain proclivi-ties, and that those proclivities have a strong bearing on how things proceed. Who the patient is, how he or she relates, is certainly not *just* a function of who he or she is with or of what is happening at the moment. Such a view, which leaves out that each person *already has* a personality before he or she comes into the ana-lyst's office or begins any new relationship, is a caricature of relational thinking, though one that is offered with surprising frequency by critics of the relational point of view (see Wachtel, 2008). Similarly, the points I have just made are in no way intended to contravene the value of conceptualizing what Bowlby has called internal working models. Rather, their aim is to *contextualize* our understanding of these models.

The seeming tension between, on the one hand, the view that people do have prevailing and pervasive characteristics that they bring into any situation even before the other person has revealed a thing about his or her own intentions or attributes and, on the other hand, the view that every feature of how we expe-rience and respond to an encounter with another person depends very signifi-cantly on how the other person behaves and what he or she is like is in fact quite readily resolved. In discussing more generally the nature of relational theorizing

(Wachtel, 2008), I have argued that our theories must clearly and prominently take into account the individual characteristics, proclivities, or personality structures that the person brings to any interaction, but that the structure of personality is always a *contextual* structure. It should be obvious that the same holds for understanding the concept of internal working models. Just as who the patient is is by no means fully determined by who the analyst is, so too the individual's attachment style is by no means a simple function of who the attachment figure is with whom he is presently interacting. At the same time, however, it is also by no means *irrelevant* who the analyst is or who the particular attachment figure is. Different aspects of the person will be brought out by different analysts or by different attachment figures. The question of whether someone is securely attached, or ambivalently attached, or avoidantly attached, and so on requires us to ask the further question: securely or insecurely attached *to whom*? This is a question that, perhaps, "officially" is always part of the attachment conception. But as one reads and hears the use of attachment concepts, it should be clear that it is rather common to hear both attachment researchers and analysts who are interested in attachment theory talk about the person's attachment status or attachment category *without* this contextualization. And, it is important to notice, this is precisely what is meant by one-person thinking – seeing the person in a fashion that assumes that the seer has no effect on the seen or that the person's attributes can be described with little or no attention to the context in which those attributes are being manifested (cf. I. Z. Hoffman, 1998).

Attachment and Schemas

A different way of reconciling the twin realities of enduring personality structures and acute responsivity to the relational field derives from an appreciation of the intersection between psychoanalytic conceptions and Piaget's concept of schemas characterized by both assimilation and accommodation. I have previously discussed in some detail (e.g., Wachtel, 1981, 2011a) how the concept of transference is rendered both more consonant with the data of clinical observation and more clinically useful when it is conceptualized in a way that links psychoanalytic concepts and observations to those of Piaget, and I have recently extended that synthesis of psychoanalytic and Piagetian thinking to the broader realm of relational theory (Wachtel, 2008). Bowlby, it turns out, was similarly influenced by Piaget's thinking and similarly melded psychoanalytic and Piagetian ideas in his concept of the internal working model (Fonagy, 2001; Marrone, 1998).[5]

My own attraction to attachment theory derives less from the attachment *categories* that have been such a central focus of the attachment literature than from an interest in the attachment *process* and in the way Bowlby's thinking about attachment draws upon the dynamic interplay between assimilation and accommodation in all facets of our experience of and response to the world we live in. Much as transference can be better understood in light of the concepts of schemas, assimilation, and accommodation (Wachtel, 1981), so too the individual's structured attachment inclinations are best seen as his or her individualized way of understanding and responding to *what is actually happening right now*. These inclinations are based on the person's developmental history and what she has made of that history, how she has understood it, interpreted it, generalized from it, created assumptions out of it. But they are *also* both maintained and modified by the world of ongoing experience. They both influence and are *influenced by* what is transpiring (cf. J. Greenberg, 2005), which is just another way of saying that they are, inevitably, characterized both by assimilation and accommodation. Attachment is less a matter of fixed categories than a process, a *dynamic* and *contextual* process, in which the structuralized residue of all the *previous* dynamic and contextual processes in which the person has participated plays a very prominent role.

From Two-Person Theory to Contextual Theory

I have been attempting thus far to highlight the two-person nature of attachment and to call attention to the ways in which discussions of attachment can so readily devolve to a one-person account. But, as I have discussed in more detail elsewhere (Wachtel, 2008), "two-person" is actually not a fully adequate way to conceptualize the psychological phenomena with which we are concerned. The one-person–two-person distinction is a first cut, a useful beginning. But it is also potentially misleading. People live not just in dyadic relationships but also in families, sibling groups, peer groups, work groups, and still larger configurations. As our daily newspapers and newscasts should make clear, nations, religions, and ethnic groups, for example, can be among the most powerful attachment objects around which human beings orient their lives, as can ideas such as psychoanalysis or organizations such as IARPP or the IPA. Many of the same dynamics that are described between infants and mothers or between husbands and wives or analysts and patients can be found in relation to these other attachment objects.[6]

Thus, it seems to me that a corrective is needed to the formulation by Mitchell (1995) that I cited earlier. Mind *is*, as Mitchell states, "inevitably embedded within a relational field" (p. 65), but that relational field is *not* always dyadic. The very roots of human evolution are misread when they are interpreted in purely dyadic terms. Yes, Bowlby and others were addressing some very crucial observations, both in terms of evolution and ethology and in terms of contemporary human psychology, when they highlighted the mother–infant bond, which is indeed a core component of our evolutionarily derived survival mechanisms. But that bond is not the only foundation of our survival. Human beings are group creatures, clan creatures, tribe creatures. In large measure, the survival of the human gene pool derived from the survival of small *groups* who shared many genes in common, and whose gene pool at times survived because individuals acting in concert created conditions for the survival of their gene *pool* even when the given individual might not live to procreate (Wade, 2006).

Looking to the present, the significance of attachment status and attachment skills and capacities in contemporary urban life is not solely a matter of one-to-one intimate relationships but also of the capacity to bond with, interact with, and sensitively read the *many* other people with whom we must cooperate and coordinate. Mirror neurons, emotional intelligence, and empathy did not evolve just to cement mothers and infants or pairs of lovers. These attributes are the glue that held together the clan, and today they are the glue that holds together the corporation, the psychology department, the PTA, or the psychoanalytic movement. The sources of pain, despair, and emptiness that bring people to our offices today are not limited to problems in a single, overridingly important dyadic relationship – though such problems certainly are a very significant part of what keeps us in business. They include as well problems with friendships, with making it in the various status hierarchies that make up our lives, and with other phenomena that go well beyond not only the dyadic model but the triangular model of Oedipal theory or the unidirectional identification of members of the group with its leader (Freud, 1921).

Appreciation of the critical importance of intimate dyadic relationships – whether in attachment theory or in relational theory – is by no means to be dismissed. But an adequate foundation for understanding the relational matrix that frames our lives requires us to understand that if two-person psychology is an advance over one-person psychology, it is because it is an instance of a larger, and ultimately more powerful reconceptualization – the move to a fully *contextual* psychology. The infant (or adult for that matter) is never simply "attached," whether securely or insecurely. He or she is attached *to* someone or something. And the nature of that attachment depends on the particular attachment object being referred to.

But more than that, it depends on the context even with regard to the attachment to a *particular* figure. That is, the idea of secure or insecure attachment, or of ambivalent, avoidant, or disorganized attachment, ultimately refers to *statistical probabilities*, to what *usually* occurs. No one is simply securely or insecurely attached, even with regard to a single attachment figure. We describe someone as securely attached when he is *mostly* securely attached – either in the sense of being securely attached to most of his attachment figures or in the sense of being securely attached to any particular attachment figure most of the time. But every single securely attached individual will look *in*securely attached some of the time, and every single insecurely attached individual will look *securely* attached some of the time.

This is not just a matter of measurement error or of trivial occasional deviations. Attention to these differences and variations is critical to promoting therapeutic change. It is part of a larger focus on the variations in behavior and experience that our patients inevitably manifest and that, if we can attune ourselves to noticing them, enables us to find the kernels of new ways of being and help our patients to develop alternative modes of behavior and experience to those that have been responsible for perpetuating their difficulties (Wachtel, 2008, 2011a). Successful therapeutic work is impeded by ways of thinking that obscure these variations and these kernels of new possibility – by the tendency to pathologize and the tendency to describe personality in terms of acontextual "inner" structures rather than in terms of contextual structures that must be understood in relation to the events and personal transactions that frame the person's life.

Moreover, it is also important to be clear that the contexts that frame and structure our lives – whether dyadic, triadic, or larger in scope – are themselves dynamic. The contexts in which we find ourselves are very largely contexts that we have ourselves contributed to creating, that we have co-created with those who participate with us in that context. Each of us is the context for those who are our own context; at the center of both social and individual psychological dynamics is a set of reciprocal feedback loops that are responsible both for the persistence of certain patterns in our lives and for the possibilities for change in those patterns. This is the essential message of cyclical psychodynamic theory. There *is* a consistency to personality, but it is a *dynamic and variegated* consistency. Whether in the realm of attachment relationships and attachment patterns, or with regard to any of the other phenomena with which psychoanalysts and psychotherapists have been concerned, it is in attention to the intersection of human *experience* and human *action* that the most adequate understanding can be found (see, for example, Shahar, Cross, & Henrich, 2004; Shahar & Porcelli, 2006; see also Chapter 3).

Mutual *actions* are as central an element in the attachment relationship as are the internal working models of each party to the relationship. Adequate understanding of attachment phenomena requires attention not just to the accumulated structures of expectation that have developed out of earlier attachment experiences, but to the "mutual doing" that is intrinsic to attachment transactions, the constant emission and registration of cues based on each other's behavior. A relationship is not just the product of two suspended brains in a vat, each with an internal working model. It is – by its very nature – two (or more) people interacting, *doing and saying things* in relation to each other or together acting upon the world.

There is certainly an enormous body of evidence that an individual's assessed attachment status tends to be relatively stable and to persist over time (Cassidy & Shaver, 2008; Grossman, Grossman, & Waters, 2005; Mikulincer & Shaver, 2007; Sroufe, Egeland, Carlson, & Collins, 2005). This is one of the robust findings that has made the area of attachment of such interest. But reports of this continuity give us just the outer surface, so to speak, not the process that lies behind it. I have already noted that what is really being measured is a depiction of the person's *average* or *modal* attachment status, not a measure that is unvarying through the days and weeks and years; our understanding of the person's central tendency must be complemented by an understanding of the exceptions if we are to be precise in our accounts or maximally effective as clinicians. But beyond this, and reflecting the dynamic contextual point of view I have been emphasizing here, it is essential to address – in the realm of attachment, as in other aspects of personality – *how* whatever continuities are observed are maintained over time. In this, one of the things crucial to take into account is that these continuities tend to be manifested in environments that *also* show continuity. Consequently, we generally don't know if the attachment status would stay the same if the environment were to change because most often the environment *does not* change.

These continuities of environment are of two sorts. The first is more linear and straightforward – most children tend to be in the same family, with the same mother, throughout their childhood. For the vast majority of children, the people who were their primary caretakers when they were first assessed in the Strange Situation at around age 1 were their primary caretakers when they were assessed later in childhood. Thus, this continuity of context is likely a major contributor to the continuity of internal model. There are obvious exceptions to this continuity of caretakers, and they largely reflect the small and large traumas that some children undergo, and that need to be taken into account in our thinking. There are also ways in which the same parents may respond quite differently to their 1-year old than to their 6-year-old or 12-year-old, or may get a job, or lose a job, become depressed, or recover from depression in the course of the child's development. Attention to such changes is, of course, also part of a contextual understanding. But the *continuities* in environment are still, in the population at large, very substantial, and it is not clear how impressive the continuities in attachment status would be if that were not the case.

It should be clear that I am *not* here making the case that all there is to attachment status is the environment, and that if you change the environment you would see an instant change in attachment status. No thinker with even a passing interest in psychoanalysis would hold such a view, and I certainly do not. Indeed, in turning to the next – and in some ways more interesting – feature of the environmental continuities, we may see that, when we take into account the crucial role of the *emotional* environment, the persistence of the child's attachment behavior contributes to the continuity of the child's environment just as the continuity of the environment contributes to the persistence of the attachment status. When considering the role of individual characteristics and environmental influences, it is rarely a matter of an either–or, unidirectional line of causation. Nor is the matter well understood, as some experimental investigators have approached it, as a matter of simply parceling out how much variance is due to the person, how much to the environment, and how much to the interaction, where the term *interaction* refers to a *statistical* concept more than a psychological one (see Wachtel, 1977b). Rather, I suggest, the most interesting, and most psychologically relevant, way of taking into account what role is played by the characteristics of the individual personality and what role by the environment is to understand how powerfully the two are intertwined, how much each is part and parcel of the other. This is, to me, what the concept of a two-person psychology is groping toward, and it is why it is clearer to think of personality traits and structures as *contextual* structures. It is the reciprocal, bidirectional nature of psychological causality that is essential to appreciate in the realm of attachment, as it is in other realms of personality development and dynamics.

Consider, for example, a typical secure child. It is virtually the definition of secure attachment status that on the basis of the child's internal working model of attachment relationships, he is likely to anticipate that his attachment figure will respond to him in a manner that is sensitive and attuned to his needs and experiences. As a consequence, he is likely to behave differently toward his attachment figure than a child whose internal working model leads him to expect a response that is unreliable, unpredictable, or poorly attuned to his own experience or that implies that it is safest to turn away from his attachment needs or from the object of those needs.

In turn, these different behaviors on the child's part have an impact on the experience and the behavior of the attachment figure, and very frequently that impact is such as to lead the attachment figure to continue to behave toward the child in the very way that has led to the child being relatively secure or insecure in the first place. For example, when the child feels comfortable experiencing and expressing a need for the parent, and responds to the parent's efforts at soothing with the kind of relief or pleasure that is generally quite gratifying to a parent, the parent is much more likely to again be responsive and available. In contrast, when the child retreats from his attachment needs, seems indifferent, disinterested, or unresponsive (the typical behavior of a child who is labeled as avoidant or dismissing), or when the child acts in ways that seem to show resentment, excessive clinginess, inability to be soothed, or any of the other behaviors characteristic of the resistant/ambivalent or preoccupied child, the mother is much less likely to be able to respond in a sensitive and embracing way. Her anxiety or anger will interfere with her responsiveness to the child's needs or make it difficult for her to persist in trying to help the child feel soothed.

None of these patterns or continuities is inevitable. Changes impacting either the parent or the child, as well as the effects of the natural and inevitable variability in the behavior and emotional state of each party from moment to moment (see, for example, the evolving literature on multiple and variable self-states – e.g., Bromberg, 1998; Davies, 1996; Harris, 1996; Howell, 2005; Slavin, 1996; D. B. Stern, 2003) can create new patterns, as implied by stochastic and chaos theories that depict how small changes can lead to crucial tipping points (Piers, 2000, 2005). The parent, for example, may overcome a troubling conflict in analysis that resolves an inhibition in her responsiveness to her child; a change in the relation between husband and wife may impact the mood and availability of the parent to the child; even a change in the family's economic circumstances may affect both the time the parent has available for the child and the mood with which he or she interacts with the child. At the same time, as these changes affect the child's evolving characteristics, the child's own reactions feed back to influence the *parent's* experience, which in turn once more affects the child's, in a virtually endless series of feedback loops that are responsible both for continuity and for change.

Contextualizing Attachment: Parallels to the Evolution of Psychoanalytic Thought

I have attempted in this chapter to illustrate how attention to attachment theory and research can contribute to the clinical endeavor in potentially innovative ways. I have emphasized as well the ways in which the potential of attachment theory to contribute to clinical theory and practice can be enhanced by a conception of attachment that is dynamic rather than categorical and two-person or contextual rather than one-person or purely internal. In advancing this approach to understanding attachment, I have also pointed to parallels between the conceptual foundations of attachment theory and those of the evolving relational branch of psychoanalytic thought. Relational theories share with attachment theory the assumption that relationships are a primary foundation of the psyche rather than a secondary anaclitic consequence of the gratification of drives. But the centrality of relationships in shaping personality development is not the only common thread between attachment theory and relational theory. Another important point of convergence between relational theory and attachment theory – at least for some leading relational thinkers[7] – is a set of assumptions about the causal structure that links early experiences to lifelong characteristics of the personality.

A crucial dividing line relates to the question of how the structuring of personality proceeds over time and, in particular, whether the past is seen as preserved via internalization, fixation, or developmental arrest or via the continuing influence of bidirectional transactions throughout the life cycle (see, for example, Mitchell, 1988; Renn, 2012; Wachtel, 2008; Westen, 1989, 2002; Zeanah, Anders, Seifer, & Stern, 1989). The first, more traditional psychoanalytic view of development essentially posits that our way of seeing and experiencing the world remains fixed in a form that resembles the perceptual and experiential inclinations of childhood because the inner world is sealed off from the impact of life experience. This idea, central to the conceptual framework of many analysts, has its origins as early as Freud's (1893) statements, regarding repressed memories, that the healthy man "always succeeds in achieving the result that the affect which was originally strong in his memory eventually loses intensity and that finally the recollection, having lost its affect, falls a victim to forgetfulness and the process of wearing-away," but that in hysteria, "an event which occurred so long ago . . . can persist in exercising its power over the subject" because, as a result of the process of repression, "these memories *have not been subject to the processes of wearing away and forgetting*" (pp. 35–36, italics added). Like the woolly mammoths occasionally found perfectly preserved under the layers of arctic ice, the paleolithic elements of the psyche, in this theory, are preserved under the layers of defenses that similarly protect them from the erosion that would occur if they were not sealed away (Wachtel, 1997).

The mature expression of this same idea was not limited to memories of actual events but applied to the broader realm of drive-related fantasy:

> Men have always found it hard to renounce pleasure; they cannot bring themselves to do it without some kind of compensation. They have therefore retained a mental activity in which all these abandoned sources of pleasure and methods of achieving pleasure are granted a further existence – a form of existence in which they are left *free from the claims of reality* and of what we call "reality-testing." (Freud, 1917, p. 370, italics added).

This same causal structure – of aspects of development or experience being split off or sealed off from influence by new experiences, and hence preserved in their original primitive or archaic form – can be seen in the causal assumptions of much object relations theorizing as well (Mitchell, 1988; Wachtel, 2008).

This is the explanatory structure from which attachment theory – which attributed a good deal of the impetus for the generation and maintenance of the individual's internal working model to what did actually happen – was seen by many analysts as unacceptably departing. But there has evolved over the years an alternative explanatory model among some psychoanalytic thinkers, in which, in varying ways, early patterns are understood as persisting not in spite of what is actually going on but because, based on the skewing of the trajectory of personality development by early experiences, the person expects – and to a significant degree *brings about* – the very experiences that will keep those early structures in place.[8] In this alternative perspective (see, for example, Wachtel, 1997, 2008; Zeanah et al., 1989; and, of course, Bowlby's writings on attachment), there is no absence of attention to the unconscious substructure of behavior and experience; but rather than viewing unconscious motives, conflicts, or fantasies as existing in a realm hermetically sealed off from the impact of reality, this view examines those unconscious structures and processes *in relation to* the ongoing events of the person's life and as both cause *and* effect. What happens in the individual's life is very significantly a product of the unconscious thoughts, perceptions, and inclinations that drive his behavior. But those unconscious structures – both as they persist and as they are subtly modified by new experiences – in turn *reflect* the impact of the events encountered. Closely examined, the unconscious phantasies that emerge in psychoanalytic work are not purely internal or archaic; they are also symbolizations of experiences that are repeatedly encountered but may not be able to be consciously represented or worked through (D. B. Stern, 1997; Wachtel, 2008, 2011a). As psychoanalysis has emphasized and illuminated, we react to events not as they occur "objectively," but as they are given *meaning* by us; and those meanings are often registered and lived out without any conscious awareness and are, moreover, generated by subjective interpretive schemas that are also very largely unconscious. But the capacity of our interpretive schemas to subjectively "remake" the events we encounter is not unlimited. The meaning given to the experience is jointly determined by the experience itself.

Such an explanatory structure – one which lends itself to noticing and articulating the vicious circles and self-fulfilling prophecies that pervasively characterize psychological life, while retaining a central interest in the unconscious – is evident in varying degrees of articulation in the wide range of two-person theories that emphasize the co-construction of experience and the mutuality (Aron, 1996) of psychological causality; in the influential revisions of the theory of transference by Gill (e.g., 1979, 1982, 1983, 1984); in the cyclical psychodynamic perspective that is at the heart of this book; in the contextual intersubjective approach of Stolorow & Atwood (1992); *and* in the theory of ongoing structuralization of the individual's internal working models in attachment theory (recall the discussion earlier of how both secure and insecure children tend to repeatedly evoke in their caretakers the very behavior that maintains their attachment status).

All of these theories are constructed upon the key psychoanalytic idea of persistent unconscious structures that exert a powerful shaping role on our experience of later events and lead us to view new experiences through the filter or lens of old expectations. But they all depart from the archaeological model of theory construction that for so long dominated psychoanalytic thought (Blum, 1999; Renn, 2012; Spence, 1982; Stolorow & Atwood, 1997; Stolorow, Orange, & Atwood, 2001; Wachtel, 2008). Rather than casting the understanding of these phenomena in terms of layers, where the more deeply buried is both earlier developmentally and more profoundly important, these alternative psychoanalytic conceptualizations highlight context, mutual and reciprocal causal patterns, and feedback loops in which the buried past is continually modified by the living present (cf. Schacter, 1996, 2001; Schimek, 1975). Such an evolving alternative paradigm for psychoanalysis, fully attentive to the phenomena that have been of central concern to analysts through the decades, but attentive as well to the ways in which human beings live not only in the past and in the psychic depths, but also in the contexts of the relationships of the present, provides a congenial medium for coherently reintegrating attachment theory and research with its psychoanalytic roots and for building most effectively on both theoretical traditions.

Notes

1. Other aspects of the dialectical relationship between the need for closeness and contact and the need for autonomy and differentiation have been explored in depth by Blatt (2008) in his distinction between anaclitic and introjective dynamics and lines of development.
2. I discuss in the following section why it is in fact better to conceive of both as *contextual* points of view rather than as two-person viewpoints.
3. Balint's (1950) and Rickman's (1957) writings on the distinctions between one-body, two-body and multi-body psychologies had already appeared, but they had not yet become the progenitors of a major theme in the psychoanalytic literature.
4. As I discuss shortly, attachment can also be to *groups* of people, or even to an abstract idea, as well as to an individual.
5. Piaget participated with Bowlby in a series of discussion groups that Bowlby organized in Geneva when he worked for the World Health Organization (Marrone, 1998). In important respects, Bowlby's conceptualization of internal working models paralleled closely Piaget's concept of dynamic schemas in psychological development.
6. We may note here a parallel to the way that Kohut ultimately expanded the meaning of what he called self-objects, so that even an *idea* can be a self-object – indeed, a self-object that one is willing to die to maintain ties with. Kohut discussed this illuminatingly with regard to the young students of the White Rose group in Nazi Germany, who fought Hitler so valiantly and went to their deaths, as Kohut (1985) describes, with "inner peacefulness and serenity" and "without a trace of fear" (p. 21).
7. Although virtually every relational theorist emphasizes the centrality of relationships (albeit with different views about the implications of this centrality for the relevance of drive theory), there is quite considerable divergence among relational thinkers regarding the causal structure of the process of development that I am addressing in this final section. See Wachtel (2008) for an examination of these divergences and their implications.
8. Some readers may see a similarity between this description and such concepts as projective identification or repetition compulsion. For a clarification of how this conceptual structure differs from these earlier concepts in rather significant ways, see Wachtel (2008).

Chapter 5

The Surface and the Depths

Reexamining the Metaphor of Depth in Psychoanalytic Discourse

The preceding chapters can be understood as presenting an alternative vision to the standard (if sometimes only implicit) psychoanalytic model of surface and depth. Here I want to examine more explicitly the images of surface and depth that undergird so much of psychoanalytic thought and to consider potential alternative ways of framing our understanding. The metaphor of depth is so thoroughly woven into psychoanalytic discourse that it is easy to *forget* that it is a metaphor and to mistake the properties of the metaphorical image for those of the phenomena we are using the image to address. Its sheer familiarity makes it difficult to recognize how it has shaped our thinking and how it has foreclosed other potential ways of understanding what we observe in our daily practice. As a consequence, our formulations about personality development, psychopathology, and therapeutic change have been constrained – and at times misdirected.

My complaint, it should be clear, is by no means with the use of metaphor per se. As this book itself amply illustrates, my own writing is absolutely drenched in metaphor (still another metaphor, of course). Indeed, it is difficult to imagine how psychological inquiry can be pursued in any meaningful manner *without* extensive use of metaphor. To attempt to do so would lead either to a stultifying impoverishment of thought or to self-deceptions in which metaphor simply goes unnoticed (cf. Lakoff & Johnson, 1980).

Even in the occasional sentence that seems quite devoid of metaphorical imagery, the trace of metaphor can usually be seen if we probe sufficiently. For the very construction of our language depends on metaphor. The etymology of our most abstract words usually reveals that they are metaphorical extensions of more concrete experiences and the words used to describe them. Our ordinary prose, said T. E. Hulme, "is the museum where the dead metaphors of the poets are preserved." (quoted in Rubenstein, 1997). Or, as Empson (1930) put it in a classic work of literary theory, "metaphor, more or less far-fetched, more or less complicated, more or less taken for granted . . . is the normal mode of development of a language" (p. 2).

Although we commonly distinguish between seemingly straightforward "words" and the "metaphors" that use them, most "words" are simply yesteryear's metaphors. Over time, as these newcomers become more and more established, they eventually become the "old money" of the linguistic community. As we come to use particular metaphorical extensions regularly, they no longer are *experienced* as metaphors, but rather become the basis for still further metaphorical extensions on *their* foundations. Many of the words we use in ordinary discourse can be traced (often from Greek or Latin roots) through many such iterations, and the addition of each new layer renders the metaphorical activity that created the previous layers still more invisible.

The traces of the construction process may be easier to discern in languages that are written in pictorial characters than in languages with alphabets like our own. Chinese words combine characters for already existing words to create new meanings, as in the much-cited example of the word for *crisis*, which combines the characters for *danger* and *opportunity*. Interestingly, this creation of new meanings by putting together already existing words seems evident even in the protolanguages of other primates. The gorilla, Koko, for example, using sign language to communicate and employing signs she had already learned, spontaneously used such essentially metaphorical constructions as *cookie-rock* to indicate a stale sweet roll and *lettuce-tree* to refer to celery (Patterson & Cohn, 1990). One may imagine that, over time and if the opportunity for using them presented itself sufficiently, these constructions would likely become words for Koko, just as metaphorically constructed units (such as *crisis*) become words for her human cousins – units of language that carry their meaning independently of the earlier units that went into their construction at one time.

In this fashion, we extend our intellectual reach by ever-greater abstracting from the concrete experiences that were the basis of mankind's earliest linguistic efforts. In this fashion, too, via the route of concatenated metaphorical extensions of still earlier metaphors, words become the one arena in which we indeed can lift ourselves by our own bootstraps.

Have I, then, come to bury metaphor or to praise it? On the one hand, as will be more than evident already, I am a lover and profligate user of metaphor. Metaphor is in many respects the vital heart of our thinking, giving it the power to grasp relationships for which our standard vocabulary may be too leaden and plodding. And indeed, our vocabulary is *almost always* too plodding for our best insights without the assistance of metaphor. And yet, for all my respect for the virtues (indeed, the absolute necessity) of metaphor, it is my intent to emphasize in this chapter the ways in which metaphor – in particular the metaphor of depth – has the potential to lead us astray.

In general, metaphor seems to be most innocent, least capable of generating confusion, when it is baldly evident *as* metaphor. The intentionally extravagant use of metaphor that I have employed thus far in this chapter was designed to *call attention* to the use of metaphor, to alert the reader to the ways we ordinarily *recognize* metaphors as such, and as a consequence take whatever illumination they provide *as* metaphorical rather than as literal. But over time, as particular metaphors become a regular and familiar part of our daily discourse, they may no longer readily announce themselves as what they are. In contrast with many of the metaphors I have employed thus far, the metaphor of depth can "pass." When we say, for example, that something is "deeply" repressed, we largely experience ourselves as being quite straightforward, not metaphorical at all. As a consequence, in a host of ways, the metaphor of depth has led us to conclusions – and to ways of proceeding therapeutically – that require rethinking.

Depth and the Imagery of Archaeology

Freud's favorite metaphors were largely spatial and military. At times, the two went together, as for example in the metaphor – used to discuss fixation and regression – of an army advancing through a territory but leaving contingents of troops at points along the way. Spatial metaphors figured prominently as well in Freud's discussions of the various systems into which he divided the mental landscape. They are at the heart of what was called the topographic model of consciousness and unconsciousness, and they appear in the later model of ego, id, and superego in the form of the roughly ovoid diagram of the psyche that appears in *The Ego and the Id* (Freud, 1923).

Perhaps most influential of all in psychoanalytic discourse, throughout its history, has been the metaphor of depth. This particular spatial metaphor had its origins in and gained its resonance from several sources. In part, it reflected Freud's lifelong preoccupation with archaeology. Like Schliemann digging for the traces of ancient Troy, the psychoanalyst was seen as digging down to deeper and deeper layers, and in the process making more and more significant discoveries (cf. Jacobsen & Steele, 1978; Mitchell, 1993). The depth metaphor and the digging metaphor, of course, are closely related; both point the analyst to probe beneath the surface, to find what was hidden, buried, obscured by material closer to the periphery, material that must be cleared away in order to see the more interesting truth below. Both as well implicitly suggest that the treasures to be found via this dig are the central aim of the enterprise.

Attention to the link between Freud's intense interest in archaeology and the metaphor of depth can help to further our understanding both of the appeal of the metaphor, its seeming naturalness for psychoanalytic discourse, and of how it can lead us astray. Archaeology, one might say, is based upon a connection between space and time. As one digs further down, one finds the traces of earlier and earlier civilizations. The very nature of our planet's physics and geology calls forth the idea – largely valid in the realm of archaeological digs, but highly problematic for psychology – that deeper is earlier, and earlier is deeper. The earth just lies that way.[1]

In the realm of psychology, however, the link between space and time is far less certain. To begin with, there is no clear "space" (cf. Schafer, 1976). Determining what is deeper cannot be measured in meters as it can in the digging of archaeologists. Indeed, depth in the psychological realm is often judged by *time*. That is, we adjudge the work to have gone more deeply when it turns up something earlier.

When this is the case, the distinction between deeper and earlier completely collapses, and we are left with tautology.

There is, to be sure, another (still metaphorical) criterion for depth that is not so thoroughly confounded. We sometimes refer to certain mental contents or processes as deeper when they are harder to get to. We may notice the patient struggling to avoid certain topics, changing the subject, denying certain logical implications of what he or she just said. We may experience a certain effortfulness on our own part in trying to bring certain experiences of the patient to light (what one might call the sweat factor in Freud's concept of resistance). This "work" that is needed to bring something to consciousness is a part of what is meant psychologically by something being more "deeply" unconscious, and it is an idea that has both logical coherence and a reasonable relation to observation.

But if there is often some sense in describing material that was harder to get to as *deeper*, there is no basis in that for inferring that the emotions or representations that become evident in such instances necessarily reflect something *earlier*. Here is where the metaphor of depth, and especially its historical link to archaeology, gets us in trouble. To be sure, the persistent evocativeness of the depth metaphor tells us that it captures *something* important about the psychological state of affairs. But if metaphors expand the reach of our thinking by constructing bridges for our thoughts from one realm to another, we should nonetheless not be misled into thinking that every property of the metaphorical referent is fully shared by that to which it is being compared. If certain thoughts can be described as "deeply" repressed – indeed, in a sense of deep that is both meaningful and interesting – that does not mean that mental ideas are layered in such a way that later ones are piled on top of earlier ones, and that one therefore reaches the earliest last and at the greatest depth. *That* is an inappropriate concreteness, an inappropriate extension from the literal physical properties of archaeological digs to the inquiries of psychoanalysis, which are both like *and* not like the former.

Interestingly, there are ways in which Freud's more classical formulations seem actually less in thrall to the archaeological metaphor than some more contemporary ways of thinking. For Freud and many classical Freudians, it was usually the Oedipal level that was most profoundly important in psychological development and in accounting for neurotic misery. Material from earlier periods that appeared in the analysis was often seen as a defense against confronting what could be called the deeper, more central issue of Oedipal conflict. This orientation, however, could only hold its hegemony for so long against the seductive pull of the archaeological metaphor from which it emerged. Today, the centrality of Oedipal dynamics in psychoanalytic theorizing has significantly declined. This is the era of the "early," of the *pre*oedipal in psychoanalysis.

Depth and Profundity

The word *profound* most often refers to a quality of especially insightful and original intellectual activity. But, apropos the discussion earlier of the way our vocabulary grows via metaphorical extensions, its origins clearly lie in the more physical image of depth. Indeed, in contrast to many words that over time have lost their ties to their original, more physical meaning (including very largely the words *insight* and *insightful* themselves), *profound* still retains that original meaning as a secondary definition, as when we refer to the profound depths of the ocean. In many contexts, this metaphorical underpinning to the word's meaning is perfectly harmless. Indeed, in many areas of discourse, the words *deep* and *profound* are used quite interchangeably, and their shared quality of being the antithesis of "superficial" thinking is perfectly compatible with clear thought.

In psychoanalysis, however, the matter is more complicated. The interlinking images embodied in the implicit equation, *more deeply unconscious equals earlier equals more profound*, have had an insufficiently appreciated impact on the way we think about unconscious processes and the origins of psychological disorder, an impact that has at times introduced significant distortions in both clinical and theoretical understanding.

The first dimension of this distortion I wish to focus on is thematic. The themes and issues that in psychoanalytic terminology are referred to as "preoedipal" have received increasing – perhaps even preponderant – attention in recent years. Some of this attention is well merited. Conflicts over dependence, attachment, nurturance, belonging, trust, self-coherence, and self-boundaries are among the most pervasive and important challenges faced by human beings and are a source of some of our most painful and intractable difficulties. Moreover, for many years the authoritative consensus that the Oedipus complex was the critical climax of the developmental drama and source of the most intense and significant conflicts led clinicians to underestimate the importance of so-called preoedipal issues. Thus, to some degree the trends of recent decades represent the redressing of an imbalance.

Now, however, the imbalance threatens to tip in the opposite direction. Where once the authority of Freud steered psychoanalytic attention inexorably to the Oedipus complex, now the compelling power of the metaphor of depth – and the equation of depth with earlier – renders the *pre*oedipal as the hard currency of psychoanalytic clinical work. Where earlier is assumed to be deeper (that is, less superficial, more profound) there will almost inevitably be an inclination to focus one's interpretive efforts in this direction. No one wishes to be perceived, or to experience herself, as superficial. Because psychoanalytic theorizing assumes that "oral" concerns about nurturance, abandonment, or the secure boundaries of self are earlier developmentally than "anal" concerns about such issues as control and order, which are in turn earlier than Oedipal or "phallic" concerns about competition, lustful desire, or transgressive guilt, there is a strong pull for therapists and theorists, in seeking to be profound (or in protecting themselves against the accusation of being superficial) to focus their interpretive efforts on the presumably earlier (and hence deeper) themes.

As Erikson (1963), Mitchell (1988), and others have pointed out, however, these various themes, whatever their links may be to particular developmental stages, are in fact important issues *throughout* the life cycle. For a given patient, *any* of them may be the most significant nexus of her difficulties, the most profound source of her psychological dilemmas and distress. One has not necessarily probed more "deeply" into the individual's psyche simply by virtue of addressing the supposedly "earlier" concerns.

Thus, while sexual longings and competitive urges are indeed powerfully shaped by longings for connection, reassurance, nurturance, cohesion, and so forth, it is erroneous to conclude from this that the latter (so-called deeper or earlier) concerns "underlie" the sexual or aggressive inclination. For it is equally true that our needs for connection, reassurance, nurturance, and self-cohesion, which continue to evolve throughout life, are given *their* continually unfolding shape by the context of other motivations and experiences in which they develop over time, including the nature of the person's sexual life or the consequences of his competitive or aggressive tendencies. The process is not one of deeper or more fundamental needs unidirectionally influencing supposedly later ones; the influence upon *each other* of the motives and concerns commonly labeled preoedipal and those commonly labeled as later is mutual and continuous. The image that best captures the state of affairs is closer to a double helix than it is to a layer cake.

Overemphasis on Pathology

A further, and even more troubling, consequence of the bias toward equating earlier with more profound is a tendency to overestimate psychopathology in people. Here the assumption that earlier is deeper interacts with another prevalent (but far from substantiated) assumption of psychoanalytic discourse – that earlier is *sicker*. If a deeper or more profound understanding of people points to emphasizing developmental levels that are earlier, and if earlier in turn implies more archaic or primitive – terms increasingly prominent in contemporary psychoanalytic discourse – then contingencies are in place that pull for perceiving greater pathology. Understanding people more profoundly subtly becomes transformed into discerning the depth of pathology that is masked by a superficially healthy exterior (see Mitchell, 1988; Wachtel, 1987, 2011a). Indeed, the claim is sometimes made that all of us have a "psychotic core" (see, e.g., Eigen, 1986).

But even apart from this last – particularly debatable – contention, it is evident that contemporary psychoanalytic theorists and clinicians, pursuing an understanding of "deep" layers of the psyche, tend to posit a greater degree of pathology in people than do therapists of other persuasions. Patients' problems are increasingly depicted as "preoedipal," and hence as deeper and more intractable than they otherwise might seem. Much of my writing on the process of psychotherapy in recent years (e.g., Wachtel, 2011a) has been particularly addressed to providing an alternative to this pathologizing tendency – an alternative, I hasten to add, that is no less attentive to the experiences, issues, and conflicts addressed by those theories that, perhaps in response to the "contingencies of profundity" discussed earlier, emphasize the so-called archaic or primitive.

The Archaeological Metaphor and the Idea
of Developmental Levels

Further contributing to the pathologizing tendency I am addressing here is the frequent depiction of patients as characterized by a particular developmental level. Here the vision engendered by the metaphor of depth and its associated archaeological imagery subtly merges with less problematic developmental conceptualizations. There is indeed good reason to view the *process* of psychological development in terms of stages in which, unless one has advanced beyond a certain point, the building blocks are not yet in place for the next step. In the course of a child's growing up, it is not inappropriate to say that he or she is not yet at the level where certain modes of thinking have been attained or are even possible (see, for example, the work of theorists such as Piaget or Werner). But when this general structure/process understanding of the course of development is confused with the psychological status of adult patients (or even of older children) – when they are depicted as stuck at some early developmental level – something goes seriously amiss.

Even with relatively severe pathology, describing the patient's functioning as at a "preoedipal level of development" can be problematic and misleading. Westen (1989), for example, in discussing borderline personality disorder, has provided a detailed account of ways in which the standard psychoanalytic assumptions about the "preoedipal" nature of these patients' functioning are inconsistent with the findings of well-conducted developmental research. Some of the defining features of borderline thought and experience, regularly depicted in the psychoanalytic literature as preoedipal, are not only markedly different from the functioning of children in the preoedipal years, but are in fact developmentally well beyond the capabilities even of Oedipal-age children. As Westen notes, the confusion arises because the psychoanalytic literature – on the basis of theoretical assumptions rather than empirical observations – routinely attributes capacities to the Oedipal child that are in fact not generally attained until the latency years or even until adolescence. Then, by the logic of the archaeological model, patients who show absences or deficiencies in these supposedly Oedipal attainments are seen as functioning at a preoedipal level. For example, with regard to borderline patients' difficulties in containing ambivalent feelings, Westen (1989) notes that the relevant developmental research indicates that, "contrary to theory, the capacity for ambivalence is not firmly established by the Oedipal period and is indeed only in its incipient stages. *Borderline splitting appears to be as much preadolescent as preoedipal*" (p. 335, italics added). He adds that, "the notion that even marginally functioning adults could operate with the cognitive representations of eighteen-month-olds, who are practically nonverbal and barely have representational intelligence, is, strictly speaking, untenable" (p. 336). Research suggests, rather, that, "the critical developmental shift to more stable, psychological, and integrated representations occurs, not in the Oedipal years, but in middle to late childhood" (p. 338).

Neither Westen's nor my own comments are meant to minimize the severe difficulties and problematic functioning evident in individuals suffering from borderline personality disorder. The object representations of borderline patients are clearly highly problematic. But they are not the object representations of an infant, and it interferes with our ability to make progress in understanding and treating this disorder when our conceptual foundations are faulty. The development of borderline patients has gone askew in important ways, but it has not simply gotten stuck at some early level. As Westen (1989) points out, in certain ways borderline adults are capable of a complexity of representation that even healthy and normal children well beyond the Oedipal stage do not manifest. Attributing their difficulties to the preoedipal stage of development impedes our understanding of what has transpired *throughout* their years of development, and even into adulthood, that has promoted unstable and malign representations and disastrous patterns of interpersonal experience.

There is little empirical evidence to suggest either that borderline patients are significantly preoedipal in their actual functioning or that the events of the first year or two of their lives account for their later difficulties more significantly than do events later in their development. Indeed, one of the most frequently reported findings regarding the childhoods of borderline patients is that they have been subjected to sexual abuse to a far higher degree than would be expected by chance (e.g., Goldman, D'Angelo, DeMaso, & Mezzacappa, 1992; Herman, Perry, & van der Kolk, 1989; Paris & Zweig-Frank, 1992). In almost all instances, this noteworthy event is an occurrence in later childhood or early adolescence, *not* in the preoedipal years.[2]

What Is the Role of Early Experience?

The critique I have offered of the equation of earlier with deeper may seem to some readers to be challenging as well the view, deeply held by most members of the psychoanalytic community, that early experiences have a crucial impact on later development. But while I do believe that the question of just how important early experience really is must be an empirical question rather than an article of faith – and indeed that at times psychoanalytic writers have paid insufficient attention to how powerful and genuinely causal can be the experiences of later childhood, adolescence, and adulthood – it is by no means my aim here to argue that early experience is unimportant. There seems to me much reason to view early events as having a particularly powerful role in shaping the direction a person's life takes. What I *am* questioning is the *way* we have understood that influence. Indeed, what I am questioning is the set of (generally unexamined) assumptions that can make it *seem* like challenging the archaeological model is equivalent to rejecting the importance of early experience per se.

The confusion about this point derives in part from a confusion associated with words such as *origins* or *roots*. If we say that some pattern in the patient's life has its origins in the earliest years of childhood or has its roots in that period, to many analysts that is akin to saying the experiences of those early years are the cause or the *explanation* for that tendency. But *when something begins* is not the same as its cause; or, put differently, *when* it begins is not the same as *why* it begins. Even more important – because even more readily confused – is understanding that even knowing why something *begins* does not tell us why it *persists*. All sorts of behaviors begin in childhood that later change or drop out. Few of us still say "I eated breakfast" or respond to competition from a younger sibling by wetting our beds. There are many powerful forces pushing for *change* in the psychological realm. Psychoanalytic discourse often tends to forget those. Rather than depicting a continuing dialectical tension between forces of change and forces of stasis, psychoanalytic theorizing tends to privilege the latter and, to a significant degree, to render the former invisible or marginal.

Zeanah, Anders, Seifer, and Stern (1989), examining the implications for psychodynamic theory of systematic research on infant development, point to a number of ways in which widely held psychoanalytic views, emphasizing fixation and developmental arrest, are inconsistent with the findings of well conducted developmental studies. Much like Peterfreund (1978) in an earlier critique (recall also the discussion earlier in this paper of the purported "preoedipal" element in borderline pathology), they argue that it is highly problematic, both theoretically and methodologically, to equate the pathological functioning of children or adults suffering from a serious mental disorder with the way normal infants supposedly function or to assume that these patients' problems arise from the persistence into later years of ways of experiencing that are an inevitable stage or phase through which all children pass but in which some poor souls get stuck. Noting a broad tendency within psychoanalytic theorizing to posit that "later problems [are] repetitions of infantile traumas [and that] the form of later pathology is determined by the sensitive period of self-development in which the trauma occurred" (p. 663), Zeanah et al. point out that such a view of development does not comport well with the available evidence. (In referring here to trauma, it is important to be clear, they are not implying that the theorists they are critiquing limit themselves to the kinds of discrete traumatic events described by Breuer and Freud (1895) in the *Studies on Hysteria*. They are alluding as well to the conflicted and fantasy-infused developmental experiences that have been at the heart of psychoanalytic theorizing for more than a century and to the notions of "developmental level" with which they are generally associated.)

As an alternative to models of fixation, regression, or developmental arrest, Zeanah et al. (1989) suggest a "continuous construction model" (p. 657), in which development proceeds throughout life as an ongoing dialectic between the developing individual's characteristics and the environmental context in which she finds herself. That context, it is important to understand, is not simply something the individual passively encounters, but is itself a product of the individual's prior and continuing choices and of her evolving personality and way of being in the world. By virtue of the particular behaviors and attitudes we elicit from others in response to the behaviors and attitudes we manifest *toward* them, and by virtue of the ways we choose to put ourselves in some kinds of situations and relationships and to avoid or retreat from others, we significantly and actively shape the environment we encounter.

In this connection, it is noteworthy to observe that even as early as 3 to 6 months of age, the children of depressed mothers elicit different behavior *from strangers* than do the children of nondepressed mothers (Field et al., 1988; Weinberg & Tronick, 1998). More specifically, in comparison to the infants of nondepressed mothers, they tend to elicit behavior from strangers that is less optimal for their further development (and hence likely to further perpetuate their disadvantage from that point forward even apart from the impact of their mothers' behavior per se). Such children, one might say, begin quite early in development to be affected not only by the impact of how their mothers responded to them but by *the impact of that impact* on the way they interact with later people; that is, the power of early experiences lies very largely in the kinds of *later* experiences they make more likely.

Viewed through a narrow lens, it might appear, as we observed these children's development, that the effects of their very early experience were indelible. But viewed from a broader perspective, it becomes clear that the impact of the early experience is mediated by countless later experiences that are the *indirect* effect of the earlier experience. The impact *appears* indelible because the behavior patterns induced by the early experience become consequential in their own right, initiating a virtually self-perpetuating process in which the subsequent experiences the developing individual encounters are in large measure a product of the patterns of behavior and perception that have already evolved but also serve to maintain that very pattern (and hence make still more such experiences likely).

It is thus apparent that we need not assume that specific patterns of psychopathology correspond to specific periods of development at which the person has gotten fixated or during which she had a particularly difficult time of it. Different people may arrive at the same fix via different routes and as a result of problems arising at different points in the course of development. The search for a theoretical structure that neatly places psychological disorders and character traits along a continuum of purported developmental levels does not do justice to what we know about the complex ways in which development proceeds as a continuing interplay between evolving personal characteristics and the environments both encountered and, over time, created by the evolving personality.

The seemingly "archaic" fantasies, yearnings, and images of self and other that are revealed by psychoanalytic exploration do not persist as a consequence of having being rendered inaccessible to the influence of new experiences by a structural split in the psyche. If one looks carefully enough, it becomes apparent that, far from being irrelevant to the so-called archaic fantasies, the new experiences play an essential role in feeding and maintaining them (Wachtel, 2008, 2011a). Both the processes by which this occurs and the psychological structures that are entailed (both as cause and persisting effect) are, to be sure, often deeply unconscious. But, while unconscious, those structures are *not* hermetically sealed off from experience; in fact, they depend for their continuation and persistence on the very experiences they regularly bring about.

The Narcissistic Personality: An Illustration

Consider, for example, the individual who manifests a narcissistic personality disorder. Competing psychoanalytic theories of this disorder posit somewhat different dynamics and early experiences to account for it (compare, for example, Kernberg, 1975, and Kohut, 1971, 1977). But there is general agreement in psychoanalytic circles that the origins of the disorder lay in the early years of life. If one looks, however, not just at what was experienced in those years but at the *continuing consequences* of the psychological structures thereby formed, one sees a picture of the effective dynamics of the disorder that differs quite significantly from the model of fixation or developmental arrest. The motives, fantasies, and defenses that evolve in the lives of narcissistic individuals have consequences; after a time, they take on a life of their own. Without understanding those consequences and those ongoing dynamics, one does not understand the patient.

The experiences of inner emptiness, fragile self-coherence, unstable self-esteem, or lack of genuine validation that plague narcissistic individuals are not just "inner" experiences that are remnants of a tragic past. They are a dynamic element in the person's *life*. When, as is characteristic of these individuals, they resort – either in the transference or in daily life – to bolstering their fragile sense of self through an overbearing, overblown, bragging stance, the implications are powerful. Two common responses elicited in others by such behavior – repelled withdrawal from an unpleasant braggart and awed admiration for a larger-than-life figure, both contribute to maintaining the painfully problematic way of life.

The first response is more obviously painful. Narcissistic individuals need to be admired, but their behavior evokes in a significant subset of people something quite the opposite. When they are either treated with disdain or threateningly seen through, the experience – far from pleasant for anyone – is especially painful for them. But because their preferred way of coping with feelings of not being valued is to puff themselves up and paint over their warts with day-glo paint, they are likely to respond to this narcissistic injury with still more of the same behavior, and thus to be confronted again with people who – genuinely – are hostile to them, repelled by them, competitive with them, or simply eager to interact with them as little as possible. And when their daily world includes more than the standard share of such experiences, it becomes fuel for still further manifestations of the same defensively motivated coping patterns, which in turn create still more of such experiences.

The poisonous consequences of the *admiration* they elicit may be less obvious at first. Admiration, after all, is the drug they seek. As is frequently reported, narcissistic individuals tend in fact to be high achievers or, even if the severity of their problems leads them to live more marginal lives, to have certain qualities or talents that can have a quite "spectacular" feeling to them. (People with strong narcissistic tendencies who do *not* have such attributes to display find it hard to maintain the narcissistic pattern and are more likely to end up simply depressed.) But the admiration elicited by the severe narcissist is different from the admiration that, in some form or another, we all seek (and, indeed, enjoy). Admiration for our real gifts and qualities is strengthening. It makes us *less* vulnerable and *less* needy for still more. It corresponds to what Kohut (1977) describes as the healthy and normal need for self-objects throughout life. In contrast, the admiration that is offered up to the narcissist is not similarly reassuring. And it is not reassuring because the very success of the narcissistic defense undermines the security it aims to bolster. The admiration the narcissist receives is not for his true qualities, for what is genuine or sustainable. It is for the inflated image he has felt compelled to put out to the world as a covering for what he experiences as an inner self that is worthless or fragile.

The dynamics of narcissism may well have their origin in the early years of life, but it is the way that the pattern generates its own ironic consequences that is most essential to understand. Once someone embarks on a life course in which inner experiences of fragility and insufficiency are defended against through self-inflation, a central building block of more solid and stable self-esteem is removed from the further construction of the self. We all require admiration for who we really are. When admiration comes instead for who we have *portrayed* ourselves as, it is false comfort. Indeed, it may end up exacerbating rather than relieving the sense of fraudulence and hollowness. The tragedy of pathological narcissism is that the person has learned to quell feelings of fraudulence by still further inflating and overselling of the self, which of course just further heightens the sense of fraudulence. That this process may go on unconsciously, and in a manner designed to deceive the self as well as others, does nothing to diminish its troubling impact or to make the quicksand in which the person has become mired any easier to extricate oneself from.

Ironically, it tends to be their expressions of vulnerability – those moments when the defense breaks down and braggadocio gives way to a painful feeling of depression, emptiness, smallness, or worthlessness – that elicit in others (including the analyst) a more empathic, caring response. Much of the work with such patients entails helping them not only to experience true warmth and caring from others that is rooted in their actual human qualities, but also to *endure* such contact. By the logic of their previous narcissistic necessities, being appreciated for their life-size rather than larger-than-life qualities may be experienced as a diminishment, even as such more realistic appreciation in fact helps to build more solid and secure psychic structure.

To whatever degree such individuals may have undergone in their earliest years the particular configuration of psychological experiences posited by psychoanalytic theorists of pathological narcissism, an account of their difficulties that is guided by the imagery of fixation or arrest at some particular level of psychic development fails to capture the powerful *dynamic* element in the perpetuation of the pattern. The profound impact of the early experience lies not in the creation of a static deficit that is carried around throughout life until a good analyst finally fills up the cavity; it lies, as discussed above in more general terms, in the kinds of *later* experiences that it makes so much more likely. The probability is great that without the early experience, the individual would not have begun the pattern just described. But without an appreciation of how the pattern is recreated over and over again by its own consequences – and by the person's further and repeated response to those consequences – we do not sufficiently understand such an individual's dilemma. The early experience is by no means irrelevant. It lays the foundation for the structures that characterize the personality for the rest of the person's life. But those structures require constant renovation to remain standing. The tragedy of psychopathology lies in the excruciating (if unwitting) skill with which the suffering individual renovates those structures again and again throughout life.

Representations of a Consequential Past, Seeds of a Consequential Future

The representations and interactional patterns that develop out of our earliest experiences are likely to be particularly influential not because the residue of the original experience is somehow lodged in the psyche like a bone in the throat, but because these representations and behavioral patterns skew the kinds of *further* experiences we have. After a period of time, it becomes virtually impossible to determine how much the child (and then adult) would remain stuck in the early established patterns if he or she were to have different experiences later, because one impact of the early experience and early skewing of the child's own behavior is that she does *not* have the same experiences as a child who has had a different start. Our earliest inclinations and characteristics evoke differential responses from others that tend to perpetuate those same inclinations and characteristics (cf. Renn, 2012).

Thus, as noted earlier, the depressed child evokes responses from others (not only from her parents but from other and later caregivers and then from peers) that are likely to immerse her in a different experiential world from that of a child who does not start out depressed. Similarly, early experiences that lead a child to be angry or irritable increase the likelihood that the child will evoke angry or rejecting behavior from others, which will in turn stir still more anger and irritability on the child's part and still more negative (and anger-generating) responses from others. Conversely, the child who early experiences secure attachment and loving responses is more likely to behave in ways that evoke still further positive responses from others, which elicit still further responses from the child that keep the positive cycle going.

These patterns of cyclical reconfirmation are not inexorable. Some children, for example, who have experienced extraordinarily difficult early years, end up showing quite remarkable resiliency (e.g., Hetherington & Blechman, 1996; O'Connor, Bredenkamp, & Rutter, 1999; Rutter, 1995). This fact in itself highlights how much more complex the developmental process is than can be captured by any simple view of the determinative impact of the earliest years. Conversely, with some children or adults, looking back to find the "roots" of their present difficulties in their early years entails a theoretically overweening fishing expedition in which what is seen is what "must have" been there rather than what one would have seen at the time. One can always read in precursors or origins, but what is essential is to understand development as a *process* – a process that is continuous and ongoing throughout life, not just the playing out of a script written in the earliest years.

Depth and the Social

The depth metaphor, and the structures of thought it evokes, contributes to marginalizing the role of social forces and institutions in psychoanalytic discourse, thereby distorting our understanding of the impact of society on personality development and impeding psychoanalytically oriented social analysis and social criticism. Sociocultural influences enter into the psychological equation from the direction of the senses, that is, from the "surface" rather than from the "depths." From the vantage point of the depth metaphor, social influences are therefore at risk of appearing "superficial." As Greenberg and Mitchell (1983) have put it,

> Within the drive/structure model [their term for the standard Freudian account and its close derivatives], social reality constitutes an overlay, a veneer superimposed upon the deeper, more "natural" fundaments of the psyche constituted by the drives. Any theory omitting or replacing the drives as the underlying motivational principle and, in addition, emphasizing the importance of personal and social relations with others is, from this point of view, superficial by definition, concerned with the "surface" areas of the personality, lacking "depth." (p. 80)

It is not only the drive model, however, that can induce such a perception. Many versions of object relations and self-psychological thinking too partake of what I have called the woolly mammoth model – a view of psychological structure and development in which certain early experiences, perceptions, and inclinations are conceptualized as essentially frozen in time, preserved in their original form like woolly mammoths buried in the arctic ice, prevented from changing and evolving over the course of development like other parts of the psyche that are not similarly walled off and preserved (Wachtel, 1997, especially pp. 26–30 and 348–349). Freud's view that when an instinctual representation is repressed, it "persists unaltered from then onwards" and that it consequently "proliferates in the dark . . . and takes on extreme forms of expression" (Freud, 1915, pp. 148, 149) has essentially been extended in more recent theorizing to conceptualizations of "primitive" or "archaic" internalized objects or self-representations. Much as with the classical Freudian approach, these more relational theories posit that certain parts of the psyche are split off from the overall course of development and that as a consequence they do not grow up as the rest of the personality does and are not generally modified by new experiences in the way that the more accessible parts of the personality are.

In these object relational and self-psychological theories, theoretical interest continues to center on the patient's "developmental level." Their common grounding in the archaeological model and its associated images of depth is signaled by a variety of questions, formulations, and concerns so pervasive in psychoanalytic discourse that they are scarcely noticed: Patients' difficulties are described as "from" the first year or two of life. The "roots" of the problem are seen in a particular developmental period or stage. The question is asked, "From 'when' is the patient's difficulty?" All of these questions point us to seek the time of life when, supposedly, a part of development got arrested, when a part of the person became permanently fixed in a preoedipal state of mind, a temporal prison from which the individual can only be released by the special kind of object relationship (or self-object relationship) that is provided uniquely by analysis. The terms *primitive* and *archaic*, so widely used by self-psychologists and object relations theorists, do not refer simply to the *quality* of the patient's perceptions or desires but to their origins in the earliest periods of psychological development. Indeed, they signal not only that the difficulties *began* in that era of the person's development, but that the person, although chronologically an adult, continues unconsciously to manifest images of self and other virtually unchanged from the very earliest years of life.

The presence of these pervasive and unexamined theoretical assumptions in relational formulations – structurally similar to those of more classically Freudian accounts though with different content – means that Greenberg and Mitchell's (1983) warning about the underestimation of the impact of social forces and contemporary interpersonal experiences has great relevance for relational theorists as well. Among these theorists too, the impact of daily concrete experiences with others – much less of social and economic arrangements, racial and ethnic stereotypes, or political values and economic trends (see Wachtel, 1983, 1999; see also Part II of this book) – is often implicitly treated as, to repeat Greenberg and Mitchell's phrase, "a veneer superimposed upon the deeper, more 'natural' fundaments of the psyche." These fundaments may now be viewed by many analysts as internalized object relations or archaic self–other representations rather than as drives, but the structure of thought remains largely the same.

In understanding how the depth metaphor marginalizes attention to the social dimension, it is important to be clear that the perception of the social as superficial is not an intrinsic or necessary consequence of interest in the unconscious determinants of human behavior and experience. Social influences themselves, after all, can be unconscious, and indeed, people can struggle against acknowledging them as fiercely and determinedly as they defend against knowledge of the wishes and fantasies more familiar in psychoanalytic discourse (see, for example, Devine, 1989; Gaertner & Dovidio, 1986; Hamilton & Gifford, 1976; Sears, 1988; Wachtel, 1999; Word, Zanna, & Cooper, 1974). But from the vantage point of the depth metaphor, such influences may still be viewed as superficial and of limited importance. The distinction between the surface and the depths that this metaphor brings to the fore consigns the social to the surface, and hence to the superficial. The social, economic, and cultural arrangements by which we live are relegated, almost without our noticing, to the role of superficial overlay. In order to appreciate the powerful *dynamic* role of social institutions and mores, to recognize fully the ways in which the shared assumptions of a society and the compelling realities of race, class, and economic status serve as co-equal shapers of the very depths of the psyche, it is necessary to consciously deconstruct the compelling and seductive image of surface and depth.

When a lens other than that of the depth metaphor is brought to bear on psychological causation, what becomes apparent is the pervasiveness of cyclical and reciprocal processes, rather than causal arrows that point in one direction (see for example, Nichols & Schwartz, 1998; Wachtel, 1987; E.F. Wachtel & Wachtel, 1986). Our most profound wishes and perceptions – that is, those that are most personal, characteristic, and momentous – are not simply inside us, reaching out to (and then modified slightly by) the world of social interaction. They are *part and parcel of* that world, entangled so totally with it that to separate one from the other is to do violence to both.

Unconscious motivations, fantasies, and conflicts play a crucial role in every aspect of our lives. But those unconscious psychological phenomena need not be conceptualized in terms of an inner world in which deep below the surface, like primeval sharks in a sunless sea, lurk "early" or "archaic" psychological organizations impervious to the experiences of ordinary living. It is precisely in elucidating the way that the depths and the surface mutually shape and, indeed, define each other that a progressive psychoanalysis can most illuminate our lives. "Depth psychology" is not about some separate realm beneath the superficial exterior of daily living, but about the richness and mystery, the multidirectionality and multicausality, the vastly tangled complexity, indeed, the *depth*, of living itself.

Notes

1. There are, of course, occasional exceptions, in which twists and eruptions in the earth's crust can partially flip things, so that an earlier geological or archaeological layer can be pushed above what had originally lain on top of it. But the general tendency is pervasive.

2. To be sure, *other* kinds of abuses and deprivations may well have occurred in those earliest years. Parents prone to abuse their children sexually in later childhood (or to tolerate such abuse by someone else) are likely to have shown other problematic features in their interactions with the child before then. Nonetheless, the prevalence of such abuse in the histories of borderline patients – a fact of massive psychological import – is one more indicator that formulations that center on the preoedipal nature of the disorder are insufficiently attentive to the ongoing realities of these people's lives and lack a sufficiently complex and comprehensive view of the process of development.

Chapter 6

Repression, Dissociation, and Self-Acceptance

Reexamining the Idea of Making the Unconscious Conscious[1]

The very first patient I ever saw, as a young graduate student, was a woman with difficulty swallowing. Any time she tried to swallow food, she would gag. Meat was especially difficult, but virtually any solid food was a problem. She was very largely living on a liquid diet. About the only food she could swallow easily was M&M's, which were serving, in a fashion not exactly in accordance with the recommended food pyramid, as the central item in her diet.

A careful medical workup revealed no physical basis for her difficulties. So she was referred to the Yale clinic for psychotherapy, and had the ill fortune to be assigned to a very raw graduate student.

Quite a few months into the treatment, it came out – for the first time – that a central feature of her childhood was continual struggles with her mother over eating. Her mother was an obese woman, weighing more than 300 pounds, and she was utterly obsessed with her daughter's eating habits. She was particularly vigilant with regard to candy, which she absolutely forbade. It will probably not surprise the reader that the food that my patient smuggled into her bedroom as a young girl, hiding it under her pillow and surreptitiously gaining forbidden pleasure when all the lights were out, was . . . M&M's.

When I heard the whole story, I was flabbergasted. I was also thrilled. There before my eyes, in my very first case, seemed to be dramatic proof of Freud's theories about repression. That this patient had forgotten about such a central event – so strikingly relevant to her difficulties – seemed almost like a gift from heaven (or at least from Vienna) to this young acolyte. But when I followed up on what felt to me like a startling revelation, the wind was taken out of my sails.

I responded to hearing her account with a comment reflecting my immersion as a graduate student in the clinical approach of psychoanalytic ego psychology, the dominant clinical approach at the time. Following Otto Fenichel's (1941) venerable recommendation that one interpret the defense first, I called attention to the fact that these remarkable recollections had taken months to bubble up to consciousness. I wanted, in essence, for her to see and acknowledge that she had been actively defending against the recall of these experiences. Moreover, I regard it as important to add from my current vantage point, I did so in the stilted manner I had been taught was the way to be professional and genuinely psychoanalytic – the stilted manner that only a beginning graduate student could follow so faithfully. "Isn't it interesting," I said, "that something so absolutely crucial to understanding your difficulties in swallowing should take so long to emerge in your consciousness!" My aim was to initiate a process of her recognizing that she had been actively keeping certain thoughts and memories out of her awareness.

Now to begin with, phrases such as "isn't it interesting?" reflect the cloak of ostensible objectivity and pseudoneutrality that were the fashion in those days. One was supposed to engage the patient's curiosity (certainly still a good thing); but the enterprise was conceived of more as like a scientific experiment in a carefully sterile environment than an engagement between two human beings.[2] Such phrasings also often reflect an unacknowledged, but significant, element of reproach. One is reminded of the Viennese-accented analysts of old Hollywood movies, stroking their beards and muttering, *"Verrry interrresting."* "Interesting," in this context, is not an acknowledgment of the patient's fascinating originality but an implicit message that maintains the analyst's position as the superior, knowing one and the patient's as the benighted self-deceiver (see Renik's [1993] discussion of Freud's railway conductor metaphor for an illuminating further discussion of this problematic feature of the traditional analytic stance). I have discussed more extensively in a book focused on the implications of the therapist's choices of wording and phrasing (Wachtel, 2011a) how the ways that therapists think about and talk to their patients can often be implicitly accusatory and demeaning (see also Wachtel, 2008, 2011b; Wile, 1982, 1984). Observing a similar phenomenon, Havens (1986) has wittily observed, "In the current interpretive climate of much psychotherapeutic work, patients sit waiting for the next insight with their fists clenched. Small wonder, for it is rarely good news" (p. 78).

My aim in the comment I made to my patient was to initiate a process of her recognizing that she had been actively keeping certain thoughts and memories out of her awareness. But perhaps partly in response to the unacknowledged stance of accusatory objectivity that characterized my beginner's imitation of the bad habits of my supervisors, but also simply reflecting her subjective phenomenological experience, the patient's response to my comment was quite matter-of-fact: "I could have told you all along. I hadn't forgotten it, it just didn't occur to me as relevant when we were talking earlier."

I think the patient was being accurate when she described her experience as one she had not forgotten but had merely not thought was relevant. If I had asked her very directly about this memory – say, "Did you and your mother struggle over food when you were a child, and were M&M's a central part of that struggle?" – I have no doubt she would have answered *yes*, and could have told me about at least the general outlines of what transpired. In that sense, it was *not* something that she "could not remember," not something that, in the simplest understanding of the term, was *repressed*. But at the same time, I also think that the memory *was* rendered inaccessible by defensive processes. But the defense being manifested is better described as dissociation. What was blocked was not the content per se but the associational network. She could remember the experience if asked about it directly, but there were inhibitions impeding the memory's *occurring to her spontaneously*. She did eventually recall it, but only after many, many months of talking about and wrestling with a problem to which the memory had striking relevance and dramatic links and affinities (even to the point of M&M's being the specific candy in the two domains). That it had not even occurred to her to make this connection, that it "never came up," suggests a very strong inhibitory process *even if* the memory remained intact and readily accessible to a direct question.

Knowing and *Really* Knowing: From Making the Unconscious Conscious to Where Id Was, There Ego Shall Be

Some years later, in reflecting on the implications of this experience, I noticed a passage in Freud that I had overlooked the first time I had read it. In "Remembering, repeating, and working-through," Freud (1914) said,

> Forgetting impressions, scenes or experiences nearly always reduces itself to shutting them off [translated in the Collected Papers, where I first read the passage, as "dissociation" of them]. When the patient talks about these "forgotten" things he seldom fails to add: "As a matter of fact I've always known it; only I've never thought of it." He often expresses disappointment at the fact that not enough things come into his head that he can call "forgotten" – that he has never thought of since they happened. (p. 148)

Perhaps the reason I overlooked this passage the first time is that in a certain sense Freud too overlooked it. That is, he obviously knew quite well the experience he was describing, but the main thrust of his writing and thought seemed to carry a different message. The very first observations Freud reported, which seem to have shaped fatefully the entire later course of psychoanalysis, *were* of matters that his patients had seemed to cast completely out of their memory, and which required struggling against great resistance to recover. Moreover, these memories were often quite dramatic (making their apparent forgetting all the more striking), and, to further heighten their impact, their recovery seemed to be associated with a quite rapid and even spectacular disappearance of often severe symptoms that had appeared to be intractable. Little wonder that these compelling observations had a powerful shaping effect on Freud's thought!

Of course, Freud also soon discovered that many of these cures were quite temporary and that he had to go back and dig for still more memories (and, in his view, *earlier* memories) in order to maintain the progress of the work. Moreover, just a few years later, he concluded that these memories were often not real memories at all but the residue of early wishes and fantasies that, in the course of time and as a result of the young child's still-fragile hold on the difference between reality and fantasy, had been stored in the psyche as actual events.

Despite these various challenges to Freud's original understanding, the idea that making the unconscious conscious was the key to therapeutic change remained central to psychoanalytic conceptions of therapeutic process and technique. And even though over time *other* conceptions of therapeutic change processes appeared in the psychoanalytic literature (as I discuss shortly) the original aim of making the unconscious conscious has really remained at the heart of the psycho-analytic enterprise to this day.

The problem is not that this emphasis on clarifying and expanding the patient's awareness is wrong or bad – who would wish to argue for ignorance, self-deception, or being out of touch with oneself? Rather, the problem is that it is *incomplete*, and that as a consequence, it does not guide us in understanding how to negotiate the sometimes *conflicting* implications of the different therapeutic processes that must be brought into play in any given case. Making the unconscious conscious is but one of the processes relevant to bringing about significant therapeutic change. Moreover, as we shall see (and as the example with which I began this chapter already illustrates), consciousness in fact is not an all-or-nothing phenomenon in which we make "conscious" what was previously "unconscious." Consciousness is a quality best discussed in terms of degrees of access or articula-tion (in this regard, see Schachtel, 1959; Shapiro, 1989; D.B. Stern, 1997).

Consciousness is also a phenomenon best understood as contextual: that is, the same thought or experience may be accessible to focal consciousness in one context and not another. As early as 1915, Freud observed that repression was not something that takes place once and for all but rather was variable and mobile. Freud's own emphasis in accounting for this variability was primarily on the quantitative factor – when the energy associated with the forbidden thought or wish intensifies, making it more likely to be expressed, it becomes more important to render it unconscious in order to avert mental pain and dangerous consequences.

From a contemporary vantage point, however, we may add that the degree to which a particular inclination feels safe enough to experience consciously or dangerous enough to need to be repressed or misrepresented in consciousness depends as well on the social mores of the situation and the degree to which others are likely to be accepting of one's feeling or of one's acting on the incli-nation. As evident in the rituals of instinctual abandonment permitted in a wide range of cultures only on certain feast days and forbidden at other times, as well as in the daily subtle adjustments made by all of us in contemporary urban societies, what may be said, felt, done, or even thought varies depending on whom we are with and what is the setting. Conveniently "forgetting" in church Sunday morn-ing what one did (or fantasized) on Saturday night is not pathological but a sign of healthy ego functioning. Recalling (especially recalling vividly) the state of consciousness of the night before might not only bring distress but also disrupt the experience of piety one is trying to maximize, an experience that is not necessar-ily insincere simply because it is the experience of an (almost inevitably) divided psyche.[3] Such forgetting, however – at least in the healthy variant – is more likely to be of the sort manifested by my M&M's patient than an inability to recall even when asked. It *just doesn't occur* to one to bring the memory to consciousness – a nonoccurring that is not a function of irrelevance but, often enough, of its *high degree* of relevance.

One conceptual medium for incorporating these new understandings was the theoretical revision that came to be called the structural theory (Arlow & Brenner, 1964; Freud, 1923). This theoretical revision was so important in the history of psychoanalysis that it gave rise to a new reigning maxim for representing the therapeutic aim of psychoanalysis: "Where id was, there ego shall be." This new vision of the therapeutic process in analysis derived from a number of important insights that modified our understanding of what it actually meant to make the unconscious conscious (that is, our understanding of the *old* reigning maxim which it at least partially replaced). To begin with, it reflected several decades in which the focus of psychoanalytic inquiry shifted to some degree from unearthing the *contents* of the unconscious to discovering the processes by which they were kept buried.

This study of the defenses pointed to several important conclusions. First, it became clear that the defenses too – that is, our active efforts to keep certain ideas or experiences out of awareness – were outside of our awareness most of the time. Moreover, like the experiences they were directed toward keeping at bay, the defenses were not only descriptively unconscious but *dynamically* unconscious; we didn't just not notice them, we *had a stake* in not noticing them, we *resisted* noticing them. As a consequence, psychoanalytic technique increasingly aimed not simply at interpreting the warded off material but at interpreting – that is, bringing to light – the defenses that *kept* the material warded off. It increasingly seemed to analysts that without bringing the defenses to consciousness – and thereby disrupting their smooth operation – material that was unearthed in one session might well be reburied by the next. This emphasis on "interpreting the defenses" was, the reader may recall, central to the way I addressed the emergence, months after therapy had begun, of my patient's recollections of her mother's preoccupation with her eating and the particular memory having to do with M&M's.

The change from making the unconscious conscious as the guiding rubric to "where id was, there ego shall be," had another crucial significance as well. Although in part the change was based on the understanding that the defenses too were often unconscious, it reflected as well a recognition that *being conscious or not* was not always the be-all and end-all of whether something was genuinely accessible or was effectively warded off. Increasingly, analysts understood that processes such as rationalization, intellectualization, and dissociation could render an impulse or experience effectively disowned *even if it was capable of entering consciousness*.

"Where id was, there ego shall be," was a conceptualization that reflected and incorporated this new understanding. In the conceptual framework of ego psychology or the structural theory, bringing into the *ego* material that had previously been part of the *id* implied a number of crucial changes in the nature and accessibility of that material. Specifically, it implied that ideas or inclinations that had been rooted in the past and more or less impervious to the corrective possibilities of new experiences would, once they gained access to the ego, be rendered more accessible not just to consciousness but to the influence of new perceptions and to modification by the thoughts and knowledge that the person already held. The language of "ego" and "id" posed a danger of reification and of images of actual "places" rather than functional relationships. But the ideas this new terminology represented were efforts, implicitly, to go beyond the overly simple idea that therapy was just a matter of making unconscious ideas conscious.

The Crucial Role of Anxiety and Experience

In further understanding the limits of the old guideline of making the unconscious conscious, it is necessary to consider the changes in the psychoanalytic understanding of anxiety and their implications for theory and for therapeutic change. As significant as were the ideas presented in *The Ego and the Id*, just three years later Freud published another work that had even more radical implications for understanding what transpires in a successful psychoanalysis – radical implications that, unfortunately, the majority of psychoanalysts (and perhaps even Freud himself) did not fully appreciate. In *Inhibitions, Symptoms, and Anxiety*, Freud (1926) implicitly introduced a new guiding criterion for the psychoanalytic process. Although it was never stated this way, we might call it: *Where anxiety was, there less anxiety (or greater freedom from anxiety) shall be.*

What Freud clarified in that 1926 work was that behind the phenomenon of repression, underlying and motivating it, was anxiety[4] – and hence, that even more fundamental than making the unconscious conscious was helping the patient to be less afraid. The anxieties Freud focused on were different from those typically addressed, say, by behavior therapists. Freud pointed us to people's fears of their own thoughts, wishes, feelings, and fantasies, not primarily to the external stimuli that behavioral therapists tend to concentrate on.[5] Moreover, many of the anxieties that were most central in the psychoanalytic scheme of things were not necessarily the *experienced* anxieties that plague the phobic or the person suffering from panic attacks. They included very centrally anxieties that are *not* experienced by the patient because they are the signal for *avoidances* that – at great cost to the individual – avert the manifest occurrence of anxiety. Indeed, it is because the sources or triggers for the anxiety are so often hidden, and because the anxiety itself is so often hidden as well, that probing what is unconscious, implicit, or warded off remains such an appropriate and important aim of the therapeutic effort.

The modes of inquiry and inference associated with psychoanalysis, I believe, remain the most powerful tools (though by no means the only tools) for *identifying* what the most salient sources of anxiety are for the patient. But much of the best work on how to effectively *reduce* that anxiety comes from other realms. My own distillation of the literature suggests that *exposure* is one of the most crucial factors contributing to the reduction of anxiety, and my understanding, as a consequence, of when psychoanalytic *interpretations* are most useful is that when they are understood as a way to promote exposure to the warded off experience they are likely to be more effective than when they are understood primarily in terms of promoting insight (Wachtel, 1997, 2008, 2011a).

One of the key factors leading to my interest in expanding my practice and my theoretical reach beyond the psychoanalytic perspective in which I was originally trained (and in which I still largely ground my thinking) was that at the time I began my integrative explorations (e.g., Wachtel, 1977a), psychoanalysis had come to seem to me too intellectualized, too much rooted in *knowing* and insufficiently rooted in *experiencing*. I became interested in exploring the possibility of using certain behavioral interventions to enhance the psychoanalytic work because behavior therapy seemed to me most of all an *experiential* therapy. This is a conceptualization that does not fit readily into the pigeonholes with which we classify the different approaches; behavior therapy, in most people's view, was put in the pigeonhole of "behaviorist," not of "experiential." But what struck me about methods like systematic desensitization, flooding, behavior rehearsal, and so forth was that they promoted direct confrontation and experiencing of the frightening and forbidden. Instead of *talking about* what troubles you, the patient in behavior therapy actually is *exposed* to it.

Unfortunately, this more experiential quality in behavioral treatments has become less prominent since behavior therapy evolved into *cognitive*-behavior therapy (CBT). Over time, cognitively focused CBT took on some of the very same problematic features that had troubled me about psychoanalytic practice at the time I began my integrative efforts to make my psychoanalytic practice more deeply experiential (Wachtel, 1977a). In the case of CBT, it became, in significant degree, an overly intellectualized effort to persuade the client that the premises underlying her thinking were "irrational," and to guide her toward thinking in ways that more closely matched the therapist's definition of rationality. Attention to affect and behavior, as a consequence, substantially declined (cf. Barlow, 2002; Burum & Goldfried, 2007; Samoilov & Goldfried, 2000; Wachtel, 2011a, 2011b; Whelton, 2004). In the hands of what I and others have critiqued as *rationalistic* cognitive therapists (see, in this regard, Arnkoff & Glass, 1992; Mahoney, 2003, 2004; Neimeyer & Mahoney, 1995; Wachtel, 2011a, 2011b), what had started out as a clinical and theoretical advance (the integration of cognition and other internal mediating processes into a therapeutic school which had paid too little attention to such influences) became a source of retreat from the client's full-bodied experience and the substitution of dry, rationalistic persuasion for engagement with the patient's vital subjective experience. Having gone out on a limb with my psychoanalytic colleagues by advocating the incorporation of methods they generally viewed at the time as superficial and clinically naïve, I was eager to show those colleagues tapes and transcripts that showed what I had learned – that the leading behavior therapists were among the most sensitive observers and clinically responsive therapists that I had encountered in my professional career. But over time, as the shift I am describing here began to accelerate, I began to feel embarrassed rather than vindicated by the videos and demonstrations I began to see in this stage of CBT's development. Some of the very same therapists I had learned so much from a few years before began to fall under the sway of the highly rationalistic visions of Aaron Beck and Albert Ellis, and instead of helping people to be directly and experientially exposed to the sources of their anxieties[6] they instead began to rationalistically try to talk people out of not only their fears, but their feelings. Anger, sadness, and other basic human emotions were labeled as "irrational," and the message was essentially that they were both faulty and unnecessary. I cringed as I watched these tapes and decided it would be prudent *not* to share them with my psychoanalytic colleagues, lest their stereotypes of behavioral and cognitive-behavioral therapy be strengthened rather than challenged.

Fortunately, in more recent years, two other trends have emerged in the cognitive-behavioral world that have been important challenges to the overly rationalistic vision that departed so radically from what had first drawn me to explore the work of the early behavior therapists. The first of these trends is a form of CBT that, far from trying to persuade people that their emotions are irrational and to disabuse them of the supposed faulty premises of their emotional experiences, instead *embraces* those experiences and takes them as the crucial starting point for any effort at change. Both dialectical behavior therapy (DBT) and acceptance and commitment therapy (ACT) begin from the premise that the crucial first step in effective clinical work is to *accept* the client's experience. There is, to be sure, a second aim, dialectically in tension with the first, of helping the client to *change* and thus, implicitly, of at least in part *questioning* or challenging the foundations of the client's difficulties. This tension between acceptance and working to promote change is a centrally important one in psychoanalytic work as well (see, for example, Bromberg, 1993; Ghent, 1995; I. Z. Hoffman, 1998; Schechter, 2007), and is one more area where there is more convergence than is often appreciated by practitioners of either.

The other important development in CBT that challenges the rationalistic version I have expressed concerns about is a growing interest in *constructivist* cognitive approaches (e.g., Feixas & Botella, 2004; Guidano, 1987, 1991; Mahoney, 1995, 2003; Neimeyer, 2009; Neimeyer & Mahoney, 1995). Here again, this is a development that is strongly paralleled in the psychoanalytic world. Constructivism is a key hallmark of the relational point of view.

Returning to the specific issue of making therapy deeply experiential rather than merely intellectual, this is of course a point on which, in principle, just about all psychoanalysts agree. The distinction between intellectual insight and emotional insight is a central idea in psychoanalytic thought. But although honoring this idea in the abstract, analysts have often not been very clear about how to *bring about* insights that are emotional rather than merely intellectual and have proceeded on assumptions (both procedural and theoretical) that can actually impede that effort.[7] More than half a century ago, Franz Alexander suggested to the psychoanalytic community that insight often *followed* change rather than being its primary engine, that new memories were as likely to emerge as a *consequence* of changes in the patient's current life patterns (achieved via a *variety* of therapeutic processes and methods) as to be their singular source (see also Fonagy, 1999). What Alexander suggested is, I imagine, what happened with the patient I discussed at the beginning of this chapter. She was in a position to bring up a set of memories that were *potentially* available all along, but only likely to actually come to mind after other work had made them less threatening. And although her *knowing* that her symptoms had their roots in these earlier experiences probably was not that central in helping her overcome them, her gradual acceptance of the *feelings* to which with those memories were linked probably *was* of crucial importance.

Approaching the "Inner World" Integratively

It is also crucial to recognize that the sources of our patients' anxieties – even of their fears of their own thoughts, wishes, and emotions – do not lie just in the past. As discussed at various points in this book, a closer analysis of the relation between the patient's way of life and the emotional imperatives or representations of self and other that are usually discussed in psychoanalytic discourse in terms of the patient's inner world reveals that that inner world is not hermetically sealed off from the rest of living. The inner world is not the unmoved mover or uncaused cause, but part of a powerful web of *reciprocal* forces, as much a *product* of the person's way of life as the cause. Such an understanding points almost ineluctably to the importance of a multifocused, integrative approach to psychotherapy.

A wide range of processes and perspectives are essential to properly conceptualize and carry out effective psychotherapy. I have already alluded to the crucial role of exposure. But it is important to understand that the sources of change are multiple and often reciprocal. Learning new ways of behaving in relation to others, for example, is crucial not just as a way of changing the manifest or "surface" patterns in a person's life, but also as a way of changing *internal* patterns of perception, cognition, and affective construction of experience. This consequence of changing manifest interaction patterns derives from the way that new ways of behaving and the new emotional signals associated with them change the feedback one receives from others, feedback which plays a crucial role in maintaining – or modifying – the internal world.

Similarly, as the patient is reintroduced to, and learns to become more comfortable with, affective experiences that had previously been warded off or denied, it becomes easier for him or her to learn new ways of expressing, modulating, and integrating those experiences. Often, at least a part of the danger experienced by the patient in relation to those affects is a result of very real deficits and deprivations that have resulted from the earlier anxiety about those affects and the consequent avoidance of those affective experiences. Learning to express our affects in ways that are socially appropriate, emotionally satisfying, and consonant with our larger life goals is a task that is, in fact, ongoing throughout life. In the course of development we engage in countless practice trials that teach us, at each developmental level, how to integrate affect into our lives in an age-appropriate manner. When we become afraid of those affects, however, we are deprived of the opportunity to hone our skills in expressing and containing them; and, ironically, we then have more reason *to be* afraid of them. This creates a self-perpetuating circle in which avoidance creates reason to avoid and hence still more avoidance ad infinitum. A wide variety of therapeutic interventions – whether conceptualized in these terms – serve to break this cycle in various ways, enabling the people we work with gradually to recover what might be called their affective birthright and to regain (and, in certain ways, to construct for the first time) a capacity to regulate, express, and enliven their lives with these affects.

Put differently, it is not just making the feeling or wish conscious that is important for therapeutic change but helping the patient to *accept* this aspect of himself. For many years, sometimes quite explicitly, sometimes without full understanding on the part of therapists of the implications of their way of proceeding, the aim of psychoanalytically guided therapies was to confront the patient with the contents of the unconscious so that he or she could *renounce* the anachronistic inclinations that were secretly harbored, but could do so in a more focused, less totalistic way than had been the case when they were unconscious. As Aron (1991) has put it,

> The ego psychological understanding of the therapeutic goal of psychoanalysis as the achievement of control and autonomy over the drives leads to a view of the working through process which emphasizes renunciation and loss, and in which the analysand must willfully abandon hopes for the fulfillment of childhood wishes. This conception is poignantly depicted in the equation of working through with the process of mourning with which it has long been compared. . . . In working through, as in mourning, the individual must painfully come to terms with abandoning a preferred pathway of libidinal discharge and needs to accept the reality of loss and its accompanying frustration. . . . The focus on gaining ego control over infantile drives, and on mastering infantile strivings by relinquishing them, lends itself to the abuses of a "maturity morality." Patients can easily come to feel that the analyst wants them to "grow up." Patients are likely to feel that the analyst is judgmental and is awaiting the day when they stop acting childishly and begin to act maturely. (Aron, 1991, pp. 90–91)

The assumptions behind such a way of proceeding can lead therapists to be unwittingly *accusatory* in their way of understanding and speaking to the patient, and thus can be decidedly countertherapeutic (see, in this regard, for example, Apfelbaum, 1980; Schechter, 2007; Wachtel, 2011a; Wile, 1984, 1985). Schechter (2007) points out that, "While the field is changing, there remains in the psychoanalytic culture a residual sense that overt support and validation, while perhaps necessary at certain moments, do not truly belong in the analysis of intrapsychic conflict" (p. 107). At the same time, Schechter points out, good interpretations in fact have an affirming validating quality that accounts for a good deal of their effectiveness. He notes along the way that, although this understanding of what is genuinely therapeutic in the analytic process has had to contend with the just-noted reluctance to be overtly supportive or affirmative, it in fact has roots in the writings of a range of prominent psychoanalytic writers, from Strachey, to Loe-wald, to Kohut, to Kris, and to numerous others. It finds its strongest expression in the emerging clinical vision of the relational point of view, with its increasing emphasis on the quality of the therapeutic relationship as a key factor in therapeutic change, a viewpoint that receives substantial support from systematic research on the sources of therapeutic change (e.g., Blatt & Zuroff, 2005; Norcross, 2002, 2010).

Increasingly, the emphasis in psychoanalytic approaches to therapy is beginning to shift from insight (that is, making the unconscious conscious) to *new relational experience* (see K. A. Frank, 1999, for a good summary and discussion of this development). In certain ways, this trend goes back as far as the innovative work of early analysts such as Ferenczi (1926) and Alexander and French (1946). It is further developed, in different ways, in the writings of Kohut (e.g., 1977), Weiss & Sampson (1986), and others. Especially relevant here is the important point made by Stolorow, Brandchaft, and Atwood (1987) that insight and the experience of a new, empathic relationship with someone who understands you are not really alternative conceptions. It is *through* the therapist's communication of accurate understanding of aspects of experience that have previously been warded off that the real sense of being understood is generated.

What Is the Role of Insight and Making the Unconscious Conscious?

Where then do I place consciousness, awareness, and insight in the overall picture of therapeutic change? I hope it is clear that my comments here are not designed to imply that consciousness or insight is unimportant. Clearly, the patient's accurate understanding of his most genuine and heartfelt aims is both a highly important goal in its own right and a prerequisite as well to devising *any* therapeutic strategy that is ethically appropriate or likely to be useful in any enduring way. How, for example, can the therapist promote exposure to the relevant cues at the heart of the patient's anxiety if neither patient nor therapist know what those cues are? But I do contend that psychoanalysts have often overestimated the role of insight, have made it more central in their understanding of how therapeutic change occurs than is consistent with the evidence. And in the process of doing so, they have ruled out or placed at the margins a wide range of potentially valuable ways of helping people change (see, e.g., Wachtel, 1997).

Put differently, the hierarchical vision of therapeutic change, with insight and interpretation regarded as royalty and other sources of change being relegated to the ranks of the commoners in the therapeutic realm, has led analysts at times to concentrate their efforts too narrowly, to conceive of what is valuable in what they do too unimaginatively, and thereby to fail *even to maximize insight itself.* Insight is more likely to be promoted by a therapy that attends to reducing the patient's anxiety and avoidance and helping him or her rebuild the behavioral and emotional capabilities that were truncated by the avoidances the anxiety had sparked. The aim of such a therapy is to promote a stronger self via fuller self-acceptance, which means not just greater *consciousness* but greater capacity to embrace, rework, and *affirm* what has been made conscious (cf. Schechter, 2007).

Combining such an aim with a meaningful search for and valuing of insight is enhanced by reconceptualizing traditional psychoanalytic distinctions between conscious and unconscious in terms of the concept of unformulated experience that has been elaborated so valuably by D.B. Stern (1997). This focus on the way that articulating and giving a more differentiated and elaborated voice to the affects, desires, and apprehensions that had been constricted and rendered largely unspoken offers a phenomenologically more astute alternative to the distinction between conscious and unconscious. Unformulated experiences are not buried or hidden or rendered unconscious after having already taken form and shape but rather have been *prevented* from taking full form and shape in the first place. The consequence of anxiety, guilt, or shame and of the defensive efforts these affects can initiate is that the troubling inclination is kept in a kind of limbo in which it is both experienced and not experienced – experienced as something vague and hard to put into words but not experienced as what it may *later* seem to be. What finally emerges in the course of the analytic or therapeutic process is not "what was there all along," but rather what was *potentially* there but was also *not allowed* to be there. What emerges, that is, is something new, something rooted in who the person has been all along but also a harbinger of whom the person is *becoming*.

Making the unconscious conscious, then, is not so much a process of unearthing or uncovering as a process of *permitting to happen*. When what is being defended against is a memory, we may encounter the seeming paradox discussed at the beginning of this chapter – a memory that seems to have been forcefully excluded from awareness while it has also all along been readily capable of becoming conscious (if only the right question were asked). What the defense largely accomplishes is to make it unlikely that the right question *will* be asked. When what is defended against is a feeling or a desire, the exclusion is in some ways more complete or severe. Whereas the right question can elicit, "Yes, that happened," even the most finely tuned question will not necessarily elicit the experience of "Yes, I want that," or "Yes, I feel that." The patient may steadfastly remain unable to acknowledge or permit those experiences.

If we look more closely at the complex phenomenology that gives rise to psychoanalytic conceptualizations, we may note that even in the realm of memory some parts of the experience are not elicitable even by "the right question." To some degree, the factual side of the memory may be elicited, but the understanding of memory that derives from contemporary research makes it clear that even this is not without complications. We now know that memories of an event or experience are, each time they are elicited, a somewhat new (and somewhat different) *construction* rather than something akin to pulling a file from a storage cabinet. The precise nature of what emerges, the exact details and sequencing of the narrative, will be modified by a host of contextual factors, including the person's psychological state and the emotional needs that are dominant at the moment. And when it comes to the feelings and intentions reflected in the events described, the vulnerability of the memory process to the need to maintain a certain image of oneself or of others will be very much greater.

Freud framed psychoanalysis primarily as a process of discovery, thereby conflating the therapeutic aims and the research aims of the enterprise. This exploratory emphasis led to crucially important new understandings of psychological dynamics, but it also constricted the imagination of analysts in thinking about the possibilities for *intervention* into the dynamics that were discovered. Making the unconscious conscious remains one important aim and means of a comprehensive therapeutic effort. But that aim and that method must be understood and pursued in a larger clinical and theoretical context. Too much of a good thing – or, more accurately, too single-minded a pursuit of a good thing – can end up being counterproductive. Pursued without sufficient regard for the *other* good things that promote therapeutic change, the search for insight can crowd out these other therapeutic forces, resulting in, as I once put it in a slightly different context (Wachtel, 1997), exquisitely articulated despair.

Notes

1. An earlier version of this chapter was presented as part of a symposium on "Unconscious processes: A perspective from the 21st century" at the 18th annual meeting of the Society for the Exploration of Psychotherapy Integration in San Francisco, California, on May 4, 2002.

2. These days, it is a certain breed of cognitive therapist who has taken on the mantle of this "objective" and "scientific" stance. And, much as psychoanalysts have discovered, in the years since the episode I am reporting here, that the relationship and the affective engagement between the parties is a crucial part of the process, many cognitive and cognitive-behavioral therapists have similarly begun to recognize the importance of the human side of the therapeutic encounter (see, for example, Gilbert & Leahy, 2007; Hayes, Follette, & Linehan, 2004; Leahy, 2008).

3. Recall of forbidden thoughts or feelings is not *necessarily* disruptive of piety. An intense sense of being a sinner may heighten rather than diminish a religious experience. But in many instances, what people seek in church is a focus on and commitment to a vision of themselves that contrasts quite considerably with their everyday choices and experiences.

4. In certain respects, Freud had always known this. He stated in his 1915 paper on repression, for example, that, "the motive and purpose of repression was nothing else than the avoidance of unpleasure" [translated, perhaps more aptly, as the avoidance of "pain" in the Collected Papers edition] (p. 153). In the same paper, however (indeed, on the same page), he also presents the formulation that the repressed impulse was *converted into* anxiety – that is, he interpreted the observation that repression and anxiety often appeared together in the same context as reflecting a discharge phenomenon in which the energy of the repressed impulse was discharged as anxiety. In his 1926 reformulation, the co-occurrence of anxiety and repression were interpreted as a *failure*

of repression; that is, as evidence that the repression was incomplete or insufficient to prevent some anxiety from occurring.

5. It is important to note here that in recent years behavioral and cognitive-behavioral therapists have begun (albeit with a somewhat different focus) also to attend to the important role of anxiety linked to stimuli associated with physiological arousal and internal, subjective experience. See, for example, Barlow, Allen, and Choate (2004).

6. As I have noted elsewhere in this book, the stimuli to which behavior therapists directed their exposure efforts tended not to be those that were central to psychoanalytic practice (albeit, in the latter case, without the process being conceptualized as one of exposure). But the efficacy of exposure as an anxiety-reducing process had relevance to psychoanalytic work as well, and indeed, when one takes into account that exposure to "external" stimuli is almost always accompanied by the evocation of unconscious fantasies and inclinations and exposure to particular fantasies, affects, or desires inevitably occurs in a real-world context, there is much reason to conclude that a sharp dichotomy between the exposures occurring in cognitive-behavioral therapy and those occurring in psychodynamic therapy is unwarranted (see Dollard & Miller, 1950; Wachtel, 1997, 2008, 2011a; Weitzman, 1967).

7. As I discuss at various points in this book, the relational movement in psychoanalytic thought, and especially its emphasis on the therapeutic impact of new relational experience (see Wachtel, 2008 for a discussion of the wide range of relational thinkers who, under different rubrics, emphasize this idea) has been an important exception to this omission. But it is also important to note (a) that the exploration of a more deeply experiential version of psychoanalytic practice is not exclusively a relational contribution, and (b) that there remain many ways in which relational theory and practice have still not fully transcended the older, constraining modes of thought from which relational theory emerged (Wachtel, 2008).

Chapter 7

Active Intervention, Psychic Structure, and the Analysis of Transference

It should already be evident to the reader that the cyclical psychodynamic perspective described in this book entails reexamination not only of the basic premises of psychoanalytic thought but of therapeutic practice as well. In the first, more theoretical aspect of the cyclical psychodynamic agenda, it overlaps quite considerably with the thrust of relational theorizing more generally. As noted in Chapter 1, cyclical psychodynamic theory and relational theory evolved separately for a number of years, but over time it became apparent that they shared so much in common that it made sense to conceive of cyclical psychodynamic theory as a version of relational theory.[1]

As we turn from theory to therapeutic practice, however, the convergence between the cyclical psychodynamic point of view and that of other relational approaches is less extensive. To be sure, there are many overlaps between the way of working that derives from a cyclical psychodynamic point of view and that associated with relational practice more generally. The way I work entails much the same examination of subjectivity and intersubjectivity as in the work of other relationalists. Consideration of unconscious and unformulated experiences; of conflict and dissociation; of the influence of early relationships and loved and feared objects – all these and much more are central both to the cyclical psychodynamic point of view and to the practices of relationalists more broadly. So too is the application of a constructivist and intersubjective perspective on these phenomena and experiences, so that rather than seeing them simply as "inside" the patient or as reflecting the therapist's "objective" insight into the patient's essential nature, the patient's experience is understood as reflecting not only his past and his already structuralized personality characteristics but also the way those patient characteristics are manifested and modified in the presence of the particular person who is his analyst or therapist and in the particular bidirectional relational experience that is being co-constructed by both.

But the separate paths of development of cyclical psychodynamic theory on the one hand and the broader relational turn with which it eventually intersected on the other reflected some significantly different views of the core elements contributing to therapeutic change and significantly different ideas about the proper boundaries around psychoanalytic thought. Relational theory, like cyclical psychodynamic theory, evolved out of an integrative effort, but it was a narrower integration that was sought by the former. What has come to be called the relational turn in psychoanalysis centered on efforts to integrate the consonant elements in interpersonal theory, self-psychology, and object relations theory. For cyclical psychodynamics, in contrast, the guiding integrative aim was broader, encompassing originally the integration of psychoanalytic and behavioral approaches (Wachtel, 1977a) and eventually moving to include systemic and experiential perspectives as well (E. F. Wachtel & Wachtel, 1986; Wachtel, 1997, 2011a, 2011b). In the last chapter, I began to discuss more explicitly the ways in which the cyclical psychodynamic perspective points to a more comprehensive, integrative therapeutic approach. In this chapter I want to extend that discussion further, considering in particular the relation between an integrative therapeutic practice that includes active interventions originally deriving from other therapeutic orientations and the traditional psychoanalytic emphasis on attention to intrapsychic structures and transference phenomena.

In considering how these differing methods and concerns fit together, I begin with a discussion of a paper by Kenneth Frank that examines some of the same questions, both because Frank has been one of the most valuable writers exploring the integration of psychodynamic and behavioral or cognitive-behavioral approaches (e.g., K. A. Frank, 1990, 1992, 1993, 2001) and because his discussion of my own writings in this realm offers an opportunity to further clarify my point of view and the ways in which it can potentially be misunderstood. In a representation of my views on psychoanalytic theory and therapeutic practice that is in most ways both accurate and highly sympathetic, and for which I am grateful on both counts, Frank (1993, p. 537) says that my work "has played down the role of inner structure and intrapsychic exploration" and that it "minimizes intrapsychic formulations." Examining what is entailed in this perception is a useful means of clarifying just what the cyclical psychodynamic conception of psychological structures is and how it bears on expanding the prospects for therapeutic intervention and therapeutic change. In addition, it affords an opportunity more generally to examine more closely what precisely we mean by intrapsychic or by inner structure.

If by intrapsychic one means an inner world that is conceived of as in no way in touch with the world of daily events, then it is correct to say that I minimize such formulations. But as Frank himself points out, analysts of a variety of orientations are increasingly appreciating that intrapsychic processes are better understood as part of an ongoing process of transaction with others and that interpersonal and intrapsychic are not really alternatives but rather two poles of a single interactive or dialectic process (see, for example, Aron, 1996; I. Z. Hoffman, 1998; Mitchell, 1988, 1993, 1997; and, indeed, K. A. Frank, 1999). When intrapsychic processes and structures are understood in this way, the approach I advocate in no way "minimizes intrapsychic formulations." Rather, what it does is rework or recast those formulations precisely for the purpose of transcending the misleading dichotomy between interpersonal and intrapsychic.

As I think about my own work in the light of Frank's discussion, it seems to me that, far from *playing down* the role of inner structure, it has had as one of its central aims to *reconceptualize just what inner structure is*. The cyclical psychodynamic account converges with the other relational approaches discussed by Frank (1993) in that it, too, understands psychic structure as "formed by, and patterned on, the model of early relationships" (p. 537). But it differs from many of its cousins in its emphasis on examining how that pattern is either maintained or modified by later experiences. What makes early relationships so fateful is their *twofold* effect on later experience. First, as psychoanalytic accounts have tended to stress, they create the schema or template through which later experiences are interpreted and understood. Through multiple and complex processes of filtering, sifting, and reorganizing, new experiences are given meaning in terms of previous experiences and the expectations, biases, fears, and wishes they have engendered. Reality, we might say, is encountered only through the midwifery of fantasy. Because interpersonal and affective events are inherently ambiguous, there is substantial latitude for the retrofitting of experience to expectation.

But there is a second way in which the past casts a shadow over the present that is equally crucial to appreciate but has received less attention in psychoanalytic quarters. As powerful as is the purely assimilative role of unconscious fantasies and expectations, as forcefully as they twist the arm of experience until it cries uncle and declares, "Yes, I see once more in this new encounter what I have always seen," the power to effect such tendentious redescription of the events of daily life does have its limits. We could not survive until adulthood, much less function effectively enough to afford an analyst's fees, were this not the case.

As foggy and idiosyncratic as our view may be of what actually transpires between us and other people, it is far from arbitrary or blithely autonomous. As Gill (1982, 1983), I. Z. Hoffman (1983), Aron (1991), Mitchell (1988), and others have argued, even the most seemingly idiosyncratic transference reactions are rooted in the actual events between patient and analyst, and this is the case in our interactions with other people in our lives as well. Were others persistently to react to us in ways that differ from our transferential expectations – transference here referring not just to what transpires between patient and analyst but rather to the pervasive tendency in all facets of our lives to experience the present in light of the past and its residue in psychic structures – those expectations would gradually be modified. The past is not an all-powerful dictator in the realm of the psyche but rather one powerful lobby in a system characterized, with homage as much to Montesquieu and Madison as to Freud, by a division of powers. The actual characteristics and intentions of the other and the social context within which the transaction occurs also insist on having their due; and the transference lobby, as it were, must settle for the same portion of the pie in the realm of the psyche that the corporate lobby must content itself with in the politics of the nation – enough to do a good deal of mischief but, fortunately, not an absolute.

But just as the corporate interests' influence is not just exercised by muscle alone but further magnified by the effects of advertising and the media more generally on the public's perception of what it wants (so that some of what should be negotiated is conceded, some of the force of opposition dissolved), so too in the psychic realm is the influence of the past magnified by the defection of its opposition. That is, where the actualities of the present could, in principle, provide at least some degree of counterbalance to the transferential impact of the past, where a persistent difference between what is expected and what actually happens could gradually chip away at the edges of those expectations, often this does not materialize. Instead, it seems, the opposition caves in and confirms the expectation, not just as seen in the distorted eyes of the transference-blinded perceiver but even as might be seen by a hypothetical unbiased observer (a concept, of course, that is a fantasy in its own right, but at times a useful one).

Put in different terms, and elaborating on the concept of accomplices discussed in Chapter 2, what is crucial to take into account is that our interpersonal perceptions are directed not to inert objects but to reactive beings, *who respond to how they are being perceived*. When we perceive a benign or friendly smile as mocking or an expression of interest as something vaguely insidious or sinister, we begin to change the other person's attitude, *not just in fantasy, but in actuality*. Initially, perhaps, it is only the considerable ambiguity of interpersonal affairs that enables us to perceive the other as mocking. But when, three, four, five, or more times, we persist in seeing a darker side to the friendly gesture, and – almost inevitably – convey that perception in some aspect of how we respond to the other (either grossly or subtly), that begins to take its toll. The other will not forever remain benignly interested and friendly in the face of such mistrust (if not outright hostility); before long he or she will begin to *feel* rather unfriendly, thereby "confirming" the first person's suspicions, since indeed the other does "show his true colors" after a while (Wachtel, 1981). Thus do prophecies become self-fulfilling and transferences become fixed and seemingly embedded in the psyche.

Put differently, we fail to appreciate the truly dynamic nature of transferential processes and psychic structures if we see only the ways in which new experiences are assimilated to old expectations. Equally crucial is the way that reality itself accommodates, as our initially distorted perceptions of others lead us to act toward them in ways that eventually induce behavior from them that maintains the plausibility of the transferential expectation. Without other people's participation – or, perhaps more accurately, with their participating in a different way (for they cannot *not* participate once they have entered our gravitational field) the inner structure would gradually change. For it is not in fact completely impervious; it only looks that way because of the unwitting cooperation it evokes. It is for this reason that I suggested in Chapter 2 that, "every neurosis requires accomplices." Without the confirmation by other people of our maladaptive expectations, those expectations would eventually shift. Indeed, that is what happens in a well-conducted, truly therapeutic analysis or therapy.[2]

Active Intervention and the Analysis of Transference

A central tenet of any integrative approach that genuinely and usefully is rooted in the psychoanalytic point of view is that the transference implications of active interventions must and can be understood and examined. It had been traditional in analytic circles to regard such interventions as intrusions in the psychoanalytic work that would inevitably obscure and distort the transference. K. A. Frank (1993) argues persuasively that such a view is based on a faulty understanding not only of active-intervention techniques but of more typical psychoanalytic practice and more traditional forms of transference analysis as well. As Frank puts it, drawing on both my own theorizing and that of Gill, "None of the therapist's responses, even silence, can avoid influencing the patient's experience; they will instead stimulate different aspects of the transference-countertransference paradigm" (p. 551).

From this perspective, the patient's reactions to so-called active interventions[3] are no less analyzable than are any of the events or experiences that occur in a more traditionally conducted analysis. In each instance, what one attempts to understand is what the therapist's behavior meant to the patient. To be sure, when the therapist offers to teach the patient specific coping skills, as Frank did with Ruth (discussed further on), she is "really" doing something, and the patient's feelings and fantasies will be a product not only of his intrapsychic proclivities but also of what his therapist was really doing. So too, however, is this the case when the therapist is silent – that is, is "really" silent – or when she offers an interpretation.

Traditionally, the silence, even the interpretation, is seen as inherently ambiguous, as sufficiently nonintrusive to be an essentially neutral stimulus, the response to which reveals the patient's inclinations more or less free of the contaminating influence of specific input. The analyst in effect disappears into the woodwork, and the patient's inner life "emerges" or "unfolds" (Wachtel, 1982a). In fact, however, whether the therapist's behavior is silence, making an interpretation, or offering coping skills, the patient's reaction will be a function of what the therapist has done (silence being one more kind of doing) as well as a function of the patient's idiosyncratic way of construing that behavior, based on previous experiences and their residue in presently existing psychological structures.

When the therapist is silent, for example, the patient may experience the silence as depriving, hesitant, rigid, adversarial, respectfully listening, profound, a sign the therapist does not know what to say, a sign she is competently professional, and so on. We have all observed the wide range of meanings patients may attribute to our silence. For many, it is such observations that seem to support the view of silence as neutral and ambiguous and of the patient's reaction to it as analyzable. Because the silence is not inherently any of these, the way the patient experiences it reflects something about the patient. Even though the therapist was "really" silent, the meaning given to the silence comes from the patient.[4]

But what happens when the therapist offers coping skills? Essentially the process is the same. The more "active" intervention is similarly ambiguous. Is the therapist being condescending? Is she warm and generous and hence eager to help? Does she lack the training to carry out her traditional role without gimmicks? Is she empathically sensitive to the patient's pain and able to see the patient's need for a little extra? Is she controlling? Does she have a superficial and mechanical understanding of human feelings? Is she open and flexible and ready to consider new approaches to the benefit of her patients? Here, too, the list is practically endless, and once again the patient's reaction, though in part determined by what the therapist is "really" doing, will also give substantial leeway for the patient's idiosyncratic way of construing interpersonal events to come through.

As a consequence, what Frank (e.g. 1992, 1993, 2001) calls action-oriented interventions can be as readily incorporated into a therapy predicated on analyzing the transference as can the more familiar modes of analytic discourse, so long as the therapist is committed to exploring the meaning to the patient of what she has done. As Frank points out clearly, the necessity to explore in this way is no greater and no less for the introduction of action techniques than it is for standard analytic procedures. Put differently, the interventions Frank describes are not just imports of foreign goods; they are relational events, and the exploration of their meaning to the patient is a crucial part of their effective use. The way Frank addresses that meaning – and the complexity of *all* analytic or therapeutic work that aims not just for symptom relief but for deep and extensive change – is nicely illustrated in a case he presents in which a patient, Ruth, is offered a number of cognitive-behavioral strategies for dealing with her panic attacks while the ongoing therapeutic work continues to be pursued from an essentially psychoanalytic point of view.

Ruth had developed character strategies for coping with her disparaging father and alternately distant and competitive mother that centered on a way of life similar to what Horney (e.g., 1945) has called the moving toward neurotic trend. She approached both parents, and then others in her life, including her analyst, through forms of silently resentful submission. When she did give expression to her wishes to be more assertive and effective in the world, these were often followed by self-harming behavior and intensified resentful submission. When there were indications that she was making progress in various aspects of her life, she would often disparage the gains, depict them as meaningless, and state that she was becoming depressed. The efforts she was making – even the successful ones – were "too difficult" and "not worth it."

At one point, in response to this pattern, Frank suggested that her way of responding to these gains – the strong message to her analyst that things were not really going as well as they might appear – "might be based on her old way of connecting with her mother, that is, of 'reassuring' her mother through her failure at a time when Ruth's personal growth might be felt as threatening" (p. 566). He noted that Ruth considered this comment by him very reflectively and that his naming the pattern seemed to enable her to at least somewhat relax her efforts to connect through what he called depressive failure. He noted as well that Ruth came in the next session with "an unusual, cautious display of pride," and told him that she felt she was "growing up a little" (p. 566). She described in particular using the relaxation, breathing, and coping skills he had taught her to manage her anxiety in class and to contribute in a satisfying way to the class discussion, something that had previously been very difficult for her to do.

Frank did not challenge or question Ruth's view that her gains derived primarily from the specifically cognitive-behavioral interventions he had made. (He had, after all, introduced these methods into the work because he thought they would be helpful to Ruth.) But, from his psychoanalytic perspective, he did view it as important to be aware of the range of meanings these interventions could have for Ruth. As he put it,

> Attentive to the possible transferential meaning of the use of the action-oriented techniques, especially in the light of Ruth's submissive relationship to her demeaning father and the conflicted wish to please him, the therapist wondered "whether my having shown you any of the coping techniques might somehow feel like a put-down, pushing you around, pressuring you, or causing you to feel that I'm better." (Frank, 1993, p. 569)

At the time, Ruth did not acknowledge any such feelings, but some time later, dealing with a different occasion, she expressed disappointment at not having been able to use these coping techniques to modulate her anxiety, and she expressed concern that she had thereby failed to please her therapist and that he would give up on her. Frank then returned to discussing with Ruth the possible meanings that introducing these methods had for her, particularly in evoking in relation to Frank some of the same conflicted feelings she experienced with her father. She desperately wanted to please her father and overtly related to him in a submissive fashion or tried (without success) to be who he wanted her to be. At the same time, she struggled with resentful and rebellious feelings toward him that felt very unsafe and that she feared would destroy whatever sense of safety and connection she could manage with him. Frank raised with Ruth the question of whether her efforts to use the coping techniques he had taught her stirred for her some of the very same feelings and conflicts. Thus, while continuing to view the cognitive-behavioral techniques he had introduced as valuable adjunctive methods in helping Ruth extricate herself from the constraining impact of the characterological strategies she had evolved to cope with her difficult family situation, Frank simultaneously aimed to illuminate for Ruth the complicated and conflicting *meanings* they had for her in the context of Ruth and Frank's relationship.

Besides exploring the ways in which Ruth's feelings toward him could be seen as replicating those toward her father, Frank also explored the nature of her conflicted ties to her mother and their additional implications for illuminating aspects of the transferential meanings of the introduction of the cognitive-behavioral coping techniques. Based on the understanding of the relationship that had developed thus far, Frank suggested that as Ruth gained confidence and manifested competence more clearly, she might fear that he would withdraw from her emotionally, as her mother did in such circumstances. Both her parents were quite attacking when Ruth did not do enough to provide for their needs, and in response to the threat she experienced, she would try to feel a measure of safety through relating in a self-disparaging or childlike way. Her feelings of safety and attachment, Frank pointed out, seemed threatened by "the emerging experience of self associated with expressiveness, accomplishment, and the recognition her efforts were beginning to receive" (p. 567).

Support for the Status Quo?

In considering the case of Ruth, it is certainly possible for the analyst who wishes to defend the status quo to find in Ruth's material what might seem to be indications that her therapist's efforts to be helpful through offering nonanalytic assistance had been counterproductive. For example, in the course of the therapy, she applied to business school and kept her application a secret from her therapist.[5] Might she have experienced his interventions as so intrusive that she needed to carve out her own space by keeping her efforts secret? At another point in the therapy, at a time when things seemed to be going rather well (or, put differently, when the therapist's interventions could be seen as having been successful), Ruth reverted to a serious symptom that she had seemed to have moved beyond. As Frank described it,

> Because there was a sense of things going well, the therapist was shocked at the beginning of the next session by the return of a set of symptoms that had not occurred for over a year. Ruth entered the consultation room carrying a magazine from the waiting room. Commenting on an article on violence, she said, "I hadn't intended to say anything, but I hurt myself again." Ruth had a history of episodically "hurting" herself by sharply and repetitively striking her face with a hairbrush. Sometimes she would persist until she caused abrasions and bleeding. At times, this behavior, which began in adolescence, also involved suicidal thoughts with images of herself hanging suffocated and lifeless at the end of a rope. In clarifying the feelings associated with the act, Ruth spoke primarily of her feelings of worthlessness. (p. 567)

Moreover, her first association to the report of this symptom was a dream about her therapist in which she entered his house through the back door, and in which further associations included the thought that the therapist was dissatisfied with how clearly she was expressing herself in the sessions and that he must see her as a "mess." She associated as well to coming in the back door as entering through the servants' entrance and that she was "not good enough to come in the front" (p. 568).

If one were so inclined, It would not be difficult to make a case for these various occurrences as indicating that the use of active interventions was experienced by Ruth as her therapist giving up on her or as not respecting her capacities to work in an analytic mode and therefore dumbing down the therapeutic work or opting for a quick fix that would clean her up, make her presentable, and then get rid of her. Themes of filth and of cleaning and indications that Ruth feared her therapist would withdraw from her, as she feared her parents would if she dared to be assertive or think well of herself, came up in Ruth's discussion of her dream and were prominent in the therapy more generally. Thus, it is not hard to make a case that Ruth had some misgivings and mixed feelings about the assistance her therapist offered, that she felt – among other feelings, it is important to note – that the reason her therapist had offered her coping techniques was that he saw her as a "mess" and did not want to engage her in all her fullness.

Such considerations, however, by no means invalidate the approach Frank has described. To begin with, transferential experiences of the sort just noted are not limited to therapeutic efforts that employ the action-oriented methods Frank describes. Such transference reactions are the stock-in-trade of all psychoanalytic work. Patients in analysis and analytic therapy *regularly* have the sorts of thoughts, feelings, and fantasies that Ruth evidenced, *regularly* construe a range of meanings in what is transpiring that may not correspond to the therapist's intentions or understanding of what she is up to. Such reactions may be evident, for example, in response to the analyst's silence; to interpretations that feel on the mark (he can see through me like I'm pitifully transparent) or off the mark (he can't see me at all; it's like I'm invisible or incomprehensible); or even to the expression of empathic resonance (he cares about me because I'm so pathetic, like a pet cocker spaniel). Far from invalidating the therapy or implying that the therapist is on the wrong track, such occurrences are generally understood as at the heart of what psychoanalytic therapy is about.

Second and equally important, the implications of Ruth's conflicted or negatively toned transferential reactions would be quite different in a therapy in which they go unnoticed or in which the therapist does not know how to deal with them than they are in a therapy where the therapist is skilled and knowledgeable in dealing with transferences. In Frank's hands, these reactions on Ruth's part are a central part of the analytic process itself. It is of the very essence of his article's message that one does not check one's understanding of analytic process or of transference analysis at the door when one enters the realm of active intervention. Indeed, as Frank points out, analytically trained clinicians may well be in the strongest position to use effectively the active intervention methods that therapists of other orientations have developed. As Frank puts it, "An integrative application that combines facilitated behavior change with analytic processes to effect in-depth personality change may be the most powerful use of behavioral-cognitive techniques" (p. 556).

The False Dichotomy between Active Methods and Standard Technique

Taken fully into account, Frank's arguments and the cyclical psychodynamic perspective from which they are partly drawn suggest that interpretations are no less active interventions than the action-oriented methods described by Frank, nor are interpretations properly understood as "neutral" (Wachtel, 1987). Interpretation differs primarily in being more *familiar* to analysts and hence more comfortable for that reason. In fact, however, interpretations and the interventions on which Frank's article focuses overlap a good deal in terms of the psychological processes they bring into play, and they overlap almost completely in terms of their implications for the transference and the possibilities of its resolution (Wachtel, 1997, 2011a).

Full appreciation of this point suggests that Frank may have been unnecessarily conservative in his conclusions. At several points in his article, Frank refers to the necessity to be "judicious" or "prudent" in using action-oriented techniques. Now certainly I am not an advocate of the injudicious or imprudent use of these methods. But Frank's language here introduces a bias that is inconsistent with the overall thrust of his arguments. The implication of the word *judicious* as he uses it in the article is that the burden of proof is on the decision to use such techniques. But Frank himself has stated (personal communication) that it is as important for the therapist to understand why he has chosen not to answer a patient's question as why he has, and it is not a very great leap to suggest as well that it is as important to understand why one has decided not to employ a particular active technique as why one has chosen to do so.

I believe it is truer to the spirit of Frank's overall argument to suggest that once one realizes that so-called action-oriented techniques are compatible with a psychoanalytic approach and that transference reactions to them are analyzable, then the therapist is confronted with a wider array of choices, *all of which* must be approached prudently and judiciously. One must think through the implications – transferential, countertransferential, and otherwise – of choosing to use these techniques and of choosing not to. Appreciating, as Frank does, the profound implications of adaptive action for achieving structural personality change, one's life as a therapist is not made simpler – more choices must be made, more options weighed – but one's potential effectiveness is correspondingly increased.

This is not to say that the outcome of the broadened prudence or judiciousness I am advocating is likely to be a therapy in which explicit action-oriented techniques predominate. There is very substantial clinical benefit to the quiet, reflective, listening, empathizing stance traditional to psychoanalytic practice. It provides the background context within which judicious and clinically sound choices can be made. In my own practice, even in the stage when I was most actively experimenting with active methods, such methods were rarely the predominant mode of the therapy. They were, rather, primarily a means of activating and making more enduring and comprehensive the working-through process (and, in much the fashion advocated by Frank, they were – and are – always approached with an eye toward their meaning to the patient, toward their transferential implications).

It is important to be aware, however, that such methods are not solely a means of promoting working through, not solely a follow-up to the exploratory activity of traditional psychoanalytic therapy. They are as well, in many cases, a potent route toward exploration in their own right. Both the use of imagery techniques and the encouragement of the patient to take active steps in daily life bring the patient into contact with new experiences and new material. Far from being a means of superficially covering over the patient's conflicts or providing a bandage, these methods are often a means of deepening the process of exploration and promoting greater access to warded off parts of the self (see, e.g., Chapter 8). This potential of action techniques must also be taken into account in making the choice, at any given point, as to whether to conduct analysis as usual or to respond to the patient's need with an intervention of the sort Frank discusses.

It should also be noted that, as one learns to use active methods more comfortably, the sharp distinction between "ordinary analyzing" and the employment of active techniques begins to fade. Perhaps the most significant implication of the approach to the role of adaptive action in structural change discussed here is that our understanding of ordinary analyzing itself is modified. Once one appreciates that silently listening and offering interpretations by no means exhaust the therapeutic possibilities of a genuinely psychoanalytic approach to people's difficulties, and once one further appreciates the logical difficulties of the notions of neutrality that for so long dominated psychoanalytic discourse (cf. Aron, 1996; Gill, 1982, 1983; I. Z. Hoffman, 1998; Renik, 1996, 1999; Wachtel, 1987), it becomes possible to weave the dimension of adaptive action into the process of interpretation itself; or, more accurately – because, as Frank makes clear, that dimension has always been latent in good psychoanalytic work – to integrate and activate this dimension more fully (Wachtel, 2008, 2011a).

In my own initial explorations of the use of active interventions (Wachtel, 1977a), the predominant form they took was as discrete events occurring against a backdrop of more or less standard analytic work (at that point in my work, with an interpersonal flavor). But over the years, I have increasingly found that the integration into my clinical work of active methods and a focus on adaptive action, as well as a focus on the patient's exposure to the sources of his fears, has yielded a more seamless synthesis, a mode of working that is at once psychoanalytic and active. This way of working aims not just to explore and understand the patient's deepest yearnings but to help him give shape to them in ways that render them more capable of being realized. Rather than engaging at some points in discrete action-oriented interventions that are completely separate from the analytic work and engaging at others times in analytic work that is more or less "standard," I have increasingly found myself working in a more fully integrated fashion than I originally conceived. In these instances, the various threads that make up the fabric of the therapy have been woven together more or less seamlessly. It is to this more seamless and comprehensive therapeutic integration that I now turn.

Notes

1. This is not to suggest that there are not also some significant theoretical *differences* between the cyclical psychodynamic point of view and that of most other relational perspectives. Some of the earlier chapters in this book reflect and depict those differences. See also Wachtel, 2008.
2. This does not mean, of course, that the analyst never inadvertently falls into the pattern, confirming rather than disconfirming the patient's expectations. Such complete avoidance of being drawn in is impossible, and if it becomes the analyst's goal, it will simply motivate her not to notice when she is doing so. Rather, the key is to achieve a reasonable balance of engagement and reflection, something akin to what Sullivan (1953) called participant observation, or what contemporary writers refer to as repairing ruptures in the therapeutic alliance (Safran & Muran, 2000; Safran, Muran, & Proskurov, 2009) or as the analysis of enactments (e.g., Aron, 2003; Bass, 2003; K. A. Frank, 2002; Maroda, 1998; D. B. Stern, 2003, 2004).
3. I call them so-called because I argue (see following) that in fact silence, interpretation, and the other features of more traditional psychoanalytic practice are no less active interventions than the interventions discussed by Frank. They are simply more familiar and hence, like the water in which a fish swims, more likely not to be noticed.
4. In fact, however, even with silence the reaction is not solely a function of the patient's proclivities. Silences really do differ, and the patient may pick up their differing qualities even if they are not overtly acknowledged. Sometimes silence is very largely an expression of resentment toward the patient; sometimes it really does reflect the therapist's fear of saying something the patient will criticize; sometimes it really is an expression of confidence in the patient's capacities; and so on. The essentially constructivist epistemology that underlies the cyclical psychodynamic approach (cf. I. Z. Hoffman, 1991) suggests that we can never state with absolute certainty what "the" meaning of the silence is. But constructivism is not nihilism. It does not deny that there are different qualities and different intents associated with various silences, and these actual properties of the interpersonal situation can have as much to do with the patient's perception as do the patient's unprompted inclinations.
5. Obviously, given that the fact of the application was a part of the case report, she later told her therapist about it.

Chapter 8

Incorporating the Panther

Toward a More Clinically Seamless Integration in Therapeutic Practice

The last chapter examined some of the implications of an integrative therapeutic strategy that combines a psychoanalytic framework with elements deriving from other orientations. As discussed in Chapter 1, the cyclical psychodynamic project is centered both on such reformulations of therapeutic aims and methods and on the reconfiguration of theory in ways that enable such integrative efforts to be coherent and more than mere eclecticism.

Much of the discussion in the earlier chapters of this book has been directed to the latter element – examining ways that psychoanalytic formulations need to be modified in light of observations that challenge more traditional modes of psychoanalytic theorizing, observations that derive both from the psychoanalytic situation itself and from the research and clinical experience associated with other therapeutic orientations. In this chapter, I wish to turn more directly to some critical elements of integrative practice.

One of the questions that students most frequently ask when introduced to the idea of integration in psychotherapy is "How do you shift from one modality to another?" They are puzzled by the mechanics of transition and disturbed at the sense of awkwardness and disruption that they envision. They lack an image of how one can go smoothly from, say, a psychodynamic mode of exploration to a behavioral mode of intervention (or vice versa). They want to know things like:

- Do you warn the patient when you're going to make a switch?
- How do you go back again?
- When do you decide to do one and when the other?
- Do you do both in the same session, or do you alternate between approaches in different sessions?
- Can one therapist do both, or should the patient see two therapists, one for the analytic work and one for the behavioral work?

These are all important questions and, indeed, even those of us who have been working in an integrative vein for some time are likely to have to acknowledge that the answers are still not always clear and that, in many instances, precise guidelines are still lacking. Part of the problem with such questions, however, is that they do not really stem from an integrative mind-set. They reflect, rather, an *eclectic* orientation, by which I mean one in which separate elements or approaches are used – in a combinative, and often creative, way that proponents of single schools would not consider, but in which those separate elements are not really fused or synthesized. There are still separate "pieces" to the therapy, and so questions of when you use one piece and when the other, when you "switch" from one to the other, and so forth naturally come to mind. Indeed, it is not surprising, in this light, that those who have advanced furthest in attempts to answer the aforementioned questions, who have spelled out the "switching" and "choosing" rules in the most precise and useful detail, have tended to be therapists associated more with the eclectic wing of the effort to transcend schooldom than the integrative wing (e.g., Beitman, 1987; Beutler, 1983; Frances, Clarkin, & Perry, 1984; Norcross, 1986a, 1986b; Prochaska, 1984).

This is not to say that those of us who regard ourselves as integrative rather than as eclectic have achieved fully the synthesis I alluded to earlier. The habits and boundaries associated with the various schools are hard to eclipse, and for most integrative practitioners, integration remains more a goal than a continuous daily reality. Eclecticism in practice and integration in aspiration is an accurate description of what integrative therapists do much of the time. There are, however, occasions when something closer to true integration is achieved, and it is worthwhile to examine those instances, for they may provide clues as to how integration may be achieved in a more thoroughgoing way.

It is my hope that the clinical examples that follow will contribute toward this end, pointing toward the evolution of a more fully integrative approach that sews together what were once separate pieces into a fabric that is coherent and seamless.

Merging and Emerging: The Case of Lillian

At the time of the excerpt I wish to discuss here, therapeutic work with the patient I shall call Lillian was focusing on her social inhibitions. We had been using imagery to help her overcome a difficulty making phone calls to clients. She was instructed, in the fashion of the behavioral technique of flooding, to imagine herself making the call and to imagine the worst possible things that could happen. As she began the imagery, something unexpected happened: Instead of picturing the consequences of her own phone conversations, she had a spontaneous image of merging with her mother, who had always been extraordinarily inhibited and who, among other inhibitions, had great difficulty making phone calls. As she and her mother inhabited the same space in the image, Lillian felt herself cringing, in a quite physical and literal fashion, much as she had sometimes described her mother as doing metaphorically.

I asked her to stay with this image and to see if she could make *this* one worse. She imagined interacting with someone who asked her "Why are you cringing?" Then, unbidden, she pictured herself *unmerging* with her mother. As she did, her mother continued to cringe, while Lillian grew larger, until she was quite large and powerful. This was scary for her at first and then very pleasant and exciting.

The imagery Lillian reported had a very spontaneous quality. Both she and I were surprised by it (though as soon as it happened it had the quality of *"Of course!"*). It did not seem at all intellectualized, deliberate, or designed to please the therapist. Yet it represented, in vivid imagistic form, a set of key issues that had been the focus of interpretive work that had gone on for some time in the therapy. As we followed it up, the "working through" involved not only a good deal of talking about the meaning of what had transpired and of its relation to Lillian's life history, but also a number of deliberate repetitions of the imagery that had earlier arisen spontaneously, repetitions that enabled her to explore further and to integrate both her longings to merge and her longings to emerge.

How would one characterize what was just described? Clearly it was not straightforward behavior therapy and most assuredly not a simple matter of conditioning. Nor, certainly, was it psychoanalysis. Moreover, although it contained elements of both, it clearly was not a simple mixture in which first a bit of one and then a bit of the other was manifested. Rather, what we see here is a kind of melding of the two approaches such that it is very difficult to see where one ends and the other begins.

Incorporating the Panther: The Case of James

Let us look now at another case, which illustrates more clearly and fully the "creative confusion" I am addressing here. James was a quite prominent member of his profession who had, to his great consternation, never passed the licensing exam. He had taken the exam five times before and had failed each time, despite the fact that his professional stature was such that his own work was occasionally addressed on the exam.

Although he presented himself as a case of "test anxiety," and informed me of that self-diagnosis in the first session, it quickly became clear that more was involved. James had grown up in a prominent Boston family and had been taught by his parents, who were quite demanding and status-conscious, that he must not only excel but also must appear to do so effortlessly.

This was not something that James was able at the outset to say directly. At first, I was merely struck by his various efforts to let me know, indirectly but most assuredly, who it was I was dealing with. He worked very hard at conveying both his stature in his profession and his social status, and he seemed very uncomfortable with being in the role of patient. In looking for a way to inquire into this tendency that did not leave James feeling criticized or put down (cf. Wachtel, 2011a), I wondered out loud if his parents had been very concerned about status and what the impact on him might have been. At this, he seemed to experience a good deal of relief and immediately relaxed some. He said yes, they were like that, and it was very oppressive.

James's conscious views were much more liberal than his parents', and this added still further to his dilemma: He could not readily acknowledge his concerns about status, or appreciate the role those concerns played in his life, because he had struggled hard to disavow them and as far as he knew he had done so. By raising them as *his parents'* concerns, I made it possible for him to begin addressing them while still maintaining his view that he himself did not endorse them, indeed while expressing his distaste for them.

Attempting to open further a path for James's exploration of attitudes I sensed were an important part of his difficulties, I then added that it must have been difficult growing up in such an environment not to adopt some of their views simply in self-defense; with their relentless emphasis on status and success, it would have been extremely painful not to attend to this himself. This comment seemed to make it a bit easier for James to take a look at his own concerns about status, most likely because it implicitly conveyed that it was *not his fault* that he felt this way.

Through this process of gentle and gradual confrontation with his disavowed status concerns, James began to recognize that in some way he had viewed the exam as a "pain in the ass" that someone like him should not have to bother with and that he felt humiliated by the impersonal, bureaucratic elements in the application and examination process, which treated him just like everyone else and made him "go through hoops." He recognized as well that he had felt apprehensive and defensive because he experienced an inner demand to outdo everyone else taking the exam while not having to engage in "grubby" preparation as others did. As a consequence of these conflicts, he came to see in this stage of the work, he had not prepared seriously enough the first time he took the exam. The combination of having to be very cool and casual about his preparation and at the same time facing puzzling and intrusive anxiety – anxiety largely prompted by the internal necessity not just to pass but to do spectacularly well *and* to do so without "sweating it" – had made it difficult to find the proper degree of diligence and calm for effective preparation. Needless to say, the pressure and the conflict over how much preparation was appropriate or enough became even greater as he took and failed the exam over and over. Helping James to gain some measure of clarity about how much he *needed* to study and how much his inner voices "allowed" him to study was an important part of this stage of the work.

This initial bit of insight-oriented work interfaced with – and in certain ways modified – the program of behavioral interventions that was to be employed. Although, as I describe shortly, I did indeed use systematic desensitization to help James overcome his test anxiety, I also concentrated more than I otherwise would have on his preparing more thoroughly for the challenge the exam represented. By helping him to see the unacknowledged feelings and ideas that had led him to treat the exam dismissively, the initial work enabled James to address the exam more seriously this time around. As he came to see, it was not just a matter of anxiety that had to be overcome. The anxiety, while in certain respects excessive, and certainly interfering with his performance on the exam, was not entirely unrealistic: it was based in part on his unacknowledged perception that he had not taken the exam seriously enough to be properly prepared.[1]

After working a good deal on the internal pressures which had led James to be dismissive toward the exam and on how he could study for it more seriously this time, we did turn to desensitization. Initially, the major axis for the development of a hierarchy was a temporal one. The images moved from a period considerably before the exam, through increasingly close approaches to his actually appearing at the door, to his sitting down at his desk, to his confronting various of the experiences he would encounter when actually taking the exam.

As we went through these images, the nature of his discomfort became clarified in a number of specific situations. Thus, when he pictured walking into the exam room he became aware of the crowd of exam takers pressing in together and experienced a strong sense of *indignity* at being pushed and at having his identity checked. This, more than any concern about failure, was his primary source of distress with these images. We discussed this in relation to the legacy of his upbringing and it led to an important discussion of his strategy for studying for the exam. He was struggling with dual inclinations to study much harder than anyone else taking the exam and to study much less. We worked on images of his being just one of the crowd until he could imagine this with little discomfort, and he found that this enabled him as well to have a much clearer sense of what would be an appropriate amount of preparation: he could do it "just like everyone else."

Similarly revealing was his reaction to the image of approaching the door of the exam building. It became clear as he immersed himself in the image that another source of discomfort was seeing the guard at the door. He recalled that the same man had been on duty on several occasions and felt very uncomfortable at the idea that this man would see that he was taking the exam still one more time. He worked on this image for much of a session, finally overcoming the anxiety when he pictured himself taking the bull by the horns and saying "good morning" instead of trying to slink in unnoticed (as he realized at some point he was doing in the image).

The most interesting developments occurred when he was picturing visiting the exam room the day before the exam. The aim in this set of imagery exercises was initially for him to acclimate himself to the setting in which the exam would take place. He was asked to look carefully around the room, to touch the various surfaces such as the desk and walls, to experience the lighting, and so forth. It was hoped that thereby some portion of the anxiety he tended to experience in the exam situation could be eliminated.

When he began the imaging, however, a fascinating series of associations and new images came forth. At first, he spontaneously had the association that the room seemed like a morgue and then that the rows of desks seemed like countless graves covering the site of a battlefield. Then he felt overcome with a feeling of impotence. I asked him if he could picture himself as firm and hard, ready to do battle. He did so (I left it ambiguous whether he should take this specifically to mean having an erection or as an image of general body toughness and readiness). He said he felt much better, stronger, and then spontaneously had an image of holding a huge sword and being prepared to take on a dragon. He associated this image to our various discussions of his treating the exam as a worthy opponent, taking it seriously yet being able to master it. He was exhilarated by this image, and I suggested he engage in such imagery at home between sessions, a suggestion he endorsed with great enthusiasm.

In the next session, we began with his again picturing himself visiting the exam room the day before the exam. For a while as he checked out the various features of the room he felt quite calm and confident but suddenly he felt a wave of anxiety, as if something were behind him. I asked him to turn around (imagistically) and see what was there. He reported seeing a large cat, a panther. Here I made a kind of interpretation. I offered that the panther represented his own power and aggression and that it was a threat to him only so long as he kept it outside of him or out of sight. I asked him if he could reappropriate the panther part of him, adding that what he was feeling threatened by was *his own* power, *his own* coiled intensity.

He pictured the panther being absorbed into himself, and the anxiety receded. I then elaborated – quite speculatively, to be sure, but in a way rooted in the understanding we had achieved together about the dynamics of his difficulty with the exam – on why it might be that he had chosen a panther in particular to represent the part of himself that needed to be reappropriated. I noted that panthers were not only strong and purposeful but were also meticulous and supremely respectful of their prey. Despite being awesome creatures, I suggested, panthers did not take their prey lightly. They did not just casually leap out whenever they saw a potential source of nourishment. They did not act as if it were beneath their dignity to stalk for hours, crawling on their bellies. Panthers, I said, were diligent students who became experts on the habits of the creatures they tracked – and experts whose expertise was the result not just of instinct or superb natural equipment but also of attention to detail and a respect for the difficulty of the task of conquest nature required of them. Their grace might look effortless, but it was far from casual; panthers were supremely serious.

Now in all this it is impossible for me to distinguish how much reflected an empathic grasp of the actual layers of meaning that led to James's experiencing that particular image and how much was simply suggestion on my part. The interpretation seems plausible, but at the very least I was gilding the lily, using the panther image to point toward attitudes I felt it would be useful for him to incorporate whether they were the actual sources of the image.[2]

What is important is that my comments were meaningful *to the patient*. Whether or not they accurately depicted the *origins* of the image, they did resonate with the ripples of meaning that the image engendered and they helped to amplify and consolidate the utility of the image itself, which was, after all, James's creation. In further work on the test anxiety and, significantly, later on his own in dealing with a range of other concerns, James, for whom imagery turned out to be a very salient modality, made great use of the panther image and its variants. He aided his efforts at relaxation, for example, by imagining himself as a big cat relaxing and licking himself. When faced with a difficult challenge he imagined again himself and the panther as one, and he felt that he didn't have to be overtly aggressive but knew deep inside he was capable of whatever was necessary. Sometimes he would even imagine himself emitting low murmuring sounds deep in his throat that, as he put it, "remind the panther that it's a panther."

One of my favorites of his spontaneous creative uses of the panther image came later in the desensitization work.[3] We were at the point of his imagining actually sitting and taking the exam when a wonderful smile appeared on his face and he told me he had just had an image that the point of the pencil with which he was writing the exam was actually the claw of the panther; that the panther was firmly within him, incorporated and channeled, and as the claws came through the tips of his fingers they were pencils which were writing out exam answers with very sharp points.

This time around, his points were indeed sharp. After having failed the exam five times previously, this time he not only passed but also did very well. I cannot of course determine whether he would have passed even without therapy of any kind, or whether a more orthodox course of either behavior therapy or psychoanalytic therapy alone (or of any other approach for that matter) would have done just as well. Only systematic research – research of a sort that will tax our powers of persistence and methodological innovation – can enable us to sort out with confidence the many questions that cases like this raise. But the case does illustrate well what can happen when integration moves beyond a little of this and a little of that and begins to be characterized by a more complete synthesis of the disparate elements. In the hands of a creative patient like James, the possibilities are intriguing.

The Evolution of an Integrative Approach

When I first noticed myself working in the way described in this chapter, I was troubled rather than pleased by it. I wondered if I was abandoning my commitment to integrating behavioral methods into my work, because in these (increasingly common) instances I was not quite doing "behavior therapy." Was I regressing to the more traditional practices of the psychoanalytic therapist, practices in which I had originally been trained and which could seem at times almost imprinted upon me?[4]

One reason for this concern was that in my earliest efforts to incorporate behavioral methods into my clinical work, when I employed methods from behavior therapy I did so in a way that was rather orthodox – even if the setting in which they were employed was not. That is, when I used these methods I looked pretty much the way a traditional behavior therapist looked when he or she used them.

Gradually, however, the dividing line began to blur between which aspects of my clinical work were behavioral and which represented the psychodynamic side. Not only did I begin to give a psychodynamic flavoring to my use of behavioral methods, but also my style of carrying through the psychodynamic side of the work – of interpreting, of communicating my understanding, and even of listening – began to be influenced by my increasing immersion in the behavioral point of view.

Some of this shift is conveyed in *Psychoanalysis and Behavior Therapy* (Wachtel, 1977a), where illustrations can be found both of the use of standard behavioral procedures and of some of the ways in which they have been modified in the effort to incorporate them into a dynamically oriented therapy. What I am describing here is how this process of synthesis has continued. In much of the work I do today, it is hard to say which is the psychodynamic and which is the behavioral. The work, one might say, is becoming more seamless. This, it seems to me, is a desirable, if sometimes confusing, state of affairs.

The questions with which this chapter began will probably never go away completely or be completely irrelevant. As we move closer to a truly integrative approach, however, they are likely to become less pressing and intimidating and their answers to take clearer shape. Aided by continually evolving efforts to understand these developments theoretically, by the elaboration of research models sufficiently complex to address the new challenges integrative work presents, and by the spontaneous creative input of patients like Lillian and James, we may perhaps hope that true improvements in our ability to help people can be forthcoming.

Notes

1. One can see here from another vantage point the circular patterns that are at the heart of the cyclical psychodynamic point of view. James's status anxieties and feelings of humiliation led him to avoid studying and to have to treat the exam lightly; this in turn led to further anxiety brought on by the unacknowledged sense of not being prepared, and to failure resulting from both the anxiety *and* the poor preparation. In turn, the failure further heightened both his anxiety about the test and his sense of humiliation and threat to his status, leading to still further avoidance and still further need to be compensatorily cavalier, and making still another failure, and the next repetition of the pattern more likely.

2. My knowledge of the behavior of the big cats, by the way, derives almost exclusively from nature programs on television, of which I am rather fond. My knowledge of the *subjective experience* of these magnificent creatures is of course based on nothing more than some good-natured anthropomorphizing combined with a touch of hokum and a dollop of whimsy. Indeed, some of the vividness of my description came from having seen a nature program the night before; but it was a program on *another* species of big cat, and I still could not say with authority whether panthers in fact spend much time on their bellies or even if they actually stalk prey for hours like lions and tigers do. (According to my earlier careful research on the matter – as a 10-year-old watching Tarzan movies – panthers do much of their hunting by leaping from tree branches.)

3. The fascinating material presented here notwithstanding, it is important to be clear that we *did* continue with the "mundane" desensitization as well, going through the hierarchy and in fact finding that we continued to encounter some points of stubborn anxiety that required diligent repetition before they yielded. Moreover, let me add that this desensitization work proceeded apace with discussions of how James was going about preparing for the exam – discussions in which our friend the panther occasionally made a useful contribution.

4. In fact, of course, I was also not quite doing psychoanalytic therapy in the traditional sense either. That was less troubling, however, both because my thinking remained firmly rooted in the psychodynamic tradition in many respects and because I had thought through more clearly and explicitly my reasons for modifying the more typical way of working in the psychodynamic vein (Wachtel, 1997).

Chapter 9

Thinking about Resistance
Affect, Cognition, and Corrective Emotional Experiences

"Resistance" is one of the most problematic and potentially counterproductive concepts in the entire field of psychotherapy. It is at the same time one of the most crucial, pointing toward perhaps the single most important factor – or, more accurately, set of factors – in determining the success or failure of the therapeutic enterprise. These two statements may seem at first to be contradictory, but as I shall elaborate further, the contradiction is more apparent than real.

Therapists of virtually all orientations report phenomena that can easily be recognized as belonging to this general domain (see, for example, Wachtel, 1982b). All therapists find that their patients behave in ways that, at least in the short run, seem to impede the progress of the therapy and that, on inspection, reflect the manifestation in the therapy itself of the same anxieties, character traits, and problematic behavior patterns that have brought the person into therapy to begin with. And good therapists of all orientations recognize that to blame the patient for these characteristics is inappropriate and counterproductive. The patient is not so much resisting the therapist's efforts as trying to hold on for dear life to whatever safety and stability he has achieved in his life. Or, from another perspective, the patient is simply "being himself," which is, of course, precisely what the therapist wants and expects him to be.[1]

Part of the challenge in conceptualizing resistance lies in this latter observation. As therapists, we want the patient to share with us the full, painful, and sometimes shameful reality of who he is and how he operates in the world. We want him to reveal to us even – or perhaps especially – those things he generally hides from other people. Indeed, we want him to reveal to us as well (again perhaps *especially*) those things he hides even from himself. Without the patient's doing this, our knowledge of him is likely to be superficial or at best hypothetical and abstract; there is no substitute for direct experience and direct observation. But the behavior patterns that create problems for him in his life are likely to create problems for him in the therapy as well, and thus the very characteristics we are (or should be) most eager to see are also the characteristics that are prone to frustrate our efforts.

Ultimately, that frustration itself is a crucial part of the process. From the vantage point of the therapist's role in the therapeutic process, the experience of frustration, as I shall discuss further below, can be a useful guide to where further inquiry is needed and where "pay dirt" lies, as well as an initiator of the exploration of enactments that must be examined and worked through for progress to be made (Aron, 2003; Bass, 2003; Black, 2003; Bromberg, 1998; K. A. Frank, 1999, 2002; Jacobs, 1986; Maroda, 1998; McLaughlin, 1991; D. B. Stern, 2003, 2004). From the vantage point of the patient's role in struggling toward meaningful therapeutic change, often it is only in working through quite directly how he thwarts his own interests or blocks access to full understanding of his yearnings, fears, and subjective experience that real progress is made. *Evading* the resistance is decidedly beside the point.

This is most clear in psychoanalytic work, but it is true in other approaches as well. This was reemphasized for me, along with the complexities and ambiguities in comparing the approach to resistance in different orientations, in participating in an exchange on resistance with therapists from a range of orientations. Davis and Hollon (1999), for example, discussing phenomena of resistance in cognitive therapy in the language of that orientation, note that

> Instances in which a client can't . . . or won't . . . complete an assignment are typically turned into opportunities to identify and explore the client's underlying beliefs and attitudes. These instances often prove particularly instructive; the very beliefs that interfere with the process of therapy are often similar in nature to the kinds of attitudes and values that complicate the pursuit of larger life goals. (p. 42)

Davis and Hollon note the parallels between this perspective on the part of cognitive therapists and the ways that psychodynamic therapists use the experience of difficulties arising in the therapeutic relationship to explore more general maladaptive relationship patterns in the patient's life. But there are important differences as well. One such difference, they say, is that cognitive therapists do not assume that resistance is as universal a phenomenon as is assumed by psychoanalysts. This is both a real difference and a difference that may be overdrawn from either direction to valorize one approach over another. Davis and Hollon, for example, describe four broad lines of explanation they believe account for clients failing to follow through on the therapeutic recommendations of cognitive therapists "client attitudes and beliefs that interfere with compliance or generate resistance; discouragement following the disconfirmation of unrealistic expectations regarding the pace of change; therapist errors that generate noncompliance or resistance; and insufficiency of the therapeutic model" (p. 52). They contend that only the first of these four is encompassed by the psychodynamic concept of resistance. Cognitive therapy, they state, "is distinct from more conventional dynamic therapies in that it does not presume that [processes of resistance] are universal or that their resolution should always be the primary working vehicle of change" (p. 52).

This distinction may be a bit exaggerated, because psychoanalytic understanding of resistance often includes the other considerations that Davis and Hollon (1999) list as separate factors influencing therapeutic failure. Patients' unrealistic expectations of the pace of change that can lead to discouragement and/or withdrawal from the therapeutic process are certainly not unfamiliar to psychoanalytic therapists; nor do the consequences of such expectations – and ideas of how to work with them – lie outside the bounds of what analysts consider in understanding the complexities of resistance. Even more germane, consideration of therapist errors that generate noncompliance or resistance is of central concern to analytic practitioners and their understanding of the multiple ways in which resistance is generated in the course of the work or in how it can be resolved. Conceptions of countertransference, of enactment, or of rupture and repair of the therapeutic alliance (Ruiz-Cordell & Safran, 2007; Safran & Muran, 2000; Safran, Muran, & Proskurov, 2009) all are central to contemporary psychoanalytic practice and to the expanded understanding of resistance as not just a phenomenon residing in the patient's psyche but a product of the co-construction (by patient *and* therapist) of the events and experiences in the session.[2]

Nonetheless, almost all readers would agree that, at the very least, working with the resistances per se is seen as more central to psychoanalytic than to cognitive therapy. In that sense, ironically, resistance is more purely seen *as resistance* by cognitive therapists than by psychoanalysts. For the latter, the phenomena that fall under the rubric of resistance are not some special realm reserved for patients who are especially recalcitrant, difficult, or, as cognitive-behavioral therapists often put it, noncompliant. Rather, these phenomena are both universal and understandable. And working with them is not a "problem" that one must deal with, but the very essence of the therapeutic enterprise, the inevitable corollary of the effort to help the patient recover contact with the parts of himself that he has been fearfully avoiding and casting out.[3] Although, as noted earlier, cognitive therapists too attend to the client's resistance at times to help him come to terms with problematic patterns and avoidances that are evident elsewhere in his life as well, this activity does not have the centrality that it does for psychoanalysis.

Neat Differences in Theory, Overlaps in the Messy Complexities of Practice

Sometimes the differences – and the similarities – between approaches are not all that easy to determine. Both cognitive therapy and psychoanalysis, for example, are often depicted in ways that overly emphasize the verbal and cognitive, and that, for each, obscure the much larger range of influences that are usually essential for significant therapeutic change in each. Thus, Davis and Hollon, in a fairly standard depiction of cognitive therapy, state that, "In cognitive therapy, the client is taught to systematically evaluate the accuracy and utility of his or her beliefs and interpretations, with the expectation that producing change in those interpretations can relieve distress and facilitate adaptive responding" (p. 35). Such a highly intellectualized account of the process of change has parallels with those descriptions of psychoanalysis that place preponderant emphasis on *insight*. In each instance, the therapist who takes this emphasis on the representations inside the person's head too literally is likely to have limited success.

Davis and Hollon note, for example, that although cognitive therapists "invariably center on the identification and evaluation of specific *thoughts* and underlying *assumptions*" (p. 35, italics added), cognitive therapy practice also often includes more strictly behavioral strategies, affectively evocative techniques, and even historical reconstruction. Demonstrating that it is the "cognitive" aspect of purportedly cognitive therapy that is crucial is a difficult case to make.

In parallel fashion, the argument that it is "insight" that is the crucial element in a well-conducted psychoanalytic therapy, although it still has some proponents, sounds increasingly quaint. In contemporary psychoanalytic thought, a much wider range of therapeutic factors is viewed as contributing to change in critically important ways. Indeed, as Eagle (1999) notes, even the once taboo notion of the "corrective emotional experience" has reentered the psychoanalytic mainstream, albeit usually in disguised form using different terminology (see following).

The "official" versions of both cognitive and psychoanalytic therapy may thus appear more arid and intellectualized than these approaches are in the hands of skillful and experienced practitioners. Moreover, even those official versions have been changing rapidly in a more clinically responsive direction. In the psychoanalytic realm, relational formulations, in which the affective interchange between the two people in the room is of central importance, have moved into the mainstream and become increasingly prominent. Similarly, in the cognitive-behavioral realm, more affectively centered approaches have increasingly challenged the drier, more abstract and cognitive versions (e.g., Burum & Goldfried, 2007; Hayes, Follette, & Linehan, 2004; Samoilov & Goldfried, 2000). Eagle's account, however, does highlight what I believe is a generally greater emphasis on the affective dimension among psychoanalysts. In his depiction of resistance, it is most centrally the person's *fear* that change will bring danger or disruption that lies at the heart of resistance, not faulty ideas. To be sure, the conceptualization of Weiss & Sampson (1986), which Eagle highly values (see also Eagle, 1984), places considerable emphasis on faulty *beliefs*, but Weiss & Sampson understand these beliefs as strongly rooted in the person's affective and relational life, and in their account the affective dimension is far more palpable than it tends to be in cognitive therapy.

Resistance and the Therapeutic Relationship

Although I have just noted that resistance (or some such phenomenon – see following regarding problems with this term) is a pervasive phenomenon in virtually all forms of psychotherapy, and even that it can be a very *useful* phenomenon for the therapeutic effort if properly understood and worked with, it is nonetheless the case that resistance can indeed be an impediment and that skillful therapeutic practice induces less resistance than less skilled practice. What one might label as "surplus" resistance is often the product of the therapist's overly rigid or mechanical application of a set of rules learned as the badge of belonging among therapists of a particular therapeutic orientation.

As authors from a range of perspectives have noted (e.g., Davis & Hollon, 1999; Eagle, 1999; Norcross, 2002, 2010; Safran & Muran, 2000), attention to the therapeutic relationship is a crucial factor in minimizing the kinds of resistance that hamper therapeutic progress. Davis and Hollon make the interesting point that clients in cognitive therapy are "in essence, being asked to suspend belief in [their] existing self-concept or world-view" and thus that participation in cognitive therapy often requires a "leap of faith" (p. 36). They note as well, following Safran and Segal (1990), that "cognitive therapy is inseparable from the interpersonal context in which it is delivered" (p. 36). Thus, establishing a relationship in which the patient or client has sufficient trust in the therapist to make that leap of faith, at least on a trial basis, is a crucial part of successful therapy.

From a different vantage point, Eagle (1999) similarly points to the crucial role of the therapeutic relationship. He notes that increased resistance can be a sign that the patient feels unsafe, and that such feelings of danger can derive from the ways that the therapist unwittingly communicates disparagement or structures the relationship in ways that are aversive or threatening (cf. Wachtel, 2011a). Eagle notes the research findings linking good therapeutic outcome to the quality of the therapeutic alliance and suggests that

> No matter how accurate or clever the therapist's interpretations may be, if the patient does not experience the therapist as helpful and supportive and as engaged with him or her in a joint effort, change is not likely to occur. (p. 29)

Put differently, the quality of the therapeutic relationship is a crucial determinant of the degree of resistance that is generated.

Again, using the relationship – and attending to the quality of the relationship – is not unique to psychoanalysis. I have already noted the relevance of these considerations in the practice of cognitive therapy. Further considering the Davis and Hollon (1999) article mentioned earlier, we may note a case they reported in which the client felt intense anxiety about performing poorly and being embarrassed on job interviews but had difficulty talking about this with his therapist because the idea of telling his therapist about his anxieties stirred still further feelings of shame; he was "not supposed" to have a hard time with such things. Only when the therapist expressed his own feelings of puzzlement and frustration at not being able to figure out what was going on did the patient begin to open up. Davis and Hollon's account emphasized an element of modeling – "the therapist's own ability to admit failure without regarding it as a threat to his self-esteem facilitated the client's own self-disclosure" (p. 40). One can note as well, however, a number of other dimensions to this set of events that illustrate the impact of the therapeutic relationship, including what systemic and strategic therapists refer to as the "one-down position." From this vantage point, people resist being forced or pressured to do something. When the therapist took the position that he was helpless to *make* the client open up to him, the client then felt more able to *choose* to do so.

It is useful to note, in this regard, that the original formulation of the resistance concept by Freud occurred in a context (see following) in which Freud was trying to wrest from the patient memories and desires that the patient was seen as trying to hide. Over time, Freud's understanding, and that of other analysts, became more sophisticated and, as Eagle (1999) points out, the primary vector shifted from a view of the patient as in essence recalcitrant and stubborn to a view that emphasized his *fear* of what might emerge. The more demeaning – and implicitly coercive – view remained in many analytic formulations, however, likely increasing the degree of resistance that analysts saw. Eagle notes, for example, Dewald's (1982) distinction between what he calls tactical resistance – deriving from the patient's anxiety about becoming aware of unconscious wishes and conflicts – and strategic resistance, which Dewald argues derives from the patient's resistance to giving up the wish to *gratify his infantile desires*. According to Dewald, in strategic resistance, the patient is "reluctant to accept in the present what is age-appropriate and realistically possible, rather than the impossible, no longer appropriate, and outmoded satisfactions and relationships" (p. 49). Such a conceptualization, in which the patient is viewed as stubbornly infantile and reluctant to "accept . . . what is age-appropriate" sets up an adversarial power struggle and is likely to result in a therapeutic relationship which, subtly or grossly, attempts to wrestle with the patient to force this infantile, recalcitrant child to "grow up" and participate more maturely and appropriately in the therapy (Aron, 1991).

This approach to resistance, rather than going *with* the resistance – empathically (and appropriately) *validating* the patient's defensive efforts (Schechter, 2007) even as the therapist also skillfully helps the patient to relinquish them – is more likely to go *against* the resistance, and thereby to increase it. A number of psychoanalytic writers in recent years have pointed to the problematic implications of viewing the patient as stubbornly holding to infantile modes of thought and as needing to *renounce* those wishes once the therapy has gotten him to achieve insight into their existence and their infantile nature (see, for example, Aron, 1991; Mitchell, 1986, 1991; Wachtel, 2008, 2011a; Wile, 1984, 1985). Aron (1991) has been particularly forceful and incisive on this matter:

> The traditional view of the analytic process emphasizes an ethic of renunciation and sacrifice in the service of health and maturity. Analysis is compared to weaning or mourning, and the focus is on pleasures which needs to be relinquished and abandoned. The focus on gaining ego control over infantile drives, and on mastering infantile strivings by relinquishing them, lends itself to the abuses of a "maturity morality." Patients can easily come to feel that the analyst wants them to "grow up." Patients are likely to feel that the analyst is judgmental and is awaiting the day when they stop acting childishly and begin to act maturely. This is not a projected transference fantasy which

needs to be analyzed as a distortion. It is often an accurate perception of the analyst's attitudes rationalized by theoretical beliefs. (pp. 90–91)

Aron (1991) adds that this attitude on the analyst's part "can lead to a prolonged impasse or perhaps worse, to a resolution of symptomatology on the basis of submission and external compliance" (p. 91). It can, as well, create a good deal of additional, *iatrogenic* resistance. There is little reason to strive wholeheartedly for insight when such "insights" point so inexorably toward renunciation. A contrasting approach to insight, central to the cyclical psychodynamic point of view, entails helping the patient to see more clearly what he really desires *so that he can more effectively achieve* those desires and better integrate them into his evolving sense of self and of life's possibilities (Wachtel, 2011a). To be sure, in the process, some of what he has strived for is likely to appear anachronistic in the context of his current life or a source of repetitive frustrations or painful experiences. But through the lens of the clinical approach described in this book (see also Wachtel, 2008, 2011a, 2011b), those problematic consequences are more likely to be the product of *already* excessive efforts to renounce his most vital strivings – related to what Kohut (1977) has called disintegration products – rather than an indication that *still more* renunciation is required. The person's yearnings, from this point of view, remain "infantile" seeming because their healthy, evolving manifestation have been hampered by fear, guilt, and shame, and consequently misrepresented and contorted. When they are reappropriated by the patient, when the therapeutic work has diminished the guilt, fear, and shame with which they have become associated, they become a source of greater vitality in living, not a dangerously infantile "regressive" underpinning to the personality.

Resistance and Corrective Emotional Experience

There is no one appropriate stance with regard to resistance, as there is no one appropriate stance in clinical work in general. Weiss (1998), for example, has commented, discussing work approached from the orientation of his joint work with Sampson and the Mt. Zion group (see, for example, Weiss & Sampson, 1986; Silberschatz, 2005), that in working with patients who "suffer primarily from the belief that they have no right either to have their own opinions or to question the opinions of authorities," it is important that the therapist particularly refrain from expressing her own opinion too insistently and that she encourage the patient's own judgments on matters. He adds, however, that "if patients suffer primarily from the belief that they do not deserve protection" (p. 421), the therapist may be more helpful by being more active and assertive, conveying to the patient that she will not be neglectful or passive as perhaps the patient's parents were. For Weiss, these various choices facing the therapist constitute a "test" which the patient unconsciously creates, a test in which the patient can see whether there is any possibility that the constricting assumptions by which he has lived his life might be able to be challenged. If the therapist "passes" the test, there is increased prospect of change. If the therapist "fails" the test, does not appreciate the nature of the familiar enactment into which she is being drawn, then change is impeded.

In discussing Weiss & Sampson's (1986) work, Eagle (1999; see also Eagle, 1984) offers a case illustration in which the patient offered a gift to his analyst. In the example Eagle describes, the analyst tactfully refused the gift, in part because it "violated the analytic contract," and salutary developments followed. As Eagle describes it,

> The patient's presentation of the gift unconsciously represented a test to determine whether or not the analyst was easily seducible. The analyst's tactful refusal of the gift constituted test passing, which then made it safe to bring into awareness and into the therapeutic session hitherto warded off material. (p. 13)

But Weiss's perspective, noted earlier, implicitly raises a question about the very analytic contract to which Eagle (1999) refers. For some patients, it may feel securely protective and, as Eagle suggests, a sign that the analyst would not be easily seduced. But as Eagle also notes, there is more than one way to understand the sequence he describes. And, however we understand this particular case, there are surely cases in which the patient's predominant childhood experience was of parents who hewed rigidly to strict rules or who could not accept that their child had something useful to offer *them*. In such cases, even tactful refusal of an offer of a gift may constitute failing rather than passing the test, whereas reflective acceptance of the gift – assuming it is not so large or significant that it creates a genuine conflict of interest or ethical breach – may be therapeutic and healing. Skillful attention to the nuances of the therapeutic relationship, and how it might constitute either a continuation or a disconfirmation of the problematic patterns established earlier in the patient's life, can go a long way toward diminishing the "surplus resistance" that can sink the therapeutic effort.

These considerations, of course, point once again to the concept, long taboo in psychoanalytic discourse, of the corrective emotional experience. It was Alexander and French (1946) who introduced the idea that the therapist should be alert to the patient's dominant problematic experiences in childhood and should strive to offer the patient a direct experience in the therapeutic relationship that provides an alternative relational model. Much like Weiss et al. (1986; see Wachtel & DeMichele, 1998), Alexander and French aimed to provide the patient with an experience that demonstrated that the assumptions and way of life that resulted from his unfortunate early experiences were not representative of human relationships in general and did not provide an unshakeable portent of what was to come if he dared to experience himself or others differently or if he dared to behave and construct his life differently from what he concluded was necessary on the basis of his interactions with his parents.

Eagle (1999) notes that the contemporary (and repackaged) versions of this concept have been shorn of the putatively authoritarian or manipulative quality that was perceived by many in the psychoanalytic community as implicit in Alexander and French's approach. Indeed, although the basic idea of the corrective emotional experience is pervasive in the work of Kohut and his followers, of Weiss and Sampson and the Mt. Zion group, and of many object relations theorists, few actually dare speak its name (cf. Wachtel, 2006, 2008; Wachtel & DeMichele, 1998). Eagle (1999, 2003) is noteworthy among psychoanalytic writers in his willingness to be explicit in referring to this idea.

Resistance and Values

Psychotherapy is not a value-free enterprise. As a consequence, determining just what constitutes resistance can be less straightforward than many discussions seem to imply. An operational definition that resistance is what the therapist sees as resistance or calls resistance might satisfy those who – as with "intelligence is what intelligence tests measure" – are soothed by such pseudoscientific mumbo-jumbo, but it does little to enable us to gain much of a foothold on what really is in the patient's interest.

Reid (1999), for example, writing on resistance from a cultural perspective, describes a case he saw while working on a Navajo reservation. A very bright young man had won a scholarship to attend college but was in danger of failing out and beset by depression. As they explored the problem, it became apparent that at the heart of his academic difficulties were frequent visits from friends and relatives from the reservation, who, right after he had received his living expenses from the scholarship, would descend on him, use the money to buy beer, feed themselves, and party. The patient, although trying to maintain his studies amid these distractions, would end up cutting classes to earn extra money, because all the money for his living expenses went to these "visits" from home. When the money ran out, these "friends" would return to the reservation, only to return for another visit when the next scholarship installment came in. It was this pattern that was leading the patient to be failing out of school, and it seemed to be a pattern he felt helpless to resist.

As Reid (1999) put it, "The solution seemed obvious to his New York City reared therapist – 'tell the free loaders that enough is enough'" (p. 72). He attempted to encourage greater assertiveness and independence on the patient's part, noting that he tried to do so subtly and noncoercively. But the patient, although clearly miserable with the state of affairs he was dealing with and the direction his life was taking, said it was impossible to act differently because he had an obligation to share whatever he had with his family and clan members. Reid asked him, "Don't they understand that they are jeopardizing your chances in college?" and the patient replied, "They don't think much of college for Indians since there are no good jobs back home. They just want me to have a good time." Exasperated, his therapist said, "Can't you tell them that you want to make something of yourself?" and received the reply "Oh, no! They would think I was trying to be better than everyone else. I would be shamed" (p. 73).

"Around and around we went," Reid said. "He was trapped between cultures and neither of us could find a way out for him. His depression was ameliorated with medication. He kept his appointments for a while, then he stopped. To my knowledge, he never completed college" (Reid, 1999, p. 73).

Was the readiness of Reid's patient to accommodate to the expectations of his friends and his tribal traditions a lack of assertiveness, and was his reluctance to take on Reid's value system (a value system which in this respect is probably shared by the vast majority of readers) a reflection of resistance? Or alternatively, as Reid suggests in later reflecting on the case, was this an instance of a therapist selling his own value system and failing to be respectful of and attentive to what mattered most to the patient? The answer to such a question is not context free. The therapist's aims and values will shape how she sees such dilemmas, which, perhaps in less obvious ways, develop in virtually all therapies.

Other examples offered by Reid highlight still other dimensions of the potential clash of cultural values and assumptions, and of the ways in which resistance can, in essence, be *constructed* as a phenomenon by the therapist's interpretation of what is transpiring. There can be many reasons beside the one Reid offers – "she is used to doing a number of things simultaneously" – for a Native American mother to bring her children into a therapy session. But what is most important in the present context is that not only may the therapist's and the patient's construction of the event differ significantly, but the therapist's wish that she *not* bring the baby may seem decidedly odd to the patient – and to her community as well.

Similar clashes of perception regarding what is right and normal regularly occur between patients and their parents (or children) as well as between patients and their therapists. Reid notes, for example, the ways in which parents who hold more traditional values may differ from their children whose values are more individualistic and less defined by the family or group.

The examples offered by Reid in discussing the role of cultural values in what might be construed as resistance share a common theme. They all reflect choices regarding a rather fundamental dilemma in human life generally, and especially one experienced by people caught between more traditional cultures and the highly individualized culture of the United States and Western Europe. This dilemma or conflict has been discussed, among others, by Fromm (1941) in terms of individuation versus aloneness, by Bakan (1966) in terms of agency versus communion and the "duality of human existence," and by Blatt (2008) in terms of interpersonal relatedness and self-definition. Modern industrialized cultures tend to emphasize the more differentiating end of each duality, emphasizing autonomy and what in psychoanalytic terms is referred to as separation-individuation (cf., Aron & Starr, 2013). Although therapists in this and similar societies probably tend to have higher regard for the relatedness dimension than the population at large, they are nonetheless usually products of the highly individualistic culture that the United States shares with other modern industrialized societies. As a consequence, they are likely to harbor values that emphasize growing *away* from the context of the family in various ways and differentiating oneself from the embedding matrix of the culture at large (cf. Wachtel, 1983). Their emphasis on relatedness is more likely to be on a kind of *voluntary* relatedness more associated with friends (and, in our divorce-prone society, with spouses) than with family, especially extended family. Other cultures, however – and people in our own culture closer to more traditional values – order the keys to the good life in quite different fashion. Apropos Weiss & Sampson's (1986) view that at the heart of many patients' difficulties is the unconscious belief that separating from one's parents and leading an independent life is tantamount to seriously harming or destroying them, it is essential to be aware that in certain cultures and subcultures it *is* experienced by parents as cruel and hurtful, and even devastating, if their children separate from them to the degree that is common – and regarded as healthy – in American society. This does not mean that we should necessarily abandon our efforts as therapists to help our patients achieve greater self-realization. But it does mean that there are often more complex value conflicts involved than we are comfortable acknowledging.

Reid emphasizes that the degree of consonance between the patient's and therapist's implicit value systems and ways of constructing the world may be a significant factor in determining how much resistance is manifested in the therapy. More than whether the therapist is psychoanalytic or cognitive-behavioral or whatever, the crucial factor may be whether the patient experiences the therapist as someone who sees the world as he does, or at the very least, as someone who understands and respects the way he sees the world.

Is Resistance the Right Term?

Freud introduced the term *resistance* at a very early stage in the history of psychoanalysis, and its formulation, I suggest, reflected the convergence of several considerations at once. To begin with, from the very outset of psychoanalysis, Freud conceptualized the therapeutic process in such a way that it was virtually coterminous with his research aim. That is, it was *discovering* what had been hidden or not understood that would be curative in his view – an assumption that was very convenient for a researcher whose research subjects were also his patients. Freud was very explicit in his more autobiographical writings that he lacked what he called therapeutic zeal. He aimed to be remembered most of all as a discoverer. Blockages in the patient's associations, premature termination of the therapy, missed sessions, and so forth were therefore not only impediments to the therapeutic process but to Freud's interest in *finding out* what was hidden in the recesses of the patient's unconscious.

Resistance, therefore, had from the beginning a double-edged quality that different therapists or different readers of the psychoanalytic literature could interpret differently. On the one hand, the notion of resistance could be read – and accurately read – as a wise and humane concept that pointed to the painful reality that the same anxieties and other difficulties that plagued the patient in his life generally were likely to show up in the therapy. It could alert the therapist to this likelihood, enabling her to be more sophisticated and effective in her efforts to help the patient and, in particular, to use the occurrence of these disruptions in the therapy room to the advantage of the therapeutic effort.

On the other hand, the parentage of the concept and the term includes, I believe, Freud's *own* interests, which did not always coincide with those of the patient as thoroughly as he liked to believe (Wachtel, 1987, Chapter 12). That is, Freud's experience, I suggest, was often of the patient resisting *his* efforts to make discoveries. The damned patient wouldn't come across with the goods!

Those who see the concept of resistance as simply *blaming* the patient, placing the locus of any lack of progress in the therapy on the patient's recalcitrance, miss (whether for reasons of ideology or narrowness of vision) the more humane and sophisticated aspects of the concept. But they are not distorting in a vacuum, as it were. There *is* such a thread woven into the concept of resistance, a thread that was inserted into the fabric of the concept at the very origins of psychoanalytic therapy and investigation and that, I believe, continues to be evident not infrequently in the ways that analysts talk about their patients. It can be said – and I would be the first to say so – that when resistance is understood in such a demeaning or adversarial way (with the patient viewed as recalcitrant, infantile, manipulative, trying to extract forbidden gratifications, and so forth – cf. Wile, 1984), this is a *miscarriage* of the concept, a *faulty* way of conceptualizing and thinking about resistance. But it is not a mistake that has no foundation in the history of psychoanalytic thought and practice.

The varied meanings of resistance lead to ambiguities that are at once evocative and hard to assign a really clear meaning. Thus Eagle (1999) refers to mental representations that are "highly resistant to change" (p. 20). What exactly does resistant to change mean here? One may call to mind the classic Henny Youngman line in which, asked the question "How is your wife?" Youngman would respond, "Compared to what?" In saying that certain representations are highly resistant to change, we can similarly ask, compared to what? That is, is the assumption that there is something inherently sticky about those representations? Is there something in the way they are coded and laid down in the nervous system that renders them less responsive to new experiences that might alter them? Or, alternatively, is what makes them *seem* more resistant to change that they are closely linked to interpersonal action sequences in which, consistent with the arguments presented in this book, their effect is to evoke behavior that recreates the same experience again? In the latter case, the representation itself might be no more resistant to change than any other representation, but merely less likely to actually be confronted with new, potentially disconfirming experiences that could activate their potential for change or accommodation.

Eagle (1999) notes, for example, that part of how early mental representations are maintained with little change over the years is that they repeatedly lead us to form and transform relationships so that they conform to our early acquired expectations and schemas. One of the primary ways that we do this is to behave in particular ways that will elicit just those responses from the other that will tend to perpetuate early relationship patterns. (p. 20)

It will be evident to the reader that this idea is a central theme of this entire book.

Resistance and Variations in Therapeutic Communication

When the concept of resistance is used problematically, the absence of therapeutic progress is essentially attributed almost exclusively to the patient. It is *the patient* who is resistant. More satisfactory conceptualizations of resistance attribute much of the variance to the therapist and/or to her techniques. From such a vantage point, resistance is at the very least a product of the dyad rather than the patient alone. The therapist, from this viewpoint, bears a greater burden of responsibility, but also has more opportunity to use her skills to reduce resistance, or at least to reduce *surplus* resistance (see earlier).

Much of my own work in recent years has been especially concerned with precisely this aim of reducing surplus resistance. Eagle (1999) notes that the cues the therapist gives out can make a substantial difference in the kind and degree of resistance that is encountered. Some of those cues are unconscious, a product of the therapist's conflicts or her countertransference. But much of what we convey to the patient is in our conscious control and can be presented in more effectively therapeutic ways if we are alert to the numerous dimensions and subtleties of our communications to the patient (Wachtel, 2011a). Reframing a patient's relapse as an opportunity rather than just a setback (see, for example, Prochaska & Prochaska, 1999) is a good example of the kind of therapeutic communication that may diminish resistance. On the other hand, Davis and Hollon's (1999) cognitive-behavioral reframing of the psychoanalytic notion of infantile motivations into "dysfunctional beliefs" (p. 41) seems to me less adequate. Saying to someone, in essence, that "you're not infantile, you're just dysfunctional" is unlikely to be especially heartwarming a message, notwithstanding the brief emotional lift the first few words might generate until the rest of the sentence is heard. (Compare in this regard Wile's [1984] discussion of similarly thin improvements in some of Kohut's reformulations of standard psychoanalytic conceptualizations.)

Practicing psychotherapy is among the most rewarding *and* most frustrating endeavors known to man. Much of what ultimately determines which of the two poles will be more dominant lies, I believe, in the balance between pejorative and empathic readings of the patient's behavior. The phenomena traditionally labeled as resistance can be a medium for either kind of reading. It is in understanding so-called resistance in more salutary and humane ways that the frustration can be reduced and the rewards (for patient and therapist alike) expanded.

Notes

1. As I noted in the end notes for Chapter 1, I use the male pronouns *he* or *his* when referring in generic terms to the *patient* and the female pronouns *she* and *her* when referring in generic terms to the *therapist*.

2. Perhaps the fourth source of therapeutic failure cited by Davis and Hollon (1999) – the inappropriateness of one's preferred therapeutic approach for this particular patient – is one that is insufficiently considered by analysts. But in this, they do not differ from therapists of any other orientation. The assumption of the superiority of one's own approach over the approach of others is by no means the exclusive possession of psychoanalytic therapists. Indeed, despite Davis and Hollon's admirable introduction of this idea in considering why cognitive therapy may sometimes fail, it has not been my experience that cognitive or cognitive-behavioral therapists are notable for the modesty of their claims about the superiority of their approach to that of psychodynamic therapy.

3. Confusion about this was introduced by the very usage of the term *resistance* by Freud, a usage that, as discussed later in this chapter, reflected his stronger aim to be a great discoverer than to be a great healer.

Chapter 10

Should Psychoanalytic Training Be Training to Be a Psychoanalyst?

The question I am raising may strike some readers as peculiar. Psychoanalytic training and training to be a psychoanalyst have been so closely associated historically that it is easy to equate the two unreflectively. But they are not necessarily the same thing, and our efforts to devise the most effective and forward-looking training model require us to be clear about the differences and their implications.

The distinction I am alluding to is between, on the one hand, training in a particular point of view and a particular set of empirical discoveries and, on the other, training in a particular technique. The conflating of the two is rooted in both the history and the language of psychoanalysis. As we are frequently reminded in the literature, the term *psychoanalysis* has three meanings: a theory of the mind; a method of treatment; and a method of research. A usual assumption that accompanies this tripartite description is that the three dovetail very nicely and enhance each other. Our theory guides our practice, which in turn (because our very method of therapy is "exploratory") provides us with new data that help us to modify and improve our theory; the new discoveries then help us to increase still further the effectiveness of our therapeutic efforts. It is a pretty picture, but I am not at all sure it is an accurate one.

This picture came closest to being accurate – indeed had a considerable degree of truth – in Freud's own work and, to some degree, in the work of some of the other early analysts. Freud was engaged in a bootstrap operation. He had to invent both his theory and his therapeutic method and – for both substantive and economic reasons – he had to rely on his practice as the chief source of his research. It is one of the marks of his genius that he could pull this off. He did indeed modify his techniques as he made new discoveries. As he gained greater understanding of the role of resistance and defenses, for example, he placed greater emphasis on their analysis as essential to effective treatment. This in turn, by directing more of his attention to resistance and defense phenomena – remember that the treatment technique was also the laboratory for his research – led to greater theoretical understanding of these phenomena, which in turn further modified the treatment technique.

But relying on his treatment method as his almost exclusive research tool had a high cost, both for therapy and for research. As Freud would be the first to point out, no gains are achieved in human affairs without some price; nothing is achieved without something else being given up. As brilliant and important as Freud's solution was, it had its limitations and introduced its own distortions. We in the psychoanalytic community, who are most of all students of conflict, must not fall into the bland and rose-colored view that the needs of research and the needs of therapy never clashed. Doing his research via the practice of his therapy was a brilliant tactic, and probably an essential one at that stage, but it had its consequences both for research and for therapy.

Consequences for Research

The consequences for research are probably more obvious. To begin with, any science that relies so exclusively on one method for gathering its data – even if the method is relatively sound – is highly vulnerable. The danger is increased very substantially when, in addition, the method is one that relies very heavily on subjective considerations and on data whose implications require elaborate inter-pretive efforts and, further, are not usually reported in their original form but as filtered through the interpretive assumptions of the reporter.[1] The danger is further compounded when the method is one in which the controls typical of scientific investigation are very largely lacking.

To be sure, analysts with a research bent are increasingly trying to do something about these limitations, engaging in such activities as systematic observation of infants and children, experimental investigations of psychoanalytic propositions, or innovative attempts to use computers, tape recorders, and other technological aids to use the therapeutic situation for research that is truly research in the mod-ern sense (e.g., Beebe & Lachmann, in press; Blatt, 2008; Bornstein & Masling, 1998; Curtis, 2009; Fonagy, Gergely, Jurist, & Target, 2002; Luborsky, 1996; Masling, 2000; Shahar, Cross, & Henrich, 2004; Shedler, Mayman, & Manis, 1993; Westen, 1998; Westen & Shedler, 2007).

Much of the impetus for these research efforts derives from concerns (of the sort just noted) regarding the status of psychoanalytic data as *evidence* for psycho-analytic propositions. But, perhaps even more important in the present context, it almost certainly derives as well from a recognition that there are very substantial limits to how much we can continue to rely on the practice of the therapeutic method we call psychoanalysis as the primary source of *new* discoveries in our field. Freud was able to do wonders with this method, both because he was an individual of unusual genius and – we should not forget – because he was essen-tially starting from scratch. The method he used was a marvelous initial explora-tory procedure. But there is good reason to think that we have discovered most of what this method as a research tool (unaided by modern technological and methodological innovations) is capable of yielding. After more than one hundred years of using this method for our research, the vein has been rather thoroughly mined. This is important for us to come to terms with, not only because it can lead us to look for other strategies of gaining further knowledge – about unconscious motives, conflicts, and mental structures, the ways early developmental experiences contribute to shaping later behavior and experience, and other topics of fundamental concern to the psychoanalytic point of view, but not necessarily best investigated via the clinical practice of psychoanalysis – but also because one key reason why the practice of psychoanalysis proper (in contrast to other therapeutic applications of the psychoanalytic point of view) is still regarded as the centerpiece of psychoanalytic training is the notion that it is through the use of this method that the continuing course of discovery in our field can best be approached.

Consequences for Therapy

I have spoken thus far about the limitations introduced by attempting to use the clinical practice of psychoanalysis as a research tool, and I have noted that a number of leading psychoanalytic thinkers have been aware of the problematic implications of this for psychoanalytic research. In contrast, the task of considering how psychoanalysis as a *therapeutic* method may have been limited by its simultaneous role as the discipline's chief method of research has scarcely begun. One might wonder, for example, whether we have assumed too readily that the exploration and uncovering that are essential to the research task of psychoanalysis also happens to be exactly what is most important in bringing about therapeutic change. That would certainly be a convenient gift for Nature to bestow on us, but Freud has taught us to be wary of Nature's ironic sense of humor. We might also wonder, in this context, whether detailed exploration of the patient's past is as essential to the therapeutic aim of helping the patient change the patterns of living which distress him – patterns which, whatever their origins, have by now been built into the warp and woof of his relationships with others and have become self-perpetuating – as it is to the research aim of understanding the etiology of the disorder.

In any event, we are left with a situation in which the aims of both research and therapy have rested upon the same method, thus giving that method a weight and centrality that is probably unparalleled in any discipline. That would not necessarily be problematic if there were clear evidence that in fact the particular clinical application of psychoanalytic thought that we call psychoanalysis proper did yield results that were special. It has been a largely unquestioned assumption in the psychoanalytic community that this is the case – that an "analysis" can produce greater change than any form of psychoanalytic *psychotherapy* (at least if the patient is "analyzable"). But in fact evidence for this assumption is lacking – at least evidence conforming with any reasonable canons; that is, evidence that does not require being convinced of the truth of the proposition to begin with in order to be persuaded.

What evidence there is regarding the comparative effectiveness of analysis proper and psychoanalytic therapy does not point to such a unique role for psychoanalysis. Wallerstein (1988, 1989), reporting on the results of the Menninger study, notes that his own expectations were considerably challenged by the study, in which full-scale analyses did not accomplish any greater discernable change than did psychotherapies that were expected to have substantially less effectiveness. As in any study, questions can be raised and I am not characterizing these finding as definitive. But clearly a report by a former president of the American Psychoanalytic Association on a study conducted at one of the foremost psychoanalytic training and treatment centers in the United States cannot be dismissed as an antipsychoanalytic diatribe.

The implications of studies such as this should not be misinterpreted. The reasonable conclusion to draw from the research conducted thus far is not the nihilistic one of a range of implacably antipsychoanalytic critics, from Eysenck, to Frederick Crews, to the keepers of the various lists of purportedly empirically supported treatments (see Wachtel, 2010). The Menninger study, like much other research (see, for example, the important review by Shedler, 2010), does show that therapies guided by psychoanalytic principles have a demonstrable therapeutic effect. Rather, the issue is that the evidence for the effectiveness of psychoanalytically conceived therapies in general is not matched by evidence for the superiority of the particular set of psychoanalytic therapies that get called psychoanalysis over those that get called psychotherapy. (I put it this way because by now the definition of "psychoanalysis" as contrasted with "psychotherapy" is a matter far more in contention than it was in the 1950s or 1960s).

Model T or Rolls-Royce?

In no other field is the original research tool and/or the original method still used with anything like the fidelity to the original that we find in psychoanalysis. To put it kindly, our ideas and methods seem to be more "enduring" than those of other disciplines; their rate of obsolescence is rather slow.

One can legitimately question, of course, how close the methods in use by analysts today really are to the original method. Clearly there have been changes over the years, from the increasing sophistication over time by Freud and other early analysts regarding the analysis of transference and resistance, to the changes later introduced by object relations theorists or self-psychologists, to the more contemporary innovations of relational analysts. But it is easy for those of us who are immersed in the field, and hence acutely aware of subtle differences, to overestimate the extent of these changes. To the outside observer, it is likely to appear that the apples have not really fallen very far from the tree. The continuities in practice over the years are impressive. The fact that for so long we could still use a term such as "classical analysis" (and that indeed some still do) with little sense of irony or embarrassment attests to that. Consider how bizarre (and terrifying) it would be if you were questioning an individual who was about to perform surgery on you and were told that he or she practiced "classical surgery."

One of the central factors constraining change in our practice is the tendency in the psychoanalytic community to draw a sharp distinction between psychoanalysis and psychotherapy. This sharp distinction – in the face of what it takes real effort not to see as a continuum – has a constraining effect on the practice both of what is called psychoanalysis and of what is called psychoanalytically oriented psychotherapy. If one introduces too much innovation, however therapeutically useful it turns out to be, one is open to the charge that what one is doing is not really analysis, it is only "psychotherapy."[2]

One effect of this is that innovations are more readily introduced in the context of psychotherapy than in analysis. But even in the realm of "psychotherapy," there is considerable constraint by virtue of the way in which the distinction is used in the psychoanalytic community. For one of the chief purposes of the dichotomy is an honorific rather than descriptive one. If we look between the lines at how the distinction is used – if we look with the hard, honest gaze Freud modeled for us – we can see that there is, not far below the surface, a clear implication that being a psychoanalyst is *better* than being a psychotherapist. Consider, for example, how different to our ears are the following two sentences: "That was not analysis, that was just psychotherapy." And: "That was not psychotherapy, it was just psychoanalysis." The first sounds unexceptionable. It is familiar and seems to make sense. We have all heard and read sentences like it many times. The second sentence, I would venture to say, might, if you read it, first strike you as a typo. It seems to make no sense. No one ever says such a thing. Nor does anyone ever refer in our literature, in any context, to "merely psychoanalysis" in the way that "merely psychotherapy" is a part of the language our ears are attuned to hear.

Given this state of affairs, it is not surprising that those who practice psychoanalytically oriented psychotherapy tend to try to model it as closely as possible after psychoanalysis itself. The differences one finds tend to be differences viewed as necessary because of exigencies of time, money, or patient characteristics; they are not differences derived from an effort to *improve* upon psychoanalysis.

Such a strategy for the development of a psychoanalytic approach to therapy makes sense only if we assume that the *procedure* or *technique* we call psychoanalysis is the best that the *intellectual tradition* of psychoanalysis can do. It is the latter, I believe, that is our real source of strength, and it is being seriously constrained by a reverence for a method that served its purpose well at the time it was developed, but which should by now be viewed as outmoded and in need of being replaced. We continue to treat psychoanalysis (in contrast with psychotherapy) as the Rolls-Royce of treatments. We might well regard it instead as the Model T – a very fine model for its time but not a cutting-edge application of what we have learned in the years since it was fashioned.

Now to some readers these comments – particularly the suggestion that the clinical method we call analysis may be outmoded – are likely to sound dismissive or even antipsychoanalytic. My intent is quite the opposite, I take psychoanalysis very seriously – seriously enough not only to have devoted much of my professional life to studying and writing about it but, even more important, seriously enough to think that its enormous potential has only begun to be fulfilled, and seriously enough to be interested in what might be holding it back. I ask you to consider: Does it seem similarly disrespectful toward another of the great geniuses in the history of Western thought – Galileo – to notice how the power of his telescope pales before the great reflector at Mount Palomar or the various electronic devices currently in use to explore the secrets of the stars and galaxies? Placed in its historical context, Galileo's telescope remains an epoch-making achievement – and not the least of the marks of its greatness is the transcendent modifications it has spawned. Do we really honor Freud by attributing to his discoveries less of a capacity to spur new inventions – new inventions of the sort that, in any fruitful sphere of scholarship, necessarily render obsolete those methods with which it began? By holding on so to the particular therapeutic method called psychoanalysis as an ideal, we betray what *should* be our ideal – the continually evolving insights into the human condition that Freud set us on the path to attaining.

These considerations lead me to a conclusion that may seem paradoxical at first but that I believe on closer examination is perfectly straightforward. The best way to be true to the psychoanalytic tradition – to the tradition bequeathed us by that great questioner of homilies and verities – is to question our commitment to the particular *method* which has also gone under the name of psychoanalysis. This does not mean abandoning that method altogether; that would certainly be premature. But it does mean a rather substantial shift in the centrality we have given that method both in our training institutes and in our literature. It means as well a closer examination of the ways that the practices that have traditionally been associated with "psychoanalysis" have almost automatically been transferred, wherever feasible, to the practices we have called psychoanalytic psychotherapy. Differences have evolved, of course, but mostly in response to difficulties or obstacles posed by particular patient characteristics. Much rarer have been explicit efforts to rethink *from the ground up* how one might employ a psychoanalytic understanding of conflict, anxiety, self- and object representation and the like, rather than assuming that any modification would be but a small variant of the way analysts have always practiced. One of the few who did try to do this was Franz Alexander, and we all know where that landed him in the esteem of the psychoanalytic community.[3]

One likely implication of the position I am developing here would be that the curriculum of any training program following this philosophy would give considerably greater weight to the various efforts which have been made in the areas of brief psychoanalytic therapy and of psychoanalytically oriented psychotherapy in general. The innovative efforts of those who were avowedly *psychoanalytic therapists* rather than psychoanalysts would not only receive greater attention than is now common in psychoanalytic training programs; they would receive a different *kind* of attention. They would be studied without a presumption that they were necessarily compromises, alloys of the "pure gold" of the classical method with various baser elements. The (heretofore heretical) notion that they might incorporate – or at least point us toward – *improvements* on the method we call psychoanalysis would be seriously explored.

A clear commitment to the psychoanalytic intellectual tradition, rather than to the practice of the particular technique we call psychoanalysis – and a clear recognition that the two commitments are not nearly as compatible as we have assumed in the past – would likely also lead to a greater interest in the relation between psychoanalytic ideas and methods and those which have been important in other therapeutic orientations. The exploration of the interface between psychoanalytic ideas and those of other clinical and theoretical traditions has been central to the development of the cyclical psychodynamic point of view (see, for example, Wachtel, 1977a, 1987, 1997; E. F. Wachtel & Wachtel, 1986), and has been a prominent theme in many of the chapters of this book. Over the years, exploration of the possibilities for integration of therapeutic approaches has greatly accelerated (see, for example, Norcross & Goldfried, 2005, Stricker & Gold, 2006), and it now seems to me that this body of work has reached a critical mass where anyone well trained in psychoanalytic psychology should be familiar with it – not just because of the specific contributions it contains, though they are clearly important, but also because of the spirit it implies about the way to approach the psychoanalytic enterprise and psychoanalytic discoveries.

Still another implication of deemphasizing training to become a "psychoanalyst" and instead highlighting the richness and fertility of psychoanalytic *ideas* is that it would further promote the application of psychoanalytic insights to other realms besides the therapeutic. Part II of this book, for example, illustrates some of the ways in which psychoanalytic ideas can be employed to better understand broad social trends and phenomena. Introducing psychoanalytic perspectives into a realm that has been very largely dominated by political and sociological perspectives adds important depth and complexity to our understanding of these phenomena and, at the same time, it offers a crucible in which to test the psychoanalytic ideas themselves, providing us, at the very least, with opportunities to refine those ideas and better understand the parameters that govern when and how unconscious fantasies, conflicts, and anxieties are expressed.

The potential of psychoanalytic psychology will not be fully realized if we continue to think of psychoanalytic training as primarily a means of preparing trainees to be psychoanalysts. The psychoanalytic tradition and its intellectual legacy are too rich and vital to be embalmed in this way. The observations that have accrued from psychoanalytic practice and the continuing developments in psychoanalytic thought – along with observations and theoretical advances deriving from other sources – point to a much wider range of new ways to help people and to engage in meaningful and generative inquiry. Some of these newer methods have already emerged and continue to evolve. Others await the creative efforts of analysts and other therapists to go beyond what they were taught by their supervisors and attend instead to the implications of those psychoanalytic discoveries that were marginalized by the very challenge they posed to received ways of working and thinking. We are in a position to inject new vitality into psychoanalysis, rooting our training in the theory and the evidence rather than in authority and tradition. We must approach the task of training new psychoanalytic psychologists with the sense that our mandate is not only to pass along what we know but also to convey what we don't know – or are not sure if we know – and to imbue in our trainees a commitment to further investigation. That commitment, and not the time-bound vehicle through which he expressed it, is Freud's lasting legacy.

Notes

1. Increasingly scientists and philosophers of science are recognizing that *all* scientific data are subject to selective and interpretive sets that bias what is reported. But the degree to which this is a problem in psychoanalysis is orders of magnitude greater.
2. For interesting further discussion of the implications of distinguishing too sharply between psychoanalysis and psychotherapy, see Aron & Starr (2013).
3. A more subtle effort to create an alternative foundation for the application of psycho-analytic ideas therapeutically was offered by Weiss and Sampson (1986). For a discussion of the ways that they tried to avoid Alexander's fate, see the exchange between Weiss (1998) and Wachtel and DeMichele (1998).

Chapter 11

Epistemological Foundations of Psychoanalysis

Science, Hermeneutics, and the Vicious Circles of Adversarial Discourse

Much fruitless and misleading debate results from a failure to appreciate that science is not one single thing but a multitude of methods and conceptual strategies that share certain common features I discuss shortly. What leads some proponents of humanistic or hermeneutic approaches to reject a natural science approach, echoing Dilthey's (1883/1991) 19th-century distinction between *Naturwissenschaften* and *Geisteswissenschaften*, is a focus on only a very narrow range of the practices that deserve to be referred to as science. *Science* is a term that refers to a host of practices that are designed to enable us to (a) accumulate and build upon systematic knowledge; and (b) do so in a way that is also designed to aid us, at least partially, in overcoming our prodigious capacity for self-deception. Any and all of the practices that human beings engage in to further their knowledge that meet these two criteria seem to me to fully merit the term science.

It is important for the reader to keep clearly in mind as I proceed that science is *not* equal to experiments (though controlled experiments are one of its powerful tools). Nor is it equivalent to positivism, to objectivism, to linear thinking. These are straw man labels that are sometimes used by analysts to defensively reject the *specter* of science, whose real threat is that it might pour cold water over some of their favorite ideas or, even worse, that it might make it possible to check on whether they are actually helping the people who come to see them.

Vicious Circles and the Epistemological Debate

Divisions between contending positions tend to be heightened when extreme positions in one direction elicit extreme positions in the other, and then each extreme position is experienced as justified by the excesses of the other side. What I am describing is a vicious circle – a phenomenon that, of course, is a central one in this entire book. One of the first things one must realize about vicious circles is that it is very difficult to determine when or how they begin. As family therapists have pointed out, the "punctuation" of a repetitive sequence is often one of the key points of difference and contention between participants in that sequence (e.g., Hoffman, 1981). Each side says the other side started it: "I am just reacting to what *they* are doing." Of course, the other side says precisely the same thing.

And each side keeps reacting to the other in a way that *keeps* the other side doing still more of the same – thus justifying their own continuation of *their* provocative behavior still again. This kind of pattern, repeated over and over, can be seen in couples, in families, and in the personality dynamics of individuals.

The same dynamic operates outside the clinical realm as well. I have previously examined, for example, how similar circular patterns can be seen in the way that societies rush madly after economic growth even while the pursuit of that growth creates social disruption and severe ecological damage, and even fails to provide very much of the satisfaction that people think will follow from having more. To understand why we are constantly frustrated, constantly feeling we need "more," and constantly failing to be satisfied with that more when we get it (and then think that somehow *still* more will do the trick), we need to understand the dynamics of the vicious circle (Wachtel, 1983).

I have seen a similarly circular pattern as well in an extensive study of race relations in the United States (Wachtel, 1999). In that realm, we may also see particularly clearly the all too common mutual *blame* part of the circle: "*We* are only doing what we do because *they* are doing what they do." And then both sides act in a way that ensures that the other side will *continue* doing the very things they complain about – and the very things that elicit their own participation in the destructive pattern still again. In this realm at least, the perpetual motion machine seems to have become a reality. Sadly and frighteningly, we now see the same pattern in the current struggles between the Western world and radical Islam. Vicious circles abound here too, with each side seeing their behavior as just a reaction to the excesses of the other – and each side *reacting* to those excesses in a way that elicits them once again.

Attention to very much the same kinds of vicious circles helps to understand how our field has become so divided over methodological and epistemological questions, especially the issue of science and the humanities or science and hermeneutics. As with all such circular patterns, the moral of the narrative depends on where one begins the description. Through the eyes of the *critics* of psychoanalysis, the narrative begins with years of psychoanalytic practice that offered very little in the nature of systematic evidence for either the assumptions underlying psychoanalytic work or the effectiveness of the treatments offered. In this version of the story – the story written by the advocates of "empirically validated treatments" and "evidence-based practice" (see Wachtel, 2010, for a critique of this approach) – these defenders of science and the testing of claims in the crucible of empirical evidence were reacting to self-indulgent irresponsibility in the psychoanalytic community and reacting as well to a stultifying conservatism in which new ideas were supported, ultimately, not by *evidence* for their validity but by whether some respected *authority* endorsed them. (And it must be acknowledged that in psychoanalytic journals, the backing for ideas more often entails citing Klein or Winnicott or Kernberg or whomever than citing systematic observations.)

From the vantage point of this narrative, then, the proponents of "science" are the brave insurgents, protecting the public by systematically evaluating the claims of the psychoanalysts and by introducing newer, briefer methods that actually have evidence that they work.

But there is another narrative that, we might say, is a version of this one through the looking glass. This opposite version of the story of "they're bad and we're good" *starts* with the demands by the science party that nothing be practiced except what has been "empirically validated" or "empirically supported" according to a rigged set of criteria (Wachtel, 2010). This demand, all too often, derives from a version of science that looks more like an obsessive-compulsive symptom than the creative and disciplined application of human intellect. It insists that nothing in the therapeutic realm can be regarded as having received empirical support unless it has been tested in a randomized controlled clinical trial. None of the other ways that science operates, none of the hundreds of kinds of methodological procedures and safeguards that are used in the wide range of sciences – from cosmology, to geology, to cellular biology, to paleontology, to countless other legitimate sciences – none of these is relevant. Only randomized clinical trials.

Imagine if Darwin's theory had to be tested via randomized controlled trials. We would have to find a granting agency that had sufficient funds (and patience) to fund a project over several billion years! We would have to find a sample of numerous alternative planets (the equivalent of patients in the randomized clinical trials paradigm) to randomly assign to prespecified conditions. Indeed, taking still another of the hallmarks of the extreme scientism camp of clinical ideology, we would have to develop a *manual* for the planets' evolution. For even if, playing along with the absurdist science fiction scenario I have just created, we found that planets in condition A evolved one kind of life and planets in condition B another, without a manual, these zealots would not be satisfied. "How do we know," they might ask, "that planet A *actually practiced* being close to a warm star and having abundant water or that planet B *actually practiced* having a meteorite hit just when its dinosaurs were thriving? Unless we can spell this out in advance, create a manual, train the planet in compliance with the manual, and make sure the planet doesn't covertly practice any funny stuff, we can't have much faith in the findings, and the proposition cannot be labeled as empirically validated.

In a great irony, the antievolution voices of so-called creationism in my own country have an implicit ally in the researchers and psychotherapists who insist that no procedure that has not been tested in randomized controlled trials should be viewed as validated. Evolutionary biology, like many sciences such as geology or cosmology, obviously cannot be approached through randomized trials or, in large measure, through controlled experiments altogether. Thus, the position taken by the extreme wing of the "empirical validation" forces in our field lines them up with the antiscience forces of the creationists. What they have in common is a very creative capacity to ignore evidence that doesn't fit well with their preconceptions and to declare doubtful and inadequate the evidence that exists.

For the absence of controlled clinical trials does not mean the absence of solid evidence. The sciences I just mentioned (geology, cosmology, etc.) do not use any equivalent of randomized clinical trials, but this does not mean that they cannot be investigated by very precise, methodologically sophisticated, or genuinely scientific research. The same holds for psychotherapy and for the theories on which it is based. There are many ways to do valid empirical assessment, and it is the totality of evidence we should be addressing, not just randomized trials (see Wachtel, 2010).

I am sometimes struck by the use of the term *gold standard* to refer to randomized clinical trials. We should remember the story of King Midas. Turning everything into gold is not always wise.

The Preoccupation with Manuals in Clinical Efficacy Research

I do not disagree that, all other things being equal, evidence of efficacy via randomized clinical trials is perhaps the strongest evidence – even if by no means the *only* relevant evidence – for the efficacy of a clinical approach. What I most forcefully do not agree with is the idea that manuals are an essential component. I certainly understand the general logic behind the manualization movement in psychotherapy research. If we are comparing two therapeutic approaches, we need to be able to be confident that what characterized the two groups was in fact the two treatments purportedly being offered. But manualization is by no means the only way to do this, and in many instances it is highly inappropriate.

To begin with, manuals are only a means toward an end, not the end itself. Even with a manual, there need to be compliance checks to ensure that the therapist is *following* the manual. But if there are compliance checks, then *they* serve – with or *without* a manual – as the means of evaluating. If the therapy being investigated is not a manualized therapy, then practitioners of the particular approach being evaluated can look at the work being done – without knowledge of the outcome, so that their judgments will not thereby be biased – and judge the degree to which the therapy approximates that approach. If there is reliability in these judgments by experienced expert practitioners of the two approaches as to which practice sample belongs to which approach (judged blindly as to outcome and purported label), we can be reasonably confident that the different conditions represent the essential and distinctive features of the different approaches.

After all, whether the therapist is in compliance with the manual is *also* ultimately a matter of judgment, also ultimately in the eye of the beholder – because fortunately, not all manualized therapies are quite as trivial as the manual concept might imply. So evaluating whether the therapist has faithfully followed the manual *also* involves a good deal of judgment and choice on the evaluator's part. The application of the manual is likely to be somewhat different with each patient, and hence, the judgment of whether the therapist is complying with the manual is not a simple matter of a checklist but a decision that has hard-to-gauge elements of ambiguity and subjectivity. Indeed, it rests on a similar evidential and epistemological foundation as the judgment that would follow from evaluating if the therapist is following a treatment approach that is *not* manualized.

What the movement toward manualization in psychotherapy research reflects – a movement whose strength derived very largely from a "gun-at-the-head" enforcement of it through the awarding (and not awarding) of research grants – is two things. First, it reflects a rather mechanical view of science, a break-it-into-pieces approach that has worked very well in quite a few areas of inquiry, but that is by no means synonymous with the scientific method. When it is employed not because it *happens to be appropriate* to a particular subdiscipline or a particular problem (which, again, it often is) but because it reflects an across-the-board insistence that without it there is no science at all, then what we have is, again, an obsessive-compulsive symptom masquerading as science.

Second, the emphasis on manuals (along with the insistence that one study a narrowly defined DSM or ICD diagnostic group) is a tendentious, thinly disguised effort to legitimatize some approaches at the expense of others, a maneuver in the economic marketplace much more than an honest effort at science. It is not just coincidence that the primary proponents of this approach to empirical validation are cognitive-behavioral and that it is an approach that *by its very definition* renders the competition not just unvalidated but *incapable of being* validated. For if one criterion for supposed empirical validation is the employment of a manual in the research, then *by definition*, a therapeutic approach that does not employ a manual cannot be "empirically validated." This is politics, not science.

Science and Intuition

Let us take a closer look at the break-it-into-pieces approach to science that is reflected in the insistence on manuals. Some concepts are actually best measured not by criteria spelled out in advance in great detail, but by broad, quasi-intuitive judgments. If they are *then* checked in other ways – for example, using the standard canons of evidence to determine whether the judgment can be reliably replicated by *another* judge who approaches the judgments independently – they are as much "scientific data" as are more molecular measurements on a detailed checklist.

The mistrust of intuition that is reflected in the insistence on manuals flies in the face of much evidence about the actual nature of scientific inquiry, even in the so-called hard sciences. The classic writings of Michael Polanyi, a prominent scientist working on the borders between physics and chemistry as well as a philosopher and historian of science, make this very clear. Polanyi (1966) has discussed in detail, as an essential part of the scientific enterprise, the "tacit dimension" of subtle observation that can be sensed but not yet articulated, and he has shown that it plays a prominent role in the so-called hard sciences as much as in our own field. It is the failure to appreciate or acknowledge this tacit dimension, the ideological mistrust of intuition, that I am referring to when I describe certain visions of the essential nature of science as obsessive-compulsive.

One early example from my own work illustrates how the power of intuition can be harnessed to the methodologies that modern science has evolved for checking on that intuition. It illustrates as well why it is scientifically impoverishing to insist on a manual or any other break-it-into-pieces methodology when that approach is not suitable to the phenomenon being studied. In the study I am referring to, conducted together with the late Jean Schimek (Wachtel & Schimek, 1970), we investigated various effects of the emotional impact of incidental stimuli. Subjects in the study free associated and made up stories to TAT cards. Unbeknownst to them, part of the study included a sound that was coming from the office next door. The sound – for half the subjects it was the sound of an argument and for the other half of light music and laughter, sounding like a happy party – was at a volume such that the words could not be made out. Later debriefing of the subjects made it clear that the subjects did not recognize that these sounds were part of the study. Moreover, although almost all of the subjects experienced the sound as incidental and did not focus on it, they could, when later questioned about it, accurately identify whether it sounded like the people next door were angry or were in a good mood.

I will not go into detail about the findings – the general thrust was that the emotional tone of the incidental stimuli did affect the emotional tone of the subjects' free associations and TAT stories; there were more angry themes in the stories when the "angry" tape was playing next door. What I do want to emphasize is that our efforts to create a "manual" for our scoring of the protocols were not only extremely time-consuming (and, indeed, obsessional feeling), they were unsuccessful. That is, we were not able to create a piecemeal set of specific behaviorally manifest items to check off that achieved high inter-rater reliability and effectively differentiated the response to the two different incidental stimuli. But we were able to achieve high levels of inter-rater reliability and to detect meaningful differences between the responses to the angry incidental stimulus and the pleasant incidental stimulus, when – instead of relying on a manual – we relied simply on our ability to perceive, in a direct and global manner, an emotional meaning in the subject's material. When, instead of creating a manual for detecting anger in the associations and stories, we simply made a global judgment of how much anger was present (blind as to which condition the stories and associations came from), we got much better and more meaningful results.

Excesses on the Other Side: Defensive Dismissal of the Scientific Canons of Evidence

This little story from the early stage of my professional career has, I think, interesting implications for both sides of the artificial divide that has been created in our field. On the one hand, it points to the importance of transcending obsessional criteria like manuals. Explicitly spelled-out criteria sometimes are the best path to knowledge, but sometimes they are an obstacle. But it is *also* important to be clear that although I have been rather hard on the proponents of "empirically validated" treatments thus far, there are equal and opposite excesses to be found among their opponents. What I have said thus far should not be taken as giving wholesale license to the self-indulgence that is the evil twin of scientism. That is, the message is not – or should not be – simply "trust my judgment." We made the effort in our study to assess the inter-rater reliability of our judgments for a reason.

What I mean by self-indulgence is well illustrated by a posting on a psychoanalytic listserve I belong to that was discussing the necessity for empirical validation of psychoanalytic ideas and the effectiveness of psychoanalytic work. The writer was a fairly well-known psychoanalytic author. I will protect him from himself by not mentioning his name. But I will quote his point of view. In joining the fray on the side of clinical observation and against systematic empirical evaluation (which, again, should not be equated with manuals or randomized clinical trials), this author said the following:

> How about this for a kind of research evidence: I now have 14 books documenting ins and outs of the creative psyche in psychoanalytically oriented work behind closed doors. What speaks through these books is the voice of authentic psychical reality – subject to correction, amplification, further work. But what is there is real. Reality speaks.

Interestingly, this same author, in the same message, informs us of his love of and fascination with science. This is a frequent, and comfortably self-congratulatory, expression of bland piety toward science, expressed by many participants in the listserve exchange I am referring to, and it seems to express a love of science as long as it doesn't interfere with their beliefs. The motto seems to be, "science for the masses, intuition for *moi*."

Put differently, rejection of the *narrow* and *political* criteria for empirical validation is appropriate, but often it disguises a rejection – sometimes smug, sometimes defensive, sometimes both – of *all* systematic efforts to validate the clinical efficacy of psychoanalysis or the ideas on which it is based. Behind banners such as postmodernism, constructivism, or hermeneutics, and employing tiresome straw man depictions of "positivists," these defenders of the faith ironically ignore some of the most fundamental implications of psychoanalysis itself – that we are extremely prone to self-deception; that this self-deception is often motivated and generally not noticed; that it serves to keep us more comfortable, to not notice what would ruffle our psychic feathers; that our very perceptions, our convictions about what we have "seen with our own eyes," are subject both to motivated and to unmotivated skews and distortions; that our memories too are suspect, and hence it is dangerous to trust them if we rely on after-the-fact recollections (the standard mode in psychoanalytic papers) rather than accounts of the session based on systematic recording. It is precisely the scientific method that has developed to deal with this state of affairs. Science, in all of its various methodological forms, is essentially a means of attempting to observe in a way that at least partly addresses our proneness to see what we want to see and remember what we want to remember.

Indeed, we might say that it is our *clinical* observations and theories that, most of all, alert us to be suspicious of those very observations and theories if not evaluated in ways more systematic than the accumulation of reports by analysts of what they remember went on in their offices last week. If our clinically based theories have any value at all, they point to an extraordinary capacity of our species to deceive ourselves, and hence to the vulnerability of purely clinically based theories without some further effort to control for this tendency. We are stuck in a closed circle if we do not have a way of evaluating our observations that does not rely on just "Trust me; I saw it in my office."

This does not mean the dictatorship of one particular methodology. Science is a term whose precise meaning is very difficult to pin down, but whose spirit is easy to detect if one is both honest and reasonably aware of the way our perceptions and convictions can lead us astray. We do not have to abandon our concern with nuances and subtleties of subjective experience or with unconscious influences on thought, feeling, and behavior in order to be scientific. Yes, it is true that the subtleties of affect and experience can be *difficult* to capture in systematic studies, and that many published studies are concerned with trivialities or superficialities that seem to working clinicians quite irrelevant to the work they do. But if we have a less ritualistic or obsessive-compulsive understanding of what science is, then there are possibilities of harnessing its safeguards while also employing the same empathic and perceptive capabilities of the clinician that she relies on in the consulting room. Remember, as one small example, the study I mentioned earlier, in which the *mechanics* or *trappings* of science did not work, but the systematic employment of ordinary emotional sensitivity proved to be both meaningful and reliable. In a similar vein, we may note Westen and Weinberger's (2004) demonstration that the old dichotomy between clinical and statistical methods is a false one, and that often what is most effectively combined in statistical fashion are not simplistic check marks on self-report instruments or the evaluations of lay observers but the sophisticated judgments of experienced clinicians – but bear in mind as well their powerful arguments that *combining* what clinicians do well and what statistical analysis does well yields the most useful and reliable knowledge.

Viewpoints and Methodologies

No one point of view "owns" science – not cognitive-behavior therapists, not neuroscientists, not practitioners of controlled clinical trials. Science is simply a way of keeping ourselves honest and, often, of amplifying our perception via new methodologies and technologies – whether they be the telescope, the microscope, the particle accelerator or, for that matter, the tape recorder.

The tape recorder, that by-now humble instrument, much more likely to be found in the rooms of children and teenagers than in high-tech laboratories, is still an insufficiently tapped resource for turning clinical process and clinical intuition into scientific data. To begin with, audio or video recording allows others to see the same material and make their own independent judgments (though there are of course differences between seeing a tape and actually being there in the affective field with the patient – no solution is perfect; there are always compromises).

Second, tape recording permits the therapist herself to check on what has been remembered. It is striking how different a sequence can be when one watches it on tape from what one has remembered (and the subtle differences are just as important as the dramatic and obvious ones). Third, sometimes it is only after watching something many times that we can see something that has, in essence, been lying there waiting for us to notice all along. In one of my very first published papers, concerned with what is communicated by body language (Wachtel, 1967), I described a pattern I did not see until I had looked at the tape more than 50 times. But once I finally noticed it, it jumped out at me and became rather obvious.

We still have not exhausted the potential of such simple methodological innovations as the audio and video recorder, not to mention the further possibilities for enhancing our observational acuity represented by methods of analyzing such data in a frame-by-frame way (e.g., Beebe & Lachmann, 2002; D. N. Stern, 1985; Tronick, 1989). This work, along with, for example, the systematic research on attachment and reflective function, which uses transcripts of tape-recorded interviews (e.g., Fonagy, 2001; Fonagy, Target, Steele, & Steele, 1998; Hesse, 1999; Main & Goldwyn, 1998) shows how *clinically meaningful* findings can derive from new observational methods that enable us to notice phenomena that we otherwise might miss, including phenomena that are close to the heart of the interests of psychoanalytic and other more clinical theorists.

Using tape recordings or transcripts derived from them is just one example of a scientific advance over just reporting what one remembers from one's sessions (memories often written down only at the end of the day or even days or years later looking back on the case). I mention the tape recorder precisely because these days it is a rather low-tech and commonplace instrument and yet it represents such a signal advance over the traditional case report, one Freud could not really imagine when he first began his work. I mention it as well because it is a method that basically retains the usual focus of the psychoanalyst. That is, it is directed to the same kind of material that the traditional case study is directed toward, recording the patient's and therapist's words and the therapist's effort to be empathically attuned to the patient's affect state. It is not a diversion from or an avoidance of those data and that effort, not a method that is restricted to check marks on questionnaires or to what is immediately consciously accessible. Doing research from an audiotape or a videotape still requires a good deal of inference and interpretation; it is not always straightforward. But the conclusions reached are more publicly accessible, more capable of being evaluated by the professional community without having to simply take the reporting analyst's word for it. Moreover, even the analyst's or therapist's subjective experience in engaging in the exchange is not excluded, because it can be provided by the therapist just as it is in the "trust me" case report. And indeed, it may be a *richer* report of the therapist's subjective experience, because it is offered, while the therapist watches the tape, with more reminders of what transpired, in response, we might say, to thick description (Geertz, 1973).[1]

In a recent book (Wachtel, 2011b) in which, based on transcripts of several sessions, I presented detailed, almost line-by-line comments on what the patient said and what I said and on my thinking and subjective experience of the process from moment to moment, I had this point vividly brought home to me. Having available transcripts and videotapes of the sessions enabled me to be reminded of my subjective experience at each point in a richness of detail that would have been impossible (and much more fictional) if I had had to rely on my inevitably sketchy and edited recollections of what transpired to reconstruct my experience. It is certainly the case that my report of my subjective experience cannot be taken as the full or accurate story; to any psychoanalytic thinker, such utterly precise and accurate access is unlikely to seem a possibility. But it is important to be clear that such is the case, of course, in the more typical psychoanalytic mode of presentation as well, based on a narrative in which the very events – the words, the sequences, the tone of voice (the book was based on watching and listening to the tapes as well as reading the transcripts) – are inevitably recalled in highly selective fashion. This more typical mode of presentation is thus not only more vulnerable epistemologically – one is likely to remember what fits with one's expectations and conveniently forget or underplay what does not – but it also, as a consequence of the same selective (and simply less complete) process, makes it less likely that the therapist will be able to reconstruct as fully and accurately her *subjective experience* of what was transpiring. Being reminded of the exact words, the exact sequence, and so forth, is almost certain to be more evocative than the more limited set of events – with, moreover, the edges shaved off that do not fit the narrative that organizes the recollection – that is an inevitable product of the limits of human memory. Thus, in addition to the greater confidence one can have in the recorded material from the point of view of evidence, it is another virtue of the use of tapes and transcripts that they are actually a better source for reconstructing the analyst's or therapist's subjectivity.

Some who object to recording sessions argue that what is most important in usefully understanding the therapeutic process is not the "facts," but the *subjective experience* of each party. From this vantage point, the version of the story told via recollection by the analyst is a more useful document because it is infused with the *meaning* that the events had (at least for the analyst). The selective editing represented by such accounts, including the unconscious dimensions of this editing, is thus seen not as an obstacle but as a form of *enhanced* reporting, guided by a filter that illuminates what really matters. I am in agreement about the first part of this argument – the "facts" need to be understood in terms of what they mean to the participants. But I am much more skeptical about the second part. To begin with, even if there are certain ways in which the unconscious processes that construct the therapist's after-the-fact narrative may reveal potentially interesting elements of her subjective experience of the sessions, it seems to me that the accuracy with which she understands *the patient's* subjectivity becomes even harder to evaluate. If the analyst's recollections are unconsciously edited to fit her subjective experience of the session, then a reader who might have a *different* understanding of what was going on for the patient is put at still a greater distance from what went on between them, making it extremely difficult to go beyond the unearned authority of the analyst presenting her account of what went on and what it meant. Moreover, to return to the issue of the analyst's access to her own subjective experience in the sessions, it must again be emphasized that in the book I was just referring to, the use of the transcript was not a *substitute* for an account of my subjective experience of participation in the session but rather was a means of *enhancing* that very account.

Apart from the homely contribution of audiotaping and videotaping, more complicated or technologically advanced ways of improving on what we can know just from sessions are, of course, also available, often in the form of some kind of physiological or neurological recording, but including many other methods as well. The point is by no means that physiological evidence is more real or solid than psychological. After all, how do we even know what a particular pattern of neural firings in the brain *means* unless we relate it to behavioral or experiential data? The "hard" physiological indicators are only as good as the "soft" psychological indicators to which they are correlated. If we do not have good, differentiated indicators in the one realm, we will not in the other. But these physiological indicators can improve our understanding very considerably nonetheless when they are combined with sensitive attention to the psychological realm. What is done under the best methods of inquiry is a kind of mutual bootstrapping. What is going on psychologically, after all, is often hard to discern or articulate or know how to organize into patterns. That is what is meant by saying that psychological matters are complex (a claim often made by those contending that they are too complex to approach via science). But just as we can understand a previously not-appreciated theme or thread in a patient's narrative by noticing that the (not yet fully developed or articulated) content is interrupted by a long pause or a puzzled or distressed look – part of what good clinicians do naturally – so too can we understand more fully the psychological meanings, the conflicts or unacknowledged desires or fears that the patient is struggling to express if we have, as an aid, information about what brain areas light up on an fMRI.

Obviously, at least as psychoanalysis or psychotherapy are presently practiced, the latter situation refers more to the laboratory than to the clinical consulting room, but it nonetheless refers to the illumination of *psychological meanings theretofore not understood or appreciated*. In both instances, what enables us to make progress is active and sensitive inquiry. In the case of the patient who becomes silent or manifests a noteworthy facial expression or shift of posture, what we do to pursue the not yet fully manifest meaning is to ask what was going through the patient's mind during the pause or just before the appearance of the particular facial expression. Similarly, in the hypothetical laboratory situation, one similarly *asks* the patient what was going on when the physiological indicator lit up. The signal from the brain scan alerts us to ask about something that might have slipped past our notice and gone unappreciated or uninterpreted. In turn, the increased differentiation and subtlety of our psychological understanding enables us to improve our methodology for brain scans, providing a new and better platform for still further cues to the investigator to notice still other potentially overlooked and subtle psychological phenomena. In principle, this mutual enhancement from one realm to the other can go on over and over, and with each iteration, we have a new platform for further advances, each building on the other.

In a different realm, closer to what today is clinically possible, the work of Luborsky and his colleagues on what he calls the symptom-context method (Luborsky, 1996) illustrates this kind of investigative bootstrapping. Luborsky's psychological inquiries are triggered by particular, characteristic, and repeated symptomatic acts or events (they can be somatic, such as a pain or a twitch, or they can be psychological, such as an experience of forgetting what one was going to say). Using those events as the starting point, he systematically investigates the context of meaning that precedes and follows the target event. By looking very closely at material that has been tape recorded, one can notice sequences and connections that are easily overlooked as the material flies by in real time.

The point, both in the real examples by Luborsky and in the hypothetical ones I am imagining vis-à-vis brain scans and other technologically assisted methods, is that the pursuit of meaning, the hermeneutic quest, is not antithetical to the process of inquiry pursued from an "external" vantage point. Rather, if the inquiry is pursued creatively and with openness to diverse sources of illumination, we find that the dichotomies often turn out to be a product of our preconceptions and biases, and that deeper and more complete understanding can be achieved by a complementary employment of, on the one hand, clinical observation and attention to subjective experience and on the other, technological aids and the systematic methods of scientific investigation.

The Contribution of Theory and the Pervasiveness of Vicious Circles

In the process of mutual influence and feedback I have been describing, in which affective and intuitive immersion in the immediacy of the clinical situation and attention to the findings of systematic research provide mutual bootstrapping, the advance of theory is a crucial third dimension. I am very much in agreement with Kurt Lewin's (1951) contention that "there is nothing so practical as a good theory" (p. 169). Having a theory that pulls together observations and findings from diverse realms of observation enables us to notice things we didn't see before and to anticipate and look for phenomena we have not yet encountered (see Wachtel, 1980). Many of the most significant new discoveries of science – the encountering of phenomena that were not even dreamed of by the best minds of previous centuries – were spurred by theories; theories that told us to look for something we would not have looked for without them.

In the arena of human behavior and experience, however, the dominant theories and disciplines have been hampered by a tendency toward building theory upon the foundation of only a limited range of observations. In the psychoanalytic realm, for example, aspects of the theory that evolved from the process of free association led to theoretical ideas (neutrality, anonymity, and abstinence, for example) that long perpetuated free association or closely related methods as the only appropriate means for psychoanalytic investigation and hence for psycho-analytic theory building. The consequence was a restricted observational field in which observations that might prove contradictory to received ideas were unlikely to be encountered. Received theory thus appeared artificially or artifactually ade-quate, but the *growth and change* of theoretical ideas through the challenge of unanticipated observations was limited.

There has, of course, been change in psychoanalytic thought and practice over the years, but that change has still proceeded within a bounded set of possibili-ties. Preoccupation with whether an idea or method was genuinely psychoanalytic often took precedence over whether it was an accurate and sufficiently inclusive account of human behavior and experience or of whether it enhanced the possi-bilities for providing patients with the help they sought (see Aron & Starr, 2013 for an excellent and comprehensive account). Many innovations that passed the second set of criteria were rejected because they didn't pass the first (that is, they were deemed "unanalytic."). In recent years, the accelerating impact of new relational ideas has been associated with new psychoanalytic *methods*, and this in turn has brought into focus new observations that require still further theoreti-cal and procedural modifications (see, for example, Aron, 1996; Mitchell, 1988, 1993, 1997; Mitchell & Aron, 1999; Wachtel, 2008). But even these advances have been constrained by a tendency to draw a boundary (even if now a somewhat more relaxed and expanded boundary) around psychoanalysis and to exclude via that boundary observations that came from proponents of approaches such as fam-ily systems and cognitive-behavioral theories.

To be sure, proponents of these latter approaches have been equally narrow. Cognitive-behavioral therapists and theorists in particular have tended to be blind to the importance of the observations that have accrued from psychoanalytic work for over a century. The Society for the Exploration of Psychotherapy Integra-tion (SEPI), the organization I mentioned in Chapter 1, has been a relatively rare venue for psychoanalysts, cognitive-behavior therapists, family therapists, and others who wish to learn from outside the artificial boundaries of their home ori-entation to exchange ideas and build more comprehensive models.

In my own efforts to recast psychoanalytic ideas in ways that can enable them to assimilate observations that derive from nonpsychoanalytic sources, the con-cept of the vicious circle, discussed in various ways throughout this chapter, has been central. Attention to vicious circles not only illuminates the dynamics of personality more fully and comprehensively, but also permits us to see how each of the major competing schools tends to focus its attention on only a part of the larger pattern that characterizes our lives, a pattern that includes both the influ-ence of the stored impact of the past and the influence of the new impact of the present context. Indeed, by attending to the larger pattern of vicious circles, we see that the very dichotomy between the inner world and the external environment is a false and misleading one. If we understand fully and properly the so-called inner world of hidden wishes, fantasies, conflicts, self- and object-representations, and so forth, we come to see that these are not just contents or forces in a separate realm inside the psyche, but reflect the alive and active ways we *respond to the world*. Looking closely, we see that the persisting unconscious fantasy, the transferential inclination, the seemingly archaic desire or fear are part of a pattern of responding to the actual world of events and experiences that we continually encounter. But the world to which they respond is not composed of the "independent variables" of the classical psychological experiment. The so-called "external" world is a function of our "internal" world as much as the internal world is a function of the external environment. Based on our wishes, fears, and fantasies, we *act*. And when we act, others respond to our actions in turn, providing input from the "external" environment that is itself a function of our "inner" proclivities and that, in turn, is further worked over and given meaning in light of those proclivities (Wachtel, 1973, 1977b, 1981, 1994, 1997, 2008).

This is much more than just what psychoanalysts have called enactments. Enactment is a concept that, although it illuminates what we actually do in the world, still usually prioritizes the internal. It is the already existing, *internal* engine of behavior that is emphasized, and the context in which it is displayed is simply the stage on which a play already written in childhood is performed. In contrast, the circular process I am emphasizing highlights the *bidirectional* nature of causality in the psychological realm. The psychological structures we discover in our therapeutic work are not simply residues from childhood. They have their *origins* in childhood, but they evolve and change in response to new circumstances. At the same time – and here is the ironic heart of the vicious circle – the circumstances are themselves largely (though by no means completely) determined by the psychic structures and inclinations we have already developed and the behavior in the real world that they generate. We do not understand people very well if we are overly inclined to see their present behavior and experience as determined by their childhoods rather than by what is actually going on in the present. But, at the same time, we do not understand very well what is going on in the present without understanding the long-standing fears and desires, the conflicts, fantasies, and subjective representations, the perceptual and cognitive proclivities that have evolved in the course of development. Neither present environmental contingencies *nor* inner representations of earlier experiences are primary. Indeed, neither has much meaning apart from the other. Such is the seamless unity that the various theories in our field have sliced up and fetishized parts of.

I have attempted, in this book and elsewhere (e.g., Wachtel, 1997, 2008, 2011a), to illustrate how these circular, self-replicating, and mutually causal processes work and what their implications are for clinical practice. I hope that in this book I have provided a reasonably clear picture of how they are manifest still again in the debate about science and hermeneutics that rages in our field today.

Note

1. Some people, of course, argue that to record a session totally changes the configuration of what is transpiring. I believe that to be a self-serving rationalization for not exposing either one's clinical skills or one's ideas to this kind of scrutiny.

Part II

Race, Class, Greed, and the Social Construction of Desire

Chapter 12

Psychoanalysis and the World of Cultural Constructions

The Contextual Self and the Realm of Everyday Unhappiness

With the present chapter, this book moves from a primary focus on the dynamics of the individual and his or her immediate interactional context to a broader concern with society as a whole and the ways that characteristics of the individual and of the sociocultural context reciprocally shape each other. Neurotic misery is not the only treatable source of suffering that can be subtracted from the unavoidable weight of everyday unhappiness. Social inequality and injustice, along with the internalization of values that obscure the differences between the genuine pursuit of satisfaction and meaning and the illusory pursuit of well-being through more and more material goods (see, for example, Kasser, 2003; Kasser & Kanner, 2003; Wachtel, 1983), represent other powerful sources of unnecessary suffering. The remaining chapters explore the implications of psychoanalytic understanding for developing better approaches to addressing these additional dimensions of human distress, which have received insufficient attention in the psychoanalytic literature. In the process, this last portion of the book also takes a closer look at some commonly held assumptions of psychoanalytic thought itself and considers how new observations deriving from attention to broader social patterns and values and from work with people from different cultural and class origins can contribute to the refinement and further development of psychoanalytic propositions.

Having become concerned some time ago about the destructive consequences – both for the earth's ecology and for the prospect of achieving a genuinely fulfilling and satisfying life – of our societal commitment to unceasing economic growth, I began to think about the values and assumptions that led us to continue to pursue such a self-defeating course. Increasingly, I was led to the conclusion that much of what was wrong was due to a misplaced effort to use economics and economic well-being as a means to solve psychological problems. Put differently, it appeared that materialistic desires for more and more "stuff" were serving both to salve and to disguise – and ultimately to exacerbate – frustrations, vulnerabilities, and suffering whose origins lay in conflicted human relationships and in the ways we learn early in life to repudiate some of our most crucial perceptions and core experiences in order to maintain the attachment ties that feel essential to the self's very survival.

The Poverty of Affluence (Wachtel, 1983) was my first effort to explore this line of thought in detail. It traced how our emphasis on economic growth created conditions which end up undermining psychological well-being and how, in turn, we have attempted to deal with that reduced sense of security and satisfaction by further efforts to produce and consume still more – with predictably unfortunate effects.

In presenting and defending this position, I had to come to terms with the claims of a number of prominent social critics (e.g., Lasch, 1979; Rieff, 1966, 1979) whose position was almost the opposite of mine. Although steeped in psychological theory and terminology, these critics' conclusion was, in essence, that we had become *too* psychological in our focus, too concerned with the self and the articulation of its passions and particularities. In examining their positions, I saw both a kernel of truth and numerous ways in which they went astray. One of the conclusions I reached was that their criticisms of psychoanalytic thought and the scrutiny of psychological experience were not really as pertinent to what was original and distinctive about psychoanalysis as to certain ways in which Freud's thought shared, in an unexamined way, some key (and problematic) assumptions of the rapidly evolving capitalist society in which it developed – assumptions which persist in our own society to this day. Because there are even more important ways in which psychoanalysis potentially contributes to a *critique* of the misunderstandings that are pervasive in our society about the true sources of satisfaction, it is essential that we sort out the liberating alternatives from the constraining assumptions and values that have been unwittingly incorporated from the social context in which it evolved.

Everyday Unhappiness

As alluded to in the title of this chapter and in the opening paragraph, Freud famously said that the aim of psychoanalysis was to turn neurotic misery into everyday unhappiness. That statement is so widely quoted in part because it reflects some of Freud's signal strengths – his pithy way with words, his capacity to convey an appealing modesty (or at least *apparent* modesty) of aims, his hard-headed realism. We see here no apocalyptic claims rooted in wishful fantasies. Rather, according to a common interpretation, what is offered in this formulation is something ultimately more valuable – the hard, cool reflections of a supreme rationalist and humanist who understood in a profound way the tragic limits of human existence.

But perhaps Freud's formulation was a bit *too* cool and modest. In effect, the question I wish to ask here is: What does psychoanalysis have to say about the everyday unhappiness itself? Can it make any contribution there as well, or is it solely a theory relevant to that misery we might call neurotic?

Certainly many of Freud's early followers had more ambitious aims. As Russell Jacoby (1983) points out in his book *The Repression of Psychoanalysis: Otto Fenichel and the Political Freudians*, even as venerable a classical analyst as Otto

Fenichel was secretly – and I use the term advisedly – committed to enlisting psychoanalysis in the search for fundamental social change. Fenichel's radical leanings (as those of Edith Jacobson and other leading psychoanalytic figures of their generation) were no secret in Europe, but they were kept under careful wraps once he came to the United States as a refugee. Jacoby reports that Fenichel was concerned both about his immigrant status in the United States during the McCarthy era and about the conservatism of the psychoanalytic establishment itself. Privately, he described himself as fighting on two fronts – against the orthodoxy of Marxist approaches, which failed to appreciate the subtleties of individual experience, and against the large number of analysts who, for their part, failed to appreciate the impact of social reality. The existence of the letters – if *letters* is the appropriate term; sometimes they ranged up to 80 pages – that were exchanged among his small circle of like-minded analysts was virtually unknown in the psychoanalytic community at large. Indeed Fenichel counseled the recipients of these letters to destroy them after reading them.

There are many significant ways in which I differ from Fenichel both in clinical matters and with regard to issues of social change. But I share his view that psychoanalysis ought to be able to illuminate our social situation and to point us in the direction of a more humane society. In exploring what the contribution of psychoanalysis might be, one place to begin would be the role of psychoanalysis in helping us to see the limits of the rationalistic calculus that now dominates our thinking about social policy. In our society, the dominant images guiding social – and often even personal – choices are those of the economist. It is no idle curiosity that perhaps the most common phrase in our society at present for conveying the idea of something being of great importance is "the bottom line."

The pervasive influence of assumptions and images unwittingly incorporated from our economic system and its corollary habits is evident even in aspects of our thinking that are not thought to be economic. One of the central ways in which economistic thinking pervades our culture (and with regard to which a psychoanalytic perspective obviously offers a clear alternative) is in the assumption that we know what we want. This assumption of transparent self-knowledge is absolutely central to the moral and social justifications for our society's veneration of the market as the mechanism for social policy decisions, a veneration that is not only an enormous impediment to progressive social change but also an obstacle to attaining what we actually do want – lives of meaning, security, and genuine satisfaction. It is, of course, an assumption that is strongly challenged by psychoanalysis.

The so-called neoclassical economics that is still a dominant strain of thought in our society is committed to taking people's choices as a given, to not examining the motivational sources of their "revealed preferences," much less the irrational thinking that often underlies them.[1] To most economists, it is impermissible either to evaluate those choices morally or to consider whether the choices people make really enhance their well-being. In Panglossian fashion, they essentially assume that if we chose to buy something, we must have wanted it, and because we are the best judge of what we want and what benefits us, we must have "maximized our utilities." Their grounding assumptions seem to imply that we are never deceived and never make mistakes.

As Nobel economics laureate Herbert Simon (1957) put it with wry skepticism, the standard economic model, assumes that every person has

> a complete and consistent system of preferences that allows him always to choose among the alternatives open to him; he is always completely aware of what his alternatives are; there are no limits on the complexity of the computations he can perform in order to determine which alternatives are best. (p. xxiii)

In a similar vein, Israeli economist Shlomo Maital (1982) noted that the "economic man" of mainstream economic theory is a virtually flawless paragon of rationality who "matches subjective value and objective price right at the precipice of his budget line, along which he or she skates with Olympian precision" (p. 147).

Complementing this view in undergirding the moral and analytical foundations of market-dominated societies is a framework that systematically excludes the *context* within which individual decisions are made. The influence of the larger social context is obscured in a number of ways. First, in addressing the moral implications of our social organization and the profoundly unequal distributions of wealth and status it yields, everything is reduced to the decisions of two parties, buyer and seller. According to the just-so story that is central to the justification of an economic system so pervaded by inequality and ecological damage (see, for example, Milton Friedman and Rose Friedman's [1980] *Free to Choose: A Personal Statement* and its critique in Wachtel, 1983), it is a system in which every economic event is an improvement. Buyer and seller decide to trade because the buyer is better off with the product than the money and the seller is better off with the money than the product. Each gains, and no one loses. Moreover, it is not only a *gain* for each, it is the very best they could possibly achieve; for if either could do better, he would promptly do so. Such is the beauty of the "free market."

Since over and over all we do is trade what we have for something we prefer still more, it would seem through this lens that life in such a system must keep getting better and better. If we turn from buying and selling to human experience, however – something economists practically forbid themselves to do – it is plain, both from formal surveys of the sense of well-being and from simply observing oneself, one's neighbors, or the evening news, that this is scarcely the case (see, for example, Easterlin, 1974; Kasser, 2003; Kasser & Kanner, 2003).

The source of the fallacy becomes evident as one looks more closely at how the assumptions of market advocates compare to the real world. Robert Frank (1985), one of the relatively few prominent economists who has been able to look reflectively at the model that guides his profession, notes that,

> In setting up formal models of economic behavior, economists almost always assume at the outset that a person's sense of well-being, or utility, depends on the absolute quantities of various goods he consumes, not on how those quantities compare with the amounts consumed by others. (p. 33)

But as Frank points out, in the real world, in contrast to the models of economists, "much evidence suggests that people do in fact care much more about how their incomes compare with those of their peers than about how large their incomes are in any absolute sense" (p. 5). He quotes with pleasure Mencken's definition of wealth as "any income that is at least one hundred dollars more a year than the income of one's wife's sister's husband" (p. 5).

Frank has also argued insightfully and persuasively that economists operate under a highly misleading picture of what people really want because they do not take into account the way in which the very operations of the market, which exclude *collective* decisions, force people into choices that resemble the Prisoner's Dilemma. The model of choice that is hawked by economists and other defenders of the market system is – to return more overtly to a central theme of this chapter – a radically acontextual one. In truth, my purchases are *not* just a matter of a decision between the seller and me. The purchases and economic decisions each of us make profoundly influence many other people in many other ways, from parents feeling helpless to deny their kids overpriced sneakers they really can't afford because "all the other kids at school are wearing them," to the effects of my purchase of an automobile on your lungs or on the earth's climate.

Now in principle, economists do take such matters into account; the concept of externalities is designed to acknowledge the impact of a particular exchange on those who were not parties to it. But the existence of externalities is most often acknowledged in the abstract and ignored in the daily operations of the market economy. Moreover, as I have discussed elsewhere (Wachtel, 1998), even if externalities were to be attended to with much greater rigor and diligence, the standard economic model does not even come close to addressing the degree to which our lives are interdependent and our choices both constrained and intertwined.

In recent decades, there have been increasing challenges to this mainstream economic view from the subdiscipline that has come to be called behavioral economics. But even the most cursory glance at what passes for political discourse in our society today makes it clear that the assumptions just discussed about the morality, rationality, and beneficent consequences of the market are still widely shared not only by economists but by the general public and are trumpeted almost as much by liberal politicians as by conservatives. In contrast, the understanding of human behavior and experience that derives from psychoanalytic theory and psychoanalytic inquiry offers us a quite different picture. Psychoanalytic theories especially highlight the ways in which we *deceive* ourselves about our wants (as well as the *conflict* between wants that can make what we consciously desire the enemy of what we want and feel even more deeply). To extricate ourselves from the prevailing idolatry of market worship and the myriad social and ecological problems such idolatry yields, it is essential to be clear how far from the truth is the claim that ours is a system in which what people end up with is what they want.

For the economist, using the methodology of so-called revealed preferences, the answer to what we want is astoundingly simple – look at our credit card statements. If with our purchases we have also bought global warming or toxins in our soil and water, or widening social inequality, well, that package of goods and damages must be what we witting, rational, utility-maximizing consumers wanted. In a clearheaded way, we have decided to trade off precisely the amount of environmental degradation we have borne for the precisely anticipated pleasure provided by the goods we have chosen. Thus, virtually by definition, any other trade-off would leave us worse off. Clearly, a psychoanalytic perspective addresses such matters rather differently, and it provides an invaluable foundation for questioning whether in fact the "preferences" we reveal in our daily forays into the marketplace should be taken as the last word about what will maximize our well being.

Parallels between the Structure of Psychoanalytic Assumptions and the Assumptions of the Socioeconomic System that Is Its Context

But if psychoanalysis helps to uncloak some of the justifying myths of the religion of the market – those that portray us as knowing exactly what we want, as making witting choices on the basis of a lucid understanding of our needs and of what brings us satisfaction – in certain ways it also *parallels and reinforces* the prevailing mythology. The efforts by critics of our economic assumptions (e.g., Galbraith, 1958, 1967) to point out how our "wants" and "needs" do not just issue spontaneously from the deepest wellsprings of our being, but rather are to a significant degree products of corporations' ceaseless messages and manipulations – messages and manipulations that may lure us further and further *away* from our true selves and true desires – have met with extraordinary resistance from an economics and political community committed to a respect for the choices exercised by consumers that does not seem matched by a respect for almost any other values. We thus still urgently need an effective and comprehensive critique of consumer desires. Psychoanalysis, as the science of desire par excellence, seems a natural foundation for such a critique. But for many years, psychoanalysis too, in its own way, offered a conception of desire as welling up spontaneously from within, and of a true self that lies in a realm apart from the world of daily social exchange and its constant flow of messages in all directions.

Our deepest desires, in this view, lie in an interior realm that can be distinguished from the "superficial" impact of the messages we continually convey to each other, including not only exchanges of an intimate or personal sort, but also about what is desirable, what "everyone" wants, what it is "normal" to want, and so forth. Perhaps this is in part why psychoanalysis has had so little to say about the economic side of our lives, about the assumptions and inclinations that shape our decisions about what job to take (the high-paying one or the gratifying and meaningful one), what products we want and need, and so forth, despite those considerations often accounting for more hours of conscious preoccupation on our patients' parts than the topics more commonly discussed in the psychoanalytic session. Psychoanalytic theories of desire tend not to address or take seriously the ways in which we create desires *in each other*, through the constant exchange of messages about what is desirable, admirable, enviable. Not only through ads, but also in the daily exchange of social clichés, we evoke in each other the images that construct our desires so extensively around material goods and purchasable experiences or socially defined signs of success. The intensity of some people's wish for a BMW instead of a Chevrolet (and the implicit denial that either vehicle will probably spend a good portion of its driving time on a crowded expressway, not the mountain road in the carefully crafted ad) or the belief that the next iteration of the iPhone or some other hot consumer item will noticeably improve one's life do not arrive via an impulse from the psychic interior. They reflect the messages and signals *we give each other*. If you want to be part of the group, you don't question such assumptions, you *affirm* them, and in so doing you further increase the bouncing back and forth of the social meme. Much of what we believe –and organize our lives around – we believe because it is what "everyone" says. We sing in chorus, believing we are expressing our individual voices, but in large measure both hearing and adding to the voice of the crowd.

For psychoanalysis to lead us beyond this self-fulfilling set of delusions and toward a way of life that is more rooted in human experience and genuine satisfaction, it needs to understand more clearly that desire is not simply an individual or "inner" experience but a socially constructed one. There are ways of being truer to ourselves or more alienated, but neither is immune from the experience – the *continuing* experience – of the mutual shaping of desire by the countless exchanges with others that constitute living-in-the-world.

In the flat, psychologically opaque model of the economist, our desires are simply properties we are endowed with, independently of any manipulations, comparisons, or socially exchanged messages. The "sovereign consumer" chooses, and the corporation merely responds to those choices. To this relentlessly, and even cruelly, superficial view of human life, which accounts for so much of the inequality and environmental havoc of our social system, psychoanalysis offers a potentially powerful alternative. But in order to achieve that potential, psychoanalysis will have to move beyond its proclivity toward hermetic interiorization to illuminate the connections between the experiences of daily life and the apprehensions and desires of the people living it. Depth, it turns out, is not a matter of how far "inside" we look, but rather of how profoundly we understand that the very distinction between "inside" and "outside" influences, between "deep" and "superficial," is a conceptual strategy that, while at first seemingly intuitively responsive to our subjective experience, is a problematic trajectory that leads us into tangles that obscure important and central features of our lives and make it more difficult to extricate ourselves from the social and environmental impasses that threaten our peace and our health.

The acontextual mode of thought I have been discussing both with regard to our society as a whole and in the early grounding assumptions of psychoanalysis reflect a radical individualism that lies at the core of many aspects of both. In the psychoanalytic realm, this view finds expression in the implicit conception of individuals as what Mitchell (e.g., 1988, 1995), Stolorow and colleagues (e.g., Stolorow & Atwood, 1994; Stolorow, Orange, & Atwell, 2001), and other critical voices in psychoanalysis have called acontextual monads, reflecting a vision of separable individual entities or isolated minds rather than human beings living in relation to a social and relational context. In the culture at large, it takes the form of assuming that it is desirable and natural to "move up" and "move away," that leaving one's family and community of origin in order to get a "better" job or bigger home is a sign of gumption and ambition. It is reflected in the ways that corporations move people from the Cincinnati office to the Atlanta office to the Denver office, with the assumption that a raise or promotion more than compensates for the tenuous ties to parents, siblings, friends, or community that such a way of life entails. We are expected, if we are really any good, to move "up, up, and away."

This phrase, of course, comes from the story of Superman, but it is an apt characterization of much of the aspirational direction of contemporary life. Superman, in fact, is a character who symbolizes more about our culture than one might at first expect. He is a hero who in one sense has a pedigree going back at least to Hercules and Samson but in another is a uniquely modern figure. The supermen of earlier myths tended to derive their strength from their parentage, from the gods and titans from whom they were descended. In one sense, this is true for our modern Superman as well; his strength derives from his being born of a people who live on a planet of vastly greater gravity than Earth's and who therefore have vastly greater muscular development than us. But what is highly significant about his story is that his extraordinary powers are only manifested once he has left home. It is only far away from the world of his fathers that he is super. Indeed, his only vulnerability is the possible encounter with a piece of home: Kryptonite, material from his home planet, is deadly to him.

One should not, of course, examine too closely the pseudoscientific foundations of the Superman story. It is intended as entertainment and presupposes a good-natured suspension of critical faculties. But it does seem interesting that contact with a piece of home does not just render him an ordinary mortal, with powers commensurate with its gravitational force (even putting aside that it takes only a little piece, which would not recreate Krypton's gravity – or that earthlings seem entirely unaffected); rather, even a little bit of home is a deadly poison. In a culture such as ours, the message seems to be, one can rise to extraordinary heights, but the pull of home is deadly.

To some degree, this way of living and this understanding of the pursuit of well-being – the tendency to seek success and achievement through moving away from the web of relationships that has, for most of human history, been the defining context for almost all people – has been evolving for some time and can be found in all parts of the world. In China, for example, the movement in recent decades from rural areas to cities constitutes the largest mass migration in human history. But as a chronic assumption that is part of the very backbone of society, it is probably most strongly evident in the United States. The noted philosopher, George Santayana (the originator of the phrase, sometimes mistakenly attributed to psychoanalytic origins, "Those who cannot remember the past are condemned to repeat it"), characterized the United States as a place "where men and even houses are easily moved about, and no one, almost, lives where he was born or believes what he has been taught" (Santayana, 1940, p. 139). His comment has important parallels with the observations of another prominent student of American life, Lloyd Warner. Warner, perhaps the foremost student of American corporate culture of his generation, suggests that,

> The most important component of the personalities of successful corporate managers and owners is that, their deep emotional identifications with their families of birth being dissolved, they are no longer closely intermeshed with the past, and therefore are capable of relating themselves easily to the present and future. They are people who have literally and spiritually left home . . . They can relate and disrelate themselves to others easily. (Warner, 1962, p. 51)

Relatedly, in another discussion of business leaders, he says,

> The mobile man first of all leaves the physical setting of his birth . . . [but] he must leave behind people as well as places. The friends of earlier years must be left, for acquaintances of the lower-status past are incompatible with the successful present. . . . But most important of all, and this is the great problem of the man on the move, he must to some degree leave his father, mother, brothers and sisters, along with the other relationships of his past. (Warner & Abegglen, 1963, p. 62)

This perhaps accounts in part for the amoral ruthlessness that is so prominent a part of much of corporate America, but it is important to note that the tendencies Warner describes in our corporate leaders have their equivalents in certain ways in a much larger segment of American society. Leaving the town or city of one's birth and moving from place to place for economic advancement is a signal feature of American life. Many more Americans move large distances from where they have lived and established whatever ties they have established than in other economically equivalent countries. The average American moves to a new neighborhood 14 times in his or her lifetime and each year, at least a fifth of all Americans move, some more than once. In contrast, in Britain the average person moves only 5 times in a lifetime, and in Japan only 4.[2] Clearly these differences have implications for the degree to which people have close ties to their neighbors, their communities, and their families.

In more recent years, this inclination toward frequent moves has diminished some, in part reflecting such factors as the decline in home prices, making it more difficult to sell one's home and move on, and in part, perhaps, reflecting deeper changes in the culture. It is noteworthy that in the 2012 presidential election, a key element in the election results was the high percentage of voters of Latin American and Asian origin who voted for Barack Obama. These more family and community oriented cultures may be modifying the more radically individualistic features that had long characterized American society and may signal a turn toward a greater appreciation of the value – and the reality – of interdependency.

To be sure, the element of hyperindividualism has by no means been simply erased from the American DNA, nor, for that matter, has it disappeared from psychoanalysis either, notwithstanding the increasing influence of the more contextual relational point of view. But there are reasons to think that, probably for different reasons, the plates are shifting in both. For many years, psychoanalytic thought clearly emphasized autonomy, differentiation, separation, to a considerably greater degree than it did interdependence and community. But increasingly this emphasis has begun to change. The introduction of a focus on interdependency by theorists such as Winnicott was an important early innovation, and the contributions over the last few decades of relational theorists have greatly amplified this alternative foundation for psychoanalytic theorizing. In the effort to apply psychoanalytic thought to the larger social realm, these emerging theoretical tendencies may have an additional arena in which to develop.

The Contextual Self

In further thinking about our interdependency and our responsiveness to the experiences and events of daily life – and in the effort to strengthen the conceptual foundations for a bridge between the individual psyche and the social order – I wish to highlight a view of the self not as an isolated property of a single individual but as itself a contextual structure or contextual phenomenon. In some ways, this understanding challenges a historical perspective, evolving for more than a century, that has emphasized the opposite direction in the evolution of the self. In this by-now mainstream analysis, the "self" is portrayed as a rather uniquely modern concept, as are the corollary ideas of conceiving of a history of the self or attempting to situate varying self-experiences in varying historical circumstances. Increasing numbers of writers in the last 50 years or so have directed their attention to the historical evolution of the experience of selfhood, and although each has given a somewhat different spin to the story, a common thread is not difficult to discern. Most have noted in one way or another the emergence of an increasingly individualistic experience of self, beginning at the time of the Renaissance and accelerating with the development of capitalism and industrialism. From selfhood as rooted in place, family, community, and tradition – a self marked by continuity, connectedness, and embeddedness – there has emerged an experience of self that is highly individual and individuated. In some ways this has been a salutary experience, yielding a degree of awareness, differentiation, and articulation of experience that enriches our lives. But in other ways this same tendency has been responsible for a sense of isolation, loss of moorings and meanings (see, for example, Rieff, 1966, 1979), and for a host of destructive movements that can be understood as desperate efforts to replace what was lost (e.g., Fromm, 1941). In recent years there has been a tendency for some theorists of the self to highlight a further transformation – one in which different *versions* of the modern individualized self are distinguished. Philip Cushman (1990), for example, has described this as a shift from a conception of the individualized self as bounded, masterful, and subjective to conceptions emphasizing instead the self as empty and fragmented.

In the chapters that follow, I build upon this tradition of social critique, but I also raise questions about some of the excesses and potentially problematic assumptions that have accompanied it. Although in important respects these accounts have been illuminating and valuable, they also contain more than a touch of hyperbole. After all, the experience of selfhood – in some manner or other – is virtually coterminous with the evolution of our self-reflective species. Surely the experience of self in the Middle Ages was never as lacking in the sense of individual identity as many of these descriptions imply. The fact that *individuals* are born, die, and feel pain ultimately alone – that however much the community may have participated in these experiences in different ways from today, they are ultimately experiences that individuals bear separately and that cannot be fully shared – must have enabled a quite considerable appreciation of separate selfhood even in the most thoroughly embedded community. Similarly, however much we may experience isolation and separateness today, not only are we in fact considerably more interdependent than the ideological accounts that undergird much of our culture acknowledge, but we are as well more connected than acknowledged by the social critics to whom I have been referring. The *tension* between the poles of embeddedness and isolation, a tension that is the very heritage of a self-conscious species, cannot be abrogated (cf. Angyal, 1951; Bakan, 1966; Blatt, 2008; Fromm, 1941). The relative strengths of these two poles can differ – and, I agree, *has* differed – from era to era and society to society in important ways; but the tension always remains, and must always in some way be reflected in people's experience.

In the remaining chapters of this book, in attempting to extend the theoretical perspective presented thus far from the clinical realm to the larger realm of society and culture, I particularly focus upon the nature of selfhood and psychological experience in relation to the social context. In the process, I aim to highlight the relational and contextual nature of the self and the problems with accounts that are overly hermetic and "internal." This does not, however, imply a view of selfhood or behavior that is conversely overbalanced to the "external," portraying us as mere playthings of the environment or of social forces. The rich understanding of subjectivity and the multilayered understanding of motivation, emotion, and conflict that are the legacy of the psychoanalytic tradition are very much part of the account I wish to present; but that understanding needs to be contextualized to serve usefully as a basis for social critique (and, indeed, as a basis for effective clinical work as well).

Psychoanalysis and the "Archaic"

Contemporary psychoanalytic formulations often look rather different from the depictions of instinctual drives and defenses against them that dominated psycho-analysis for so many years. Instead of emphasizing forces and energies and per-emptory strivings after bodily pleasure, the newer formulations tend to focus on primitive internalized images of self or other and on powerful fantasized images of desired or feared relationships and attachments. But in their deepest core, they often retain the basic theoretical structure of the earlier id psychology – depicting parts of our psychic life as cut off from maturation and from influence by the outer world.

Put differently, theories deriving from this (often not very closely examined) theoretical core – whether classical drive theories or contemporary relational or object relational theories – postulate that something remains primitive in the psyche and persists in spite of all that is going on around us. Because these early psychological structures or inclinations (whether conceived of in terms of drive-related desires or fantasies, internalized objects, or some other con-ceptual tool) have been split off from the evolving ego – the part of the psy-che that is in touch with perceptual reality and responsive to its ever-changing indications – they do not change as circumstances change nor do they learn from experience. In that sense, they are divorced from the context, seen as having little or nothing to do with the person's life as it is actually being lived in the present.

But, as I have discussed from a clinical vantage point in the preceding chapters, there is another way of understanding the seemingly archaic or infantile manifes-tations of psychological experience that pays full attention to their intensity and the ways they can lead us in potentially dangerous or problematic directions yet has vastly different implications. Closer inspection suggests that these apparently archaic and anomalous inclinations and experiences persist not in spite of, but pre-cisely *because of*, the way the person is living his or her life. Although seemingly unrealistic and out of touch with reality, they in fact reflect, symbolically express, and often perpetuate the conditions and experiences of everyday life. This understand-ing is especially important in using psychoanalytic insights to understand how such critical elements of human social life as race, class, and culture both shape and are shaped by unconscious symbolization, construction, and perceptual idiosyncrasies.

The Contextual Self and the Larger Social Order

The desires we manifest in the marketplace, economists insist, must never be questioned, never be related to the manipulations and circumstances of life in a culture in which the failure to have more each year than the year before seems at times like the only human tragedy acknowledged. At its best, psychoanalysis offers a powerful alternative to this point of view that, while celebrating individual choice, has an extraordinarily impoverished understanding of the individuals who are doing the choosing. In the following chapters, I will present an approach to psychoanalytic social analysis, rooted in the cyclical psychodynamic point of view, that attempts to cast our understanding of the dynamics of unconscious thought and motivation in a way that also takes into account race, class, ethnicity, culture, and the concrete economic and power relationships that are so important a part of people's daily experience of satisfaction or of "everyday unhappiness."

Notes

1. The emergence of the subfield of behavioral economics represents an important exception to this tendency. Behavioral economics is very much attentive to the ways that our choices often deviate quite considerably from conventional economic conceptions of rationality. But behavioral economists, though an increasingly important voice in their profession, still remain very much a minority at this point, both in academia and in the government agencies where decisions are made daily that deeply affect our lives.
2. See http://voices.yahoo.com/census-bureau-report-Americans-move-too-much -2983301.html. For an earlier account portraying similar trends but examining them in more detail, see Jasper (2000).

Chapter 13

Full Pockets, Empty Lives

Probing the Contemporary Culture of Greed

The great strength of psychoanalysis is not so much in its answers as in its questions. Psychoanalysis is, most of all, a point of view that probes beneath the surface of the obvious and raises questions about what we have comfortably assumed. Perhaps the most important product of a well-conducted analysis is increased curiosity. What is dull and settled becomes *interesting*. As a consequence, what was locked in becomes potentially changeable. The vagaries of professional status and the economics of insurance reimbursement lead our profession to emphasize its parallels with medicine. But in reality, our roots lie much more in philosophy. Socrates, much more than Hippocrates, was Freud's precursor. The questioning dialogue, rather than the definitive diagnosis, is the hallmark of the psychoanalytic method and of its benefits and virtues.

In keeping with this emphasis, my main aim in this chapter is to try to make the reader curious, to lead him or her to *notice*, and to find at least a little bit *odd*, some of the standard assumptions and characteristics of our society's way of life. Only secondarily do I aim to offer some speculative psychoanalytic hypotheses regarding their sources and dynamics. In essence, I approach life in contemporary American society in much the way a good psychoanalyst or psychotherapist approaches issues of character with an individual patient. Such work often includes a process of making *ego-alien* problematic assumptions and choices that had been ego-syntonic, thereby leading the patient to *look at* what he has previously simply taken for granted. I wish here to do something similar with regard to aspects of our lives as members of the contemporary consumer society in which we are, often unreflectively, immersed.

Thus, I want to turn the reader's scrutiny to the material side of our lives – to how, for example, we decide what we "need," whether we are doing well or not well, whether we have enough or feel we are deprived or need more. I would like to stimulate reflection about what we ordinarily regard as standard and reasonable assumptions about what our economic aims should be, about what is appropriate and healthy for us to want or to expect, both as individuals and as a society. I would like as well to consider how, in our daily experience as consumers and as citizens, we defensively isolate those assumptions from their consequence – the potentially irreversible damage we are doing to the environment in our relentless pursuit of what we think is the good life; the vast inequalities we are generating; the way we are increasingly rationing health care, supposedly because we "can't afford" more extensive coverage, notwithstanding the proliferation of iPhones, iPads, flat-screen TVs, and the like even in a time of economic downturn or the fact that the average home today is 50% larger than the homes people lived in in the affluent 1950s and 1960s (Rozhon, 2000).

In this context, I would like as well to invite reflection on the dynamics that lead so many in our society to persist in single-minded pursuit of economic goals, despite the strong indication from many well-conducted studies that economic success plays a strikingly small role in people's sense of happiness or well-being and that our society's vastly increased consumption over the decades has not been accompanied by any corresponding increase in happiness or contentment, either economically or more generally (Kasser, 2000; Kasser & Ryan, 1993; Myers, 2000; Sirgy, 1998).

From another vantage point, I would like to look at the role of envy and greed in contemporary life. Envy and greed are both individual experiences and characteristics of the culture at large, and in certain ways they are a bridge between the two. On both levels, they are capable of infecting our motivational system, driving us in directions that may be counter to our real interests. Envy is the more easily identified and precisely defined of the two experiences; greed is a term whose meaning is more ambiguous and variegated. If greed can be a raging river, rising out of control, envy is often one of its major tributaries. Seeing what others have is one of the powerful influences that stirs greater and greater desires, desires that over time may become autonomous of envy. We may want not just what others have but *more* than others have, or more for more's sake – regardless of any reasonable need on our part. From a different angle – and here I am beginning the task of parsing out the varied psychological meanings of greed – we may want more for the purpose of bolstering self-esteem.

The term *greed* is usually a pejorative, denoting a morally culpable attitude. But once we see the behaviors typically associated with greed as, partially, entailing a defense of fragile self-esteem, we begin to view the phenomena in a more differentiated and complex manner. Even apart from a psychological understanding of the dynamics of greed, there are exceptions to the generally opprobrious connotation of the term. We hear mainstream economists, business leaders, and libertarians advocate turning to the market to resolve human dilemmas that, through the ages, have been addressed from perspectives that included concern with morality, justice, or equity. For them, those of us who critique the directions in which our society is heading should just back off and let people be "free to choose" (Friedman & Friedman, 1980). The desire for more (and more, and more) is the source of "incentives" and, in their utopian picture, sparks innovation, creates jobs, and lifts all boats. That some are in yachts and some in scows is of little concern.

If for economists, greed is the engine of social progress, a form of enlightened self-interest, for many other thinkers, back to the ancient time when the myth of King Midas first took shape, greed has been seen rather as a form of self-deception, a kind of false consciousness in which what really matters is obscured by a pressing and single-minded focus on material wealth. Not infrequently, greedy individuals, or institutionalized greed, can cause considerable harm to others. But the insight in the Midas story points to what might be called the *tragedy of insatiability*. The greedy individual may be morally reprehensible, but he is also likely to be unable to achieve genuine contentment or satisfaction. Indeed, one of my central interests is understanding the *difference* between the individual who strives restlessly but does experience satisfaction as a result and the individual for whom insatiability is a curse, for whom the desire for money and wealth is a hunger that cannot be slaked.

In attempting to consider the psychological import of greed and its impact, the psychoanalytically inclined may well think to turn to Melanie Klein and her followers. Writers in the Kleinian tradition have focused on envy and greed far more than thinkers in any other psychoanalytic school (Boris, 1986; Klein, 1957). Their take on greed, however, is narrowly focused on speculative notions of the destructive fantasies infants supposedly have while feeding at the breast, fantasies in which the simple and nourishing act of sucking is presumed to be laden with meanings of devouring, destroying, tearing apart, and so on. It provides little that is of any use for exploring links between psychological experience and broader social trends, links that are essential to understand if we are to attempt any systematic changes in what might be described as a *culture* of greed that shapes our lives – including our "inner" lives – in countless ways. Apart from the absence of any real evidence for these extraordinarily concrete Kleinian formulations, these understandings are far too hermetic, far too focused on an inner world that is further from the world of everyday social reality than is Neptune or Pluto.

In this connection, I was happy to be able to address these issues in the context of the annual Karen Horney lecture of the Association for the Advancement of Psychoanalysis,[1] because Horney was one of the few major psychoanalytic theorists who *did* bring the social context squarely into her theorizing as a psychoanalyst. Her first book, we may recall, was *The Neurotic Personality of Our Time* (Horney, 1937). Those last three words, *of our time*, were a striking departure from the vision that had guided psychoanalytic theorizing up to that point. Horney was contending that the phenomena analysts observed in the psychoanalytic situation were society- and era-specific. A central message of that work was that *society matters*, that psychoanalysis was no less deep for taking into account the social, but rather, more accurate and comprehensive.

It is important to understand that a perspective in which social values and institutions play a much more significant role than is common in psychoanalytic theorizing is in no way inconsistent with the common psychoanalytic view that the phenomena we observe in our patients arise early in their childhoods. Horney's theoretical perspective paid quite considerable attention to what happens in childhood. She wrote clearly and forcefully about the ways in which parental attitudes and behavior shaped the experience of the developing child and about the vulnerability of the child in the course of growing up. But she understood neurosis not simply as reflecting fixations or developmental arrests, but as the product of continuing choices and actions made throughout life (Horney, 1939, 1945). In some psychoanalytic theorizing, the postoedipal years seem almost a kind of afterlife, in which we receive our just rewards or punishments for the person we have already become by age 5 or 6. Not for Horney. In Horney's theory, as in cyclical psychodynamic theory, which draws considerably on Horney's ideas, the early years matter, but they matter largely because of the kind of later years they are likely to make more probable. If our fate seems sealed rather early, it is because the sealer and the sealee are one and the same. The person we have *become* is the strongest influence on the person we continue to be. Applying this perspective to the phenomena of greed, envy, and materialism, it is apparent that – whether one is analyzing individual character traits or manifestations at the level of society as a whole – these phenomena reflect a complex set of interconnections and feedback loops.

What Do Money and Possessions Mean in Our Lives?

In attempting to understand just what money and possessions mean in people's lives, one of the first things worth noticing is how concrete and literal money appears to be to most people. Nothing seems more objective, more straightforward than dollars and cents. We refer in everyday parlance to "cool cash," because – mistakenly, as it happens – we regard it to be so different from hot affects.

We know, of course, that money can evoke passions. The murder mystery would not be such a perennially popular genre were that not the case. But the murder mystery is a simple genre, one we do not regard as needing explanation because the passions themselves are viewed as transparent. We may not fully understand, may not be able to identify with, may react with fascinated horror at some of what people *do* to get money, but the authors of such stories count on our understanding (or thinking we understand) quite fully and readily why the characters involved *want* it.

Money seems simple to us because in a certain sense it is thoroughly one dimensional, possessing quantity but none of the qualities that so complicate and enrich our lives. When it comes to money, there is only *more* or *less*. When traveling, one may notice that the currency of some nations is far more beautiful than the United States' rather uninteresting bills of a rather unappealing shade of green. Yet American currency is among the most desired throughout the world because it holds its *quantity* better than many others. It is true that we use phrases like *clean money* and *dirty money*, but that refers to the way the money is earned, not the money itself. Money itself *has* no qualities, only quantity.

It is this ability to know everything there is about money just by counting it that makes money appear so straightforward and concrete. And yet, almost nothing is more symbolic in its very nature. Money only has meaning as something that stands for something else – as a social phenomenon, as part of a web of interpersonal obligations, and as a symbol of individual aspirations, fantasies, desires.

As a consequence of our misunderstanding of money, this seemingly most literal and concrete element in our lives paradoxically leads us away from our actual experience and toward our *fantasies* about our experience. Money makes us *think* we know exactly what we are talking about when we do not. It substitutes for self-knowledge, or at the very least delays our inquiry into what we really want. It is a medium to promote *forestalling* a clear sense of what we want. What money means is "I don't know yet what I want, but when I do, here is something I can get it with." If you know what you want, you exchange your money for it, and then you no longer have the money. Of course, we may save, even while knowing for what we are saving. But even then, we are still in the realm of fantasy. We think this is what we want, but it is only after we have bought it that we can really know. And, as every one of us has experienced, it is scarcely uncommon to regret a purchase after it is made. It has been said that man is the only animal that can feel sad after sex. Perhaps what makes money seem sexy is that we can similarly feel sad after buying something.

Closest to the surface, of course, money is a symbol of success. One of its meanings – quite apart from what it can buy – is what it says about us. Veblen's (1899) insights into conspicuous consumption were controversial and original at the beginning of the last century, but today they are commonplace. Less commonly appreciated are the ways that money and material possessions fulfill other imperatives, having more to do with deeper levels of the psyche.

In "Character and Anal Erotism," Freud (1908) early put forth the idea that, in the unconscious, money stands for feces. In part, he suggested, this equation results from the relinquished aim of direct anal pleasures being given over to *another* form of playing with and holding onto something dirty. Money represents a transformation of preoccupation with material that society regards with disgust to material on which society places the highest value. Ferenczi (1952) extended this notion in his paper "The Origin of the Interest in Money," tracing a presumed sequence whereby anal pleasures give way to interest in mud, then to dirt, and eventually through a sequence to money.

Fenichel (1938), in his classic paper "The Drive to Amass Wealth," found much of value in these analyses, as he did in related conceptualizations by Abraham and by Jones, both again emphasizing the putatively "anal" meaning of money. But he cites approvingly as well a compendium by the French psychoanalyst Odier, of a much wider range of potential symbolic meanings of money, which included

> milk, food, mother's breast, intestinal contents, feces, penis, sperm, child, potency, love, protection, care, passivity, obstinacy, vanity, pride, egoism, indifference toward objects, autoeroticism, gift, offering, renunciation, hate, weapon, humiliation, deprivation of potency, besmirching, degradation, sexual aggression, anal penis. (p. 85)

The point is well taken that money can come to have almost any meaning in the unconscious of any particular individual. Nonetheless, Fenichel also notes, "nothing justifies the assertion that the symbolic significance of money is more important than its real significance" (p. 85). Indeed, the overall thrust of Fenichel's paper is to make room for both the irrational and the rational sources of our interest in money. Among the former, he emphasizes especially two meanings: (1) "the will to power," which he develops less along the lines of Nietzsche or of Adler and more with regard to narcissism and the wish to recapture feelings of infantile omnipotence; and (2) "the will to possessions," a category he uses to elaborate on the anal conceptualizations noted earlier and to relate them to issues of holding onto body parts and – in the specific link to feces – to what had seemed like it belonged to us but could be taken away.

Among the "rational" meanings that he emphasizes, Fenichel stresses the straightforward ability to satisfy our various needs that money affords and, on a social or sociological level, the ways in which the social structure requires the accumulation of money. Here Fenichel (1938) notes that, "a capitalist, under penalty of his own destruction, *must strive to accumulate wealth*" (p. 73, italics in original). We may see here that Fenichel – notwithstanding his role in the psychoanalytic movement as virtually the guardian of psychoanalytic orthodoxy for his generation – was in fact quite dissatisfied with the exclusively intrapsychic emphasis of the psychoanalytic mainstream and its inattention to the powerful impact of social and economic forces. Indeed, as discussed in the previous chapter, Fenichel was passionately committed to a vision of psychoanalysis as a foundation for radical social change. Certainly his mode of analysis is in many ways dramatically different from Horney's and from the version of psychoanalysis that guides this book and this chapter, but his understanding similarly emphasizes the necessity to take into account the way that social forces and structures on the one hand and the impact and dynamics of individual experience on the other reciprocally shape each other and give each other their meaning and direction.

An Illustrative Case

In further pursuing this theme, I now turn to a case. In part, I offer it as a further extension of our understanding of the role that money and material success play in people's lives and of the dynamics of insatiability. But I offer it as well as a jumping-off point for considering the limits of a purely psychological understanding and to provide a basis for exploring where a more social or cultural perspective is needed to round out the picture. I also offer it as an illustration of where my own tunnel vision shaped the way I understood the patient's experience. Even for someone as concerned as I have been throughout my career with integrating a social dimension more firmly into psychoanalytic discourse, it is easy, when sitting within the four walls of the consulting room, to make society largely disappear.

Stanley, a successful corporate executive, had difficulty enjoying his quite substantial success in any sustained way. He alternated between, on the one hand, taking pleasure in his accomplishments and relishing images of himself as a dashing man about town and, on the other, seeing himself as a dull, mediocre, pathetic man seeking younger women to bolster his self-esteem but unable to commit himself to them when they were interested. In the course of the work, it became increasingly apparent that guilt over having succeeded where his father was perceived as having failed made it difficult to enjoy the fruits of his success, or even to experience it freely as success. He had grown up in a home in which his mother was frequently disparaging of his father, and his financial success, as a consequence, was to a significant degree a forbidden triumph, both savored and feared.

His attraction to younger women further exacerbated and complicated the largely Oedipal nature of his conflicts. On the one hand, younger women were "safer." As he himself put it, they were less "motherly," they were a "fresh start" that got him away from his family. On the other hand, in the corporate world in which he moved, they were, as he also put it, the coin of the realm, a symbol of success that further exacerbated his guilt.

While there was much value to this way of looking at Stanley's dynamics, it was insufficient. The simple dichotomy that had dominated Stanley's understanding of his childhood years – disparaged father and cherished son – eventually gave way to a vision of a more complex configuration. The guilt of the Oedipal winner was only one part of his struggle. At another level, he, too, was disparaged by his mother, but disparaged in a very particular way. Stanley suffered from a particular fantasy that he had internalized from his mother, a fantasy of himself as slothful, needing to be pushed and prodded, having as his natural state one of inactivity that he had constantly to counter. His mother loved him dearly but saw him as someone with enormous potential who needed to be prodded constantly in order to fulfill it. The image he had internalized from his mother's experience of him and of her relationship with him was of himself as naturally inert and as needing to be eternally vigilant or he would do nothing at all.

This image of himself was activated not only in his work life but also even in his recreational life. He would push himself to go out almost every night, to be at jazz clubs and bars until all hours of the morning, even when he had a very full work schedule the next day. It is scarcely surprising that he would experience a certain degree of relief when, for one reason or another, one of his planned forays was canceled. But that relief, a perfectly natural consequence of his grueling schedule of work and play, was for him further confirmation that he was in fact slothful by nature. Why else, he thought, would anyone be pleased to have a fun evening canceled and actually enjoy just staying home and watching television!

Not surprisingly, given the pattern in which Stanley was enmeshed, whenever he would "catch" himself being lazy he would redouble his efforts to crack the whip and keep himself from being mired in sloth. So further Herculean demands would issue forth, with the inevitable result that he was once again set up to feel the forbidden relief when a break in the schedule was forced on him.

Over time, it became apparent that to be content with his present job, notwithstanding its high income and substantial prestige, clashed with the influence of a very central introject, the mother of childhood who had to "push" her adored child so he would be the fulfillment of her dreams instead of the "slug" he would be without her as the motivator. In essence, to experience himself as *self*-motivated, as capable of reasonable self-regulation and naturally present élan and vigor, felt like a betrayal and like a loss of the mother whose love – and whose opposition to his imagined inertia – was experienced as essential to his psychic equilibrium.

The observations just described vis-à-vis the case of Stanley readily lend themselves to an understanding in terms of Fairbairn's (1952) ideas about the development of internalized objects. These ideas were very largely initiated by Fairbairn's observations of the surprising loyalty to their parents shown by children who had been severely abused. These children would construct and accept terribly painful disparaging and blaming images of themselves rather than give up the fantasy of a tie to an ultimately benign parental figure who provided meaning, life, and (oddly) safety in a world otherwise terrifyingly arbitrary.

In understanding this dynamic, and its relevance for the themes of the present chapter, it is important to be clear that the abuse need not be physical, nor need it even be what ordinarily passes for verbal abuse. The abuse that leads to the internalization can also consist – as in the case of Stanley – of the parent's insatiable *expectations* of the child, of demands that are not couched as demands but that, when internalized, serve as an internal voice, a voice both cherished and terrifying, that drives the individual throughout life, never leaving him or her content with what has been achieved or accumulated.

My own clinical experience suggests that this kind of parental injection of insatiable expectations is not uncommon. I suspect that it is, as well, a dynamic that is especially characteristic of societies like ours, marked by vast opportunity, but also by intense competition, enormous variations in how much wealth and income is achieved, and powerful consequences resulting from which end of the economic spectrum one ends up on.

The Social Structuring of Motivation

The social context in which any given psychological configuration is manifested is crucial. Returning to the case of Stanley, for example, one may wonder whether the same dynamics would have been evident if Stanley had grown up in a different society – say in an Indian village, or in China under Mao – where the opportunity structure, the role models, the shared assumptions and imperatives were different. Not only would the possibilities of playing out his conflicts have been different, quite possibly the very nature of his introjects would have been. Mother might still have had some concerns about whether Stanley was energetic enough, but the very valuing of his being hard driving, much less the sense that enormous variations in his future life circumstances would flow from the choices he made about how hard and single-mindedly to work, would likely have been considerably diminished. Stanley would still have had an inner world, but it would have been a *different* inner world. That difference in itself should tell us that the inner world is not quite as "inner" as some of our theoretical language seems to imply, not as hermetically sealed off from the influence of larger social forces or of the circumstances and experiences of daily life.

A wide variety of features of our own society increase the likelihood that the configuration of psychological forces that evolves in an individual will find its structuring and expression in the materialistic end of the spectrum and will contain elements of insatiability. We are all familiar with the quip, "when the going gets tough, the tough go shopping." It is hard to imagine that quip emerging from Castro's Cuba, and certainly not from a tribe in the Amazon. Ours is a society that offers shopping as a solution to feelings of emptiness, worthlessness, low mood, and so forth. Many people report that shopping creates for them feelings of symbolic renewal, of being "good to themselves," a sense of "I deserve it," that, if often a bit hollowly defensive, nonetheless is momentarily bolstering. For many in our society, shopping is a form of self-medication, with the same momentary improvement in mood and the same potential side effects as more chemical versions of self-medicating.

Many aspects of American life pull very strongly for defining our desires and our sense of the good life in primarily material terms – most obviously advertising and the mass media, but also, for example, the very structure of our neighborhoods. For many Americans, the mall is the only really public space they know, the only place they go to "get out" or to be in the presence of other people. Wealth and income also determine, to a particularly significant degree in our society, whether one's children will be well educated, whether it is safe to walk the streets around one's home, and a variety of other crucial facets of life that are in themselves not directly purchased but that are highly correlated with income. One may not particularly want a big house, a fancy car, or expensive clothes or jewelry, and yet may still feel it is essential for a good life to have a high income (R. H. Frank, 2007, 2011).

For many Americans, however, success *is* defined materialistically; money and possessions are sought very largely as an end in themselves and serve as the validator of their worth and definer of their needs and desires. Indeed, so widespread is this feature of American subjectivity that some readers may wonder why I am bothering to state it at all. The sky is blue, the grass is green, and people like to have more money. What else is new?

But wanting to have more money is not the same as organizing a great deal of one's life around maximizing that dimension. All other things being equal, we would certainly have reason to wonder about someone who chooses less rather than more. But all other things are *not* equal. The pursuit of money and material goods as a central life aim often comes at a rather high price (Wachtel, 1983). There are trade-offs implicit in the choices people make, and a better understanding of those trade-offs is, in fact, one of the contributions that a psychological examination of life in the consumer culture can offer.

Few people believe or openly avow that having more money or material goods is the primary motivator or goal in their lives. Most people would certainly *say* that a good relationship or a warm family or happy children count more. But the reality of American life is often quite different. The actual choices and trade-offs people make may be quite at odds with what they say they want. This should come as no surprise to a psychoanalytic readership.

What may be more at odds with the conventional psychoanalytic view is the way that social and individual influences interdigitate in shaping this pattern. We are accustomed to distinguishing between "deep" sources and "surface" influences (see Chapter 5) and, in doing so, we often implicitly downgrade the role of the social. Perhaps even more problematic, we isolate it. That is, we may acknowledge that social structures and social influences make a difference – how can we not if we are reasonably sentient participants in the world around us – but we treat these social influences as separate, as having to do with something else than what we concern ourselves with as psychoanalysts.

Living in a consumer culture that converts our needs into commodities, and in the process – by again turning everything into dollar values – into quantities, shapes the very core of our being. Whatever potential for envy, greed, or insatiability is laid down in the earliest years of life is activated and exaggerated by certain cultural contexts, just as it may be more adaptively channeled and reworked in others. Even the mundane details of daily living can reverberate with the dynamic forces more familiar to psychoanalytic thinkers to yield a structuring of the psyche that is replicated over generations.

Consider, for example, a simple observation. All of our theories of development assume that when parents have time to be with their children, and when that time is relaxed, attentive, and responsive to the child's needs, the outcome will be better than if parents are tense, distracted, pressed for time, and resentful of the demands that parenthood presents. Usually, our clinical theories depict the difference between the two kinds of parenting as a consequence of the individual characters of the parents. Our journals and case reports are filled with accounts of patients' parents depicted as narcissistic, depressed, or lacking in empathy. If, however, we expand our focus, it becomes apparent that nurturingly engaged parental availability is also powerfully dependent on aspects of the larger social context, including matters as simple and straightforward as how long a commute Mom and Dad have to and from work, how chronically infuriating the traffic conditions are, how many hours they work and whether they have a work setting that is stressful and authoritarian or cooperative and promoting of their creative input, and whether their income and spending patterns permit them to pay their bills on time or whether they are in debt and hounded by creditors. Psychoanalytic discourse usually disdains such seemingly "surface" considerations. After all, does not the impact of any of these depend on the individual's character structure? Not everyone who drives home in heavy traffic comes home irritated at his or her kids.

But in fact, the omission of the simple and straightforward can be a real gap in psychoanalytic understanding. Yes, character structure will mediate the impact of almost any external situation. But at the same time, character does not operate in a vacuum. Character is not really adequately described from a solely intrapsychic framework. Character is a proclivity to act in certain situations – to *experience* those situations – in particular, idiosyncratic ways, and to experience and act in other situations in other ways that are *equally* idiosyncratic or pathognomonic. The same situation will elicit quite distinct reactions from people who have had different developmental experiences or who manifest different personality types. This much psychoanalysis recognizes clearly and emphasizes. What it often does not appreciate sufficiently is the converse of this observation – that the same character structure will eventuate not just in different behavior but also in radically different *experience* in different situational contexts. Put simply, context matters.

The picture that emerges from this analysis is one of very substantial specificity. Specifics of character, upbringing, and context all are determinative, and they interact in complex, mutually causal feedback patterns to yield still more specificity. No wonder psychological research, so often searching for generalizations, is so hard to conduct effectively. But my message is certainly not one of epistemological nihilism. If we must be wary of our generalizations, we must also probe the edges of the specifics to find larger contours. Society is not destiny, any more than character, in any purely intrapsychic sense, is destiny. But the modal experiences that are promoted in any particular society will have modal consequences.

One of the most important, but most often overlooked, dimensions mediating those modal consequences is the mutual influence of each of our choices and purchases on our neighbors, the reciprocal ratcheting up of what is standard and expected that, without our really sensing or understanding it, changes our perception of what is right, natural, appropriate (R. H. Frank, 1985, 2007). To understand how this works, consider a different but related phenomenon, the perception of what "looks right" in clothing. Simply by living in our society, we come to have a gut-level, automatic, unmediated-by-cognition sense of how wide a tie or jacket lapel should be or where a hemline should fall on a skirt. That socially shaped sense feels simply like straightforward perception, like just seeing what looks right. But when the fashion changes, over time our perception changes as well. The tie that looked perfectly fine comes to look too narrow or too wide, the hemline that looked just right comes to look too high or too low. Those of us less inclined to be slaves to fashion may try to resist this manipulation and may succeed for a while. But over time it is virtually impossible to override through cognition what is so powerfully communicated, on an immediate perceptual-affective level, by the experience of living in society with others.

So too – with even greater consequence – does our sense of what we *need* get shaped and changed by the experience of living in society. What are experienced as the standard accoutrements of an ordinary lifestyle in the United States are very different from what they are in Bangladesh, and they are quite different in the United States today than they were in the 1950s or 1960s, when (perhaps in contrast to today's perceptions) we were described as "The Affluent Society" (Galbraith, 1958). Today's average family would find unsatisfactorily small the home that the average family found perfectly ample back then, and would likely additionally experience as a deprivation the absence of air conditioning, dishwasher, clothes dryer, or other items that were relatively scarce luxury items back then (see Wachtel, 1983, for a more detailed description of how middle class standards were defined in the 1950s and 1960s and how standards for luxury and necessity change over time without the changes even being noticed).

Our sense of what we need has escalated substantially. What people perceived as quite satisfactory in that earlier era of relative affluence (again see Galbraith, 1958) would leave most Americans today feeling pinched and deprived. Economists tell us that a rising tide lifts all boats. But they deny the comparative effect that is so obvious to casual observation and so well documented by social psychologists. When the tide rises, everyone still feels they are at sea level. The envy toward those in the bigger boats is not reduced by the increase in the average size of the vessels. When all boats get larger, the average person's boat still feels like "just a boat."

At some level, I think, most Americans are aware that something is awry in the kind of consumerism our society spawns.[2] We know that there are many among us who by no means share in the general prosperity of our society and countless millions more throughout the world who get by on even less; and we know, at least at some level, about the impact of our escalating consumption patterns on the environment. What is less likely to be clearly perceived is that the ways members of our society organize their lives in pursuit of these continually escalating consumption standards are not always beneficial to their relationships or their children. It is perhaps the guilt or shame they feel in the unacknowledged recognition that their children often pay a price for what they need to maintain their own self-esteem in a highly competitive society that accounts for that great American mantra, "I'm doing this for my family." This mantra is usually uttered by parents who work too many hours or who tear their children out of schools and friendship groups to move to a bigger home or to pursue a promotion or a better paying job in another city.

The irony is that these very choices, which deprive children of the things that really matter in their lives, are likely to lead these children to turn to material goods for comfort, to define their needs not in interpersonal or experiential terms but in terms of status and the right material objects. Then, to further compound the irony, this response on the children's part is likely to validate to parents the perception that their children "need" these material stand-ins for emotional well-being. Indeed, looking ahead for a longer period of time, we may see how the children whose motivational structures have been shaped by such experiences will in turn manifest similar choices when they grow up and become parents, and hence will pass the entire pattern along to their children.

We are looking here at the psychological consequences of the way our society, our economy, our total way of life defines what are "the good things in life." Whether we are thinking of an investment banker, whose seven-figure salary requires him to be out of town three or four days a week making deals, or a psychoanalyst whose six-figure salary requires her to be seeing patients until 8 p.m. or 9 p.m. each night, one must wonder if the children or the family might be better off with *three quarters* of the income and a larger chunk of parental time. This is not usually the choice that people capable of garnering large incomes make in our society, however, and not because they are simply flawed people but because the social context makes such a choice very difficult.

Note here that I am talking about parents who work long hours not to put bread on the table but to ensure that their children grow up in a large house in a wealthy suburb, with a large-screen television in the family room, clothing displaying the "right labels," sneakers costing enough to make one a potential murder victim in some neighborhoods, and so forth. Note also that I am not talking about parents who are bad people or who necessarily have flawed characters. The very point I am addressing is that living in our society shapes the way we experience our needs, our vision of what is normal or essential for a decent life, for feeling *average*. To point to the fault in the individual parent is to miss the phenomenon itself. Shared social values and assumptions pervade the very heart of people's motivational structures, impacting powerfully on the choices they make in the most intimate aspects of their lives. They often determine as well whether one has the time or the psychic energy to be the kind of parent who can provide his or her children with the experiences that can inoculate them against substituting money and status for intimacy and genuine self-esteem.

Money as a Self-Object

In thinking further about how such patterns get maintained, and how the more intrapsychic dimensions intersect with the more manifestly social, it is useful to consider here a contribution from self-psychology. One of the most important theoretical modifications in psychoanalysis in recent decades was Kohut's recognition that the need for what he called selfobjects was not a once-and-for-all requirement of early childhood. Rather than self-objects being the building blocks for the construction of a fully autonomous self – one sound and cohesive enough no longer to need self-objects to keep itself healthy and together – self-objects, Kohut (1977) eventually concluded, were a necessity throughout life.

Viewing this observation from a different vantage point, one might say that the older psychoanalytic ideal of separation and individuation misrepresented as an end or as the singular direction of healthy development what is in fact one pole of an ongoing dialectic in human life (cf. Blatt, 2008). Far from separation and individuation being, in themselves, criteria of health, it is the capacity to make use of connection – of continuing and essential connection – that enables useful individuation at all. We do not put away our need for experiences of validation from others once we have achieved coherent selfhood.

In our society, however, many aspects of our lives make it difficult to obtain the necessary validation. If we consider the observations that Erich Fromm (1955) offered in his account of the marketing personality as the character structure most likely to be generated by the dynamics of our social system, we see a pattern that places significant obstacles in the path of developing truly validating relationships over the course of adult life. In order to feel validated, we must feel *known*; but in order to sell ourselves, to impress people in a market-dominated society, we must often deceive, covering over the very qualities – the vulnerabilities, conflicts, uncertainties – for which the healing impact of empathy and validation are most needed. Further compounding this unfortunate pattern is that when others too are selling themselves, when others too are hiding their vulnerabilities and exaggerating their strengths, there is a kind of mutual intimidation. Thus, each is discouraged from being too deeply self-revealing and encouraged instead, in subtle ways that are largely unconscious, to be strategic rather than intimate in most relationships. And, in the fashion discussed earlier with regard to how children may defensively develop a materialistic orientation toward life to cope with the deprivations arising from their parents' materialism, people caught in this mutual game of marketing and self-presentation are likely to virtually despair of receiving real affirmation and understanding and instead to emphasize even more intensely the substitute for genuine human connection that the marketing orientation represents.

Moreover, when people work long hours in order to chase after an ever-escalating standard of material consumption – and when even their time nominally away from work is significantly engaged with their cell phones and computers and with shopping – time for friendships and other relationships that can serve to maintain the emotional infrastructure is greatly diminished. Add to this that 1 in 5 Americans moves every year – most often in search of a higher paying job or to a bigger house – and the emotional infrastructure becomes even less stable.

If people need self-objects throughout life but lead lives that impede the maintenance of close ties, then they are placed in circumstances of considerable vulnerability. The need does not go away, but the ways people attempt to satisfy the need may end up serving to keep raw the very wounds they are meant to heal. In Kohut's conceptualization, the self-object is generally another person, although, in a variant also discussed by Kohut (1985), it may be an ideal to which one attempts to be true. But for many in our society, I suggest, money or material possessions or the status of one's job come to serve as substitute self-objects. They hold the self together, as best it can be held in that fashion.

In still another irony, however, the costs of seeking to sustain selfhood in this way leave the person on such a track less able to develop alternative, and more satisfactory, self-object relations. The things we must do to make money and possessions the fount of our selfhood or prime buttress of our self-esteem keep us further stuck in needing money and possessions as self-objects, further alienated from more human sources of psychic nourishment. On the most surface level, moving frequently to keep getting a better job and higher income, or working long hours that leave little time for friends or family, disrupt continuity of relationships, the sense of community, and the maintenance of intimacy. Moreover, at a deeper level, the patterns of relating that are associated with depending on money and possessions as self-objects influence and impoverish the way one relates to other people. The very quality of these relationships further increases the need for the compensatory, but not really satisfactory, use of these objectified attributes as self-objects, keeping the individual on a treadmill from which it is difficult to step off.

For some in our society, in addition to money being a self-object, the corporations for which they work have served a similar function. As they move through the corporate ranks, from the Denver office to the Atlanta office, to the Houston office, close friendships may be difficult to maintain, so the corporation itself becomes the constant, the source of whatever affirmation is experienced. Increasingly, however, even this meager source of attachment is being compromised. Loyalty, in both directions, has been considerably diminished. People who have worked for decades for one corporation are being let go in the service of downsizing and remaining competitive, and, from a reverse perspective, individuals who might have organized their lives around rising within a single corporate structure are opting to seek out new opportunities on their own. We are told that in the unfolding century, people should anticipate changing not only jobs but also careers a number of times throughout their working lives. Thus, the function corporations have served as substitute self-objects is likely to be diminished, and with this further diminishing of the available self-object structures, we may expect still greater dependence on money and possessions as the ultimate fungible self-object.

No one says to oneself, "I think I'll seek my self-objects in money and possessions" or "I think I'll validate myself and hold my self together with money." What I am describing is something that goes on unconsciously, adding further to the dismay and internal pressure to have more money. When people do not even *know* just what function money is serving in their lives, thinking rationally about it become even more difficult. The bewilderment and constant hunger that comes with being dependent on money in ways that are so poorly understood just adds further to the vicious circles I have been describing.

The Self and Its Context

I have threaded back and forth in this chapter between the contents and conflicts of the unconscious and the mores and institutions of society. The relation between the two is itself one of my primary concerns, perhaps as much so as the specifics of how greed, materialism, and discontent are generated and perpetuated in our lives. The quest for more and more money and material goods fills a hunger that comes from elsewhere. It is the task of psychological analysis to discover from where that hunger comes. But it is also important to see how that hunger is perpetuated by the small details of the lives we lead and the larger contours of the society in which we live, which both reflects and structures our characters.

The aim, central to psychoanalysis, of restoring intimacy and authentic selfhood is a noble one, and psychoanalysis does have a great deal to contribute on this score. But expanding the realm of the genuine and the intimate cannot be achieved defensively by constructing a moat that seals off the inner world from the world of everyday life and of society. To restore authentic selfhood, we must appreciate and understand the forces that oppose and undermine it. In some parts of the world, it is authoritarian regimes, whether of religious fundamentalists or ideologues of the right or left. In most of the industrialized world, it is runaway materialism and the socially sanctioned and socially amplified greed for goods. The moment we leave our consulting rooms, this all-pervasive feature of contemporary life is inescapably and powerfully evident to us. Indeed, more than we wish to admit, it is inescapably and powerfully evident *in* us.

The need is great to transcend the hermetic image of the subjective or inner world as somehow formed just by the space between mother and infant but untouched by Apple, MasterCard, or Nike. To transcend that hermetic image, psychoanalysis itself must become less hermetic. Right now psychoanalysis is isolated from sociology, economics, history, even the rest of psychology. There is a great need for us to move beyond that isolation, both because we have something to learn from these other disciplines and because we have something to contribute. We are familiar with the idea of keeping up with the Joneses. What we have not paid sufficient attention to is the way we keep up with the Joneses' introjects, the way in which the drivenness and vulnerabilities we acquire in childhood combine with the different pressures of everyday life to yield a pattern of striving that we think is ours but that, in important ways, lives through us rather than expressing our deepest and most genuine needs and inclinations. As we combine the insights that have accrued from psychoanalytic exploration with the understandings that derive from the other disciplines that study human behavior and the quotidian understandings and insights that guide our thinking when we are not wearing our cap as psychoanalysts or psychotherapists, we are likely to be in a better position both to help our patients and to contribute to the resolution of some of our pressing social dilemmas. What we have learned in our work with individual patients is too important to restrict to the consulting room – and what we have learned in our lives as members of society is too important to *keep out* of the consulting room.

Notes

1. An earlier version of this chapter was delivered as the 2001 Annual Karen Horney lecture to the American Institute of Psychoanalysis.
2. I do not mean to imply here that what I am describing is unique to the United States. To greater or lesser degree, similar patterns are evident in other industrialized nations and even in parts of the Third World.

Chapter 14

Greed as an Individual and Social Phenomenon

In this chapter, I wish to further explore the phenomenon of greed, this time from the vantage point of Sidney Blatt's influential two-configurations model (Blatt, 2008), which stresses the dual (and sometimes competing) needs for relatedness and self-development. Over the past 25 years, the two-configurations model has been one of the most innovative and important contributions to our understanding of personality dynamics and development. The model stresses the development of personality along two key dimensions – the establishment of mature, satisfying interpersonal relationships, and the formation of a cohesive, effective self or identity. In much of his writings, Blatt has termed the first line of development *anaclitic* or *relational*, and he has referred to the second line as *introjective* or *self-definitional*. The model has been particularly prominent in research on psychopathology in general and depression in particular. But the two-configurations model is rooted as well in a still-broader vision. It explores and elaborates on a tension that has been noted by thinkers about human nature throughout the centuries. Humans are both part of nature and apart from nature – separate, differentiated beings and a part of a larger whole that is absolutely essential for their survival. We suffer from our knowledge of our separate existence and from our awareness of the future – and hence of death. At the same time, this awareness is our essential defining quality as human and the foundation of all that is unique to our species.

Much as with nature, society too is both the context that makes our lives possible and the womb from which we struggle throughout life to emerge. The warm nurturing waters of human contact and social connection in which we swim and from which we derive our social and psychological nutrients are also waters that threaten to engulf and drown us. Anxiety is almost inevitable in negotiating this Janus-faced dilemma that is quintessential to our species. If we secure too strongly our connection with nature, society, or the key relational figures in our lives, we are in danger of losing our uniqueness, our identity, indeed our very sense of selfhood or being. But if we dedicate ourselves too single-mindedly to creating a self, even to being true to our perceived inner yearnings and perceptions, we run an equally terrifying risk – losing touch with the very ground of our being, our intimate connection with – indeed our inseparability from – the larger context of nature and of society. Different cultures pull for a resolution of this tension in one direction or the other – the distinction between individualistic and collectivist cultures is a widely applied one in cross-cultural research (Triandis, 1995) – but in fact people in *every* culture experience these competing pulls. The proportions and the modal behaviors or values may differ, but the need to deal with the fundamental conflict is common to all.

One particularly important feature of the two-configurations model, setting it apart from almost all of the other approaches to this core dilemma in human life, is its grounding in the traditions both of psychoanalysis and of empirical psychological research. On the one hand, in contrast to more speculative or anecdotally rooted understandings, the two-configurations model has been put repeatedly to the test of systematic controlled research. On the other hand, however, unlike formulations about personality that are derived rather exclusively from factor analyses of questionnaires or some other simplifying methodology that purchases seeming precision at a high cost, the two-configurations model is rooted as well in the complex vision of personality development that derives from psychoanalysis. Thus, like all psychoanalytic conceptualizations, it is dynamic, rather than categorical. The two configurations are not alternative categories into which people are put. They are not even "percentages of variance," with people conceptualized as showing a little of this, a little of that. Rather, they are inclinations or orientations *in tension*. As is true of all psychoanalytic formulations, at the center of this model are conflict, paradox, and an ongoing need to come to terms with powerful and competing inclinations.

People do differ in the degree to which they manifest anaclitic or introjective tendencies, and it is true that an extreme overweighting in either direction is likely to be associated with pathology. But health is not measured by the degree to which the person achieves a 50–50 balance. Balance is indeed important, but it is a *dialectical* balance, a balance that reflects the ongoing dynamic effort to reconcile conflicting needs and proclivities. The optimal balance for any particular person is a reflection of that person's genetic inheritance, early developmental experience, later developmental experiences, and, very importantly, the interpersonal and societal context in which the person's behavior and experience are manifested. This means not only that the social and relational context in which the person's orientation *developed* is crucial, but also that the context in which it is *presently* manifested can elicit, in differing configurations and proportions, quite different facets of the complex whole that is the person. The same individual who is especially concerned with separation, competency, and self-definition in one context may well be more concerned with a sense of belonging or being nurtured and cared for in another. This is not an inconsistency but a reflection of the inherently contextual nature of personality and the specificity of human experience (Wachtel, 2008, 2011a).

Introjective and Anaclitic Orientations as Bound Opposites

Although the concept of introjective and anaclitic lines of development points to a fundamental tension in almost all of us, it does not imply two separate "types" of people. Not only are the two orientations woven together empirically, in the readily observed variability and contextuality of their manifestations, they are not even *conceptually* independent. By this, I do not mean that they are not distinct or that they are not clearly delineated conceptually. Rather, what I mean is that they are conceptualized in a way that illuminates their quality of being not simply opposites but *bound* opposites, opposites in a kind of intrinsic tension, such that each inclination is powerfully and fundamentally shaped by the other. It is out of the very way that we attempt to merge, attach, root ourselves in the other or in society that our need for separation, boundaries, or self-definition emerges and is heightened. And it is in our very efforts to define ourselves as separate and self-sufficient that our need for connection is fueled. One side cannot be achieved without, as a very feature of achieving it, the other being introduced anew. We cannot resolve the tension by choosing one or the other but only by continually and creatively weaving them together in the fabric of our lives.

In this conceptualization, the two-configurations model resembles Piaget's complementary processes of assimilation and accommodation. Here too, each process cannot be adequately understood, cannot even really be defined, without reference to the other. Consider, for example, what happens when a child who has developed an initial schema of *dog* comes into contact with a kind of dog that he has not seen before, say a Chihuahua or a Great Dane. When the child learns to include either of these new experiences in his schema of dog, he is clearly assimilating them to that schema. But in the very effort to do this, the child is also accommodating the schema to take them in. It is no longer the *same* schema, simply because it is now a schema that includes these new outliers that previously were not part of the child's vision of what the category dog included. It is the very act of assimilation that produces the accommodation and the very act of accommodation that enables the assimilation. Neither could proceed without the other.

Social Implications of the Model: Bound Opposites and the Phenomenon of Greed

The understanding of the two-configurations model in terms of bound opposites, of dynamic rather than categorical distinctions, has important implications not only for how we view personality development and psychopathology but also for how we understand many phenomena that are central to the operation of our society as a whole. Any society, and especially one as complex as ours, has as one of its central challenges reconciling these two essential features of human psychology. A society that fails to make room for what might be called the anaclitic side of life, for our continuing need for relatedness and our continuing dependence on each other throughout life, breeds alienation and leaves people enormously vulnerable to the vagaries of nature, markets, or other sources of potential disaster. Even the hardest of hard-right ultra-individualistic ideologues (or at least those who have any hope of being electable) acknowledge that we need some kind of safety net for those who are in need. Reliance on individual responsibility alone is a recipe for disaster, both socially and individually.

At the same time, if a society makes insufficient space for self-definition, if the need for boundaries, relative autonomy, or the development of the unique aims and values that create a distinct identity are persistently thwarted, the result is likely to be stultifying conformity and an absence of initiative and motivation. The now-defunct Soviet Union might be thought of as an example of such a society.

The task of a society is to create a way of life in which these two strands of human nature interact in a dynamic and creative way, with neither predominating to a degree that it crowds out the other. As with individuals, distortions and hypertrophies can develop in societies too, but as with individuals, these hypertrophies always have a price and are inherently unstable. Ideologues may, in one sense, almost be defined by their failure to appreciate the dialectical nature of human needs and motivations.

Greed as a Social Phenomenon

In this chapter, I wish to focus on one particular realm in which the social and the psychological converge and in which the two-configurations model provides potential illumination – the phenomenon of greed. I choose greed as my focus both because it is a topic I have explored in my own research and because it is especially central to the dynamics of our society. At least since the time of Adam Smith, it has been clear that greed can be a powerful engine of economic growth and productivity. As Smith (1776, Book I, Chapter II: 2) put it, in a widely quoted passage, "It is not from the benevolence of the butcher, the brewer, or the baker that we expect our dinner, but from their regard to their self-interest."

To be sure, greed and self-interest are not necessarily the same. And a strong case can be made that Smith used the latter term (that is, *self-interest*) precisely because he meant that, rather than greed. But Smith's thinking has been retrofitted, one might say, by an ideological strain that has become, in many respects, the dominant one in our society. The constant stimulation of desire for more and more material goods in all of us and the single-minded pursuit of that experienced need for more and more by each individual in the society is seen by leading voices in the American academic and political life as the fuel that ignites our economy and that is necessary to make us a strong and prosperous nation. In the ideology that has gained such problematic strength in our society in recent years, explicit concern with the feelings and needs of others, except insofar as those feelings and needs are important to discern for the purposes of marketing and product development, is not only unnecessary but also misguided. Attention to the needs of the community as a whole or to its least privileged members impairs the remarkable alchemy through which the invisible hand of the market most effectively turns the base metal of individual greed into social gold.

Interestingly, if we turn to Adam Smith himself, we see that from the outset he understood that the wish for more for oneself must be pursued both in tension with and, from a broader perspective, in concert with – or in the term I introduced earlier, in *bound opposition to* – another equally crucial set of human motivations and inclinations. Smith discussed this second crucial dimension under the rubrics of natural sympathy and moral sentiments. A good society – indeed, even a society that is capable of functioning well economically – depends on a degree of trust and trustworthiness that enables people to count on the honesty, integrity, and good will of those with whom they interact and without which even the capacity to engage effectively in hard-nosed negotiation breaks down. When greed alone prevails, greed itself is thwarted; when each person has no inhibition in maximizing profit by providing cheap, damaged, or dangerous goods, none can engage intelligently in trade.

Moreover, Smith's vision of a good society goes beyond simply the modicum of honesty required for the pursuit of self-interest to be reasonably enlightened. As Smith (1759) put it in *The Theory of Moral Sentiments*:

> All the members of human society stand in need of each other's assistance. . . . Where the necessary assistance is reciprocally afforded from love, from gratitude, from friendship and esteem, the society flourishes and is happy. All the different members of it are bound together by the agreeable bonds of love and affection. . . . Society . . . cannot subsist among those who are at all times ready to hurt and injure one another. (pp. 124–125)

In a contemporary context, writers like the political scientist Robert Putnam (2000) have made similar points about our own society and the challenges it faces.

In essence, then, the dynamics of greed in a well-functioning society must be dialectically balanced, as must the anaclitic and introjective tendencies in a healthy personality. Putting together the conceptual frameworks of Sid Blatt and Adam Smith, we may say that ambition, striving for success, and seeking to stand out are essential components of a vital society and economy but only when balanced by a corresponding element of caring, concern, solidarity, or fellow feeling for others. When the first is lacking, interdependence regresses to dependency, and one may perhaps depict the society itself as problematically anaclitic, lacking dynamism, productivity, innovation, or willingness to take risks or to lead. When the second is lacking, one may think of the society as problematically introjective, the alienated, competitive struggle among hostile and isolated monads described by social critics from Hobbes (1651) to Marx (1964) to Fromm (1941, 1955).

Insatiability and Heedlessness

Given its importance both in individual lives and in our society as a whole, greed has been a rather neglected topic in the psychological literature. Among psychoanalytic discussions of the topic, a Kleinian perspective has been particularly prominent (e.g., Boris 1986; Emery, 1992; Klein, 1957). These writings, although at times suggestive, have tended to be breathtakingly speculative. They have also given enormous emphasis (perhaps, one might say at the risk of a bad pun, overweening emphasis) to the experience of the infant at the breast. Consequently, they offer few paths toward understanding the ways in which variations in greed among individuals and societies are related to larger social phenomena.

In part, the neglect of the concept of greed – both in the psychoanalytic literature and in the larger literature of psychology in general – reflects the origins of the concept of greed not in the empirical tradition of psychological research but in the judgmental tradition of moral exhortation. It reflects as well the considerable ambiguity and imprecision in our usage of the terms *greed* and *greedy*. If one, for example, looks through the literally thousands of references to greed in the Lexis-Nexis index of newspapers, magazines, and other news and media sources, it is readily apparent that the variations in tone, nuance, and connotative and denotative reference point are enormous. In thinking about these varied uses and meanings of the term, I have provisionally, in my own research, attempted to introduce some order by distinguishing between two broad classes of usage – greed as *insatiability* and greed as *heedlessness*.

In some ways, the former may be seen as pointing to how greedy individuals hurt (or at least frustrate) themselves, and the latter to how, through their greed, they hurt others. The distinction, like almost all distinctions in the psychological realm, is by no means hard and fast. Thus, for example, King Midas might well serve as a poster child for the insatiability dimension. As rich as he was, it was simply not enough. And ultimately, the story of Midas is clearly a story of how greed brings ruin to the greedy person himself. But we can certainly agree that things do not go well for Midas's daughter either. And indeed, the insatiability of the greedy person has almost inevitable impact on others.

Similarly, if we consider who might be the poster child for the second meaning of greed – heedlessness – a good candidate might be Gordon Gekko, the character in the film *Wall Street* (Pressman & Stone, 1987). Gekko's signature statement, "Greed is good," comes from the mouth of a man who is amorally indifferent to the impact of his actions on others. He wants his, and the devil take the hindmost. Yet at the same time, two things are worth noticing. First, Gekko hardly seems like a genuinely happy or fulfilled man. His greed has an impact on him as well. Second, one important sign of his discomfort with his total indifference is his need to rationalize it. This rationalization, "Greed is good" is the mantra of our entire economic system, a claim that, ultimately, selfish behavior not only does not hurt others but also is essential to everyone's welfare. Recall here Adam Smith on the butcher and the baker (purged, of course, of Smith's insights about the moral sentiments).

Greed and the Two-Configurations Model

Can the two-configurations formulation shed any further light on the distinction I have been discussing thus far? Perhaps we might speculate that the insatiability dimension has some relationship to the anaclitic line of development and the heedlessness dimension to the introjective. Might we, for example, see a disguised or altered expression of what Blatt has called anaclitic in the greedy person's insatiable hunger, in feelings of emptiness and lack of support and nurturance that fuel a relentless sense of needing more? Similarly, in greed marked more by the dimension of heedlessness, are we observing a pathology of drivenness and self-definition, an inability to integrate the needs and feelings of others into one's own aims either because the boundaries of the self, perceived at one level as too permeable, are defensively bolstered and hardened or because driving voices from within drown out the voices of other people's needs and experiences?

To be sure, insatiability can derive from an unquenchable desire for achievement or at least for signs of achievement. And, conversely, what I am calling heedlessness can at times derive from a sense of entitlement that comes from feeling, "I have never received the love and protection I desire from others." So there is not a simple one-to-one correspondence, and this, of course, is not surprising because the two configurations Blatt has studied do not reduce simply to greed, nor does greed reduce to those two configurations. They are potentially related but by no means equivalent concepts.

Nonetheless, exploring the ways in which greed, materialism, and consumerism do and do not map onto the two-configurations model can add illuminating dimensionality to our understanding of the social and motivational implications of greedy behavior. At times, we may note, an overly materialistic orientation is a means toward independence from other people, toward a substitution of *things* for people. But at other times, it can be almost the opposite. In one patient I saw a number of years back, for example, who had a seemingly insatiable desire for material things, those material things were clearly in the service of ingratiating himself with others or of making himself attractive to them, a sadly ineffective effort to connect with other people, rather than to be independent.

Stimulated by the two-configurations model, one might suggest that, in contrast to the distinction between insatiability and heedlessness (though partially overlapping with that distinction), the various manifestations of greed might also be usefully categorized according to whether the primary aim is one of *filling* up the self with good stuff or one of *shoring* up the self with signs of achievement and success. Although the (anaclitic) fear of being a hungry self (or a lonely self) and the (introjective) fear of being a weak self are by no means totally independent, they do represent different loadings or emphases that, as in other arenas in which roughly the same distinction has been applied, can have quite significant implications.

From the vantage point of the two-configurations model, we may ask about greedy behavior whether it supports primarily the sense of belonging, being connected, being taken care of or, in contrast, of being masterful and bounded, to use for this latter orientation the terminology emphasized by Cushman (1990) in another application of psychological perspectives to the analysis of social issues. And one thing that immediately becomes clearer from this vantage point, and quite interesting as well, is that although one might think of greed as something that disrupts social ties, and of the greedy person as unpopular as a result of greed, we may also see that certain forms of greed (and of the related phenomena of materialism and consumerism) are largely designed to make oneself more desirable or attractive to others. These efforts may not succeed (as many neurotic tendencies do not succeed), but that is at times their aim, and whether we are considering the implications for treating an individual in psychotherapy or of working to change problematic social trends, it is useful to understand the distinctive motivational configurations that underlie the pattern with which we are concerned. When someone wants lots of money, expensive clothes, a big house, all the signs of success, sometimes it is to enhance the sense of self-efficacy and independence, but at other times it is a way of winning people over. The two-configurations model helps us to see more clearly a distinction between kinds of greed or motives for greed that may not be immediately evident in the morphology of the behavior itself.

Put differently, people who are particularly driven by feelings (conscious or unconscious) of dependency, neediness, or emptiness, who need to be filled up by others, who manifest inclinations toward more hysterical forms of personality organization, may well be more inclined, when greedy, to be hungry, to feel they need more and more simply because they do not have enough. At the same time, because their greed is anaclitically rooted, they may be wary of alienating others, may be hesitant to offend by *actually* taking more than their fair share, even as their *desires* feel endless and their capacity to feel they have enough is limited. As the two-configurations model helps us to understand, greed of this sort may be characterized more by resentfulness than by actual accumulation; such people feel perpetually unsatisfied but also perpetually prevented from acting to take or get what they think they need.

In contrast, people more focused on self-definition, on the maintenance of clear boundaries between self and other, or on struggling with feelings of inadequacy or insufficient power or independence, may be more likely, when greedy, to be characterized by the dimension I have called heedlessness. Their greed is, one might say, less pathetic and more aggressive. That is, they are struggling less with feelings of needing to be filled up and more with feelings of needing to be strong and dominant. Fine-tuning themselves to the needs of others in order to elicit protection and nurturance from them is less of concern than making sure that others are not dominating or disdaining them. The need for more and more is, one might say figuratively, to display the musculature of the body's surface, rather than to fill its empty interior. Thus, the heedlessness dimension of greed may be expected to bear some relationship to the introjective dimension of Blatt's two-configurations model, with its emphasis on boundaries, separation, and self-definition.

Greed, the Anaclitic-Introjective Distinction, and Horney's Tripartite Model of Moving Toward, Away, and Against

The distinctions that I have been discussing thus far overlap in interesting ways with Horney's (1945) conceptualization of the moving-toward and the moving-against neurotic trends, with an additional and more complex relation to what she refers to as the moving-away trend. Like the two-configurations model, Horney's conceptualization is often mistakenly viewed as a typology when it is in fact a depiction of inclinations in tension, competing inclinations of the same individual, even if, as with the anaclitic-introjective distinction, individuals may be identifiable as occupying different ends of the continuum with regard to their relative emphasis on one or the other of these inclinations.

It is perhaps easiest to see how the anaclitic or dependent dimension corresponds to the moving-toward trend in Horney's scheme. In both, there is an experience (sometimes conscious, sometimes mostly unconscious) of intense neediness and of turning to others for support and nurturance. If greed is characterized by an overtone of either of these tendencies, it will be greed of the insatiably hungry variety, and although the *expression* of this hunger or the resentment or despair it generates may alienate others, the strongest underlying *aim* is to cement the ties to them, to prevent the feared occurrence of abandonment, to maintain a sense of safety or well-being through being protected, cared for, loved.

The introjective or self-differentiation dimension also maps usefully onto Horney's theoretical scheme but, in this instance, it seems to partake of both the moving-against trend and the moving-away. The distinctions between the moving-against and the moving-away trends are manifold and fundamental, but in the present context perhaps what is most important is that in the former category (the moving-against), one is still very closely tied to others and needs them, even if that need is less evident because the need is expressed through dominance. But whereas one cannot be dominant or dominating without the presence and participation of others, one can be independent, or at the very least can strive for independence and experience oneself as independent, quite apart from any connection to others. In the sense that the self-definition dimension is one in which the firmness of the *boundaries* of the self is at issue, with a desire for more sharply defined boundaries or a fear that the boundaries are dangerously permeable, it is a dimension of experience that overlaps quite considerably with what is implied in Horney's moving-away trend. If we view this motivational configuration from the vantage point of greed and materialism, the function of a vast cache of material goods is to substitute for people and to diminish the need for them because one *has* (in the most literal sense) whatever one needs.

However, in the sense that the introjective dimension refers to being self-critical around themes of adequacy, success, admirability, and so forth, it overlaps significantly as well with the moving-against trend, in which anxiety is warded off through what might be called – seemingly paradoxically but actually quite straightforwardly – a "desperate" show of strength. Indeed, some of the vulnerability of the individual who is plagued by negative or depressive feelings along the introjective dimension may be usefully understood in terms of the failure of the moving-against strategy really to liberate the person from the "taint" of needing others – that is, as Horney describes, the persistence of neediness beneath the bravado or, more accurately, the persistence of conflict between wanting to dominate and wanting to be taken care of.

Thus, from the vantage point of the two-configurations theory, the moving-away trend may be seen as occupying a position further along the self-definition dimension, a position even more radically dedicated to eliminating or erasing the vulnerability that inheres in needing people (or in *acknowledging* one's need for people). It would be of considerable interest to conduct research, inspired by both the Blatt and the Horney conceptualizations, that examines where people's experience and behavior sort into a tripartite model (corresponding to the dimensions of toward, against, and away) and where they sort into a bipolar model, as implied in the related but nonetheless distinct two-configurations perspective. In the pursuit of greater understanding of the psychological dynamics of greed, similar attention to parsing out where a two-configurations model captures most of the variance and where a tripartite model is preferable would be a useful issue to explore.

The Intersection of the Individual and the Social

For all of the difficulties and ambiguities in the concept of greed, I have chosen to make it a focus of this chapter – and an important element in work I am currently pursuing beyond this chapter – because it seems to me a key nexus between some of our most pressing social problems and the more private discontents that plague many individually in our society. Psychoanalytic theorizing and discourse have often paid insufficient attention to the impact of the values, institutions, pressures, assumptions, and messages of the larger social system on people's sense of well-being or of distress and unhappiness. Although the larger agenda of psychoanalysis has always included a concern with how the values and institutions of society seep into (as they are also shaped by) the psychological depths of the individual, the carrying out of this agenda has often been hampered by a priori assumptions about the inordinate impact of early familial experiences. These assumptions tend to render society but a distant shadow or ghostly epiphenomenon, simply the elaboration of patterns that have already been well set before the child begins elementary school.

If psychoanalytic social criticism is to be vital, it must take seriously the impact of real social and economic forces without reducing them simply to manifestations of the intimate sphere writ large. At the same time, the strength of a psychoanalytic analysis lies in highlighting the ways in which the impact of those larger social forces is complicated by and intertwined with unconscious emotional pulls and attitudes, conflict, and the struggle to keep certain experiences out of awareness, and the anxiety and vulnerability that neither riches nor power can quell.

One key to illuminating this enormously complex set of interconnecting force fields lies in the elaboration of both the phenomenology and the motivational underpinnings of whatever psychological phenomena are being investigated.

In pursuing better understanding of the phenomenon of greed, the distinctions that Blatt has explored and articulated in the evolving two-configurations model seem to me of great value. The suggestions offered in this chapter are speculative, one provisional way of applying the model that is based on both my recent immersion in the study of greed as a psychological phenomenon and extrapolations stimulated by the two-configurations theory. In emphasizing the conceptualization of bound opposites in the two-configurations theory, I have tried to highlight the dynamic nature of a framework that is sometimes misunderstood to be merely categorical and to show how this dynamic understanding of a key dialectic in human development has applications and potentials well beyond its original areas of application.

Chapter 15

Psychoanalysis, Psychotherapy, and the Challenges of Race and Class

It has been noted by a variety of observers that in its origins psychoanalysis was a rather revolutionary challenge to the comfortable assumptions of the status quo, but over the years it has become an establishment profession that fits easily into the practices and social structure of our highly unequal society (see, for example, Jacoby, 1983, and Aron & Starr, 2013). Most who hold this view do not question that psychoanalysis provides needed help to suffering individuals or that its practice embodies genuinely humane and socially valuable understanding of human suffering. The critiques are, after all, mostly critiques from within. Rather, the concern embodied in these critiques of psychoanalysis is that the focus of psychoanalytic inquiry has become too narrow, addressing certain sources of human misery but largely ignoring others that are equally important. As noted earlier, neurotic misery is not the only treatable source of suffering that can be subtracted from the sum of everyday unhappiness that we mere mortals cannot avoid. Social inequality and injustice represent another powerful source of unnecessary suffering that, in principle, can be modified and diminished.

I believe that psychoanalysis has something useful to contribute in this latter realm as well, and in what follows I wish to offer some ideas about the ways in which that contribution might be made. The question of how psychoanalysis can contribute to addressing social inequality and injustice can be approached both in a narrow and a broad fashion. Viewed narrowly, the question becomes primarily one of treatment: How can we make psychoanalytic treatment available to a wider range of patients, especially to those who have been socially marginalized? What are the ways in which our treatments must be modified in order for them to be appropriate for patients other than those for whom the treatment was originally devised? Viewed more broadly, the relevant questions still *include* this first set of concerns, but then go well beyond to inquire not only about psychoanalytic *therapy* but psychoanalytic *theory* or the psychoanalytic point of view: How can the psychoanalytic perspective deepen our understanding of the needs and dilemmas of those whom society has treated unjustly and dismissively, and how can those insights be applied, not only in direct therapeutic ways but in efforts at social and political reform?

I concentrate in this chapter particularly on the second or broader question, but consistent with my comment that the second question includes the first, I begin with some of the ways in which psychoanalytic *treatment* can be brought to bear in serving disenfranchised populations.

Psychoanalytic Therapy and Middle-Class Values and Lifestyle

There can be little question that psychoanalysis began as an approach directed toward the middle and upper classes. The case studies in the literature of the first decades of psychoanalysis clearly depict a world of relative privilege (even as they also, of course, describe intense human suffering). This reflected not just the matter of who could pay for analysis but also a view of the psychological state of the lower classes that suggested that they did not have the inner resources to benefit from the insights psychoanalysis had to offer.

Freud's unexamined class biases were evident in his explanation of the "puzzle" that hysteria was no more frequent in the lower classes than in the more cultivated classes. At a stage in his thinking when he viewed actual traumatic events as an essential part of the etiology, he regarded this absence of higher rates of hysteria among the lower classes as a challenge because "everything goes to show that the injunction for the sexual safeguarding of childhood is far more frequently transgressed in the case of the children of the proletariat" (Freud, 1896, p. 207). Thus, given this view that sexual abuse was much more likely to occur in the lower classes, he needed an explanation for why hysteria was not also more likely to occur. His answer was that the more delicate morality of upper class children would be more likely to require them to *repress* the trauma. As he put it, "the ego's efforts at defence depend upon the subject's total moral and intellectual development," and since such development was not as great in the lower classes, "the fact that hysteria is so much rarer in the lower classes than its specific aetiology would warrant is no longer entirely incomprehensible" (pp. 210–211). This view of the contrasting moral development of the upper and lower classes accounts in part for Freud's later conclusion that, in applying psychoanalysis to the psychological problems of the lower classes, one must "alloy" the "pure gold" of psychoanalysis with suggestion in order to create a psychotherapy for the masses (Freud, 1918).[1]

In the ensuing years, there have been a variety of efforts to apply psychoanalytic insights and methods to a range of patients beyond those who were the primary initial target of the treatment. Phrases like the *expanded scope* of psychoanalysis have become common. Relatively few of these efforts, however, have been directly addressed to expanding the scope of psychoanalysis explicitly in terms of class or ethnicity. The expansion has been most frequently addressed in terms of different *diagnoses* (see Altman, 2011 and Perez-Foster, Moskowitz, & Javier, 1996 for important exception).

Applications of psychoanalysis to borderline disorders, narcissistic disorders, and psychotic disorders have been the primary areas of expansion.[2] These efforts have creatively and importantly extended the range of psychoanalytic techniques and increased our appreciation of the applicability of psychoanalytic ideas. They have in certain ways radically altered our understanding of what is required for the patient to be accessible to what psychoanalysis has to offer, and many kinds of patients that were once conceived of as unanalyzable are now part of the regular case load of many psychoanalytic therapists. But these innovations have largely been directed, at least in their initial applications, toward middle class patients who happen to have these more severe diagnoses. Far fewer of the innovations and expansions of psychoanalytic reach have been explicitly directed toward broadening the range not of diagnosis but of class, race, ethnicity, and culture.

This is not to say that psychoanalysis has not been extended into this latter realm. Many clinicians working in the public hospitals and clinics that serve the poor have had psychoanalytic training, and they have learned to apply psychoanalytic insights and methods to this work. Moreover, the expansion in the view of analyzability that initially largely derived from a diagnostic vantage point before very long led to other changes and other expansions. Once the expectable transferences of middle class neurotics ceased to define the boundaries of psychoanalytic applicability, the differing behavior patterns, values, and ways of relating that are associated with class and culture could also be accommodated. Before very long, the expansion of *diagnostic* applicability became readily intertwined with an expansion of cultural applicability. The psychoanalytic literature contains far fewer papers about race and culture than it does about borderline and narcissistic disorders; but psychoanalytic *practice* – especially as it is manifested outside the boundaries of the private practice setting – has made more of a shift.[3]

Differential Treatments for Rich and Poor?

It is difficult to deny that stereotypes and prejudices have played a role in the kinds of mental health services offered to rich and poor. As far back as Hollingshead and Redlich's classic study of social class and mental illness, it was apparent that the poor were much less likely to be seen as appropriate for exploratory psychotherapy (Hollingshead & Redlich, 1958), and in significant ways this pattern persists into the present. I am in agreement with those who argue that biases have often led to a negative and dismissive attitude toward poor and minority patients that sees them as not appropriate for the same kind of treatment that is offered to the middle and upper classes. And I believe that we should indeed stretch ourselves to accommodate our modes of practice to the needs, habits, values, and expectations of patients from outside a middle class context. With but a moderate amount of accommodation – and an attitude that *respects* the differing values and assumptions of nonmainstream patients rather than viewing them simply as an unfortunate necessity to accept – the treatments available to the middle classes *can* be applied to many of the poor.

I question, however, whether our assumption should necessarily be that the poor are best served by finding ways to make their treatment as close as is practically possible to what is offered the middle class. We have been misled, I suggest, by the legacy of Freud's image of the "pure gold" of analysis. Offering those of other cultural traditions a therapy designed to be as close as possible to what was crafted for the privileged classes implicitly accepts as "standard" or superior the mores, habits, and preferences of the latter.

Changing the approach to fit a new cultural context does not mean watering it down. Alloys, after all, are quite often stronger and more resilient than a single "pure" ingredient. Thus, in approaching therapeutic work with patients who are poor or members of a minority group, it is useful to approach it as a task in which we can *learn something* about analysis itself. That is, we are not simply accommodating a rather perfect product to unfortunate necessities, but are being afforded an opportunity to gain some perspective on what we have assumed is essential or intrinsic to our task but may be simply a cultural artifact – or even an impediment.

Psychoanalysis as a Culture

The practice of psychoanalysis has a cultural dimension not only because it has been so closely associated with the middle class cultures of North America and Western Europe. It has evolved, over time, into a more specific culture as well – a culture that may be experienced as alien even by many members of the white middle class. The perspective on their unexamined assumptions that white middle class therapists may gain when they work with individuals whose class or ethnic identities differ from their own can thus be helpful not only in their work with these individuals specifically but even with members of their own ethnic and class group, whose experience of confusion in entering into our arcane rituals may be obscured by a misleading sense of cultural familiarity. Put differently, in attempting to alloy the "pure gold" of psychoanalysis to adapt it to new cultural groups, we may in fact create something new that is more effective even with the original population to which psychoanalysis has been applied.

It is particularly evident, for example, in working with populations outside the middle class mainstream, that they need to be *introduced* to the method, to be told more explicitly and in more detail than is commonly the practice what their participation in the process is to be and what the therapist's participation is to be. It is useful, further, to explain more than we are accustomed to *why* we set things up the way we do, how it works, and what the advantages are of doing things the way we do. It may be tempting to view this as a "compromise" because of the expectations and characteristics of the population being addressed. But in fact, there is good evidence that such preparation is useful for middle class patients as well.

What is required of us, however, in working with a broader range of patients, is more than just explaining why we do things the way we do. At times, what is required is that we do things differently. (Such explaining is itself doing things differently, of course, but I am referring here to still further changes.) Here again, we can learn something useful from the experience. There has developed an increasingly prevalent tendency in recent years to adopt the idea of "the frame" of therapy as if there is an inherently right and natural way to do things and every-thing that deviates from it is suspect. If the therapist deviates, she is corrupting the process, and the patient will, at least unconsciously, be troubled by it; and if it is the patient who seeks to modify "the frame," he is seen as engaging in some kind of manipulation or resistance that is ultimately inimical to his interests (and that it is thus the therapist's duty to steadfastly refuse to participate in, lest the patient feel endangered by the therapist's weakness or corruptibility).

It is extremely difficult, however, to be successful in therapeutic work with patients outside the white middle class if one maintains traditional notions about "the frame." Here again, it is important to be open to the lessons such experiences may teach about the validity of our conventional ideas of the therapeutic frame even with white middle class patients. Psychoanalysis is not a finished product that, in fundamentalist fashion, is already perfect and can only be corrupted. The practices that have evolved are by no means the only logical derivations from the observations that lie at the heart of the psychoanalytic point of view. They are, to some degree, historical accidents, and it is very unlikely that they represent the final word about what a psychoanalytic understanding can achieve. Reaching out to new populations thus is not simply a matter of applying the received method as faithfully as possible, and accommodating when unfortunate necessity forces a compromise upon us. Rather, the lessons learned as new variations evolve in applying psychoanalytic ideas to new populations have considerable potential to improve our work with the original population to which psychoanalysis was applied as well.

Most analysts today are inclined to view their work with *any* patient as hold-ing benefits for the analyst as well as the patient. We are used to thinking that we have something to learn from the patient as well as vice versa. In extending analytic work to patients from other cultural and class orientations, such a view is especially important. If such efforts to reach out are not to be tainted with condescension and unwitting cultural arrogance, it is important to keep clearly in mind that as we apply analysis to new groups, we learn something about analysis. If we start with the assumption that we are bringing pure gold to those who can accept only base metals, we not only do a poor job in helping those to whom we apply our noblesse oblige, we also deprive ourselves of a very valuable learning opportunity.

What the Poor and Culturally Different Have to Teach Us about Psychoanalytic *Theory*

Working with new populations confronts us not just with questions about psycho-analytic *technique*, but with questions about theory as well, about the assumptions that we ordinarily take for granted. Have we, for example, overemphasized the vectors of separation and individuation in our view of healthy development? Are we tuning in to universal developmental processes in our conceptualizations, or do those conceptualizations reflect, to a degree that is hard to calculate, presumptions that are built into the particular set of lenses our culture bequeaths to us? When we look at questions such as Is it normal or healthy for adult children to live in the same home as their parents until they are married? Where do grandparents live? Who sleeps in the same bed? What kind of loyalty is owed to one's mother and father and what kinds of choices do those loyalties require? and so forth, we find that other cultures reach quite different conclusions than upper middle class white culture tends to, and that, indeed, even that culture offered quite different answers some time back in time.[4] At present, white middle class culture in North America is highly individualistic – far more so than most other cultures in the world – and there is a risk that we may read this individualism into our vision of healthy psychological development. The encounter of psychoanalysis with patients from other cultural frames of reference can be a useful corrective to our hard-to-assess tunnel vision.[5]

Much the same can be said about our notions of attachment. Much of our thinking is rooted in assumptions about the preeminent importance of a single attachment figure. But village life in parts of the third world seems to offer a different model of attachment, one that is more communal. Within our own society as well, there are subcultures in which the boundaries around the nuclear family are far less impermeable.

Discussing the resources and communal values evident in the African American community, for example, the distinguished African American sociologist Andrew Billingsley (1992) notes that the strengths of the African American family are obscured when it is viewed through a lens that takes the middle class white family as standard and normal. These strengths include being able to rely on extended family to a much greater degree than in the typical middle class white family, so that many children of single parents have in fact several meaningful and available parental figures. They include as well a much greater readiness in the African American community for people to take care of children who are not formally related to them. Stack (1975), in studying patterns of nurturance in African American communities, has described these tendencies as entailing what she calls fictive kin. Addressing the phenomenon to which Stack was referring, Billingsley (1992) noted that his own children

> have so many "aunts," "uncles," and "cousins" unrelated to them by blood that they can hardly keep track of them. Whenever they are in need, however, or reach a particular transition in their lives, they can count on assistance from these "appropriated" family members. (p. 31)[6]

It is to be expected that greater confrontation by psychoanalysts with such alternative family structures, if approached with an open mind and with a set to accommodate theoretically as well as to assimilate to existing conceptions, will lead to important modifications in our conceptualizations of the nature of attachments, object representations, and a variety of other key psychoanalytic ideas.

Where Does the Greatest Contribution of Psychoanalysis Lie?

The discussion thus far has distinguished between two different relationships between psychoanalysis and the needs of the disadvantaged. One, I have suggested, lies in providing direct treatment. Here the emphasis is on addressing one immediate way in which the poor and marginalized have been shortchanged: Something valuable that is available to the better off is considerably less available to them. But psychoanalysis can also be of great value as a guide to how to *think about* the inequalities and injustices in our society, enabling us to better understand the anxieties, conflicts, and defenses that are differentially induced in the privileged and the less privileged by our inequalities and that must be addressed if we are to be effective in overcoming those inequalities. (See Wachtel, 1999, for a detailed discussion of racial and ethnic stereotyping and the nature of the impasse we face in race relations and of how psychological and psychoanalytic perspectives can be combined with political and economic efforts to make those efforts more likely to succeed.)

Each of these roles for psychoanalysis or, for that matter, contemporary cognitive science has substantial value. But, it might be said, the first attempts to treat the disadvantaged, whereas the second attempts to treat disadvantage itself. The first, in essence, works within the circumstances of our inequalities and tries to repair part of the damage. The second addresses the reasons for the persistence of injustice and inequality per se. Both kinds of effort are necessary. Psychoanalysts, by and large, are clinicians, not social reformers, and working within the system to provide whatever healing we can to those who have been its victims does not constitute an endorsement of the injustices. Indeed, without this component, reform efforts alone essentially write off a good part of a generation.

But it is important to be clear that psychoanalytic understanding can play a role in a more fundamental change in our systemic inequalities as well. For this to proceed, it is essential that psychoanalytic insights into the sources of inequality and impediments to change be strongly integrated with attention to history, politics, and economics (see Wachtel, 1999). There are real differentials of power and access to resources that cannot be reduced to fantasy. The psychoanalytic perspective can offer kinds of understanding that are at times severely lacking in the more purely political or economic thrust that is more common to efforts at achieving social justice. It cannot, however, replace those efforts but can only complement them.

On the other hand, it is often the case that more politically or economically oriented approaches to understanding injustice lack precisely what psychoanalysis offers. Economists often appear to be the last of the pre-Freudians in the intellectual world. For all their imposing equations, their thinking about human behavior is based on a hyperrational model that is likely to seem quaint at best to anyone with any exposure to psychoanalysis. As I discussed in a previous chapter, in the economists' vision, we always know exactly what we want, our goals do not conflict in problematic ways but are clearly prioritized, and we pursue our aims so effectively that what we end up with is virtually defined as what makes us most happy. The prodigious human capacity for self-deception, so obvious to psychoanalysts, has little room in the Panglossian vision that underlies the economists' numbers (see, e.g., Maital, 1982; Simon, 1957; Wachtel, 1983), and injustice too all too readily dissolves from view, since the market's allocations are assumed to provide the optimal distribution of resources (see Katz, 1989; Wachtel, 1983, 1999).

Political approaches to understanding social inequality similarly can benefit from the perspective that psychoanalysis has to offer. *Conflict* in the political worldview is rarely seen as intrapsychic. Instead, it is almost exclusively addressed as *between* people or groups of people, whose needs or aims are seen as relatively clear and singular, but conflicting. Psychoanalysis provides important wisdom in precisely the opposite direction. Psychoanalysts are perhaps most of all experts in the many ways the human psyche is internally divided. Applying this perspective to the political realm and the nature of our social divisions, psychoanalysis offers both hope and fresh understanding. People or groups who are simply written off as reactionaries or racists, or, from the opposite end of the spectrum, as lazy, hostile, or thoroughly alienated from so-called middle class values, may be seen as having more complex potentialities and more multiple inclinations, each vying for expression. Some aspects of their psychological makeup may be submerged by their circumstances and their current resolution of their competing urges and visions, but alternative possibilities and inclinations are rarely absent. As a consequence, strategies of social change, rather than simply attempting to *defeat* the other side, may be directed toward finding better ways to win them over, to create the circumstances that bring out the more progressive and helpful aspects of their psychological configuration.

Psychoanalysis offers a second corrective as well to the starkly confrontational vision that infuses much political discourse and frequently underlies efforts at political change. Just as the emphasis in psychoanalysis on internal conflict offers an alternative to the image of implacable opposition often guiding political struggle, so too does the psychoanalytic emphasis on empathy. Certainly analysts are quite thoroughly aware of human beings' capacity to be in direct and even hostile conflict with each other. Interpersonal and intergroup conflict or the capacity for violence are by no means absent from the psychoanalytic vision, as any readers of Freud's trenchant and often sobering social writings is well aware. But psychoanalysis offers us as well the image of empathy, the effort to approach another human being in a way that *understands* his or her needs and inclinations, that understands how the world looks through the other person's eyes.

In the face of patients' negative transference reactions or anger at the analyst, analysts do not write the patient off as an enemy but seek to understand the perceptions that produced the anger. Moreover, they reach that understanding in large part by looking within themselves and finding within themselves the same potential and the same fundamental psychological inclinations. Sullivan's view that "we are all much more simply human than otherwise" is shared by analysts of all persuasions, and it is a valuable foundation for addressing racial, ethnic, and class conflicts in a way more likely to admit of resolution.

There are indeed very real and significant divergences in the interests of rich and poor, capitalists and workers, haves and have-nots. Ignoring that reality leaves us with empty sentimentality. But the seemingly hard-headed view of inevitable and intractable conflict is more a self-fulfilling prophecy than a direct look into the stark face of reality. It is very largely a *contingent* truth, a truth whose inevitability is spuriously confirmed by the actions it prompts and the consequences it sows. The application of an empathic perspective to those whose political views one wishes to challenge is not the same as accepting the injustices that might be a product of their views. It is, rather, a means of approaching those injustices in a way more likely to yield a genuine resolution instead of a quite possibly pyrrhic victory in a culture war virtually without end. The application of a psychoanalytically sophisticated guiding vision to complement the understanding of power politics, economic self-seeking, or the fallout of historic injustices can increase the likelihood that those fighting for justice will not only win but also will be pleased with the results of their victory.[7]

Beyond the Adversarial Mind-Set

A further implication of the foregoing arguments is that overcoming the divisions in our society that perpetuate pain and injustice requires that we move beyond the either–or and us–them thinking that has tended to characterize American political life. The divisions and inequalities that pervade our society have their origins in real and enormous injustices, from slavery and legally enforced segregation to prejudices, discrimination, and vastly different opportunities for some groups than for others. But the perpetuation of those injustices is by now more complicated. The simple assignment of victims and victimizers, good guys and bad guys, requires a diligently maintained tunnel vision. Enough individuals actually fit more or less well the assigned role in this simplified drama to maintain the stereotypes, but the vast majority of the population does not. Most people, on both sides of our various divides, are complicated and often compromised, capable of acts of kindness and understanding but also of cruelty and heedlessness. Which side is brought out depends, one might say, on the clinical skill that is often so sorely lacking in the political arena.

Our conceptualizations have consequences, and the self-fulfilling prophecies they frequently promote can have tragic consequences. I have written elsewhere, for example (Wachtel, 1999), of the ways that expanding our definition of racism – finding "racism" in a host of acts and attitudes that several decades ago would never have elicited this label – has had the ironic consequence of obscuring what is perhaps the more pervasive failing of the white population in its relations with people of color – *indifference*. Indifference, the radical failure of empathy for, caring about, or identification with other human beings because they are per-ceived as "other," often does not entail the active hostility or disparagement more commonly associated with the concept of racism; but its effects can be equally destructive. Moreover, reconceptualizing the white contribution to the perpetua-tion of our inequalities as indifference is not an instance of "plea bargaining." As I have noted in a more extended discussion of the implications of our expansion of the contexts in which the term *racism* is applied, "indifference in the face of severe human suffering is not a minor offense" (Wachtel, 1999, p. 39).

Describing the white contribution in terms of indifference, however, has the advantage of being more likely to make contact with whites' subjective experience than does the overuse of the term racism to the point where it begins to lose its meaning. The aim of such a reconceptualization is not to enable whites to avoid responsibility but precisely the opposite – to make it possible for them to *take* responsibility, to *acknowledge* their role in perpetuating our patterns of inequality. Psychoanalysts most of all know that making people feel guilty does not always lead to more moral behavior. Much of the time, quite the opposite can result. The guilty person feels angry at those who made him feel guilty or defends against the guilt in ways that contribute to denial of the harm. Effective efforts to get people to change must be attuned to the subtleties of conflict, defense, and self-perception.

In similar fashion, bludgeoning the defenses does not necessarily produce insight. Unless our account of what the person's motivational state is can make some contact with the person's phenomenological experience, our interpretations become arid intellectual exercises. The patient must *feel* that what we are saying is true of *him*. So too is this the case in efforts at political or social reform. Learning from the psychoanalytic model, social reformers can fashion their interpretations in ways that are more likely to be effective communications than mere catharses.

The Crucial Role of Vicious Circles

Racial mistrust and misunderstanding and the perpetuation of social injustice are realms in which the operation of vicious circles, a central theme of this entire book, plays a very central role (Wachtel, 1999). Those vicious circles operate at many levels, some close to the observational heart of psychoanalytic concerns, some seemingly at a quite different level of abstraction. When psychoanalysis becomes overly identified with the study of an "inner world" – and especially when that inner world is conceptualized or described in hermetic fashion unre-lated to the events of daily life – psychoanalytic insights can seem to have little to contribute to the resolution of our major social problems. It is quite possible, however, to recast psychoanalytic formulations in ways that continue to address the unconscious dynamics traditionally of psychoanalytic concern and yet are simultaneously attentive to the actualities of race, class, poverty, or the myriad daily realities that occupy center stage in most other theories of human behavior. To unite psychoanalysis and social and historical reality in this way, the analysis of vicious circles is a key conceptual tool (Wachtel, 1983, 1999).

Vicious circles are endemic to the perpetuation of our racial and class injustices. We find them in virtually every realm of our societal life and at every level of our individual and collective psyches. If one considers, for example, the relation between crime and "white flight," we may readily see how, on the one hand, prerational white aversions – rooted in unexamined racist preconceptions that can be understood psychoanalytically (e.g., Fanon, 1967; Kovel, 1984), social psychologically (e.g., Gaertner & Dovidio, 1986; Sears, 1988), historically (e.g., Jordan, 1977), or from numerous other vantage points – lead to the isolation of people of color, restricting their opportunities and creating what Massey and Denton (1993) have called a culture of segregation. At the same time, the behaviors that result from that culture (see, e.g., Anderson, 1990; Majors & Billson, 1992) – a culture so largely attributable to both hostility *and* indifference on the part of whites – can further frighten whites and lead to strengthening still further the white aversion that perpetuates it (Gaertner & Dovidio, 1986; Kovel, 1984; Wachtel, 1999).

The key to understanding the origins of this by-now tragically self-perpetuating sequence is not hard to find if we look back in history. The injustices – largely *one-sided* injustices with clear victims and oppressors – are easy enough to find. But if we look at the behaviors of blacks and whites in the present – people born into a situation not initially of their making, but from very early likely to live out the roles that society has differentially created for them – it is not as easy to tell who is reacting to whom. Or perhaps it would be more accurate to say that *each* is reacting to the other, but neither is very able to see very clearly the ways that the other is reacting to *him*. As I discuss in more detail in the next chapter, family therapists call this the problem of punctuation, and it makes determining where the sequence begins and ends – roughly equivalent to whose fault is it, or "who started?" – an often fruitless exercise. It is the very difference in the way that the two sides punctuate the sequence that keeps it going. And it is only when they can begin to recognize that in fact it is more a circular pattern in which *both* sides are caught that a resolution can begin to be fashioned.

I offer a range of illustrations of how these vicious circles in the realm of race relations work in the next chapter (see also Wachtel, 1999). By and large, they tend to operate largely automatically, with very little awareness of many of the cues and subjective experiences that set them off and perpetuate them and with even less awareness of the way in which they do constitute a circular and mutually maintained pattern rather than the simple linear reaction to the other that they are likely to be experienced as. Understanding of these circular patterns is a critical tool for facilitating the integration of social and psychological levels of analysis and overcoming the implicit assumption that these are competing and even incompatible perspectives. The concern with individuals' unconscious motivations, conflicts, representations, and defenses that is associated with the psychoanalytic perspective and the attention to issues of race, class, history, politics, and economics that is so prominent in the other disciplines that study human behavior are equally essential components of a comprehensive understanding of the dilemmas we face. It is a particular concern of cyclical psychodynamic theory to achieve the integration of these pseudocompeting perspectives. Investigators and commentators from a range of viewpoints can potentially contribute to this process if they are open to the impact of the real-world events and socio-historical contexts that are a crucial part of all our patients' lives. What is required is to return to the issue with which Part II of this book began – the multiple sources of everyday unhappiness and the multiple levels on which it can be reduced. Psychoanalysis is a powerful tool, whose uses still are far from exhausted. In expanding those uses, we expand the very meaning of psychoanalysis itself.

Notes

1. For a somewhat different perspective on the call for a psychotherapy for the masses, see Aron and Starr, 2013.
2. There has been a whole other realm of extensions and expansions directed toward work with children. I am focusing here primarily on work with adults.
3. Apropos the discussion in Chapter 10, these clinical practices were not usually "psychoanalysis" but rather psychoanalytic psychotherapy or psychoanalytically informed psychotherapy.
4. At the time of the American Revolution, for example, it was standard procedure for adult male strangers to share a bed at an inn.
5. It is worth noting that even among whites in North America, the term *ethnic* is still used for those subcultures that hold to earlier, less individualistic ideas about family, community, and the like.
6. For further discussion of the strengths that black families bring to bear in addressing the stresses and challenges they confront, see also Boyd-Franklin (2003); Johnson and Staples (1993); Taylor, Jackson, and Chatters (1997).
7. One is reminded here of the witticism sometimes employed to describe the less than salutary results that can derive from a struggle for justice in which hatred and dehumanization of the presumed oppressor is the guiding vision: "Before, our society was characterized by the oppression of man by man. Now it is exactly the opposite."

Chapter 16

The Vicious Circles of Racism
A Cyclical Psychodynamic Perspective on Race and Race Relations

I wish in this chapter to further explore some of the ways in which a psychoanalytic perspective can help illuminate the complexities of race relations and other interethnic and intercultural strife. The racial divisions and tensions that continue to create disharmony in our society are a product of many factors; they are most certainly *not* simply a matter of "psychical reality." Very real historic crimes and abuses, very real differences in economic circumstances, in educational opportunities, in the neighborhoods in which blacks and whites grow up, and in a host of other powerful life circumstances are central to the differing status of blacks and whites in our society. I do believe, however, that psychoanalysis – and a psychological perspective more generally – can be of great value in helping us address these real-world differences and finding a way to move past the mind-sets on both sides that maintain them.

In focusing on the persistence of large and painful divisions and continuing inequities, I do not mean to imply that we have not made progress in resolving our racial divisions and injustices. When we look back to the circumstances before the onset of the modern civil rights movement, we must be struck by the enormity of what has been achieved. Many people still alive can remember a world in which, in many parts of the United States, African Americans were legally required to attend separate schools, drink from separate water fountains, and use separate bathrooms from whites in many parts of our country; and in which, *throughout* the nation, blacks were discriminated against openly and with impunity. In contrast, I am writing these words at a time when a black man is president of the United States.

And yet, despite all these advances, with a clear-eyed gaze one can look around at an America *right now* in which much of what I described in the preceding paragraph *still* seems to be the case. Whites and blacks *still* tend to live in different neighborhoods, to attend different schools, to be in different classes even within the same schools, to marry within their race, not across races, and so forth (see, for example, Massey & Denton, 1993). The average incomes of whites is *still* much greater than the average income of blacks; the unemployment rate of African Americans is still significantly higher (and among African American teenagers is *enormously* higher); the infant mortality rate in some inner-city neighborhoods is higher than in Bangladesh.

So what has actually changed? Much of what has changed (and this is where psychoanalysis begins to be relevant) is in what it is acceptable to say or even to feel. We have moved from a system of overt and socially accepted discrimination to one of *covert* distinctions and aversions, to a system where most of us – even so-called *liberal* whites – profess one principle and live by another (for example, express a strong belief in equal opportunity in education or housing, but live in mostly white neighborhoods with mostly white schools, or send their children to mostly white *private* schools). That is a situation ripe for the kind of understanding that psychoanalysis offers. Psychoanalysis is a discipline quintessentially devoted to examining our self-deceptions and self-delusions, especially those that make us appear purer and more virtuous than we really are.

But I am *not* focusing here – or at least not primarily – on unconscious racism. Unconscious racism exists, to be sure, and it is in fact one part of the total configuration keeping us locked into our divisions and inequalities. But the idea of unconscious racism – at least among progressives with any taste for psychoanalysis at all – has become a cliché. It is *too easy* an idea; in an odd way it is comforting, because even if it entails a certain amount of self-accusation among progressive or liberal whites who endorse the idea, it accords easily with the dictates of their superegos (actually, of *our* superegos, because I include myself in this category). It excoriates oppressors and absolves victims, makes the complicated mess of our contemporary society into a morality play with clear good guys and bad guys – a kind of splitting on a grand scale. And even if the bad guys happen to be *us* – it is no secret that psychoanalysts are disproportionately white – we know from other psychoanalytic work that such self-blame can at times be oddly comforting. Fairbairn, for example, built much of his theorizing around the observation that abused and abandoned children preferred holding on to a positive vision of their parents even at the expense of this requiring a *negative* view of themselves. As he put it, "it is better to live as a sinner in a world ruled by God than as a saint in a world ruled by the devil" (Fairbairn, 1952).

There are few sinners *or* saints in the story I wish to tell here, but there are plenty of complicated, conflicted people, people flawed and decent at the same time, people driven to act in ways that cause trouble for both themselves and others without understanding terribly well what the larger forces are that have shaped their behavior and their experience. In other words, people as they look through a psychoanalytic lens.

Viewed specifically from the vantage point of the cyclical psychodynamic version of psychoanalytic thought, the individual's history is – as in all psychoanalytic accounts – a crucial part of the explanation for why a person is caught in a particular troubling life pattern. But the impact of that history is mediated by the psychological forces and structures it has left as a residue. Most of all, the history has its influence by the way it generates a *further* history – a further history that, all too often, bears a tragic resemblance to what came before. Early experiences set into motion patterns that become virtually self-perpetuating, or at least self-perpetuating once the role of the behavior of others is also brought into the picture. I have described this process as one in which other people are drawn into the pattern as accomplices (see Chapter 2), and have argued that we cannot understand personality adequately without attending to the characteristic accomplices that play a crucial role in maintaining it.

A similar dynamic relation between past and present can be discerned in the impact of the history of our entire nation upon our stubborn divisions and inequalities. Here too, as in the psychoanalytic realm, understanding of the history is of great importance; how can anyone appreciate the meaning of our patterns of racial division without taking into account the brute facts of slavery and segregation? But here too as well, accounts that explain the present in terms of the history *directly*, without understanding the countless mediating events between then and now, are misleading and are likely to lead us to overlook crucial factors in the perpetuation of the pattern.

Consider, for example, the demeaning stereotypes about African Americans that developed as a justification for the evils of slavery. Those stereotypes, in one sense, have their origins deep in our history. They are among the factors, going back hundreds of years, which form the foundation of our present patterns of inequality, division, and mistrust. But those stereotypes are not just a residue from the past. They have a dynamic and ongoing history that is even more tragic and more tangled than it might appear at first glance, and if we are finally to overcome them, we need to take that more complex story into account.

Stereotype Anxiety and Disidentification with the Academic

To understand how this is the case, let us turn to the work of social psychologist Claude Steele. Steele (e.g., Steele, 1997; Steele & Aronson, 1995) studied the performance of very bright black and white Stanford undergraduates on a set of extremely difficult and challenging test items. When the items were presented as a test of intellectual ability, the black students performed significantly more poorly than the whites. When, however, Steele told the students that these were just experimental items that did not have anything to do with individual ability, the black students did every bit as well as the whites *on the very same items*. Steele explains these and related findings in term of stereotype anxiety; in the condition in which the students thought their intellectual abilities were being evaluated (the standard condition of testing in most circumstances), anxieties were evoked in the African American students that reflected their concerns about confirming stereotypes about black intellectual ability. That anxiety – rather than any difference in the actual capacity to do well on the test items – accounted for the poorer performance, as attested to by the successful performance of the African American students on the very same items when the meaning of the test was framed differently. Steele has performed an elegant series of studies to demonstrate that the anxiety creating the differential in performance is specifically stereotype anxiety, operating over and above any other forms of test anxiety that may be shared by black and white students alike.

In some ways, Steele's studies are reassuring to those of us working to over-come racial stereotyping and discrimination. As I have discussed in *Race in the Mind of America* (Wachtel, 1999), for example, Steele's findings provide one key element – there are many others – in challenging the specious arguments of *The Bell Curve*, Richard Herrnstein and Charles Murray's (1994) work of right-wing political advocacy disguised as science. But there are troubling implications of Steele's findings and theorizing as well. For example, in one of the many varieties of vicious circles operating in the realm of race, the poorer performance that sometimes results from the impact of stereotyping has the ironic effect of *strengthening* the stereotypes. If African Americans do more poorly on intellectual achievement tests – *even if* that poor performance is a product of the impact of stereotypes – then the stereotypes will seem to be "confirmed." I have called this process one of *pseudo*-confirmation (Wachtel, 1999), but it is unfortunately no less powerful for being specious.

What is the bearing of psychoanalysis on these findings or of these findings on psychoanalysis? Steele, after all, is not a psychoanalyst but a social psychologist working within the tradition of empirical social psychology. To begin with, it is important to note that the psychological processes to which Steele's work is addressed go on largely outside of awareness. The African American students are not really aware that they are being influenced by anxiety over stereotypes as they take the tests; the white students are largely unaware of the ways that they see the world through the lens of stereotypes or of the many ways they contribute to *perpetuating* those stereotypes; and neither group is aware of the circular and repetitive nature of the pattern in which they reciprocally participate.

Intersecting in a different way with phenomena familiar to psychoanalytic observers is another consequence of the stereotype anxieties that Steele has been addressing – a still more troubling process that Steele labels disidentification with the entire realm of academic achievement. In contrast to students from elite universities who are the African American subjects in most of Steele's studies – individuals who have, all in all, managed quite successfully to *battle* the constraining influence of stereotypes – a great many other African American young people respond in quite a different way. Discouraged about the prospect of succeeding in the academic realm, they protect their self-esteem by *not trying* to do well in school, by *disengaging* from the academic realm and seeking self-esteem from other kinds of activities entirely. As Steele puts it (Steele & Aronson, 1995), the self-concept becomes redefined

> such that school achievement is not a basis of self-evaluation nor a personal identity. This protects the person against the self-evaluative threat posed by the stereotypes, but may have the byproduct of diminishing interest, motivation, and ultimately achievement in the domain. (p. 797)

Here again, of course, we confront still another vicious circle. If, in order to protect their self-esteem against the painful impact of stereotypes, they do not invest in school to the same degree as white children do, and hence do not do as well, this serves to *reinforce the stereotypes still further*, both for themselves and for the next cohort of African American children entering school a few years after them and finding (again through a process of pseudo-confirmation) that the "reality" they encounter is that African American kids don't do well in school. Here we see, in a fashion that should be familiar to the psychoanalytic observer, a process in which defensive efforts to ward off threats to self-esteem have ironic and unanticipated consequences. The disidentification to which Steele refers does bring short-term comfort, but as is the case with those defensive efforts more familiar in psychoanalytic work, that short-term comfort is purchased at the price of quite considerable long-term disadvantage.

A number of large-scale studies have reported findings that converge with and bolster Steele's theorizing about disidentification. The theory of disidentification emphasizes the need to put oneself on the line, to really *care* about school success, in order to have a reasonable prospect of doing well. In essence, one's self-esteem must, to a certain degree, depend on school success. Obviously, such dependence can go too far. We have all seen cases in which the patient lacked a stable core sense of self, in which self-esteem was *very problematically* tied to a need for continuing success, and in which any failure to meet a rather excessive and ultimately unmeetable standard resulted in severe narcissistic injury. This, of course, is not what Steele is referring to in his concept of identification and disidentification from the academic realm. While in our psychoanalytic work we frequently aim to liberate people from the tender mercies of a narcissistically demanding superego and to help them build a stable sense of self-worth less dependent on their latest achievement, no reader of this chapter would have achieved his or her advanced degree with the kind of defensive insouciance about school success to which Steele and other researchers on disidentification are pointing.

The troubling finding of several studies that examined the responses of a large national sample of children and adolescents is that between the 8th and 12th grades, the correlations between self-esteem and school performance plummeted for African American youths, eventually reaching a level close to zero, while that for young people from other groups stayed substantial (Osborne, 1995, 1997). In part, this detaching of self-esteem from school performance reflects the influence of the stereotypes discussed by Steele; in part it reflects the psychological impact of decrements in performance that have already accumulated as a result of prior encounters with stereotyping and with a host of other privations; and in part it reflects antiacademic peer pressures that grow from the same soil.

Regarding those peer pressures, still another study, based on a sample of 20,000 American teenagers, found that

> peer pressure among Black and Latino students *not* to excel in school is so strong in many communities – even among middle class adolescents – that many positive steps that Black and Latino parents have taken to facilitate their children's school success are undermined. (Steinberg, 1996, p. 47)

Here again, much of what happens is out of awareness. There is, to be sure, a conscious *portion* of the process. A number of observers (e.g., Comer & Poussaint, 1992; Franklin, 1993; Ogbu, 1991; Steinberg, 1996) have noted a quite explicit disparagement of academic achievement among African American youth, a deriding of school success as "acting white," that both rationalizes the individual's turning away from academic pursuits and serves to keep in line peers who otherwise might threateningly achieve – and hence breach the defense that disidentification entails.

Like all defenses, disidentification is typically not recognized *as* a defense, as a way of warding off anxiety. Rather, it serves to keep out of focus the very anxiety it is designed to ward off. If school doesn't *matter*, if it is just something for white folks, then one doesn't need to *worry* about school. Also, like other forms of defense more familiar in psychoanalytic discourse, it bolsters self-esteem, at least in the short run: A number of studies have indicated that, notwithstanding the lower overall socioeconomic status of African Americans and their poorer performance in school – that is, on a *group* basis, with many high-achieving exceptions – the self-esteem of African American youths is not lower than that of other groups, and, by the measures employed (often relatively superficial questionnaire measures), sometimes appears to be higher. But this bolstering of self-esteem comes at a very high cost. As the cyclical psychodynamic view particularly emphasizes, defensive efforts are likely in the long run to strengthen the very circumstances of threat they are designed to defend *against*. In the case of the defense of disidentification with academics, this ironic consequence of defending is particularly clear: The disidentification makes good school performance much less likely, thereby perpetuating the circumstances that required the use of the defense in the first place.

This tendency to disparage activities in which one's group tends to do poorly – even if that poor performance is by no means intrinsic to the group's capacities – is not unique to the situation African Americans encounter. It has been found in numerous studies of the ways that stigmatized groups of all kinds maintain self-esteem in the face of unfair treatment and disparagement. Research on how people attempt to maintain self-esteem in the face of experiences of stigmatization indicates that members of stigmatized groups employ several strategies quite regularly: (a) Whether the stigmatization is based on race, ethnicity, disability, or any other characteristic, they tend to interpret failure as a result of *prejudice and discrimination by others* rather than as reflecting directly on the self; (b) they compare their performance and their position in society only to that of other members of their own group, not to that of individuals from more privileged groups, thereby protecting themselves from comparisons with people who may be doing better; and (c) they selectively devalue activities in which their group performs poorly and emphasize those in which it excels (see Crocker & Major, 1989).

These responses help to mitigate the impact of unfair stigmatization, and in the process they can be of great value in enabling people to persist in the face of adversity. But each of them can also have ironic consequences that contribute to maintaining the individual in the very circumstances that made these maneuvers necessary in the first place. The vicious circles thus engendered, explored in my book *Race in the Mind of America* (Wachtel, 1999), play a substantial and generally unappreciated role in maintaining our society's damaging and unjust divisions.

For example, the lower test scores and school achievement of African Americans derive from a host of circumstances – both historic and ongoing – that would suppress development of the full potential of any group subjected to them. But once maintaining self-esteem in the face of lower test scores includes the strategies I have just noted, further consequences develop that are likely to perpetuate the very failures to which those strategies were a response. For example, bolstering self-esteem by attributing failure to prejudice and discrimination can create a *stake* in seeing prejudice and discrimination, an internal necessity that skews perceptions and interpretations of events. Moreover, because perceptions of racism and bias are, after all, rooted in part in real experiences – viewing our society as continuing to embody a good deal of racism is certainly not something they are "making up" – the boundary between inner necessity and outer reality can be difficult to locate. To the degree that this perceptual necessity, deriving from the need to protect self-esteem, leads to overestimation of the degree of racism that persists in our society, it can undermine academic motivation; the conviction that "one way or another I will be excluded" can make it difficult to persist against hardships that are, after all, real and significant.

Similarly, when self-esteem is in part maintained by comparing oneself only to members of one's own group, it can engender motivation to limit contact with the majority and to experience oneself as belonging to a group apart. Real assimilation is thus likely to be experienced as almost impossible to accomplish and, indeed, as undesirable even if possible. But once again, the very success of this strategy in maintaining self-esteem has ironic and circular consequences. For this protection offered by separateness once again creates a stake in keeping separate. And in a society where the greatest educational and economic opportunities reside in institutions that have historically been predominantly white, the result of keeping separate is likely to be continued marginalization, lesser economic and educational success, and, most ironic and damaging of all, still further need to keep separate as a consequence. Thus the circle turns again and again, creating its own justification through the very adversity it engenders.

Finally, as I have already discussed with regard to disidentification with academics and the imputation that studying or succeeding in school is acting white, the third common strategy noted by researchers on stigmatization – disparaging those activities in which one's group has been less successful – can create still other self-fulfilling prophecies, in which the defense against an assault to self-esteem contributes to the perpetuation of that same assault. Thus, in a host of ways, powerful motivational forces, rooted in the experience of marginalization, neglect, and oppression, may lead African Americans and other stigmatized minorities to resist efforts to become a fully participant member of the larger society. And the terrible irony in this clearly understandable adaptive strategy is that, once again, it is likely to perpetuate the very conditions that produced the stigmatization in the first place. Strategies that maintain self-esteem in the short run may keep members of these groups outside the mainstream in the long run – perpetuating the need to continue to use such strategies (see again *Race in the Mind of America* [Wachtel, 1999]).

White Participation in Maintaining Our Unjust Divisions

The still larger tragedy in this set of vicious circles is that the process I have just described – a process in which failures as well as problematic behaviors and attitudes may be generated by the very efforts of African Americans to defend against the impact of being mistreated and devalued – interacts with different but equally problematic tendencies in the *white* community that *also* serve to perpetuate the uneasy and socially corrosive state of race relations in our society. There is a pervasive tendency in American society for whites to distance themselves from African Americans and to ignore the injustices that African Americans endure or the privileges that accrue to whites. The behavior and attitudes that result in the black community in response to those tendencies among whites end up, in powerful ways, strengthening those very tendencies among whites, as they provide both a rationalization for preexisting, though often denied, inclinations and a measure of "real experience" that contributes to a sense among some whites that their attitudes are not prejudices but responses to real characteristics.

The tangle is difficult to unravel because these white attitudes are a complex mixture of irrational, long-standing, and defensively influenced internalized schemas on the one hand, and perceptions of actual events and circumstances on the other – perceptions which themselves, of course, are by no means literal but, like all perceptions, constructions rooted in the interaction between actuality and inner necessity. With sufficient pseudo-confirmation, the degree to which these attitudes are rooted in fears and fantasies with strong irrational and unconscious elements can be easy to push aside.

Also pushed out of awareness is the way these fears and aversions on the part of whites lead both to personal interactions and to social policies that contribute to perpetuating our continuing social dilemmas. The central role of whites' participation in the vicious circles in which we are caught is often left out by white observers, who may be receptive to seeing how *blacks* have gotten caught in some kind of vicious circle that entraps them in maladaptive behavior, but are much more hesitant to notice how *their own* attitudes and behaviors contribute to perpetuating the pattern.

As with the patterns I noted earlier among African Americans, this white participation in the perpetuation of our racial divisions and our mutual suspicions goes on very largely out of awareness. It is no longer acceptable in many circles to voice – or even to permit oneself to experience subjectively – prejudiced views that once were quite common and overt. In an influential line of research, David Sears, a social psychologist at UCLA, examined the ways that racist ideas go underground and get expressed indirectly. Sears (1988) distinguishes between old-fashioned racism – overt and obvious – and what he calls "symbolic" racism, an affective attitude toward blacks that is rationalized by being packaged in another set of values that are more acceptable. The symbolic dimension of expressing unacknowledged affective attitudes is evident, as Sears sees it, in the importance to people of issues such as busing and affirmative action even when, as Sears's data reveal, these issues may have little personal impact on the person holding the attitude – for example, people with strong attitudes about busing who do not themselves have a child in the public schools. In Sears's view, his data suggest that in many instances the attitudes that whites hold about these issues are "an irrational response to long-standing predispositions rather than a reasonable response to the realities of life" (p. 53).

John McConahay, one of Sears's early collaborators, later slightly reframed their conceptualization, suggesting that the attitudes their work addressed might be better called modern racism than symbolic racism, because even "old-fashioned" racism was largely symbolic (McConahay, 1982). That is, as Joel Kovel has suggested from a more psychoanalytic perspective (Kovel, 1984), blacks may evoke in whites a range of distorted affective reactions that have little to do with the reality of who they are or how they behave. Both in old-fashioned and quite overt racism and in the more subtle and disguised forms more common today, irrational meanings are evoked that are symbolically mediated.

Frantz Fanon (1967), writing as a psychoanalyst as well as a revolutionary advocate, described in particularly chilling terms the roots of that symbolic mediation:

> *In Europe, the black man is the symbol of Evil.* . . . The torturer is the black man, Satan is black, . . . when one is dirty one is black – whether one is thinking of physical dirtiness or of moral dirtiness. It would be astonishing, if the trouble were taken to bring them all together, to see the vast number of expressions that make the black man the equivalent of sin. In Europe, whether concretely or symbolically, the black man stands for the bad side of the character. As long as one cannot understand this fact, one is doomed to talk in circles about the "black problem." (pp. 188–189)

Kovel (1984), building his psychoanalytic analysis of white racism in part upon Fanon's observations, suggested that,

> Whatever a white man experiences as bad in himself, as springing from what Fanon described as an "inordinate black hollow" in "the remotest depth of the European consciousness," whatever is forbidden and horrifying in human nature, may be designated as black and projected onto a man whose dark skin and oppressed past fit him to receive the symbol. (pp. 65–67)

These projections can take many forms, some obvious and some more subtle. But in Kovel's view, an important key to understanding the overall attitudinal structure that is expressed in the many different contents and details lies in a distinction between two overarching poles in the dynamics of racism – dominative and aversive. These two types are not completely independent or antithetical; in many individuals they may overlap quite substantially. But they have somewhat different psychological roots, and over time their implications can differ quite substantially. As Kovel (1984) describes the distinction,

> In general, the dominative type has been marked by heat and the aversive type by coldness. The former is clearly associated with the American South, where, of course, domination of blacks became the cornerstone of society; and the latter with the North, where blacks have so consistently come and found themselves out of place. The dominative racist, when threatened by the black, resorts to direct violence; the aversive racist, in the same situation, turns away and walls himself off. (p. 32)

Presently, it is aversive racism that dominates. The dominative form corresponds to a significant degree to what Sears called old-fashioned racism, and as he noted, that attitude has become rather thoroughly disreputable in most quarters of our society, without racism itself necessarily disappearing. Today it is aversive racism – that more elusive and more readily disguisable set of attitudes – that is most at the heart of our difficulties. And flushing out that more easily rationalized and covered-over set of attitudes requires an ingenuity in teasing out unacknowledged attitudes and feelings that should be quite familiar to the psychoanalytically inclined. Sears, McConahay, and their colleagues attempted to lay bare these less conscious and acknowledged forms of racial feeling and prejudice largely through a series of cleverly fashioned questionnaires, in which people answered questions designed to tap more subtle dimensions of their experience without giving the clues so obvious in most questionnaires that indicate fairly clearly that "if I answer this question *yes*, I'm saying I'm a racist."

Other researchers have explored the less conscious dimensions of whites' racial attitudes by devising revealing situations in which the actual behavior of whites toward blacks was revealed in unobtrusive ways that sidestepped conscious defenses. In one study, for example, the subjects, all of whom were white, were told that the study was concerned with examining the process of interviewing. In fact, however, the study was actually designed to examine differences in the ways whites interact with other whites and with African Americans. Half the (white) subjects were paired with white interviewees and half with blacks. The aim was to assess the subjects' emotional attitudes in ways that were difficult to fake. Thus, not only were their attitudes assessed through their actual behavior rather than what they said in response to explicit questions, but the *dimensions* of behavior examined consisted not of obvious indicators such as whether they were being friendly or fair, but a variety of nonverbal behaviors of which the subjects were unlikely even to be aware. Among the observations of the study, for example, were that the white inter-viewers sat further away when they were interviewing African Americans than they did when the interviewees were white; that these white interviewers made more speech errors when talking to African Americans; and that they ended the interviews with African Americans sooner than they did with whites (Word, Zanna, & Cooper, 1974).

It is worth noting that here again, we are likely to be encountering a process that is better understood as part of a series of vicious circles than a simple linear event of one group responding to the altitudes of the other. On the one hand, the subtle ways in which the white subjects in the study unwittingly (but pow-erfully) conveyed lesser respect or interest to black interviewees represent one of *many* such experiences likely to be encountered by African Americans who interview for jobs or university admissions with white interviewers. But in turn, as a *consequence* of being repeatedly subjected to such experiences (whether con-sciously intended), African American interviewees of white interviewers might be expected (*also* often without consciousness or intention) to be more anxious, unfriendly, or guarded than white applicants. And this, in turn, via another repeti-tion of the process of pseudo-confirmation, is likely to lead still other white inter-viewers, encountering in their interactions with African Americans the legacy of these African Americans' experiences in *previous* interactions with whites, to again, perhaps without consciousness, manifest the same kind of behavior noted in the study, reinforcing still again the understandable (but not necessarily *under-stood*) resentment or wariness on the African Americans' part that will be experi-enced by the *next* whites they interact with, who will in turn (again likely without much awareness) repeat *their* role in perpetuating the cycle.

Other researchers have employed still other methods to assess how whites may give expression to attitudes of which they are largely unaware or which they vig-orously deny. In one study, for example (Gaertner & Dovidio, 1986), the sub-jects – all white – were asked to complete a complex task together with another person, who they thought was also a subject in the research. In half the pairs, the other person was assigned the role of supervisor in the task; for the other half, the other person was assigned the role of subordinate. In fact, the other person was not really a subject but was a collaborator in the research, and in each of the two conditions (supervisor or subordinate) the collaborator was white for half the sub-jects and African American for the other half. The actual focus of the study was on what happened when the collaborator "accidentally" knocked over a container of pencils, which fell to the floor. The results were striking. When the person who knocked over the pencils was black, almost all the white subjects helped him pick up the pencils *when* the black person was in the role of subordinate; but only a little more than half of the white subjects did so when the black person was a supervi-sor. On the other hand, when the *white* collaborator knocked over the pencils, the white subjects were much more likely to help pick them up when the other was in the role of supervisor than in the role of subordinate. These findings suggest that, with other whites, the general tendency to be deferent to and help out an authority figure was evident even in the artificial circumstances of such an experiment. But when these white subjects interacted with blacks, the tendency was reversed. They were *less* likely to help when the black person was in a superior position. This striking reversal suggests that there was unacknowledged discomfort or resentment at the black being in the position of superior rather than subordinate.

Again, the study looked at behavior and attitudes, and at aspects of the interaction between blacks and whites, that were highly unlikely to have been conscious for the subjects and that, indeed, might well have been vigorously denied if pointed out. The findings also suggest still another facet of the vicious circles that are likely to be endlessly initiated and repeated between people of the two groups as they interact. What, after all, are likely to be the attitudes of African Americans – whether in subordinate *or* supervisory capacities – in encountering these powerful, but unacknowledged and officially covert attitudes? And what, in turn, are likely to be the attitudes of whites in encountering African Americans' responses to behaviors of theirs that they are not even aware they have manifested? Mutual mistrust and misunderstanding, and the perpetuation of a pattern that is ultimately problematic for both, is the likely result.

A variety of such circles repeat themselves in countless variations day after day, and they likely constitute, at this point in time, the primary engine that drives our continuing divisions and inequalities. What is essential to understand, if we are to have a chance to break these circles, is that – as family therapists put it – the punctuation is arbitrary. That is, once a circle of this sort has come into play, it is difficult if not impossible to indicate who started. We know, of course, who started in historical terms. It is painfully clear that all of these circular processes have their origins in the criminal act of bringing people to these shores as slaves centuries ago. But in the present, looking at how black and white children are socialized and at the experiences they are likely to have with each other as they grow up, it is much more difficult to say what is the chicken and what is the egg. Members of each group respond to what they "see" and what they experience as they interact with each other, and the behavior of each tends to bring out in the other precisely what they expect (and, all too often, what they resent or disdain).

To be sure, the process is aided by prejudices that parents – wittingly and unwittingly – *teach* their children. The kids are not blank slates basing their views solely on direct experience; they enter their first encounters with members of the other group already harboring attitudes that have the potential to keep the social impasse going. But the *persistence* of those attitudes is usually richly reinforced by direct experience, and direct experience of a sort that is mutually and reciprocally (if often not consciously) perpetuated in the ironic fashion that, over and over, creates causes out of consequences.

The Convergence between Social and Clinical Impasses

Such a circular process of problematic patterns being maintained by the very misery and havoc they create is, of course, by no means unique to the realm of race relations. It has been a central theme of this book that our understanding of the *clinical* phenomena that have been at the heart of psychoanalytic concern from the very beginning is *also* enhanced by an appreciation of the circular nature of the binds that characterize our patients' lives. Wherever human suffering and the perpetuation of irrational and destructive ideas blights the social or psychological landscape, we are likely to be in the presence of vicious circles. Understanding the nature of those circles, and resisting the temptation to reduce them to simple linear story lines, is the first step in overcoming them. In race relations as in neurotic suffering, the tendency to perpetuate our problems by our very efforts to deal with them is pervasive. So too, however, is our capacity – at least potentially – to finally recognize the pattern in which we are caught and, with time and effort, to change the patterns that entrap us.

References

Alexander, F., & French, T. (1946). *Psychoanalytic therapy.* New York, NY: Ronald Press.

Allen, J. G., Fonagy, P., & Bateman, A. W. (2008). *Mentalizing in clinical practice.* Arlington, VA: American Psychiatric.

Altman, N. E. (2011). *The analyst in the inner city: Race, class, and culture through an analytic lens.* Hillsdale, NJ: Analytic Press.

Anderson, E. (1990). *Streetwise: Race, class, and change in an urban community.* Chicago, IL: University of Chicago Press.

Angyal, A. (1951). *Neurosis and treatment: A holistic theory.* New York, NY: Wiley.

Apfelbaum, B. (1980). Ego analysis versus depth analysis. In B. Apfelbaum, M. H. Williams, S. E. Greene, & C. Apfelbaum (Eds.), *Expanding the boundaries of sex therapy* (pp. 9–36). Berkeley, CA: Berkeley Sex Therapy Group.

Arlow, J., & Brenner, C. (1964). *Psychoanalytic concepts and the structural theory.* New York, NY: International Universities Press.

Arnkoff, D. B., & Glass, C. R. (1992). Cognitive therapy and psychotherapy integration. In D. K. Freedheim (Ed.), *History of psychotherapy: A century of change* (pp. 657–694). Washington, DC: American Psychological Association.

Aron, L. (1990). One person and two person psychologies and the method of psychoanalysis. *Psychoanalytic Psychology, 7*(4), 475–485.

Aron, L. (1991). Working through the past – Working toward the future. *Contemporary Psychoanalysis, 27,* 81–108.

Aron, L. (1996). *A meeting of minds: Mutuality in psychoanalysis.* Hillsdale, NJ: Analytic Press.

Aron, L. (2003). The paradoxical place of enactment in psychoanalysis: Introduction. *Psychoanalytic Dialogues, 13*(5), 623–631.

Aron, L. (2006). Analytic impasse and the third: Clinical implications of intersubjectivity theory. *International Journal of Psychoanalysis, 87*(2), 349–368.

Aron, L., & Starr, K. (2013). *A psychotherapy for the people: Toward a progressive psychoanalysis.* New York, NY: Routledge/Taylor & Francis Group.

Bakan, D. (1966). *The duality of human existence: Isolation and communion in Western man.* Boston, MA: Beacon Press.

Balint, M. (1950). Changing therapeutical aims and techniques in psycho-analysis. *International Journal of Psychoanalysis, 31,* 117–124.

Barlow, D. H. (2002). *Anxiety and its disorders: The nature and treatment of anxiety and panic* (2nd ed.). New York, NY: Guilford Press.

Barlow, D. H., Allen, L. B., & Choate, M. L. (2004). Toward a unified treatment for emotional disorders. *Behavior Therapy, 35*(2), 205–230.

Bass, A. (2003). "E" enactments in psychoanalysis: Another medium, another message. *Psychoanalytic Dialogues, 13*(5), 657–676.

Beebe, B. (2000). Coconstructing mother – infant distress: The microsynchrony of maternal impingement and infant avoidance in the face-to-face encounter. *Psychoanalytic Inquiry, 20*(3), 421–440.

Beebe, B., & Lachmann, F. M. (1998). Co-constructing inner and relational processes: Self- and mutual regulation in infant research and adult treatment. *Psychoanalytic Psychology, 15*(4), 480–516.

Beebe, B., & Lachmann, F. M. (2002). *Infant research and adult treatment: Co-constructing interactions.* Hillsdale, NJ: Analytic Press.

Beebe, B., & Lachmann, F. (2003). The relational turn in psychoanalysis: A dyadic systems view from infant research. *Contemporary Psychoanalysis, 39*(3), 379–409.

Beebe, B. & Lachmann, F. (in press). *The origins of attachment.* New York, NY: Routledge.

Beitman, B. D. (1987). *The structure of individual psychotherapy.* New York, NY: Guilford Press.

Benjamin, J. (1988). *The bonds of love: Psychoanalysis, feminism, and the problem of domination.* New York, NY: Pantheon Books.

Benjamin, J. (2004). Beyond doer and done to: An intersubjective view of thirdness. *Psychoanalytic Quarterly, 73*(1), 5–46.

Benjamin, J. (2010). Where's the gap and what's the difference? The relational view of intersubjectivity, multiple selves, and enactments. *Contemporary Psychoanalysis, 46*(1), 112–119.

Betchen, S. J. (2005). *Intrusive partners – elusive mates: The pursuer-distancer dynamic in couples.* New York, NY: Routledge.

Beutler, L. E. (1983). *Eclectic psychotherapy: A systematic approach.* New York, NY: Pergamon Press.

Bibring, E. (1954). Psychoanalysis and the dynamic psychotherapies. *Journal of the American Psychoanalytic Association, 2*(4), 745–770.

Billingsley, A. (1992). *Climbing Jacob's ladder: The enduring legacy of African-American families.* New York, NY: Simon & Schuster.

Black, M. J. (2003). Enactment: Analytic musings on energy, language, and personal growth. *Psychoanalytic Dialogues, 13*(5), 633–655.

Blatt, S. J. (2008). *Polarities of experience: Relatedness and self-definition in personality development, psychopathology, and the therapeutic process.* Washington, DC: American Psychological Association.

Blatt, S. J., & Zuroff, D. C. (2005). Empirical evaluation of the assumptions in identifying evidence based treatments in mental health. *Clinical Psychology Review, 25*(4), 459–486.

Blum, H. P. (1999). The reconstruction of reminiscence. *Journal of the American Psychoanalytic Association, 47*(4), 1125–1143.

Boris, H. N. (1986). The "other" breast: Greed, envy, spite and revenge. *Contemporary Psychoanalysis, 22*(1), 45–59.

Bornstein, R. E., & Masling, J. M. (Eds.). (1998). *Empirical perspectives on the psychoanalytic unconscious.* Washington, DC: American Psychological Association.

Boston Change Process Study Group. (2007). The foundational level of psychodynamic meaning: Implicit process in relation to conflict, defense, and the dynamic unconscious. *International Journal of Psychoanalysis, 88*(4), 843–860.

Bowers, K. S. (1973). Situationism in psychology: An analysis and a critique. *Psychological Review*, *80*(5), 307–336.

Boyd-Franklin, N. (2003). *Black families in therapy: Understanding the African American experience* (2nd ed.). New York, NY: Guilford Press.

Breuer, J., & Freud, S. (1895). Studies on hysteria. In Freud, S., *The standard edition of the complete psychological works of Sigmund Freud* (Vol. 2, pp. 1–305). London, UK: Hogarth Press.

Bromberg, P. (1993). Shadow and substance: A relational perspective on clinical process. *Psychoanalytic Psychology*, *10*(2), 147–168.

Bromberg, P. M. (1998). *Standing in the spaces: Essays on clinical process, trauma, and dissociation*. Hillsdale, NJ: Analytic Press.

Burum, B. A., & Goldfried, M. R. (2007). The centrality of emotion to psychological change. *Clinical Psychology: Science and Practice*, *14*(4), 407–413.

Cassidy, J., & Shaver, P. R. (Eds.). (2008). *Handbook of attachment: Theory, research, and clinical applications* (2nd ed.). New York, NY: Guilford Press.

Cohn, J. F., & Tronick, E. Z. (1988). Mother–infant face-to-face interaction: Influence is bidirectional and unrelated to periodic cycles in either partner's behavior. *Developmental Psychology*, *24*(3), 386–392.

Comer, J. P., & Poussaint, A. F. (1992). *Raising black children: Two leading psychiatrists confront the educational, social and emotional problems facing black children*. New York, NY: Plume.

Crocker, J., & Major, B. (1989). Social stigma and self-esteem: The self-protective properties of stigma. *Psychological Review*, *96*(4), 608–630.

Curtis, R. C. (2009). *Desire, self, mind, and the psychotherapies: Unifying psychological science and psychoanalysis*. Lanham, MD: Jason Aronson.

Cushman, P. (1990). Why the self is empty: Toward a historically situated psychology. *American Psychologist*, *45*(5), 599–611.

Davies, J. M. (1996). Linking the "pre-analytic" with the postclassical: Integration, dissociation, and the multiplicity of unconscious processes. *Contemporary Psychoanalysis*, *32*(4), 553–576.

Davis, D., & Hollon, S. D. (1999). Refraining resistance and noncompliance in cognitive therapy. *Journal of Psychotherapy Integration*, *9*(1), 33–55.

Devine, P. G. (1989). Stereotyping and prejudice: Their automatic and controlled components. *Journal of Personality and Social Psychology*, *56*(1), 5–18.

Dewald, P. A. (1982). Psychoanalytic perspectives on resistance. In P. Wachtel (Ed.), *Resistance: Psychodynamic and behavioral approaches* (pp. 45–68). New York, NY: Plenum.

Dilthey, W. (1883/1991). *Introduction to the human sciences* (Collected writings: Vol. 1). Princeton, NJ: Princeton University Press.

Dimen, M., & Goldner, V. (2002). *Gender in psychoanalytic space: Between clinic and culture*. New York, NY: Other Press.

Dollard, J., & Miller, N. E. (1950). *Personality and psychotherapy: An analysis in terms of learning, thinking, and culture*. New York, NY: McGraw-Hill.

Eagle, M. N. (1984). *Recent developments in psychoanalysis: A critical evaluation*. New York, NY: McGraw-Hill.

Eagle, M. (1999). Why don't people change? A psychoanalytic perspective. *Journal of Psychotherapy Integration*, *9*(1), 3–32.

Eagle, M. (2003). Clinical implications of attachment theory. *Psychoanalytic Inquiry*, *23*(1), 27–53.

Eagle, M.N., & Wolitzky, D.L. (2009). Adult psychotherapy from the perspectives of attachment theory and psychoanalysis. In J.H. Obegi & E. Berant (Eds.), *Attachment theory and research in clinical work with adults* (pp. 351–378). New York, NY: Guilford Press.

Easterlin, R.A. (1974). Does economic growth improve the human lot? Some empirical evidence. In P.A. David & M.W. Reder (Eds.), *Nations and households in economic growth: Essays in honor of Moses Abramowitz* (pp. 89–125). New York, NY: Academic Press.

Eigen, M. (1986). *The psychotic core.* Northvale, NJ: Jason Aronson.

Emery, E. (1992). The envious eye: Concerning some aspects of envy from Wilfred Bion to Harold Boris. *Melanie Klein and Object Relations, 10*(1), 19–29.

Empson, W. (1930). *Seven types of ambiguity.* New York, NY: New Directions.

Erikson, E.H. (1950). *Childhood and society.* New York, NY: Norton.

Erikson, E.H. (1959). *Identity and the life cycle.* New York, NY: International Universities Press.

Erikson, E.H. (1963). *Childhood and society.* New York, NY: Norton.

Fairbairn, W.R.D. (1952). *An object-relations theory of the personality.* New York, NY: Basic Books.

Fanon, F. (1967). *Black skin, white masks.* New York, NY: Grove Press.

Feixas, G., & Botella, L. (2004). Psychotherapy integration: Reflections and contributions from a constructivist epistemology. *Journal of Psychotherapy Integration, 14*(2), 192–222.

Fenichel, O. (1938). The drive to amass wealth. *Psychoanalytic Quarterly, 7,* 69–95.

Fenichel, O. (1941). *Problems of psychoanalytic technique.* New York, NY: Psychoanalytic Quarterly Press.

Ferenczi, S. (1926). *Further contributions to the theory and technique of psycho-analysis.* London, UK: Hogarth Press.

Ferenczi, S. (1952). The origin of the interest in money. In *First contributions to psychoanalysis.* London, UK: Hogarth Press.

Field, T., Healy, B., Goldstein, S., Perry, S., Bendell, D., Schanberg, S., . . . Kuhn, C. (1988). Infants of depressed mothers show "depressed" behavior even with nondepressed adults. *Child Development, 59*(6), 1569–1579.

Fonagy, P. (1991). Thinking about thinking: Some clinical and theoretical considerations in the treatment of a borderline patient. *International Journal of Psychoanalysis, 72*(4), 639–656.

Fonagy, P. (1999). Points of contact and divergence between psychoanalytic and attachment theories: Is psychoanalytic theory truly different. *Psychoanalytic Inquiry, 19*(4), 448–480.

Fonagy, P. (2001). *Attachment theory and psychoanalysis.* New York, NY: Other Press.

Fonagy, P., Gergely, G., Jurist, E.L., & Target, M. (2002). *Affect regulation, mentalization, and the development of the self.* New York, NY: Other Press.

Fonagy, P., Gergely, G., & Target, M. (2008). Psychoanalytic constructs and attachment theory and research. In J. Cassidy & P.R. Shaver (Eds.), *Handbook of attachment: Theory, research, and clinical applications* (2nd ed., pp. 783–810). New York, NY: Guilford Press.

Fonagy, P., Target, M., Steele, H., & Steele, M. (1998). *Reflective-functioning manual, version 5.0, for application to adult attachment interviews.* London, UK: University College London.

Fosshage, J.L. (2003). Fundamental pathways to change: Illuminating old and creating new relational experience. *International Forum of Psychoanalysis, 12*(4), 244–251.

Frances, A., Clarkin, J.F., & Perry, S. (1984). *Differential therapeutics in psychiatry: The art and science of treatment selection.* New York, NY: Brunner/Mazel.

Frank, K.A. (1990). Action techniques in psychoanalysis – background and introduction. *Contemporary Psychoanalysis, 26*(4), 732–756.

Frank, K.A. (1992). Combining action techniques with psychoanalytic therapy. *International Review of Psychoanalysis, 19*(1), 57–79.

Frank, K.A. (1993). Action, insight, and working through outlines of an integrative approach. *Psychoanalytic Dialogues: The International Journal of Relational Perspectives, 3*(4), 535–577.

Frank, K.A. (1999). *Psychoanalytic participation: Action, integration, and integration.* Hillsdale, NJ: Analytic Press.

Frank, K.A. (2001). Extending the field of psychoanalytic change: Exploratory–assertive motivation, self-efficacy, and the new analytic role for action. *Psychoanalytic Inquiry, 21*(5), 620–639.

Frank, K.A. (2002). The "ins and outs" of enactment: A relational bridge for psychotherapy integration. *Journal of Psychotherapy Integration, 12*(3), 267–286.

Frank, R.H. (1985). *Choosing the right pond: Human behavior and the quest for status.* New York, NY: Oxford University Press.

Frank, R.H. (2007). *Falling behind: How rising inequality harms the middle class.* Berkeley, CA: University of California Press.

Frank, R.H. (2011). *The Darwin economy: Liberty, competition, and the common good.* Princeton, NJ: Princeton University Press.

Franklin, A.J. (1993). The invisibility syndrome. *Family Therapy Networker, 17*(4), 32–38.

Freud, S. (1893). On the psychical mechanism of hysterical phenomena. *The Standard Edition of the Complete Psychological Works of Sigmund Freud* (Vol. 3). London, UK: Hogarth Press.

Freud, S. (1896). The aetiology of hysteria. *The Standard Edition of the Complete Psychological Works of Sigmund Freud* (Vol. 3). London, UK: Hogarth Press.

Freud, S. (1908). Character and anal erotism. *The Standard Edition of the Complete Psychological Works of Sigmund Freud* (Vol. 9). London, UK: Hogarth Press.

Freud, S. (1914/1957). Remembering, repeating, and working-through (Further recommendations on the technique of psycho-analysis II). *The Standard Edition of the Complete Psychological Works of Sigmund Freud* (Vol. 12). London, UK: Hogarth Press.

Freud, S. (1915/1958). Repression. *The Standard Edition of the Complete Psychological Works of Sigmund Freud* (Vol. 14). London, UK: Hogarth Press.

Freud, S. (1917). Introductory lectures on psycho-analysis. *The Standard Edition of the Complete Psychological Works of Sigmund Freud* (Vol. 16). London, UK: Hogarth Press.

Freud, S. (1918). Lines of advance in psycho-analytic therapy. *The Standard Edition of the Complete Psychological Works of Sigmund Freud* (Vol. 17). London, UK: Hogarth Press.

Freud, S. (1921). Group psychology and the analysis of the ego. *The Standard Edition of the Complete Psychological Works of Sigmund Freud* (Vol. 18). London, UK: Hogarth Press.

Freud, S. (1923/1961). The ego and the id. *The Standard Edition of the Complete Psychological Works of Sigmund Freud* (Vol. 19). London, UK: Hogarth Press.

Freud, S. (1926/1959). Inhibitions, symptoms, and anxiety. *The Standard Edition of the Complete Psychological Works of Sigmund Freud* (Vol. 20). London, UK: Hogarth Press.

Friedman, L. (2002). What lies beyond interpretation, and is that the right question? *Psychoanalytic Psychology, 19*(3), 540–551.

Friedman, M., & Friedman, R. (1980). *Free to choose: A personal statement.* New York, NY: Harcourt.

Fromm, E. (1941). *Escape from freedom.* New York, NY: Holt, Rinehart, & Winston.

Fromm, E. (1955). *The sane society.* New York, NY: Rinehart & Co.

Gaertner, S.L., & Dovidio, J.F. (1986). The aversive form of racism. In J.F. Dovidio & S.L. Gaertner (Eds.), *Prejudice, discrimination, and racism* (pp. 61–89). Orlando, FL: Academic Press.

Galbraith, J.K. (1958). *The affluent society.* Boston, MA: Houghton Mifflin.

Galbraith, J.K. (1967). *The new industrial state.* Boston: Houghton Mifflin.

Geertz, C. (1973). Thick description: Toward an interpretative theory of culture. In C. Geertz (Ed.), *The interpretation of cultures.* New York, NY: Basic Books.

Gerson, M.J. (2010). *The embedded self: An integrative psychodynamic and systemic perspective on couples and family therapy.* New York, NY: Routledge.

Ghent, E. (1989). Credo – The dialectics of one-person and two-person psychologies. *Contemporary Psychoanalysis, 25*(2), 169–211.

Ghent, E. (1995). Interaction in the psychoanalytic situation. *Psychoanalytic Dialogues, 5*(3), 479–491.

Gilbert, P., & Leahy, R.L. (Eds.). (2007). *The therapeutic relationship in the cognitive behavioral psychotherapies.* New York, NY: Routledge.

Gill, M.M. (1979). The analysis of the transference. *Journal of the American Psychoanalytic Association, 27*(Suppl.), 263–288.

Gill, M.M. (1982). *Analysis of transference.* New York, NY: International Universities Press.

Gill, M.M. (1983). The interpersonal paradigm and the degree of the therapist's involvement. *Contemporary Psychoanalysis, 19*(2), 200–237.

Gill, M.M. (1984). Psychoanalysis and psychotherapy: A revision. *International Review of Psychoanalysis, 11*, 161–179.

Goldman, S.J., D'Angelo, E.J., DeMaso, D.R., & Mezzacappa, E. (1992). Physical and sexual abuse histories among children with borderline personality disorder. *American Journal of Psychiatry, 149*(12), 1723–1726.

Goldner, V. (1991). Toward a critical relational theory of gender. *Psychoanalytic Dialogues, 1*(3), 249–272.

Gottlieb, R.M. (2010). Coke or Pepsi? Reflections on Freudian and relational psychoanalysts in dialogue. *Contemporary Psychoanalysis, 46*, 87–99.

Greenberg, J. (2005). Conflict in the middle voice. *Psychoanalytic Quarterly, 74*(1), 105–120.

Greenberg, J., & Mitchell, S.A. (1983). *Object relations in psychoanalytic theory.* Cambridge, MA: Harvard University Press.

Greenberg, L.S. (2002). *Emotion-focused therapy: Coaching clients to work through their feelings.* Washington, DC: American Psychological Association.

Greenberg, L.S. (2004). Emotion-focused therapy. *Clinical Psychology & Psychotherapy, 11*(1), 3–16.

Greenberg, L. S. (2008). Emotion and cognition in psychotherapy: The transforming power of affect. *Canadian Psychology, 49*(1), 49–59.

Greenberg, L. S., & Goldman, R. N. (2008). *Emotion-focused couples therapy: The dynamics of emotion, love, and power.* Washington, DC: American Psychological Association.

Greenberg, L. S., & Pascual-Leone, A. (2006). Emotion in psychotherapy: A practice-friendly review. *Journal of Clinical Psychology, 62*(5), 611–630.

Greenberg, L. S., & Paivio, S. C. (1997). *Working with emotions in psychotherapy.* New York, NY: Guilford Press.

Greenberg, L. S., & Watson, J. C. (2006). *Emotion-focused therapy for depression.* Washington, DC: American Psychological Association.

Grossman, K. E., Grossman, K., & Waters, E. (Eds.). (2005). *Attachment from infancy to adulthood: The major longitudinal studies.* New York, NY: Guilford Press.

Guidano, V. E. (1987). *Complexity of the self: A developmental approach to psychopathology and therapy.* New York, NY: Guilford Press.

Guidano, V. E. (1991). *The self in process.* New York, NY: Guilford Press.

Hamilton, D. L., & Gifford, R. K. (1976). Illusory correlation in interpersonal perception: A cognitive basis of stereotypic judgments. *Journal of Experimental Social Psychology, 12*(4), 392–407.

Harris, A. (1996). The conceptual power of multiplicity. *Contemporary Psychoanalysis, 32*(4), 537–552.

Harris, A. (2005). *Gender as soft assembly.* Hillsdale, NJ: Analytic Press.

Havens, L. (1986). *Making contact: Uses of language in psychotherapy.* Cambridge, MA: Harvard University Press.

Hayes, S. C., Follette, V. M., & Linehan, M. M. (Eds.). (2004). *Mindfulness and acceptance: Expanding the cognitive-behavioral tradition.* New York, NY: Guilford Press.

Herman, J. L., Perry, J. C., & van der Kolk, B. (1989). Childhood trauma in borderline personality disorder. *American Journal of Psychiatry, 146*(4), 490–495.

Herrnstein, R., & Murray, C. (1994). *The bell curve: Intelligence and class structure in American life.* New York, NY: Free Press.

Hesse, E. (1999). The adult attachment interview: Historical and current perspectives. In J. Cassidy & P. R. Shaver (Eds.), *Handbook of attachment: Theory, research, and clinical applications* (pp. 395–433). New York, NY: Guilford Press.

Hetherington, E. M., & Blechman, E. A. (Eds.). (1996). *Stress, coping and resiliency in children and families.* Mahwah, NJ: Lawrence Erlbaum.

Hirsch, I. (1998). The concept of enactment and theoretical convergence. *Psychoanalytic Quarterly, 67*(1), 78–101.

Hobbes, T. (1651/1968). *Leviathan* (C. B. MacPherson, Ed.). Harmondsworth, England: Penguin.

Hoffman, I. Z. (1983). The patient as interpreter of the analyst's experience. *Contemporary Psychoanalysis, 19*(3), 389–422.

Hoffman, I. Z. (1991). Toward a social-constructivist view of the psychoanalytic situation. *Psychoanalytic Dialogues, 1*(1), 74–105.

Hoffman, I. Z. (1998). Ritual and spontaneity in the psychoanalytic process. Hillsdale, NJ: Analytic Press.

Hoffman, L. (1981). *Foundations of family therapy: A conceptual framework for systems change.* New York, NY: Basic Books.

Hoffman, L. (1998). Setting aside the model in family therapy. *Journal of Marital and Family Therapy, 24*(2), 145–156.

Hollingshead, A., & Redlich, F. (1958). *Social class and mental illness: A community study.* New Haven, CT: Yale University Press.

Horney, K. (1937). *The neurotic personality of our time.* New York, NY: Norton.

Horney, K. (1939). *New ways in psychoanalysis.* New York, NY: Norton.

Horney, K. (1945). *Our inner conflicts: A constructive theory of neurosis.* New York, NY: Norton.

Howell, E. F. (2005). *The dissociative mind.* Hillsdale, NJ: Analytic Press.

Jacobs, T. J. (1986). On countertransference enactments. *Journal of the American Psychoanalytic Association, 34*(2), 289–307.

Jacobsen, P. B., & Steele, R. S. (1978). From present to past: Freudian archaeology. *International Review of Psychoanalysis, 6,* 349–362.

Jacoby, R. (1983). *The repression of psychoanalysis: Otto Fenichel and the political Freudians.* New York, NY: Basic Books.

Jasper, J. M. (2000). *Restless nation: Starting over in America.* Chicago, IL: University of Chicago Press.

Johnson, L. B., & Staples, R. (1993). *Black families at the crossroads: Challenges and prospects.* San Francisco, CA: Jossey-Bass.

Jordan, W. D. (1977). *White over black: American attitudes toward the Negro, 1550–1812.* New York, NY: Norton.

Kasser, T. (2000). Two versions of the American dream: Which goals and values make for a high quality of life? In E. Diener & D. R. Rahtz (Eds.), *Advances in quality of life theory and research* (pp. 3–12). Dordrecht, Netherlands: Kluwer Academic.

Kasser, T. (2003). *The high price of materialism.* Cambridge, MA: MIT Press.

Kasser, T., & Kanner, A. D. (Eds.). (2003). *Psychology and consumer culture: The struggle for a good life in a materialistic world.* Washington, DC: American Psychological Association.

Kasser, T., & Ryan, R. M. (1993). A dark side of the American dream: Correlates of financial success a central life aspiration. *Journal of Personality and Social Psychology, 65*(2), 410–422.

Katz, M. (1989). *The undeserving poor: America's enduring confrontation with poverty.* New York, NY: Pantheon.

Kazdin, A. E. (2006). Arbitrary metrics: Implications for identifying evidence-based treatments. *American Psychologist, 61*(1), 42–49.

Kazdin, A. E. (2008). Evidence-based treatment and practice: New opportunities to bridge clinical research and practice, enhance the knowledge base, and improve patient care. *American Psychologist, 63*(3), 146–159.

Kernberg, O. (1975). *Borderline conditions and pathological narcissism.* New York, NY: Jason Aronson.

Klein, M. (1957). *Envy and gratitude: A study of unconscious sources.* New York, NY: Basic Books.

Kohut, H. (1971). *The analysis of the self: A systematic approach to the psychoanalytic treatment of narcissistic personality disorders.* New York, NY: International Universities Press.

Kohut, H. (1977). *The restoration of the self.* New York, NY: International Universities Press.

Kohut, H. (1985). *Self psychology and the humanities: Reflections on a new psychoanalytic approach.* New York, NY: Norton.

Kovel, J. (1984). *White racism: A psychohistory.* New York, NY: Columbia University Press.

Kuhn, T. S. (1962). *The structure of scientific revolutions*. Chicago, IL: University of Chicago Press.

Lakoff, G., & Johnson, M. (1980). *Metaphors we live by*. Chicago, IL: University of Chicago Press.

Laplanche J., & Pontalis, J. B. (1973). *The language of psycho-analysis*. New York, NY: Norton.

Lasch, C. (1979). *The culture of narcissism*. New York, NY: Norton.

Leahy, R. L. (2008). The therapeutic relationship in cognitive-behavioral therapy. *Behavioural and Cognitive Psychotherapy, 36*(6), 769–777.

Lewin, K. (1951). *Field theory in social science: Selected theoretical papers*. New York, NY: Harper & Row.

Loewald, H. W. (1960). On the therapeutic action of psycho-analysis. *International Journal of Psychoanalysis, 41*, 16–33.

Luborsky, L. (1996). *The symptom-context method: Symptoms as opportunities in psychotherapy*. Washington, DC: American Psychological Association.

Lyons-Ruth, K. (1999). The two-person unconscious: Intersubjective dialogue, enactive relational representation, and the emergence of new forms of relational organization. *Psychoanalytic Inquiry, 19*(4), 576–617.

Mahoney, M. J. (1995). *Cognitive and constructive psychotherapies: Theory, research, and practice*. New York, NY: Springer.

Mahoney, M. J. (2003). *Constructive psychotherapy: A practical guide*. New York, NY: Guilford Press.

Mahoney, M. J. (2004). Synthesis. In A. Freeman, M. J. Mahoney, P. Devito, & D. Martin (Eds.), *Cognition and psychotherapy* (2nd ed.). New York, NY: Springer.

Main, M., & Goldwyn, R. (1998). *Adult attachment classification system*. Unpublished manuscript, University of California, Berkeley, CA.

Maital, S. (1982). *Minds, markets, and money: Psychological foundations of economic behavior*. New York, NY: Basic Books.

Majors, R. G., & Billson, J. M. (1992). *Cool pose: The dilemmas of black manhood in America*. New York, NY: Lexington Books.

Malatesta, C. Z., Culver, C., Tesman, J. R., & Shepard, B. (1989). The development of emotion expression during the first two years of life. *Monograph of the Society for Research in Child Development, 54*(1–2), Serial No. 219, 1–33.

Maroda, K. J. (1998). Enactment: When the patient's and analyst's pasts converge. *Psychoanalytic Psychology, 15*(4), 517–535.

Marrone, M. (1998). *Attachment and interaction*. London, UK: Kingsley.

Marx, K. (1964). *The economic and philosophic manuscripts of 1844* (D. J. Struik, Ed. & Trans.). New York, NY: International.

Masling, J. M. (2000). Empirical evidence and the health of psychoanalysis. *Journal of the American Academy of Psychoanalysis, 28*(4), 665–686.

Massey, D. S., & Denton, N. A. (1993). *American apartheid: Segregation and the making of the underclass*. Cambridge, MA: Harvard University Press.

McConahay, J. B. (1982). Self-interest versus racial attitudes as correlates of anti-busing attitudes in Louisville: Is it the buses or the blacks? *Journal of Politics, 44*(3), 692–720.

McLaughlin, J. T. (1991). Clinical and theoretical aspects of enactment. *Journal of the American Psychoanalytic Association, 39*(3), 595–614.

Messer, S. B. (2000). Applying the visions of reality to a case of brief psychotherapy. *Journal of Psychotherapy Integration, 10*(1), 55–70.

Mikulincer, M., & Shaver, P. R. (2007). *Attachment in adulthood: Structure, dynamics, and change*. New York, NY: Guilford Press.

Mischel, W. (1968). *Personality and assessment*. New York, NY: Wiley.

Mitchell, S. A. (1986). The wings of Icarus: – Illusion and the problem of narcissism. *Contemporary Psychoanalysis, 22*, 107–132.

Mitchell, S. A. (1988). *Relational concepts in psychoanalysis: An integration*. Cambridge, MA: Harvard University Press.

Mitchell, S. A. (1991). Wishes, needs, and interpersonal negotiations. *Psychoanalytic Inquiry, 11*(1–2), 147–170.

Mitchell, S. A. (1993). *Hope and dread in psychoanalysis*. New York, NY: Basic Books.

Mitchell, S. A. (1995). Interaction in the Kleinian and interpersonal traditions. *Contemporary Psychoanalysis, 31*(1), 65–91.

Mitchell, S. A. (1997). *Influence and autonomy in psychoanalysis*. Hillsdale, NJ: Analytic Press.

Mitchell, S. A. (1999). Attachment theory and the psychoanalytic tradition: Reflections on human relationality. *Psychoanalytic Dialogues, 9*(1), 85–107.

Mitchell, S. A., & Aron, L. (Eds.). (1999). *Relational psychoanalysis: The emergence of a tradition*. Hillsdale, NJ: Analytic Press.

Modell, A. H. (1984). *Psychoanalysis in a new context*. New York, NY: International Universities Press.

Myers, D. G. (2000). *The American paradox: Spiritual hunger in an age of plenty*. New Haven, CT: Yale University Press.

Napier, A. Y. (1978). The rejection-intrusion pattern: A central family dynamic. *Journal of Marriage and Family Therapy, 4*(1), 5–12.

Neimeyer, R. A. (2009). *Constructivist psychotherapy*. London, UK: Routledge.

Neimeyer, R. A., & Mahoney, M. J. (Eds.). (1995). *Constructivism in psychotherapy*. Washington, DC: American Psychological Association.

Nichols, M. P., & Schwartz, R. C. (1998). *Family therapy: Concepts and methods*. Needham Heights, MA: Allyn & Bacon.

Norcross, J. C. (1986a). *Handbook of eclectic psychotherapy*. New York, NY: Brunner/Mazel.

Norcross, J. C. (1986b). *Casebook of eclectic psychotherapy*. New York, NY: Brunner/Mazel.

Norcross, J. N. (2002). *Psychotherapy relationships that work: Therapist contributions and responsiveness to patients*. New York, NY: Oxford University Press.

Norcross, J. N. (2010). The therapeutic relationship. In B. L. Duncan, S. D. Miller, B. E. Wampold, & M. A. Hubble (Eds.), *The heart and soul of change: Delivering what works in therapy* (2nd ed., pp. 113–141). Washington, DC: American Psychological Association.

Norcross, J. N., & Goldfried, M. R. (Eds.). (2005). *Handbook of psychotherapy integration* (2nd ed.). New York, NY: Oxford University Press.

O'Connor, T. G., Bredenkamp, D., Rutter, M. (1999). *Infant Mental Health Journal, 20*, 110–129.

Ogbu, J. (1991). Immigrant and involuntary minorities in comparative perspective. In M. A. Gibson & J. U. Ogbu (Eds.), *Minority status and schooling: A comparative study of immigrant and involuntary minorities*. New York, NY: Garland.

Osborne, J. W. (1995). Academics, self-esteem, and race: A look at the underlying assumptions of the disidentification hypothesis. *Personality and Social Psychology Bulletin, 21*(5), 449–455.

Osborne, J. W. (1997). Race and academic disidentification. *Journal of Educational Psychology*, *89*(4), 728–735.

Paris, J., & Zweig-Frank, H. (1992). A critical review of the role of childhood sexual abuse in the etiology of borderline personality disorder. *Canadian Journal of Psychiatry*, *37*(2), 125–128.

Patterson, F. G. P., & Cohn, R. H. (1990). Language acquisition by a lowland gorilla: Koko's first ten years of vocabulary development. *Word*, *41*, 97–143.

Perez-Foster, R. M., Moskowitz, M., & Javier, R. A. (1996). *Reaching across boundaries of culture and class: Widening the scope of psychotherapy.* Lanham, MD: Rowman & Littlefield.

Peterfreund, E. (1978). Some critical comments on psychoanalytic conceptualizations of infancy. *International Journal of Psychoanalysis*, *59*, 427–441.

Piers, C. (2000). Character as self-organizing complexity. *Psychoanalysis and Contemporary Thought*, *23*, 3–34.

Piers, C. (2005). The mind's multiplicity and continuity. *Psychoanalytic Dialogues*, *15*(2), 229–254.

Polanyi, M. (1966). *The tacit dimension.* London, UK: Routledge.

Pos, A. E., & Greenberg, L. S. (2007). Emotion-focused therapy. The transforming power of affect. *Journal of Contemporary Psychotherapy*, *37*(1), 25–31.

Pos, A. E., Greenberg, L. S., & Elliott, R. (2008). Experiential therapy. In J. L. Lebow (Ed.), *Twenty-first century psychotherapies: Contemporary approaches to theory and practice* (pp. 80–122). Hoboken, NJ: Wiley.

Pressman, E. R. (Producer), & Stone, O. (Director). (1987). *Wall Street* [Motion picture]. United States: Twentieth Century Fox.

Prochaska, J. O. (1984). *Systems of psychotherapy: A transtheoretical analysis* (2nd ed.). Homewood, IL: Dorsey Press.

Prochaska, J. O., & Prochaska, J. M. (1999). Why don't continents move? Why don't people change? *Journal of Psychotherapy Integration*, *9*(1), 83–102.

Putnam, R. (2000). *Bowling alone: The collapse and revival of American community.* New York, NY: Simon & Schuster.

Reid, T. (1999). A cultural perspective on resistance. *Journal of Psychotherapy Integration*, *9*(1), 57–81.

Renik, O. (1993). Analytic interaction: Conceptualizing technique in light of the analyst's irreducible subjectivity. *Psychoanalytic Quarterly*, *62*(4), 553–571.

Renik, O. (1996). The perils of neutrality. *Psychoanalytic Quarterly*, *65*(3), 495–517.

Renik, O. (1999). Playing one's cards face up in analysis: An approach to the problem of self-disclosure. *Psychoanalytic Quarterly*, *68*(4), 521–530.

Renn, P. (2012). The silent past and the invisible present: Memory, trauma, and representation in psychotherapy. New York, NY: Routledge.

Rickman, J. (1957). *Selected contributions to psycho-analysis.* Oxford, UK: Basic Books.

Ricouer, P. (1970). *Freud and philosophy: An essay on interpretation.* New Haven, CT: Yale University Press.

Rieff, P. (1966). *The triumph of the therapeutic: Uses of faith after Freud.* Chicago, IL: University of Chicago Press.

Rieff, P. (1979). *Freud: The mind of the moralist.* Chicago, IL: University of Chicago Press.

Rozhon, T. (2000, October 22). Be it ever less humble: American homes get bigger. *The New York Times.* Retrieved from www.nytimes.com/2000/10/22/weekinreview/ideas-trends-be-it-ever-less-humble-american-homes-get-bigger.html

Rubenstein, B.B. (1997). On metaphor and related phenomena. In R.R. Holt (Ed.), *Psychoanalysis and the philosophy of science: Collected papers of Benjamin B. Rubenstein, M.D.* (pp. 123–171). Madison, CT: International Universities Press.

Ruiz-Cordell, K.D., & Safran, J.D. (2007). Alliance ruptures: Theory, research, and practice. In S.G. Hofmann & J. Weinberger (Eds.), *The art and science of psychotherapy* (pp. 155–170). New York, NY: Routledge.

Rutter, M. (1995). Psychosocial adversity: Risk, resilience & recovery. *South African Journal of Child and Adolescent Psychiatry, 7*(2), 75–88.

Safran, J.D., & Muran, J.C. (2000). *Negotiating the therapeutic alliance: A relational treatment guide.* New York, NY: Guilford Press.

Safran, J.D., Muran, J.C., & Eubanks-Carter, C. (2011). Repairing alliance ruptures. *Psychotherapy, 48*(1), 80–87.

Safran, J.D., Muran, J.C., & Proskurov, B. (2009). Alliance, negotiation, and rupture resolution. In R.A. Levy & J.S. Ablon (Eds.), *Handbook of evidence-based psychodynamic psychotherapy: Bridging the gap between science and practice* (pp. 201–225). Totowa, NJ: Humana Press.

Safran, J.D., & Segal, Z.V. (1990). *Interpersonal process in cognitive therapy.* New York, NY: Guilford Press.

Samoilov, A., & Goldfried, M.R. (2000). Role of emotion in cognitive-behavior therapy. *Clinical Psychology: Science and Practice, 7*(4), 373–385.

Santayana, G. (1940). Materialism and idealism in American life. In A.T. Johnson & A. Tate (Eds.), *America through the essay.* New York: Oxford University Press.

Schachtel, E.G. (1959). *Metamorphosis: On the development of affect, perception, attention, and memory.* New York, NY: Basic Books.

Schacter, D.L. (1996). *Searching for memory: The brain, the mind, and the past.* New York, NY: Basic Books.

Schacter, D.L. (2001). *The seven sins of memory: How the mind forgets and remembers.* Boston, MA: Houghton Mifflin.

Schacter, D.L., Norman, K.A., & Koutstaal, W. (1998). The cognitive neuroscience of constructive memory. *Annual Review of Psychology, 49,* 289–318.

Schafer, R. (1976). *A new language for psychoanalysis.* New Haven, CT: Yale University Press.

Schafer, R. (1997). *The contemporary Kleinians of London.* Madison, CT: International Universities Press.

Schechter, M. (2007). The patient's experience of validation in psychoanalytic treatment. *Journal of the American Psychoanalytic Association, 55*(1), 105–130.

Schimek, J.G. (1975). A critical re-examination of Freud's concept of unconscious mental representation. *International Review of Psychoanalysis, 2*(2), 171–187.

Sears, D.O. (1988). Symbolic racism. In P.A. Katz & D.A. Taylor (Eds.), *Eliminating racism: Profiles in controversy* (pp. 53–84). New York, NY: Plenum.

Shahar, G., Cross, L.W., & Henrich, C.C. (2004). Representations in action (Or: action models of development meet psychoanalytic conceptualizations of mental representations). *Psychoanalytic Study of the Child, 59,* 261–293.

Shahar, G., & Porcelli, J.H. (2006). The action formulation: A proposed heuristic for clinical case formulation. *Journal of Clinical Psychology, 62*(9), 1115–1127.

Shapiro, D. (1965). *Neurotic styles.* New York, NY: Basic Books.

Shapiro, D. (1989). *Psychotherapy of neurotic character.* New York, NY: Basic Books.

Shedler, J. (2010). The efficacy of psychodynamic psychotherapy. *American Psychologist, 65*(2), 98–109.

Shedler, J., Mayman, M., & Manis, M. (1993). The illusion of mental health. *American Psychologist, 48*, 1117–1131.

Silberschatz, G. (2005). *Transformative relationships: The control mastery theory of psychotherapy.* New York, NY: Routledge.

Simon, H. A. (1957). *Models of man.* New York, NY: Wiley.

Sirgy, M. J. (1998). Materialism and quality of life. *Social Indicators Research, 43*(3), 227–260.

Slade, A. (1999). Attachment theory and research: Implications for the theory and practice of individual psychotherapy with adults. In J. Cassidy & P. R. Shaver (Eds.), *Handbook of attachment: Theory, research, and clinical applications* (pp. 575–594). New York, NY: Guilford Press.

Slade, A. (2004). Two therapies: Attachment organization and the clinical process. In L. Atkinson & S. Goldberg (Eds.), *Attachment issues in psychopathology and intervention* (pp. 181–206). Mahwah, NJ: Lawrence Erlbaum Associates.

Slade, A. (2008). The implications of attachment theory and research for adult psychotherapy: Research and clinical perspectives. In J. Cassidy & P. R. Shaver (Eds.), *Handbook of attachment: Theory, research, and clinical applications* (2nd ed., pp. 762–782). New York, NY: Guilford Press.

Slavin, M. O. (1996). Is one self enough? Multiplicity in self-organization and the capacity to negotiate relational conflict. *Contemporary Psychoanalysis, 32*(4), 615–625.

Smith, A. (1776). *An inquiry into the nature and causes of the wealth of nations.* Oxford, UK: Clarendon Press.

Smith, A. (2002) [1759]. Knud Haakonssen, ed. *The Theory of Moral Sentiments.* Cambridge, UK: Cambridge University Press.

Spence, D. P. (1982). *Narrative truth and historical truth: Meaning and interpretation in psychoanalysis.* New York, NY: Norton.

Sroufe, L. A., Egeland, B., Carlson, E. A., & Collins, W. A. (2005). *The development of the person: The Minnesota study of risk and adaptation from birth to adulthood.* New York, NY: Guilford Press.

Stack, C. (1975). *All our kin: Strategies for survival in a Black community.* New York, NY: Harper & Row.

Steele, C. M. (1997). A threat in the air: How stereotypes shape intellectual identity and performance. *American Psychologist, 52*(6), 613–629.

Steele, C. M., & Aronson, J. (1995). Stereotype threat and the intellectual test performance of African Americans. *Journal of Personality and Social Psychology, 69*(5), 797–811.

Steinberg, L. (1996). Ethnicity and adolescent achievement. *American Educator, 20*(2), 28–35, 44–48.

Stern, D. B. (1997). *Unformulated experience: From dissociation to imagination in psychoanalysis.* Hillsdale, NJ: Analytic Press.

Stern, D. B. (2003). The fusion of horizons: Dissociation, enactment, and understanding. *Psychoanalytic Dialogues, 13*(6), 843–873.

Stern, D. B. (2004). The eye sees itself: Dissociation, enactment, and the achievement of conflict. *Contemporary Psychoanalysis, 40*, 197–237.

Stern, D. N. (1985). *The interpersonal world of the infant.* New York, NY: Basic Books.

Stern, D. N., Sander, L. W., Nahum, J. P., Harrison, A. M., Lyons-Ruth, K., Morgan, A. C., . . . Tronick, E. Z. (1998). Non-interpretive mechanisms in psychoanalytic therapy: The "something more" than interpretation. *International Journal of Psychoanalysis, 79*(5), 903–921.

Stolorow, R. D., & Atwood, G. E. (1992). *Contexts of being: The intersubjective foundations of psychological life*. Hillsdale, NJ: Analytic Press.

Stolorow, R. D., & Atwood, G. E. (1994). The myth of the isolated mind. *Progress in Self Psychology, 10*, 233–250.

Stolorow, R. D., & Atwood, G. E. (1997). Deconstructing the myth of the neutral analyst: An alternative from intersubjective systems theory. *Psychoanalytic Quarterly, 66*(3), 431–449.

Stolorow, R. D., Brandchaft, B., & Atwood, G. E. (1987). *Psychoanalytic treatment: An intersubjective approach*. Hillsdale, NJ: Analytic Press.

Stolorow, R. D., Orange, D. M., & Atwood, G. E. (2001). World horizons: A post-Cartesian alternative to the Freudian unconscious. *Contemporary Psychoanalysis, 37*(1), 43–61.

Stricker, G., & Gold, J. (Eds.). (2006). *A casebook of psychotherapy integration*. Washington, DC: American Psychological Association.

Sullivan, H. S. (1953). *The interpersonal theory of psychiatry*. New York, NY: Norton.

Taylor, R. J., Jackson, J. S., & Chatters, L. M. (Eds.). (1997). *Family life in Black America*. Thousand Oaks, CA: Sage.

Triandis, H. (1995). *Individualism & collectivism*. Boulder, CO: Westview Press.

Tronick, E. (1989). Emotions and emotional communication in infants. *American Psychologist, 44*(2), 112–119.

Veblen, T. (1899). *The theory of the leisure class: An economic study of institutions*. New York, NY: Macmillan.

Wachtel, E. F., & Wachtel, P. L. (1986). *Family dynamics in individual psychotherapy: A guide to clinical strategies*. New York, NY: Guilford.

Wachtel, P. L. (1967). An approach to the study of body language in psychotherapy. *Psychotherapy: Theory, Research and Practice, 43*(3), 97–100.

Wachtel, P. L. (1973). Psychodynamics, behavior therapy, and the implacable experimenter: An inquiry into the consistency of personality. *Journal of Abnormal Psychology, 82*(2), 324–334.

Wachtel, P. L. (1977a). *Psychoanalysis and behavior therapy: Toward an integration*. New York, NY: Basic Books.

Wachtel, P. L. (1977b). Interaction cycles, unconscious processes, and the person situation issue. In D. Magnusson & N. Endler (Eds.), *Personality at the crossroads: Issues in interactional psychology* (pp. 317–331). Hillsdale, NJ: Lawrence Erlbaum Associates.

Wachtel, P. L. (1979). Karen Horney's ironic vision. *New Republic, 106*(1), 22–25.

Wachtel, P. L. (1980). Investigation and its discontents: Some constraints on progress in psychological research. *American Psychologist, 35*(5), 399–408.

Wachtel, P. L. (1981). Transference, schema, and assimilation: The relevance of Piaget to the psychoanalytic theory of transference. *Annual of Psychoanalysis, 8*, 59–76.

Wachtel, P. L. (1982a). Vicious circles: The self and the rhetoric of emerging and unfolding. *Contemporary Psychoanalysis, 18*(2), 273–295.

Wachtel, P. L. (Ed.), (1982b). *Resistance: Psychodynamic and behavioral approaches*. New York, NY: Plenum.

Wachtel, P. L. (1983). *The poverty of affluence: A psychological portrait of the American way of life*. New York, NY: Free Press.

Wachtel, P. L. (1987). *Action and insight*. New York, NY: Guilford Press.

Wachtel, P. L. (1991). The role of accomplices in preventing and facilitating change. In R. Curtis & G. Stricker (Eds.), *How people change: Inside and outside therapy* (pp. 21–28). New York, NY: Plenum.

Wachtel, P.L. (1994). Cyclical processes in psychopathology. *Journal of Abnormal Psychology, 103*(1), 51–54.

Wachtel, P.L. (1997). *Psychoanalysis, behavior therapy, and the relational world.* Washington, DC: American Psychological Association.

Wachtel, P.L. (1998). Alternatives to the consumer society. In D.A. Crocker & T. Linden (Eds.), *Ethics of consumption: The good, justice, and global stewardship* (pp. 198–217). Lanham, MD: Rowman & Littlefield.

Wachtel, P.L. (1999). *Race in the mind of America: Breaking the vicious circle between blacks and whites.* New York, NY: Routledge.

Wachtel, P.L. (2003). Full pockets, empty lives: A psychoanalytic exploration of the contemporary culture of greed. *American Journal of Psychoanalysis, 63*(2), 101–120.

Wachtel, P.L. (2006). The ambiguities of the "real" in psychoanalysis. *Psychoanalytic Perspectives, 3*(2), 17–26.

Wachtel, P.L. (2008). *Relational theory and the practice of psychotherapy.* New York, NY: Guilford Press.

Wachtel, P.L. (2010). Beyond "ESTs": Problematic assumptions in the pursuit of evidence-based practice. *Psychoanalytic Psychology, 27*(3), 251–272.

Wachtel, P.L. (2011a). *Therapeutic communication: Knowing what to say when* (2nd ed.). New York, NY: Guilford Press.

Wachtel, P.L. (2011b). *Inside the session: What really happens in psychotherapy.* Washington, DC: American Psychological Association.

Wachtel, P.L., & DeMichele, A. (1998). Unconscious plan, or unconscious conflict? *Psychoanalytic Dialogues, 8*(3), 429–442.

Wachtel, P.L., Kruk, J.C., & McKinney, M.K. (2005). Cyclical psychodynamics and integrative relational psychotherapy. In J.C. Norcross & M.R. Goldfried (Eds.), *Handbook of psychotherapy integration* (2nd ed., pp. 172–195). New York, NY: Oxford University Press.

Wachtel, P.L., & Schimek, J.G. (1970). An exploratory study of the effects of emotionally toned incidental stimuli. *Journal of Personality, 38*(4), 467–481.

Wade, N. (2006). *Before the dawn: Recovering the lost history of our ancestors.* New York, NY: Penguin.

Wallerstein, R.S. (1988). Psychoanalysis and psychotherapy: Relative roles reconsidered. *Annual of Psychoanalysis, 16,* 129–151.

Wallerstein, R.S. (1989). The psychotherapy research project of the Menninger Foundation: An overview. *Journal of Consulting and Clinical Psychology, 57*(2), 195–205.

Wallin, D.J. (2007). *Attachment in psychotherapy.* New York, NY: Guilford Press.

Warner, W.L. (1962). *The corporation in the emergent American society.* New York, NY: Harper & Row.

Warner, W.L., & Abegglen, J. (1963). *Big business leaders in America.* New York, NY: Atheneum.

Weinberg, M.K., & Tronick, E.Z. (1998). The impact of maternal psychiatric illness on infant development. *Journal of Clinical Psychiatry, 59*(Suppl. 2), 53–61.

Weiss, J. (1998). Patients' unconscious plans for solving their problems. *Psychoanalytic Dialogues, 8*(3), 411–428.

Weiss, J., Sampson, H., & Mount Zion Psychotherapy Research Group. (1986). *The psychoanalytic process: Theory, clinical observation, and empirical research.* New York, NY: Guilford Press.

Weitzman, B. (1967). Behavior therapy and psychotherapy. *Psychological Review, 74*(4), 300–317.

Westen, D. (1989). Are "primitive" object relations really preoedipal? *American Journal of Orthopsychiatry*, *59*(3), 331–345.

Westen, D. (1998). The scientific legacy of Sigmund Freud: Toward a psychodynamically informed psychological science. *Psychological Bulletin*, *124*(3), 333–371.

Westen, D. (2002). The language of psychoanalytic discourse. *Psychoanalytic Dialogues*, *12*(6), 857–898.

Westen, D., & Morrison, K. (2001). A multidimensional meta-analysis of treatments for depression, panic, and generalized anxiety disorders: An empirical examination of the status of empirically supported therapies. *Journal of Consulting and Clinical Psychology*, *69*(6), 875–899.

Westen, D., & Shedler, J. (2007). Personality diagnosis with the Shedler-Westen Assessment Procedure (SWAP): Integrating clinical and statistical measurement and prediction. *Journal of Abnormal Psychology*, *116*(4), 810–822.

Westen, D., & Weinberger, J. (2004). When clinical description becomes statistical prediction. *American Psychologist*, *59*(7), 595–613.

Westen, D., Novotny, C. M., & Thompson-Brenner, H. (2004). The empirical status of empirically supported psychotherapies: Assumptions, findings, and reporting in controlled clinical trials. *Psychological Bulletin*, *130*(4), 631–663.

Whelton, W. J. (2004). Emotional processes in psychotherapy: Evidence across therapeutic modalities. *Clinical Psychology & Psychotherapy*, *11*(1), 58–71.

Wile, D. B. (1982). *Kohut, Kernberg, and accusatory interpretations*. Paper presented at the symposium "Do we have to harm clients to help them?" American Psychological Association Convention, Washington, DC.

Wile, D. B. (1984). Kohut, Kernberg, and accusatory interpretations. *Psychotherapy*, *21*(3), 353–364.

Wile, D. B. (1985). Psychotherapy by precedent: Unexamined legacies from pre-1920 psychoanalysis. *Psychotherapy*, *22*, 793–802.

Winnicott D. W. (1960). The theory of the parent–infant relationship. *International Journal of Psychoanalysis*, *41*, 585–595.

Winnicott, D. W. (1975). Through paediatrics to psycho-analysis. *International Psycho-Analytical Library*, *100*, 1–325.

Wolff, P. H. (2001). *Why psychoanalysis is still interesting*. Paper presented at the annual meeting of the Rapaport-Klein Study Group, Stockbridge, MA.

Word, C. O., Zanna, M. P., & Cooper, J. (1974). The nonverbal mediation of self-fulfilling prophecies in interracial interaction. *Journal of Experimental Social Psychology*, *10*(2), 109–120.

Zeanah, C. H., Anders, T. F., Seifer, R., & Stern, D. N. (1989). Implications of research on infant development for psychodynamic theory and practice. *Journal of the American Academy of Child and Adolescent Psychiatry*, *28*, 657–668.

Index

acceptance and commitment therapy 90
accomplices in life patterns: becoming
    33–8; race relations and 208–9;
    transference and 100–1
achievement disidentification 210–14
acontextual mode of thought 160–2
actions, mutual, and attachment relationship
    61
active intervention 101–4, 106–8
affective experiences, learning to accept
    and deal with 91–2
African Americans 200, 209, 210–11;
    see also race relations
Alexander, F. 90–1, 93, 124, 136
anaclitic/relational development: greed
    and 191; introjective/self-definitional
    development and 185–6; moving-
    toward trend and 192; overview of 184,
    185; society and 186–7
anxiety: achievement disidentification and
    210–14; making unconscious conscious
    and 88–91; stereotype 209–10
archaeological metaphor 69–70, 73–4
archaeological model of theory construction
    64–5, 66
"archaic" self-representations 80–1, 166
Aron, L. 4, 92, 99, 122–3
Association for the Advancement of
    Psychoanalysis 170
attachment theory: Andrew case example
    51–5; contextualizing attachment 63–6;
    cultural differences and 200; integrative
    approach and 7; overview of 50–1;
    schemas and 58–9; secure attachment
    55–8; two-person theory and 59–63
Atwood, G. E. 65, 93, 162
authentic selfhood, restoration of 182–3
aversive racism 216

Bakan, D. 126
Beck, Aaron 90
Beebe, B. 48
behavioral economics 167n.1
behavior therapy: effectiveness of methods
    of 14–15; as experiential way of
    working 23; incorporation of methods
    of 15–16, 112–16; origins of cyclical
    psychodynamics and 10–21
The Bell Curve (Herrnstein and Murray)
    210
Billingsley, Andrew 200
Blatt, S. J. 126, 184, 188, 193, 194
bootstrapping, mutual 149–50
borderline personality disorder and
    developmental levels 73–4
bound opposition 185–7, 188
Bowlby, John 50, 56, 58
Brandchaft, B. 93

CBT (cognitive-behavior therapy) 23,
    89–90
change: contextual point of view and
    60–1; forces of 75; hierarchical vision
    of 93–4; insight and 90–1, 93–5, 120;
    making unconscious conscious as key to
    85–8; outside therapy room 36–8; see
    also resistance
character, development of 177–8
"Character and Anal Eroticism" (Freud)
    172
circular patterns 17, 128–9; see also
    vicious circles
class and race see inequality and injustice;
    race relations
clinical trials, controlled 140–2
cognitive-behavior therapy (CBT) 3, 23,
    29, 89–90, 96, 118–21, 129

cognitive therapy 118–20, 121
comparison with others, role of 178–9
confirmation and disconfirmation 8–9
conflict, views of 202–4
consciousness, as phenomenon 86;
    see also unconscious, making
    conscious
consequential past and future 79–80
constructivism 6, 90, 108
constructivist 29
constructivist cognitive approaches 90
consumerism see money and possessions
contextual point of view: attachment
    theory and 58, 59–66; critique of Mischel
    and 17–20; overview of 5–6, 17
contextual self 164–7
continuous construction mode; 75
corporations, as self-objects 182
corrective emotional experience and
    resistance 123–5
countertranference, role of 26, 47, 119,
    129
Crews, Frederick 134
cultural context in cyclical psychodynamic
    theory 23–4, 27
cultural values: psychoanalysis and 196–7,
    198–9; resistance and 125–7
Cushman, Philip 165, 190–1
cyclical psychodynamics: constructivism
    and other shared themes 6; family
    systems thinking and 21–2; humanistic-
    experiential and emotion-focused
    therapies and 22–3; implications for
    daily clinical work 27–8; inner world,
    intimate world, world of culture and
    society, and 24–8; as integrative
    137; integrative aims of 7–8; one-
    person, two-person, and contextual
    points of view 4–6; origins of 10–21;
    overview of 3–4, 97–8; perspective
    on race relations 207–9; psychological
    development and 8–10; social and
    cultural context and 23–4; see also
    vicious circles

daily life see everyday experiences
Davis, D. 118–20, 121, 129
default position 4–5, 28
defenses: dissociation and 84–5; structural
    theory and 87
Denton, N. A. 205
depth metaphor: imagery of archaeology
    and 69–70; overview of 67, 69;

pathology and 72; profundity and 70–2;
    sociocultural influences and 80–2
developmental levels, concept of 73–4,
    80–1
Dewald, P. A. 122
dialectical behavior therapy 90
dichotomous view of human beings 33
Dilthey, W. 139
disconfirmation and confirmation 8–9
discrimination, attribution of failure to
    212–13
disidentification with academic achievement
    210–14
disintegration products 123
dissociation, as defensive process 84–5
dominative racism 216
"The Drive to Amass Wealth" (Fenichel)
    172–3

Eagle, M. 55, 120, 121, 122, 124–5, 128–9
early experiences: importance of 8–10;
    narcissistic personality case illustration
    77–9; representations, interactional
    patterns, and 79–80; role of 74–7
eclectic orientation 110
economic goals, pursuit of 169, 172–3,
    176–7, 179–80
economic growth, destructive consequences
    of 155–6
economic system: influence of assumptions
    from 157–60; psychoanalysis as
    paralleling and reinforcing mythology
    of 160–4
economists, hyperrational model of 201–2
Ellis, Albert 90
emotional environment and attachment
    behavior 62
emotion-focused therapy and cyclical
    psychodynamics 22–3
empathy 202–4
empirical validation 142–6
Empson, W. 67
enactments 26, 35, 47, 108, 118, 152
"envelope of insignificant differences"
    9–10
environment, continuities in, and
    attachment status 61–2
envy 169
epistemological foundations of
    psychoanalysis: clinical efficacy
    research and 142–3; contribution of
    theory, and pervasiveness of vicious
    circles 150–2; dismissal of evidence and

144–6; science, intuition, and 143–4; vicious circles and 139–42; viewpoints, methodologies, and 146–50
epistemology, two-person 4
Erikson, E. H. 11, 21, 71–2
essentialist mode of thought 57
ethnic, use of term 206n.5
everyday experiences: attention to 36–8; as confirming "infantile" wishes, feelings, and fantasies 9–11; inner world and 46–9
everyday unhappiness 155–60
experiential therapy 88–9, 90–1
exposure and reduction of anxiety 88–9
externalities, concept of 159

Fairbairn, W.R.D. 175, 208
family systems thinking and cyclical psychodynamics 21–2
Fanon, Frantz 215
fantasies 10, 46, 76–7, 85, 96
fashion and perception 178
feminist thought 7
Fenichel, Otto 83, 156–7, 172–3
Ferenczi, S. 93, 172
fixation, emphasis on 75–6
Frank, Kenneth 98–9, 101, 102–6
Frank, Robert 158–9
free association 46–7
French, T. 93, 124
Freud, Sigmund: "Character and Anal Eroticism" 172; class biases of 196; on dissociation 85; on everyday unhappiness 156; exploratory emphasis of 95; Inhibitions, Symptoms, and Anxiety 88; metaphors of 69; "pure gold" of analysis and 197; repetitive compulsion concept of 28–9n.4; repression and 80, 83, 86; resistance and 122, 127–8; techniques and research of 131–2
Fromm, E. 126, 180–1, 188

gifts given to analysts 124
Gill, M. M. 65, 99, 101
greed: insatiability, heedlessness, and 188–9; moving-toward, moving-against, and moving-away trends, and 192–3; overview of 169–70; as social phenomenon 187–8; social problems, private discontents, and 193–4; two-configurations model and 184, 189–91
Greenberg, J. 3–4, 7, 80, 81

Hartmann, Heinz 10
Havens, L. 84
heedlessness, greed as 189
Herrnstein, Richard 210
Hobbes, T. 188
Hoffman, I. Z. 4, 6, 48, 58, 99, 108
Hollingshead, A. 197
Hollon, S. D. 118–20, 121, 129
Horney, K. 21, 31, 102, 170–1, 192–3
Hulme, T. E. 67
humanistic-experiential therapy and cyclical psychodynamics 22–3; see also experiential therapy

iatrogenic resistance 123
inderdependency and contextual self 164–6
individuation 126–7, 164–5
inequality and injustice: differential treatment issues 197–8; lessons about psychoanalytic theory and 199–200; political worldviews and 203–4; psychoanalytic contribution to issues of 195–6, 201–3; psychoanalytic therapy, middle class values, and 196–7; vicious circles and 204–6; see also race relations
infancy: evolution of personality and 48; greed and 170, 188–9
infantile modes of thought 122–3
Inhibitions, Symptoms, and Anxiety (Freud) 88
inner world: approaching integratively 91–3; concepts of 24–5; daily life and 46–9; false dichotomy between external environment and 151–2; link to outer world 39–46; society and 175–6, 182–3; see also depth metaphor
insatiability 170, 189–90
insight: change and 120; as following change 90–1; role of in making unconscious conscious 93–5
integrative aims of relational theory and cyclical psychodynamics 7–8, 137; see also active intervention; integrative practice
integrative approaches to inner world 91–3
integrative practice: elements of 109–10; evolution of 115–16; James case illustration 111–15; Lillian case illustration 110–11
internal working models 57, 58, 62–3, 65

interpersonal theory 25–6
interpretation: as affirmative and
    supportive 92–3; of defenses 87;
    explicit 54–5; as exposure 89; of
    transference 46–7
intimate world, concepts of 25–7
intrapsychic processes, concept of 98–9
introjective/self-definitional development:
    anaclitic/relational development and
    185–6; greed and 191; moving-against
    and moving-away trends and 192–3;
    overview of 184, 185; society and
    186–7
intuition and science 143–4
"Isn't it interesting" phrase 84

Jacoby, Russell 156–7

Klein, Melanie 170, 188
Kohut, H. 78, 93, 123, 125, 180, 181
Kovel, Joel 215–16
Kuhn, T. S. 12

Lewin, Kurt 150
Loewald, H. W. 93
Luborsky, L. 150

Maital, Shlomo 158
manuals in clinical efficacy research,
    preoccupation with 142–4
Marx, K. 188
Massey, D. S. 205
materialism see greed; money and
    possessions
McConahay, John 215
Menninger study 133–4
mental health services, race, and class
    197–8
metaphor, use of 67–8; see also depth
    metaphor
Midas story 169–70, 189
Mischel, Walter, Personality and
    Assessment 13–14, 17–20, 21
Mitchell, S. A. 3–4, 5, 7, 56, 59, 71–2, 80,
    81, 99, 162
modes of thought: acontextual 160–2;
    essentialist 57; infantile 122–3
monadic language 56
money and possessions: case illustration
    173–5; meaning of 171–3; as self-
    objects 180–2; social structuring of
    motivation for 175–80
moral development, Freud views of 196

motivation, social structuring of 175–80
moving for economic advancement 162–4
moving-toward, moving-against, and
    moving-away trends 192–3
Murray, Charles 210

narcissistic personality case illustration 77–9
neurological recording 149–50
neurosis/neurotic patterns: case illustration
    32–8; defined 31–2; Horney and 170–1,
    192–3; staying power of 31
The Neurotic Personality of our Time
    (Horney) 170

Object Relations in Psychoanalytic Theory
    (Greenberg and Mitchell) 3–4
object relations theory 64–5, 80–1
observational methods 108n.2, 146–7
Oedipal dynamics 69, 71
"one-down position" 121–2
one-person theories 5
one-person thinking 58
"The Origin of the Interest in Money"
    (Ferenczi) 172
others, therapeutic impact of 35
outer world, link to inner world 39–46
overtracking case example 51–5

panther imagery 114–15
participant observation 108n.2
pathology, overemphasis on 72
perceptions, interpersonal 100
personality: borderline, and developmental
    levels 73–4; descriptions of 60–1;
    environment and 61–2; evolution of, and
    infancy 48; as fixed vs. co-constructed
    64–6; narcissistic 77–9; reciprocal actions
    and 49; two-configurations model and
    184–5; see also neurosis/neurotic patterns
Personality and Assessment (Mischel)
    13–14, 17–20, 21
Peterfreund, E. 75
phrasing, therapist choice of 83–4
physiological recording 149–50
Piaget, Jean 25, 58, 186
Polanyi, Michael 143
political approaches to social inequality
    202
political worldviews 203–4
The Poverty of Affluence (Wachel) 156
predispositions and early experiences 8–10
prejudice, attribution of failure to 212–13
"preoedipal" themes 71–75

"primitive" self-representations 80–1
profundity and depth 70–2
projective identification 49n.4
pseudo-confirmation process 210
psychic structure 98–101
psychoanalysis: "archaic" and 166;
    critiques of focus of 195; cultural
    dimension of 198–9; curiosity and
    168; expanded scope of 196–7; goal
    of 182–3; habits of thought of 20–1;
    inequality, injustice, and 195–6, 201–3;
    isolation of 183; meanings of term 131;
    origins of cyclical psychodynamics and
    10–21; psychotherapy distinguished
    from 134–5; relational movement
    in 3–4, 93, 97–8; as social group or
    network 12; see also epistemological
    foundations of psychoanalysis;
    interpretation; therapeutic practice;
    therapists; transference
Psychoanalysis and Behavior Therapy
    (Wachtel) 21, 116
psychological development, dynamics of
    8–10
punctuation, problem of 205
pursuer and distancer pattern, clinical
    illustration of 40–3
Putnam, Robert 188

Race in the Mind of America (Wachtel)
    210, 213
race relations: cyclical psychodynamic
    perspective on 207–9; stereotype
    anxiety, academic disidentification,
    and 209–14; vicious circles and 205–6;
    white community and 214–18; see also
    inequality and injustice
rationalistic cognitive therapists 89–90
received version of psychoanalysis 12
Redlich, F. 197
reframing resistance 129
regression, emphasis on 75–6
Reid, T. 125–6, 127
Relational Concepts in Psychoanalysis
    (Mitchell) 4
relational development see anaclitic/
    relational development
relational theory: attachment theory
    and 64; integrative aims of 7–8;
    shift in psychoanalytic approaches to
    incorporate 3–4, 93, 97–8; theorists of
    21; see also two-person point of view
repair of ruptures 108n.2

repression: anxiety and 88–91; Freud
    theory of 80, 83, 86
The Repression of Psychoanalysis (Jacoby)
    156–7
research: clinical efficacy 142–6;
    treatment method as tool of 131–4
resistance: corrective emotional
    experience and 123–5; overview
    of 117–19; terminology for 127–9;
    theory compared to practice and
    119–20; therapeutic relationship and
    120–3; values and 125–7; variations in
    therapeutic communication and 129
revealed preferences methodology 160

Safran, J. D. 121
Sampson, H. 93, 120, 123–4, 125, 127
Santayana, George 163
Schechter, M. 92–3
schemas 25, 58–9; see also internal
    working models
Schimek, Jean 144
science: defensive dismissal of canons
    of evidence in 144–6; defined 139;
    intuition and 143–4
Sears, David 215
secure attachment 55–8
Segal, Z. V. 121
segregation, culture of 205, 213
self-definitional development see
    introjective/self-definitional
    development
self-esteem: greed and 169; school
    performance and 209–14
self-fulfilling prophecies 203, 213–14
self-objects 66n.6, 180–2
self-psychological theory 80–1
self-representations, "archaic" 80–1, 166
self-states, multiple 11–12
self-understanding from outside in: Arlene
    clinical example 44–6; Karl clinical
    example 40–3; overview of 39–40
separation-individuation conflict 126–7,
    164–5, 180, 184–5
SEPI (Society for the Exploration of
    Psychotherapy Integration) 22, 151
session-centric tendencies 47
sexual abuse and borderline personality
    disorder 74
Shapiro, D. 31
shopping, as form of self-medication 176
silence, experience of 101–2
Simon, Herbert 158

situational context *see* contextual point of view
Smith, Adam 187–8
social context in cyclical psychodynamic theory 23–4, 27
social inhibitions case illustration 110–11
social order and contextual self 166–7
society: contributions of psychoanalysis to 157; inner world and 175–6, 182–3; material side of 168–9; motivation and 175–80; phenomena as specific to era and 170; psychoanalytic approach to 168; two-configurations model and 186–7; *see also* inequality and injustice; race relations
Society for the Exploration of Psychotherapy Integration (SEPI) 22, 151
spatial metaphors of Freud 69; *see also* depth metaphor
Stack, C. 200
standard techniques: false dichotomy between active methods and 106–8; support for 104–6
stasis, forces of 75
status concerns case illustration 111–15
Steele, Claude 209–10, 211
stereotype anxiety 209–10
stereotypes of African Americans 209, 210–11
Stern, D. B. 13, 34, 94
Stern, D. N. 48
stigmatization 212–13
Stolorow, R. D. 65, 93, 162
strategic resistance 122
structural theory 87–8
subjective experience of sessions 148–9
subjectivity 25, 148–9
Sullivan, Harry Stack 9–10, 21, 26, 49n.3, 108n.2, 203
Superman story 162
surface metaphor 67, 80–2
surplus resistance 121, 124, 129
symbolic racism 215
systematic desensitization 112–13

tactical resistance 122
tape recordings 146–7
"the frame" of therapy 198–9
theory: contribution of, and vicious circles 150–2; interpersonal 25–6; lessons about from poor and culturally different

199–200; object relations 64–5, 80–1; one-person 5; self-psychological 80–1; structural 87–8; *see also* attachment theory; cyclical psychodynamics; relational theory
The Theory of Moral Sentiments (Smith) 188
therapeutic change *see* change
therapeutic impact of others 35
therapeutic practice: changes or innovations in 134–8, 197–8; overview of 97–101; as research tool 131–4; *see also* integrative practice
therapeutic relationship and resistance 120–3, 129
therapists: assumptions of superiority of approaches by 130n.2; choice of wording and phrasing of 83–4; judicious and clinically sound choices of 106–7; as potential accomplices 36; subjective experience of 148–9; unconscious tests for 54, 123–4
tracking and attachment 52–3
training programs 136–8
transcripts 147–8
transference: analysis of 101–4; defense of status quo and 104–6; dynamic nature of 99–101; interpretation of 46–7; Piagetian thinking and 58
Tronick, E. 48
two-configurations model: greed and 189–91; overview of 184–5; social implications of 186–7; *see also* anaclitic/relational development; introjective/self-definitional development
two-person point of view: anchor points of 48–9; attachment theory and 55–8, 59–63; evolution of 47–8; overview of 4–6, 12–13; *see also* relational theory

unconscious, making conscious: id, ego, and 85–8; integrative approaches to inner world 91–3; overview of 83–5; role of anxiety and experience in 88–91; role of insight in 93–5
unconscious racism, concept of 208
unconscious tests for therapists 54, 123–4

values: middle class, and psychoanalytic therapy 196–7; resistance and 125–7
Veblen, T. 172

vicious circles: clinical phenomena and 218–19; disidentification with academic achievement and 210–11, 212–13; epistemological 47, 139–42; inequality, injustice, and 204–6; pervasiveness of 150–2; in race relations 217, 218; stereotypes and 210

Wachtel, Ellen F. 21–2
Wallerstein, R. S. 133–4
Wall Street (film) 189
Warner, Lloyd 163
Weinberger, J. 146
Weiss, J. 93, 120, 123–4, 125, 127

Westen, D. 73, 74, 146
"Where id was, there ego shall be" conceptualization 87–8
white participation in perpetuation of racial divisions 214–18
Winnicott, D. W. 48, 164
woolly mammoth model 80
world of society and culture, concepts of 27; *see also* cultural context in cyclical psychodynamic theory; cultural values; society

Zeanah, C. H. 75
zone of interaction, intermediate 26